Surviving Schizophrenia

A Family Manual

Revised Edition

E. Fuller Torrey, M.D.

PERENNIAL LIBRARY

HARPER & ROW, PUBLISHERS, New York

Cambridge, Philadelphia, San Francisco, Washington
London, Mexico City, São Paulo, Singapore, Sydney

To those suffering from schizophrenia and their families, who daily must face challenges worthy of Prometheus and find patience worthy of Job

Royalties have been assigned to the National Alliance for the Mentally Ill.

Permissions acknowledgments appear on pages xvii–xviii.

SURVIVING SCHIZOPHRENIA: A FAMILY MANUAL *(Revised Edition)*. Copyright © 1988, 1983 by E. Fuller Torrey. All rights reserved. Printed in the United States of America. No part of this book may be used or reproduced in any manner whatsoever without written permission except in the case of brief quotations embodied in critical articles and reviews. For information address Harper & Row, Publishers, Inc., 10 East 53rd Street, New York, N.Y. 10022. Published simultaneously in Canada by Fitzhenry & Whiteside Limited, Toronto.

Designed by Erich Hobbing

Library of Congress Cataloging-in-Publication Data

Torrey, E. Fuller (Edwin Fuller), 1937–
　　Surviving schizophrenia.

　　Bibliography: p.
　　Includes index.
　　1. Schizophrenia—Popular works.　I. Title.
RC514.T633　1988　　616.89'82　　87-45673
ISBN 0-06-055119-4　　88 89 90 91 92 MPC 10 9 8 7 6 5 4 3 2 1
ISBN 0-06-096249-6 (pbk.) 88 89 90 91 92 MPC 10 9 8 7 6 5 4 3 2

Surviving

Schizophrenia

A Family Manual

By the same author

Ethical Issues in Medicine
Witchdoctors and Psychiatrists
The Death of Psychiatry
Why Did You Do That?
Schizophrenia and Civilization
The Roots of Treason

As for me, you must know that I shouldn't precisely have chosen madness if there had been any choice.

VINCENT VAN GOGH, 1889, in a letter to his brother, written while he was involuntarily confined in the psychiatric hospital at St.-Rémy

ABOUT THE AUTHOR

A clinical and research psychiatrist in Washington, D.C., Dr. E. Fuller Torrey specializes in schizophrenia. He was graduated magna cum laude from Princeton University and with honors from the McGill University School of Medicine; he received his training in psychiatry from Stanford University, where he also took a master's degree in anthropology. He has worked in general medicine, as well as psychiatry, spending two years as a Peace Corps physician in Ethiopia and one year each in a neighborhood health center in New York's South Bronx and in the Indian Health Service in Alaska. Twice he was awarded Commendation Medals by the U.S. Public Health Service.

Dr. Torrey's work in psychiatry has included four years as a Special Assistant to the Director of the National Institute of Mental Health and eight years as a clinical psychiatrist at St. Elizabeths Hospital in Washington, D.C. He has also done field research on schizophrenia in Ireland and Papua New Guinea. Currently he is continuing research on the causes of schizophrenia and also is affiliated part-time with the Public Citizen's Health Research Group. He has written or edited nine books, including *The Roots of Treason: Ezra Pound and the Secret of St. Elizabeths*, which was nominated by the National Book Critics Circle as one of the five best biographies of 1983. He has also written over one hundred lay and professional papers, and appeared on numerous television programs, including "Donahue" and "60 Minutes."

CONTENTS

ILLUSTRATIONS

PREFACE

When I completed the first edition of this book there were just over one hundred local chapters of the National Alliance for the Mentally Ill (NAMI), the organization of families of the seriously mentally ill. As I complete the second edition, NAMI has grown to over eight hundred chapters; this growth and maturation of an advocacy group for the most neglected of America's citizens is the single most exciting development of those years.

At the same time that NAMI has come of age there has been additional research, establishing even more emphatically the biological bases for schizophrenia and manic-depressive psychosis as brain diseases; they are nothing more, and nothing less, than diseases like multiple sclerosis, Alzheimer's disease, and Parkinson's disease. Finally, during these years the public at large has become aware of the disaster of deinstitutionalization, with thousands of seriously mentally ill persons, released and untreated, crowding passersby in city streets and parks. From such public awareness have come indignation and demands that the seriously mentally ill be treated more humanely than being dumped onto the nation's sidewalks.

The second edition of this book reflects these developments and the increasing sophistication of individuals and families who suffer from schizophrenia. They want to know why the system of care is so inadequate, how the disease should be treated, and how to live with the disease. All parts of the book have been expanded, but especially those chapters having to do with treatment and rehabilitation. Knowledge about schizophrenia is essential for individuals and families; it will not remove the pain of the disease but may at least make it bearable.

On the horizon there are increasing hopes for schizophrenia—

hopes for more research to find the causes, hopes for more effective treatments. These hopes can become reality not by wishing, but by informed and action-oriented advocacy groups. There is no question that the treatment of persons with schizophrenia can be improved if only we have the will to do so.

PREFACE TO THE FIRST EDITION

"Your daughter has schizophrenia," I told the woman.

"Oh, my god, anything but that," she replied. "Why couldn't she have leukemia or some other disease instead?"

"But if she had leukemia she might die," I pointed out. "Schizophrenia is a much more treatable disease."

The woman looked sadly at me, then down at the floor. She spoke softly. "I would still prefer that my daughter had leukemia."

This book is a product of a thousand such conversations. Conceived in the darkness of despair, it was fathered by education and mothered by hope. It is written for families whose lives are currently touched by schizophrenia. My sister is afflicted; perhaps your brother, aunt, or son is also. The book provides a scientific framework for understanding its symptoms, causes, and treatment and suggests how families can come to terms with the disease. Above all, the book tries to dispel the multitude of myths and alleviate the millstone of guilt which families have been condemned to carry by mental health professionals; surely this has been Original Psychiatric Sin.

Schizophrenia is a cruel disease. The lives of those affected are often chronicles of constricted experiences, muted emotions, missed opportunities, unfulfilled expectations. It leads to a twilight existence, a twentieth-century underground man. The fate of these patients has been worsened by our propensity to misunderstand, our failure to provide adequate treatment and rehabilitation, our meager research efforts. A disease which should be found, in the phrase of T. S. Eliot, in the "frigid purgatorial fires" has become through our ignorance and neglect a living hell.

Perhaps it is a disease whose time has come. There are rays of hope—research, treatment, the organizations of families and friends. If this book contributes just a little toward bringing schizophrenia out of the Slough of Despond and into the mainstream of American medicine then it will have accomplished its purpose.

ACKNOWLEDGMENTS

I am indebted to many individuals for assistance in creating this book. Jim and Carol Howe and David Shore contributed many useful suggestions on the text. Leslie Scallet helped collect information on current state mental health laws. Lynne Saunders of the National Alliance for the Mentally Ill and Paolo del Vecchio of the National Mental Health Consumer's Association identified state contact persons for their organizations. Jeffrey Aarons helped with the illustrations. The staffs of the WAW Division and St. Elizabeths Hospital medical libraries were unfailingly helpful. Judy Miller provided excellent typing services. Lou AvRutick originally found a home for the book at Harper & Row, where Carol Cohen nurtured it to maturity. Above all I am indebted to my wife, Barbara, for the essential but ineffable ingredients that make writing a book possible.

Portions of chapters 1 and 8 are borrowed with permission from *Care of the Seriously Mentally Ill*, which I wrote with Sidney M. Wolfe, and part of chapter 13 from my article in the *British Journal of Psychiatry*.

I am also grateful to the following:

Richard Abrams for permission to reprint excerpts from his book review in the *American Journal of Psychiatry*.

Joseph H. Berke for permission to reprint excerpts from *Mary Barnes: Two Accounts of a Journey Through Madness*.

Malcolm B. Bowers and Science Press for permission to reprint excerpts from *Retreat from Sanity: The Structure of Emerging Psychosis*.

Eliot T. O. Slater for permission to reprint excerpts from *Clinical Psychiatry*.

Andrew McGhie and The British Psychological Society for permission to reprint excerpts from an article in the *British Journal of Medical Psychology*.

British Journal of Psychiatry for permission to reprint excerpts from an article by James Chapman.

Journal of Abnormal and Social Psychology for permission to reprint excerpts from an article by Anonymous.

Anchor Press and Doubleday for permission to reprint excerpts from *These Are My Sisters*, by Lara Jefferson.

Presses Universitaires de France for permission to reprint excerpts from *Autobiography of a Schizophrenic Girl*, by Marguerite Sechehaye.

W. W. Norton and Company for permission to reprint excerpts from *In a Darkness*, by James A. Wechsler.

National Schizophrenic Fellowship for permission to reprint excerpts from *Coping with Schizophrenia*, by H. R. Rollin.

G. P. Putnam and Sons for permission to reprint excerpts from *This Stranger, My Son*, by Louise Wilson.

University Books for permission to reprint excerpts from *The Witnesses*, by Thomas Hennell.

D. V. Jeste and *Comprehensive Psychiatry* for permission to quote from an article.

J. G. Hall and *Lancet* for permission to quote from an article.

Nancy J. Hermon and Colin M. Smith for permission to quote from a presentation at the 1986 Alberta Schizophrenia Conference.

The Medical Letter, Psychological Bulletin, Psychology Today, and *Schizophrenia Bulletin* for permission to quote from articles.

Mrs. Gilda Nelson for permission to quote from poems by her deceased son, Robert L. Nelson.

Dr. Bernhard Bogerts for permission to utilize photographs of the brain.

Surviving
Schizophrenia

A Family Manual

I

OUT OF THE CLOSET

Schizophrenia is to psychiatry what cancer is to medicine: a sentence as well as a diagnosis.

W. Hall, G. Andrews, and G. Goldstein,
Australian and New Zealand Journal of Psychiatry, 1985

Schizophrenia, I said. The word itself is ominous. It has been called "one of the most sinister words in the language." It has a bite to it, a harsh grating sound that evokes visions of madness and asylums. It is not fluid like *démence,* the word from which "dementia" comes. Nor is it a visual word like *écrassé,* the origin of "cracked," meaning that the person was like a cracked pot. Nor is it romantic like "lunatic," meaning fallen under the influence of the moon (which in Latin is *luna*). "Schizophrenia" is a discordant and cruel term, just like the disease it signifies.

And just like the treatment—or more accurately lack of treatment—to which those with this disease are subjected. For many people with schizophrenia it is an open question whether, except for medications, they fare any better now than they did one hundred or more years ago. In 1843, for example, Dorothea Dix appeared before the Massachusetts Legislature to decry "the state of insane persons confined within this Commonwealth in cages, closets, cellars, stalls, pens, chained, naked, beaten with rods, and lashed into obedience." In 1985 witnesses testified before the Senate Subcommittee on the Handicapped regarding staff abuse of persons confined in mental hospitals, including "kicking or otherwise striking patients, sexual advances and rape, verbal threats of injury and other forms of intimidation."

In 1843 Miss Dix also testified about insane persons placed for a

1

fee with "masters." One such man had been kept in an unheated outhouse for a year "and there had frozen his feet which were now reduced to shapeless stumps. Despite his inability to walk about, chains were nevertheless fastened about his stumps for fear that he might *crawl* forth from his present cell and do some damage." In 1982 *The New York Times* reported on nine mental patients, placed for a fee with a foster home operator, who were kept in a shed with no toilet or running water and "two vicious dogs chained outside the small room" to ensure that they did not run away.

In 1848 a man in New York was not admitted to the local insane asylum because it was crowded. Shortly thereafter, instructed by his voices, he killed his mother and father, then removed their hearts, which he roasted and ate. In 1986 a man in New York was not admitted to the local psychiatric hospital because it was crowded. Shortly thereafter, instructed by voices telling him to kill, he carried a sword aboard a Staten Island ferry and slashed two strangers to death. A year earlier a woman who had been released from another New York psychiatric hospital against medical recommendations pushed a stranger into the path of a subway train. As she was being led away by police, the woman cried: "I'm sick, I'm sick, and I have no one."

In 1824 a New York State report on insane paupers severely condemned the practices of "passing on" and "dumping" such persons from town to town, transporting them to the next town at night and leaving them "in the hope that their inability to give coherent accounts of themselves would make it difficult, if not impossible, to trace them back to their original places of settlement." In 1984 newspapers described the practice in Texas of taking busloads of severely mentally ill persons from the Austin State Hospital and dumping them at the Houston bus station, and in Arizona of taking mentally ill homeless persons and putting them on buses for Los Angeles; locally it was sometimes referred to as "Greyhound Therapy."

The 1824 report also described "a poor unfortunate lunatic, of the age of eighteen or twenty years, [who] was left in the street in the winter, and in the night whose feet were in consequence badly frozen; he could give no intelligible account of himself." In the 1980s newspapers regularly reported seriously mentally ill persons freezing on the streets in winter. So commonplace had it become that when a homeless man froze to death a few blocks from the White House, the *Washington Post* "routinely reported his death as a minor part of a weather story." The front page of *The New York Times* featured a picture of a city worker "trying to give lunch to a man who lives in a box in Battery Park." The picture showed a makeshift shelter made of pieces of cardboard on a park bench. And in Massachusetts, when "two small defenseless street people" were beaten to death, the local newspaper editorialized that it was like having "rabbits forced to live in the company with dogs."

For those afflicted with schizophrenia, or for those of us with family members afflicted, it is becoming increasingly difficult to avoid the reality that society has failed this group abysmally. We would like to believe otherwise, to believe apologists for state departments of mental health, for the National Institute of Mental Health, and for the American Psychiatric Association. We would like to believe that mental hospitals really are not *that* bad, that board-and-care homes really do a *nice* job, and that mentally ill homeless persons *prefer* to live on the streets. The people described in the media, we like to say, are exceptions. But the exceptions keep growing, appearing in our line of vision, more and more of them until it is no longer possible to see them as exceptions. We wake up one morning and suddenly realize that these people are not exceptions at all but rather are the rule. The care and treatment of persons with schizophrenia is the single biggest blemish on the face of contemporary American medical and social services; when the social history of our era is written, the plight of these persons will be recorded as a national scandal.

HOW MANY PEOPLE HAVE SCHIZOPHRENIA?

Studies of schizophrenia have shown that approximately one out of every hundred persons in the United States will be diagnosed with schizophrenia during his or her lifetime. In some areas of the world the incidence is lower (e.g., tropical Africa), while in others it is higher (e.g., Scandinavia, western Ireland); see chapter 13. In terms of how many people in the United States have schizophrenia at any given time (in contrast to lifetime rates of one in one hundred), estimates of this number vary depending on recovery rates, mortality rates, and diagnostic definitions. A conservative estimate of the number of persons with schizophrenia in the United States today, based on recent prevalence studies (see chapter 13), would be 1.2 million people.

It should be noted that this number is for schizophrenia alone; it does *not* include those with manic-depressive psychosis, severe depressions, cases of psychosis due to other causes (see chapter 4), or severely disturbed children. The 1.2 million persons are those with symptoms of schizophrenia today. If those who have had schizophrenia and completely recovered (see chapter 5) are also included, then the estimate would be approximately 1.6 million persons. This is the same number of persons who live in Nebraska or Utah, or who live in Vermont and New Hampshire combined, the same number who live in Alaska, Delaware, and Wyoming put together. Every year another 43,000 persons are diagnosed with schizophrenia for the first time. Every day another 118 persons are diagnosed with schizophrenia for the first time. And these figures are only for the United States.

But these are just numbers. They have little meaning for most people, like the numbers of people killed in a flood in India or in an earthquake in Turkey. The numbers fail to evoke the human suffering and personal tragedy which accompany the disease. It is a tragedy which goes on, year after year, for those who recover only partially or not at all. Schizophrenia is, as the epigraph for the chapter says, a sentence as well as a diagnosis. The result is often a life sentence for both the person afflicted and for the family. No release. No parole. No time off for good behavior.

Despite its being a common disease, schizophrenia is remote to most people. A remarkable number of people do not even know what schizophrenia is. A recent survey of college freshmen found that 64 percent of them believed "multiple personalities" to be a common symptom of schizophrenia. Schizophrenia has nothing to do with multiple or split personalities—the Sybils or Three Faces of Eve—which is in fact a very rare condition classified as a dissociative disorder. We also use the term "schizophrenia" loosely and broadly in our everyday language to signify ambivalent feelings or the pursuit of two contradictory goals at the same time. A Secretary of the Treasury says that "schizophrenia crippled our economic policy." Other officials speak of "a schizophrenia in the Atlantic Alliance" and "our schizophrenic foreign policy process." Such usage of the term further confuses people about what schizophrenia really is.

Schizophrenia is sometimes also used interchangeably with the term "psychosis." Psychosis means loss of contact with reality. Most, but not all, persons with psychosis do in fact have schizophrenia. However, the category "psychosis" also includes manic-depressive psychosis (now officially called bipolar disorder), so for the sake of precision it is preferable to say schizophrenia if that is what you mean. This distinction will become clearer in chapter 4, where manic-depressive psychosis is discussed. In common usage, when the term "psychotic" is used it implies the loss-of-reality symptoms found in both schizophrenia and manic-depressive illness.

WHERE ARE THEY?

If in fact schizophrenia is such a common disease, then why is it so invisible? It is invisible because we have become experts in hiding it. Schizophrenia lurks in the closets, hiding behind euphemisms like "nervous breakdown" or "bad case of nerves." It stands quietly behind lace curtains but nobody bothers to mention it. It is the aunt who used to live with them but then moved; what they don't add is that she moved to the state hospital. It is the son who got in trouble in late adolescence and is now said to be living in Pennsylvania; what they don't add is that he is committed to the state hospital there. It is the sister who tragically committed suicide over, it is rumored, a love affair; what they don't add is that she committed suicide because she was plagued by voices and chose not to live with her disease. We hide it, hoping nobody will tell, hoping nobody will find out. It is a stigma.

The stigma of schizophrenia makes it all the more tragic. Not only must persons affected and their families bear the disease itself, but they must bear the stigma of it as well. People with schizophrenia are the lepers of the twentieth century. The aunt, son, or sister hidden in the closet may be discovered at any minute, and then the word will be out. Disaster, Dishonor, Disgrace. The magnitude of schizophrenia as a national calamity is exceeded only by the magnitude of our ignorance in dealing with it.

For it is only our ignorance which continues to keep people with schizophrenia in the closet. It is only our lingering mystical mentality, our heritage of examining entrails to predict the future, our aversion to the evil eye, which keeps us from putting schizophrenia into its proper 1980s perspective. Schizophrenia is a brain disease, now definitely known to be such. It is a real scientific and biological entity, as clearly as diabetes, multiple sclerosis, and cancer are scientific and biological entities. It exhibits symptoms of a a brain disease, symptoms which include impairment in thinking, delusions, hallucinations, changes in emotions, and changes in behavior. And, like cancer, it probably has more than one cause. Thus, though we speak of schizophrenia and cancer in the singular, we really understand them as being in the plural; there are probably several different kinds of schizophrenia of the brain, just as there are several different kinds of cancer of the brain.

The occasions when we become most publicly aware of schizophrenia are, unfortunately, those during which someone with the disease commits a violent act. Such murders are widely publicized, in contrast to the 18,500 murders each year in the United States committed by individuals not mentally ill, which are usually reported only as local news. In reality only a small fraction of people with schizophrenia are dangerous, and then usually because their illness has not been treated or has been treated inadequately, or they have refused treatment. Violent crimes committed by persons with schizophrenia are sometimes publicized because of the background of the person, as when John Bradley, All-American hockey goalie and honors student at Bowdoin College, brutally killed his father and mother. Sometimes it is publicized because of the status of the victim, as when Dennis Sweeney killed former Congressman Allard Lowenstein because he believed Lowenstein controlled electrodes implanted in his brain and a radio receiver implanted in his teeth. Or when Lois Lang, a homeless woman diagnosed with paranoid schizophrenia, walked into a Wall Street firm and killed the chairman of the board because she believed she owned part of the firm.

The problems of the seriously mentally ill have reached into the White House itself, making it difficult for anyone to ignore. In 1983, the son of President Reagan's tax attorney, a young man with chronic schizophrenia, bludgeoned his mother to death. The only other son had also been diagnosed with schizophrenia and had committed suicide two years previously. In 1981, the nation had been shocked when John Hinckley, another young man with schizophrenia treated by a psychiatrist, shot and almost killed the President.

It is unfortunate that it is these isolated episodes of violence that force our attention onto the seriously mentally ill. Most such individuals are passive and meek, incapable of providing or caring for themselves because of their illnesses. For every person with schizophrenia who commits a crime, at least ten—maybe one hundred—are the victims of a crime. But only rarely are these crimes publicized, as in the case of Phyllis Iannotta, a homeless, 67-year-old, mentally ill woman who was found stabbed to death. In her pocket was a can of Friskies turkey-and-giblet cat food and a plastic spoon.

There is remarkably little hard information on where the 1.2 million persons with schizophrenia in the United States are living or receiving care. The Director of the National Institute of Mental Health (NIMH), testifying before the Senate Committee on Appropriations in late 1986, said that NIMH could account for only 42 percent of such individuals; for the other 58 percent their living and care arrangements were unknown. This shocking admission, by the federal agency which is responsible for maintaining such information, marks one more indication of the neglect this disease has suffered.

If all sources of information on persons with schizophrenia are synthesized, it is possible to construct a reasonably accurate picture of where they are living on any given day. The chart on the next page shows the whereabouts of the 1.2 million persons currently diagnosed with this disorder.

Hospitals: 85,461. In 1980 in the United States patients with the diagnosis of schizophrenia occupied hospital beds in the following numbers:

State and county hospitals	59,463
Veterans Administration hospitals	10,105
General hospitals	7,052
Beds in Community Mental Health Centers	5,204
Private hospitals	3,637
Total	85,461

Nursing Homes: 165,000. In 1986 it was estimated that 1.5 million Americans lived in nursing homes. A 1977 study found that 11 percent of nursing home residents had been classified as "purely chronically mentally ill," and another 5 percent had a diagnosis of chronic mental illness with some physical disability. No diagnostic breakdown of these mentally ill nursing home patients is available but it is known that most have been placed there as transfers from state hospitals. A reasonable estimate of the percentage of patients among such transfers who would have a diagnosis of schizophrenia would be two-thirds. This means that, based on the 1986 nursing home population, approximately 165,000 persons with schizophrenia now reside in such institutions.

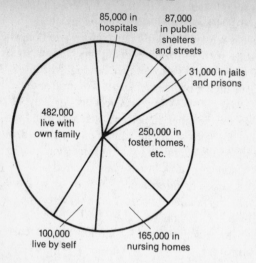

DISTRIBUTION OF PERSONS WITH SCHIZOPHRENIA:
1.2 MILLION TOTAL

85,000 in hospitals

87,000 in public shelters and streets

31,000 in jails and prisons

482,000 live with own family

250,000 in foster homes, etc.

100,000 live by self

165,000 in nursing homes

Public Shelters and Streets: 87,000. The number of homeless persons who live on the streets and in public shelters is one of the great political footballs of the 1980s. Estimates by different government agencies have ranged from 250,000 to 2,500,000. Two separate studies in 1984 and 1985 concluded that there were approximately 350,000 homeless people in the United States. The percentage of homeless persons with schizophrenia is also controversial; studies in Washington, Boston, and Philadelphia all found between 36 and 39 percent of the homeless had that diagnosis, but a study in Los Angeles found only 14 percent. If it is assumed that 25 percent of 350,000 homeless people have schizophrenia, that would mean 87,000 such persons are living on the nation's streets and in public shelters. That is approximately the same number who are in hospitals on any given day. In surveys of these people done to date it has also been found that less than 10 percent of them are receiving any treatment for their illness.

Jails: 31,000. In 1985 there were approximately 750,000 people in jails and prisons in the United States. Studies of prisoners in California, Colorado, and Oklahoma found that 6.7 percent, 5.0 percent, and 5.2 percent respectively were psychotic. The average of these three studies is 5.6 percent, and based on prevalence studies it is reasonable to assume that three-fourths of these have schizophrenia (and the other fourth mostly manic-depressive psychosis). Thus, if 4.2 percent of 750,000 prisoners have schizophrenia, then there are approximately 31,000 persons with this illness in America's jails and prisons.

There is also evidence that individuals with schizophrenia who are picked up by the police for minor offenses are more likely to be charged by the police and put in jail; in one study of a county prison it was found that "psychotic inmates were four times more likely to have been incarcerated for less serious charges such as disorderly conduct and threats." The recent trend veers toward the criminalization of psychotic behavior. Tragic consequences have already become apparent. In Georgia, for example, a young man with schizophrenia—"voted friendliest boy in the Whigham High School class of 1978"—was put in jail for a robbery committed while obviously psychotic. In jail his antipsychotic medication was discontinued, and "a few days later [he] gouged out his left eye with his fingers."

Foster Homes, etc.: 250,000.   These are supervised living arrangements set up for patients discharged from mental hospitals. They go by a variety of names: foster homes, halfway houses, board-and-care homes, county homes, etc. The common denominator of them all is that the person living there pays several hundred dollars a month for room and board and varying degrees of supervision; in most cases the money comes from some form of social security payments (see chapter 9). Nobody knows for certain how many persons live in such homes or what percentage of them have schizophrenia. Estimates based on the total amount of social security funds going to individuals with psychoses suggest the number of such persons as at least 500,000. It is reasonable to assume that at least half of these have schizophrenia and are living in foster homes, etc.

Living by Self: 100,000.   This number is just a guess as nobody knows how many persons with schizophrenia are able to live alone. The group includes those persons whose symptoms are under good control (usually with medication), many of whom are holding jobs and leading virtually normal lives. It also includes those who are renting rooms in rundown "SRO's" (single-room-occupancy hotels) and living a marginal though independent existence utilizing their social security checks.

Living with Family: 482,000.   The families of persons with schizophrenia are the single most important primary care providers. In rural areas it is common to find more than half of all persons with this disease living at home. Nobody knows precisely how many persons with schizophrenia live with their families, but most authorities suspect that it is greater than the number living in foster homes, board-and-care homes, etc. In many cases it is a substantial hardship for the family to have the ill family member live with them, but they are reluctant to put the person back into a state system which they may view as brutal and demeaning, or to turn the person out into the streets.

WHAT IS THE COST OF THE DISEASE?

To ask a question about the cost of schizophrenia is, in one sense, meaningless. Anyone who has a family member with schizophrenia knows that its magnitude and tragedy are light-years beyond calculation in dollars and cents. At the same time we live in a society with finite resources and, whether we like it or not, cost-benefit thinking is part of the allocation of those resources. The decision-making process is a political one in which—either explicitly or implicitly—questions are asked, such as the following: How much does the disease cost? How much money can be saved by finding better treatments? What is the cost-benefit ratio of spending more research funds on this disease? Because such questions arise, it is important to understand the cost of schizophrenia.

The cost of schizophrenia, like any disease, can be calculated in a variety of ways. The economic cost for treating a single case of the disease can be assessed. Or the cost of treating all known cases can be added together. Lost wages because of the disease can be added, as well as the cost of social support (e.g., room and board, rehabilitation programs) needed to keep the person functioning over many years. The cost for treating schizophrenia can also be compared with the cost for treating other diseases, such as heart disease. Finally, but most difficult, the noneconomic cost of schizophrenia can be considered.

The cost for treating a case of schizophrenia in which the person recovers is not unreasonable compared with other serious diseases. The person usually requires hospitalization for a few weeks and then medication for several months. If the person is not among the fortunate one-quarter of patients who recover completely (see chapter 5), then the costs multiply rapidly.

Estimates have been made of the direct care cost for treating Sylvia Frumkin, the woman described in Susan Sheehan's *Is There No Place on Earth for Me?*, who over 18 years had 27 different admissions to hospitals for schizophrenia. The total cost of her care was estimated to be $636,000, which included only hospitalizations, halfway houses, and foster homes. It did not include outpatient medication costs, emergency room services, general health care, social services, law enforcement services needed to return her to the hospital, legal services, court costs, lost wages, or even the direct care costs incurred by Ms. Frumkin's family. I have made a similar approximation of direct care costs for my sister, who has had schizophrenia for over 30 years and who has required hospitalization most of that time; the direct care costs for hospitalization in New York State mental hospitals alone during that time total almost $1.5 million. Such costs, I would submit, are not unusual for persons with severe schizophrenia.

When attempts are made to multiply the cost of treating one individual with schizophrenia by all people who have this disease, then estimates become simply "guesstimates." Schizophrenia varies clinically from mild to severe, and individuals with this disease vary greatly over the years in the services they require. What is known is that the total annual cost of state psychiatric hospitals was $4.5 billion in 1983, and another $2.3 billion in federal social security funds was paid to individuals with psychoses. Various government officials have estimated the total annual cost of schizophrenia in the United States at $10 to $20 billion in 1975, $18 billion in 1982, and $36 billion in 1986. Dr. Richard Wyatt, a leading researcher on this disease, estimated the annual cost in 1983 at $48.2 billion and projected to the year 2007 when he said the cost would reach $155 billion a year.

The problem with most cost estimates done to date is that they do not fully consider the magnitude of the disease. Because schizophrenia usually begins between the ages of 17 and 25, and because only one-quarter of people who get it recover completely, the economic cost of the disease must include the fact that approximately 1.2 million persons have been raised and educated through childhood and adolescence, with all the costs associated, only to become disabled at precisely the moment they are supposed to become economically contributing members of society. Most of the 1.2 million persons with this disease continue to require services such as occasional hospitalization, foster homes, subsidized income, court costs, social services, outpatient psychiatric services, etc. People with schizophrenia are not old or beyond their economically most productive years when they become sick, such as patients with Alzheimer's disease. Nor do they die relatively quickly, such as happens to many patients with cancer. If a fiendish economist from another planet were trying to devise a disease which would force our society to incur the maximum costs, then he (or she) could not do better than schizophrenia. Schizophrenia is economically a three-time loser: society must raise and educate the person destined to become afflicted, most people with the disease are unable to contribute economically to society, and at the same time many of them require costly services from society for the rest of their lives.

The cost of schizophrenia has also been compared with other diseases. In Australia the direct and indirect costs for schizophrenia were compared with heart attacks. Despite the fact that heart attacks affect twelve times more people than schizophrenia does in Australia, the overall direct and indirect costs per case of schizophrenia are six times greater than those for heart attacks. These costs did not include pension or social security costs which, since persons with schizophrenia live much longer than persons with heart attacks, would make the disparity even greater.

The huge economic cost of schizophrenia leads directly to the question of economic benefits of research on this disease. As will be discussed in chapter 6, schizophrenia is the most underresearched disease in the western world. In the Australian study referred to above, for example, it was found that research on schizophrenia received only one-fourteenth the funds lavished upon research on heart attacks. In terms of the relative cost of these diseases to society, this is a foolish allocation of research funds on economic grounds alone. In the United States a calculation has been made that if research discoveries could reduce the cost of schizophrenia by only 10 percent by 1998, the savings that would accrue over the following decade would total $180 billion.

None of the cost calculations discussed so far have included the largest cost of all—the cost to the family. This includes economic costs such as hospitalization and medications, as well as lost wages when a mother, for example, has to quit her job to remain at home with her schizophrenic son. Much more important is the noneconomic cost of schizophrenia for families. This cost is incalculable. It is the effect of raising an apparently normal child through childhood, then watching that child develop a chronic disease. It is the guilt of suspecting that you have done something to cause the disease in your family member, the fear of not knowing what the person may do next, the uncertainties and unpredictabilities of schedules and family life, and the broken marriages which are direct consequences of having someone with schizophrenia in the family. Cerebral palsy and Down's syndrome are tragedies for families of newborns; cancer and Alzheimer's disease are tragedies for families of the elderly. There is no known disease, however, with noneconomic costs so great as for schizophrenia. It is the costliest disease of all.

WHO IS RESPONSIBLE FOR CARE?

Given the numbers of people with schizophrenia and its staggering cost, who bears responsibility for providing care? Since 1766, even before the United States existed, the primary burden for the care of seriously mentally ill individuals has fallen on individual states. In that year Governor Francis Fauquier went before the Virginia House of Burgesses and asked them to approve funds for the opening of a public mental hospital. He told them:

> It is expedient I should . . . recommend to your Consideration and Humanity a poor unhappy set of People who are deprived of their Senses, and wander about the Country, terrifying the Rest of their Fellow Creatures. A legal Confinement and proper Provision ought to be appointed for these miserable Objects, who cannot help themselves. Every civilized Country has a Hospital for these People, where they are confined, maintained and attended by able Physicians, to endeavour to restore to them their lost Reason.

His request was approved and, after many delays, the first American hospital exclusively devoted to seriously mentally ill individuals was opened at Williamsburg in 1773. Other states were slow to follow Virginia's lead until Kentucky opened a state mental hospital in 1824 and South Carolina in 1828. In 1828, Horace Mann went before the Massachusetts Legislature and proclaimed: "The insane are the wards of the state."

In the ensuing years few people have doubted or challenged that dictum, although in some states the responsibility has been passed down to the counties. One of the few who did so was Dorothea Dix, who in 1848 tried to get Congress to appropriate federal land which could be used to benefit the mentally ill. She said that the seriously mentally ill, beset by "miseries and disqualifications brought upon them by the sorest afflictions with which humanity can be visited . . . are the wards of the nation." Congress did eventually pass a modified version of her request in 1854, but the bill was vetoed by President Franklin Pierce, who feared that if he set such a precedent the states would transfer the responsibility for all indigent people to the federal government. No other challenge to the state's responsibility for the seriously mentally ill took place until the community mental health center movement of the 1960s (see chapter 8).

It is now clear that with few exceptions the states have failed in their responsibility to provide care for persons with schizophrenia. Their failure has been compounded by failures of the National Institute of Mental Health to provide leadership on research; of the American Psychiatric Association, American Psychological Association, and National Association of Social Workers to provide leadership at the professional level; and of the National Mental Health Association to provide leadership at the advocacy level. The failures are conspicuous, deplorable, egregious. The failures continue day after day, month after month, and their consequences accrue to each of the 1.2 million persons with schizophrenia and to their families.

Isn't it time to change this? This is after all the twentieth century, not the twelfth. Isn't it time to bring psychiatry out of the Dark Ages and face schizophrenia for exactly what it is—a brain disease in need of research, sick individuals in need of services, the most tragic disease in western civilization. It is not necessary to accept the status quo on schizophrenia. It can be changed by those who are afflicted and by their families.

Every society has had within it individuals who, through no fault of their own, were unable to care for themselves. The care offered to these individuals has varied considerably from society to society over the centuries. Many proposals have been put forward regarding the truest index of a civilization—gross national product, control of world markets, growth rate, number of people subjugated, production of artistic or literary masterpieces, religiosity of the people, etc. Perhaps the most accurate index of civilization is the care it provides to those unable to care for themselves. This may be progress, the rest just existence.

Until attention and energy are focused on those with schizophrenia, they will continue to be with us—gazing vacantly at the bare walls of deteriorating state hospitals, living in roach-infested boarding houses, haunting back alleys of the inner city as in some modern Twilight Zone. They stand mute, their backs to the walls of vacant buildings, the gargoyles of our civilization.

RECOMMENDED FURTHER READING

Andrews, G., W. Hall, G. Goldstein, et al. "The Economic Costs of Schizophrenia." *Archives of General Psychiatry* 42 (1985): 537–43. This is a summary of the Australian study of the costs of schizophrenia and comparison with the costs of heart attacks.

Deutsch, A. *The Mentally Ill in America.* New York: Columbia University Press, 1937. Provides a nice summary of nineteenth-century efforts to treat the seriously mentally ill in America.

———. *The Shame of the States.* New York: Harcourt, Brace and Company, 1948. This is a classic study of American mental hospitals in the 1940s. The shame of the states at that time has evolved into the shame of the streets today.

Lamb, H. R., ed. *The Homeless Mentally Ill.* Washington, D.C.: American Psychiatric Association, 1984. This is a collection of papers from the APA's Task Force on the Homeless Mentally Ill.

Valdiserri, E. V., K. R. Carroll, and A. J. Hartl. "A Study of Offenses Committed by Psychotic Inmates in a County Jail." *Hospital and Community Psychiatry* 37 (1986): 163–66. This paper is the best evidence to date of a disturbing trend—the criminalization of psychotic behavior.

2

THE INNER WORLD OF MADNESS:
VIEW FROM THE INSIDE

What then does schizophrenia mean to me? It means fatigue and confusion, it means trying to separate every experience into the real and the unreal and not sometimes being aware of where the edges overlap. It means trying to think straight when there is a maze of experiences getting in the way, and when thoughts are continually being sucked out of your head so that you become embarrassed to speak at meetings. It means feeling sometimes that you are inside your head and visualising yourself walking over your brain, or watching another girl wearing your clothes and carrying out actions as you think them. It means knowing that you are continually "watched," that you can never succeed in life because the laws are all against you and knowing that your ultimate destruction is never far away.

Schizophrenic patient, quoted in Henry R. Rollin,
Coping with Schizophrenia

When tragedy strikes, one of the things which make life bearable for people is the sympathy of friends and relatives. This can be seen, for example, in a natural disaster like a flood and with a chronic disease like cancer. Those closest to the person afflicted offer help, extend their sympathy, and generally provide important solace and support in the person's time of need. "Sympathy," said Emerson, "is a supporting atmosphere, and in it we unfold easily and well." A prerequisite for sympathy is an ability to put oneself in the place of the person afflicted. One must be able to imagine oneself in a flood or getting cancer.

Without this ability to put oneself in the place of the person afflicted, there can be abstract pity but not true sympathy.

Sympathy for those afflicted with schizophrenia is sparse because it is difficult to put oneself in the place of the sufferer. The whole disease process is mysterious, foreign, and frightening to most people. It is not like a flood, where one can imagine all one's possessions being washed away. Nor like a cancer, where one can imagine a slowly growing tumor, relentlessly spreading from organ to organ and squeezing life from the body. No, schizophrenia is madness. Those who are afflicted act bizarrely, say strange things, withdraw from us, and may even try to hurt us. They are no longer the same person—they are *mad!* We don't understand why they say what they say and do what they do. We don't understand the disease process. Rather than a steadily growing tumor, which we can understand, it is as if the person has lost control of his/her brain. How can we sympathize with a person who is possessed by unknown and unseen forces? How can we sympathize with a madman or a madwoman?

The paucity of sympathy for those with schizophrenia makes it that much more of a disaster. Being afflicted with the disease is bad enough by itself. Those of us who have not had this disease should ask ourselves, for example, how we would feel if our brain began playing tricks on us, if unseen voices shouted at us, if we lost the capacity to feel emotions, and if we lost the ability to reason logically. This would certainly be burden enough for any human being to have to bear. But what if, in addition to this, those closest to us began to avoid us or ignore us, to pretend that they didn't hear our comments, to pretend that they didn't notice what we did? How would we feel if those we most cared about were embarrassed by our behavior each day?

Because there is little understanding of schizophrenia, so there is little sympathy. For this reason it is the obligation of everyone with a relative or close friend with schizophrenia to learn as much as possible about what the disease is and what the afflicted person is experiencing. This is not merely an intellectual exercise or a way to satisfy one's curiosity but rather to make it possible to sympathize with the person. For friends and relatives who want to be helpful, probably the most important thing to do is to learn about the inner workings of the schizophrenic brain. One mother wrote me after listening to her afflicted son's descriptions of his hallucinations: "I saw into the visual hallucinations that plagued him and frankly, at times, it raised the hair on my neck. It also helped me to get outside of *my* tragedy and to realize how horrible it is for the person who is afflicted. I thank God for that painful wisdom. I am able to cope easier with all of this."

With sympathy, schizophrenia is a personal tragedy. Without sympathy, it becomes a family calamity, for there is nothing to knit people together, no balm for the wounds. Understanding schizophrenia also helps demystify the disease and brings it from the realm of the occult to the daylight of reason. As we come to understand it, the face of madness slowly changes before us from one of terror to one of sadness. For the sufferer, this is a significant change.

The best way to learn what a person with schizophrenia experiences is to listen to someone with the disease. For this reason I have relied heavily upon patients' own accounts in describing the signs and symptoms. There are some excellent descriptions scattered throughout English literature; the best of these are listed at the end of this chapter. By contrast one of the most widely read books about a "schizophrenic," Hannah Green's *I Never Promised You a Rose Garden,* is not at all helpful. It describes a patient who, according to a recent analysis, should not even be diagnosed with schizophrenia but rather with hysteria (now often referred to as somatization disorder).

When one listens to persons with schizophrenia describe what they are experiencing and observes their behavior, certain abnormalities can be noted:

1. Alterations of the senses
2. Inability to sort and interpret incoming sensations, and an inability therefore to respond appropriately
3. Delusions and hallucinations
4. Altered sense of self
5. Changes in emotions
6. Changes in movements
7. Changes in behavior

No one symptom or sign is found in all schizophrenic patients; rather the final diagnosis rests upon the total symptom picture. Some patients have much more of one kind of symptom, other patients another. Conversely, there is no single symptom or sign of schizophrenia which is found exclusively in that disease. All symptoms and signs can be found at least occasionally in other diseases of the brain, such as brain tumors and temporal lobe epilepsy.

ALTERATIONS OF THE SENSES

In Edgar Allan Poe's "The Tell-Tale Heart" (1843), the main charac-ter, clearly lapsing into a schizophrenialike state, exclaims to the reader, "Have I not told you that what you mistake for madness is but overacuteness of the senses?" An expert on the dark recesses of the human mind, Poe put his finger directly on a central theme of madness. Alterations of the senses are especially prominent in the early stages of schizophrenic breakdown and can be found, according to one study, in almost two-thirds of all patients. As the authors of the study conclude: "Perceptual dysfunction is the most invariant feature of the early stage of schizophrenia." It can be elicited from patients most commonly when they have recovered from a psychotic episode; rarely can patients who are acutely or chronically psychotic describe these changes.

The alterations may be either enhancement (more common) or blunting; all sensory modalities may be affected. For example, Poe's protagonist was experiencing predominantly an increased acuteness of hearing:

> True!—nervous—very, very dreadfully nervous I had been and am! but why will you say that I am mad? The disease had sharpened my senses—not destroyed—not dulled them. Above all was the sense of hearing acute. I heard all things in the heaven and in the earth. I heard many things in hell. How, then, am I mad? Harken! and observe how healthily—how calmly—I can tell you the whole story.

Another described it this way:

> During the last while back I have noticed that noises all seem to be louder to me than they were before. It's as if someone had turned up the volume. . . . I notice it most with background noises—you know what I mean, noises that are always around but you don't notice them. Now they seem to be just as loud and sometimes louder than the main noises that are going on. . . . It's a bit alarming at times because it makes it difficult to keep your mind on something when there's so much going on that you can't help listening to.

Visual perceptual changes are even more common than auditory changes. Two patients described it as follows:

> Colours seem to be brighter now, almost as if they are luminous painting. I'm not sure if things are solid until I touch them.

I seem to be noticing colours more than before, although I am not artistically minded. The colours of things seem much clearer and yet at the same time there is something missing. The things I look at seem to be flatter as if you were looking just at a surface. Maybe it's because I notice so much more about things and find myself looking at them for a longer time. Not only the colour of things fascinates me but all sorts of little things, like markings in the surface, pick up my attention too.

And another noted both the sharpness of colors as well as the transformation of objects:

Everything looked vibrant, especially red; people took on a devilish look, with black outlines and white shining eyes; all sorts of objects—chairs, buildings, obstacles—took on a life of their own; they seemed to make threatening gestures, to have an animistic outlook.

In some instances the visual alterations improved the appearance:

Lots of things seemed psychedelic; they shone. I was working in a restaurant and it looked more first class than it really was.

In other cases the alterations made the object ugly or frightening:

People looked deformed, as if they had had plastic surgery, or were wearing makeup with different bone structure.

People were pulling hideous faces.

People were deformed, squarish, like in plaster.

Colors and textures may blend into each other:

I saw everything very bright and rich and pure like the thinnest line possible. Or a shiny smoothness like water but solid. After a while things got rough and shadowed again.

Sometimes both hearing *and* visual sensations are increased, as happened to this young woman:

These crises, far from abating, seemed rather to increase. One day, while I was in the principal's office, suddenly the room became enormous, illuminated by a dreadful electric light that cast false shadows. Everything was exact, smooth, artificial, extremely tense; the chairs and tables seemed models placed here and there. Pupils and teachers were puppets revolving without cause, without objective. I recognized nothing, nobody. It was as though reality, attenuated, had slipped away from all these things and these people. Profound dread overwhelmed me, and as though lost, I looked around desperately for help. I heard people talking, but I did not grasp the meaning of the words. The voices were metallic, without warmth or color. From time to time, a word detached itself from the rest. It repeated itself over and over in my head, absurd, as though cut off by a knife.

Closely related to the overacuteness of the senses is the flooding of the senses with stimuli. It is not only that the senses become more sharply attuned but that they see and hear everything. Normally our brain screens out most incoming sights and sounds, allowing us to concentrate on whatever we choose. This screening mechanism appears to become impaired in many persons with schizophrenia, releasing a veritable flood of sensory stimuli into the brain simultaneously.

This is one person's description of flooding of the senses with auditory stimuli:

Everything seems to grip my attention although I am not particularly interested in anything. I am speaking to you just now, but I can hear noises going on next door and in the corridor. I find it difficult to shut these out, and it makes it more difficult for me to concentrate on what I am saying to you. Often the silliest little things that are going on seem to interest me. That's not even true: they don't interest me, but I find myself attending to them and wasting a lot of time this way.

And with visual stimuli:

Occasionally during subsequent periods of disturbance there was some distortion of vision and some degree of hallucination. On several occasions my eyes became markedly oversensitive to light. Ordinary colors appeared to be much too bright, and sunlight seemed dazzling in intensity. When this happened, ordinary reading was impossible, and print seemed excessively black.

Frequently these two things happen together.

I can probably tell you as much or more about what really went on those days than lots of people who were sane: the comings and goings of people, the weather, what was on the news, what we ate, what records were played, what was said. My focus was a bit bizarre. I could do portraits of people who were walking down the street. I remembered license numbers of cars we were following into Vancouver. We paid $3.57 for gas. The air machine made eighteen dings while we were there.

In these disturbing circumstances I sensed again the atmosphere of unreality. During class, in the quiet of the work period, I heard the street noises—a trolley passing, people talking, a horse neighing, a horn sounding, each detached, immovable, separated from its source, without meaning. Around me, the other children, heads bent over their work, were robots or puppets, moved by an invisible mechanism. On the platform, the teacher, too, talking, gesticulating, rising to write on the blackboard, was a grotesque jack-in-the-box. And always this ghastly quiet, broken by outside sounds coming from far away, the implacable sun heating the lifeless immobility. An awful terror bound me; I wanted to scream.

An outsider may see only someone "out of touch with reality." In fact we are experiencing so many realities that it is often confusing and sometimes totally overwhelming.

As these examples make clear, it is difficult to concentrate or pay attention when so much sensory data is rushing through the brain. In one study more than half of people who had had schizophrenia recalled impairments in attention and in keeping track of time. Mark Vonnegut expressed it as follows:

Had someone asked me about what was going on, I would have had quite a bit of trouble taking the questions seriously and even more trouble getting my voice and words to work right. I would have been much more interested in their clothes or face than the questions and would have thought they were really asking something much deeper. I was on my way to Vancouver, and knew it most of the time, but if asked where I was, that would have been a long way down the line of answers that came to mind.

As did this patient:

Sometimes when people speak to me my head is overloaded. It's too much to hold at once. It goes out as quick as it goes in. It makes you forget what you just heard because you can't get hearing it long enough. It's just words in the air unless you can figure it out from their faces.

Sensory modalities other than hearing and vision may also be affected in schizophrenia. Mary Barnes in her autobiographical account of "a journey through madness" recalled how "it was terrible to be touched. . . . Once a nurse tried to cut my nails. The touch was such that I tried to bite her." Another patient described the horror of feeling a rat in his throat and tasting the "decay in my mouth as its body disintegrated inside me." Increased sensitivity of the genitalia is occasionally found, explained by one patient as "a genital sexual irritation from which there was no peace and no relief." I recently took care of a young man with such a sensation who became convinced that his penis was turning black. He countered this delusional fear by insisting that doctors—or anyone within sight—examine him every five minutes to reassure him. His hospitalization was precipitated by his having gone into the local post office where a girlfriend worked and asking her to examine him in front of the customers.

Another aspect of the overacuteness of the senses is a flooding of the mind with thoughts. It is as if the brain is being bombarded both with external stimuli (e.g., sounds and sights) and with internal stimuli as well (thoughts, memories). One psychiatrist who has studied this area extensively claims that we have not been as aware of the internal stimuli in persons with schizophrenia as we should be.

> My trouble is that I've got too many thoughts. You might think about something, let's say that ashtray, and just think, oh! yes, that's for putting my cigarette in, but I would think of it and then I would think of a dozen different things connected with it at the same time.

> My concentration is very poor. I jump from one thing to another. If I am talking to someone they only need to cross their legs or scratch their heads and I am distracted and forget what I was saying. I think I could concentrate better with my eyes shut.

And this person describes the flooding of memories from the past:

> Childhood feelings began to come back as symbols, and bits from past conversations went through my head. . . . I began to think I was hypnotized so that I would remember what had happened in the first four and a half years of my life. . . . I thought that my parents had supplied information about the nursery school teacher and pediatrician to someone—perhaps my husband—with the hope that I would be able to straighten myself out by remembering the early years.

Perhaps it is this increased ability of some schizophrenic patients to recall childhood events which has mistakenly led psychoanalysts to assume that the recalled events were somehow causally related to the schizophrenia (as will be discussed in chapter 6). There is no scientific evidence to support such theories, however, and much evidence to support contrary theories.

A variation of flooding with thoughts occurs when the person feels that someone is inserting the flood of thoughts into his/her head. This is commonly referred to as thought insertion and when present is considered by many psychiatrists to be an almost certain symptom of schizophrenia.

> All sorts of "thoughts" seem to come to me, as if someone is "speaking" them inside my head. When in any company it appears to be worse (probably some form of self-consciousness), I don't want the "thoughts" to come but I keep on "hearing" them (as it were) and it requires lots of will power sometimes to stop myself from "thinking" (in the form of "words") the most absurd and embarrassing things. These "thoughts" do not mean anything to me and cause "lack of concentration" in whatever I am doing at work, etc. When listening to music I find that the words of the song come to me involuntarily, or if I don't know the particular song that is being played, I seem to "make up words" to the song against my will. Another thing similar to the above is the fact that if there is any banging or suchlike noise going on, I do the same thing, which is to "think-up" words to "rhyme"—as you might say—with whatever noise I can hear.

With this kind of activity going on in a person's head, it is not surprising that it would be difficult to concentrate.

> I was invited to play checkers and started to do so, but I could not go on. I was too much absorbed in my own thoughts, particularly those regarding the approaching end of the world and those responsible for the use of force and for the charge of homicidal intent. By nightfall my head was all in a whirl. It seemed to be the Day of Judgment and all humanity came streaming in from four different directions.

Concentrating on even as simple a task as walking from one building to another may become impossible.

> Fear made me ill; just the same I ran out to visit a friend who was staying at a nearby sanatorium. To get there, a way led through the woods, short and well marked. Becoming lost in the thick fog, I circled round and round the sanatorium without seeing it, my fear augmenting all the while. By and by I realized that the wind inspired this fear; the trees, too, large and black in the mist, but particularly the wind. At length I grasped the meaning of its message: the frozen wind from the North Pole wanted to crush the earth, to destroy it. Or perhaps it was an omen, a sign that the earth was about to be laid waste. This idea tormented me with growing intensity.

When all aspects of overacuteness of the senses are taken together, the consequent cacophony in the brain must be frightening, and it is so described by most patients. In the very earliest stage of the disease, however, before this overacuteness becomes too severe, it may be a pleasant experience. Many descriptions of the initial days of becoming schizophrenic are descriptions of heightened awareness, commonly called "peak experiences"; such experiences are also common in manic-depressive illness and in getting high on drugs. Here is one patient's description:

> Suddenly my whole being was filled with light and loveliness and with an upsurge of deeply moving feeling from within myself to meet and recipro-cate the influence that flowed into me. I was in a state of the most vivid awareness and illumination. What can I say of it? A cloudless, cerulean blue sky of the mind, shot through with shafts of exquisite, warm, dazzling sunlight.

Many patients interpret such experiences within a religious framework and believe they are being touched by God.

> Before last week, I was quite closed about my emotions; then finally I owned up to them with another person. I began to speak without thinking beforehand and what came out showed an awareness of human beings and God. I could feel deeply about other people. We felt connected. The side which had been suppressing emotions did not seem to be the real one. I was in a higher and higher state of exhilaration and awareness. Things people said had hidden meaning. They said things that applied to life. Everything that was real seemed to make sense. I had a great awareness of life, truth, and God. I went to church and suddenly all parts of the service made sense. My senses were sharpened. I became fascinated by the little insignificant things around me. There was an additional awareness of the world that would do artists, architects, and painters good. I ended up being too emotional, but I felt very much at home with myself, very much at ease. It gave me a great feeling of power. It was not a case of seeing more broadly but deeper. I was losing touch with the outside world and lost my sense of time. There was a fog around me in some sense, and I felt asleep. I could see more deeply into problems that other people had and would go directly into a deeper subject with a person. I had the feeling I loved everybody in the world.

A few weeks before my illness I began to regress into success daydreams somewhat similar to, though not quite as naive and grandiose as, those I had had during the early adolescence. I was puzzled by this tendency, though not greatly alarmed because it hardly seemed that my daydreaming self was a part of my adult ethical self. At the onset of panic, I was suddenly confronted with an overwhelming conviction that I had discovered the secrets of the universe, which were being rapidly made plain with incredible lucidity. The truths discovered seemed to be known immediately and directly, with absolute certainty. I had no sense of doubt or awareness of the possibility of doubt. In spite of former atheism and strong antireligious sentiments, I was suddenly convinced that it was possible to prove rationally the existence of God.

In view of such experiences it is hardly surprising to find excessive religious preoccupation listed as a common early sign of schizophrenia.

Sensations can be blunted, as well as enhanced, in schizophrenia. Such blunting is more commonly found late in the course of the disease whereas enhancement is often one of the earliest symptoms. The blunting is described "as if a heavy curtain were drawn over his mind; it resembled a thick deadening cloud that prevented the free use of his senses." One's own voice may sound muted or faraway, and vision may be wavy or blurred: "However hard I looked it was as if I was looking through a daydream and the mass of detail, such as the pattern on a carpet, became lost."

One sensation which may be blunted in schizophrenia is that of pain. Although it does not happen frequently, when such blunting does occur it may be dramatic and have practical consequences for those who are caring for the person. It is now in vogue to attribute such blunting to medication, but in fact it was clearly described twenty and thirty years before drugs for schizophrenia became widely available. There are many accounts in the older textbooks of surgeons, for example, being able to do appendectomies and similar procedures on some schizophrenic patients with little or no anesthesia. One of my patients had a massive breast abscess which was unknown until the fluid from it seeped through her dress; although this is normally an exceedingly painful condition, she insisted she felt no pain whatsoever. Nurses who have cared for schizophrenic patients over many years can recite stories of fractured bones, perforated ulcers, or ruptured appendixes which the patient said nothing about. Practically, it is important to be aware of this possibility so that medical help can be sought for persons if they look sick, even if they are not complaining of pain. It is also the reason that some people with schizophrenia burn their fingers when they smoke cigarettes too close to the end.

It may well be that there is a common denominator for all aspects of the alterations of the senses discussed thus far. All sensory input into the brain passes through the limbic area in the lower portion of the brain. It is this area that is most suspect as being involved in schizophrenia, as will be discussed in chapter 6. The limbic system filters this sensory input, and it is likely that disease of this system accounts for many or most schizophrenic symptoms. Norma Mac-Donald, a woman who published an account of her schizophrenic illness in 1960, foresaw this possibility in a particularly clear manner several years before psychiatrists and neurologists understood it, and she wrote about her conception of the breakdown in the filter system.

At first it was as if parts of my brain "awoke" which had been dormant, and I became interested in a wide assortment of people, events, places, and ideas which normally would make no impression on me. Not knowing that I was ill, I made no attempt to understand what was happening, but felt that there was some overwhelming significance in all this, produced either by God or Satan, and I felt that I was duty-bound to ponder on each of these new interests, and the more I pondered the worse it became. The walk of a stranger on the street could be a sign to me which I must interpret. Every face in the windows of a passing streetcar would be engraved on my mind, all of them concentrating on me and trying to pass me some sort of message. Now, many years later, I can appreciate what had happened. Each of us is capable of coping with a large number of stimuli, invading our being through any one of the senses. We could hear every sound within earshot and see every object, hue, and colour within the field of vision, and so on. It's obvious that we would be incapable of carrying on any of our daily activities if even one-hundredth of all these available stimuli invaded us at once. So the mind must have a filter which functions without our conscious thought, sorting stimuli and allowing only those which are relevant to the situation in hand to disturb consciousness. And this filter must be working at maximum efficiency at all times, particularly when we require a degree of concentration. What had happened to me in Toronto was a breakdown in the filter, and a hodge-podge of unrelated stimuli were distracting me from things which should have had my undivided attention.

INABILITY TO INTERPRET AND RESPOND

In normal people the brain functions in such a way that incoming stimuli are sorted and interpreted; then a correct response is selected and sent out. Most of the responses are learned, such as saying "thank you" when a gift is given to us. These responses also include logic, such as being able to predict what will happen to us if we do not arrive for work at the time we are supposed to. Our brains sort and interpret incoming stimuli and send out responses hundreds of thousands of times each day. The site of this function is also thought to be the limbic system, and it is intimately connected with the screening function referred to above.

A fundamental defect of schizophrenic patients' brains is their frequent inability to sort, interpret, and respond like normal brains. Textbooks of psychiatry describe this as a thought disorder, but it is more than just thoughts which are involved. Visual and auditory stimuli, emotions, and some actions are misarranged in exactly the same way as thoughts; the brain defect is probably similar for all.

We do not understand the human brain well enough to know precisely how the system works; but imagine a telephone operator sitting at an old plug-in type of switchboard in the middle of your limbic system. He or she receives all the sensory input, thoughts, ideas, memories and emotions coming in, sorts them, and determines those which go together. For example, normally our brain takes the words of a sentence and converts them automatically into a pattern of thought. We don't have to concentrate on the individual words but rather can focus on the meaning of the whole message.

Now what would happen if the switchboard operator decided not to do the job of sorting and interpreting? In terms of understanding auditory stimuli, two schizophrenic patients describe this kind of defect:

> When people are talking I have to think what the words mean. You see, there is an interval instead of a spontaneous response. I have to think about it and it takes time. I have to pay all my attention to people when they are speaking or I get all mixed up and don't understand them.

> I can concentrate quite well on what people are saying if they talk simply. It's when they go on into long sentences that I lose the meanings. It just becomes a lot of words that I would need to string together to make sense.

One pair of researchers described this defect as a receptive aphasia similar to that found in some patients who have had a stroke. The words are there but the person cannot synthesize them into sentences, as explained by this person with schizophrenia:

> I used to get the sudden thing that I couldn't understand what people said, like it was a foreign language.

Difficulties in comprehending visual stimuli are similar to those described for auditory stimuli.

> I have to put things together in my head. If I look at my watch I see the watchstrap, watch, face, hands and so on, then I have got to put them together to get it into one piece.

> Everything is in bits. You put the picture up bit by bit into your head. It's like a photograph that's torn in bits and put together again. If you move it's frightening. The picture you had in your head is still there but broken up. If I move there's a new picture that I have to put together again.

One patient had similar problems when she looked at her psychiatrist, seeing "the teeth, then the nose, then the cheeks, then one eye and the other. Perhaps it was this independence of each part that inspired such fear and prevented my recognizing her even though I knew who she was."

It is probably because of such impairments in visual interpretation that some persons with schizophrenia misidentify someone and say he or she looks like someone else. My sister with schizophrenia does this frequently, claiming to have seen many friends from childhood who I know in fact could not have been present. Another patient with schizophrenia added a grandiose flair to the visual misperception:

> This morning, when I was at Hillside [Hospital] I was making a movie. I was surrounded by movie stars. The X-ray technician was Peter Lawford. The security guard was Don Knotts . . .

Persons with schizophrenia, it might be said, frequently cannot see the forest for the trees and, even when they can, the forest appears changed.

In addition to difficulties in interpreting individual auditory and visual stimuli in coherent patterns, many persons with schizophrenia have difficulty putting the two kinds of stimuli together.

> I can't concentrate on television because I can't watch the screen and listen to what is being said at the same time. I can't seem to take in two things

like this at the same time especially when one of them means watching and the other means listening. On the other hand I seem to be always taking in too much at the one time and then I can't handle it and can't make sense of it.

I tried sitting in my apartment and reading; the words looked perfectly familiar, like old friends whose faces I remembered perfectly well but whose names I couldn't recall; I read one paragraph ten times, could make no sense of it whatever, and shut the book. I tried listening to the radio, but the sounds went through my head like a buzz saw. I walked carefully through traffic to a movie theater and sat through a movie which seemed to consist of a lot of people wandering around slowly and talking a great deal about something or other. I decided, finally, to spend my days sitting in the park watching the birds on the lake.

These persons' difficulties in watching television or movies are very typical. In fact it is striking how few schizophrenic patients on hospital wards watch television, contrary to what is popularly believed. Some may sit in front of it and watch the visual motion, as if it were a test pattern, but few of them can tell you what is going on. This includes patients of all levels of intelligence and education, among them college-educated persons who, given little else to do, might be expected to take advantage of the TV for much of the day. On the contrary, you are more likely to find them sitting quietly in another corner of the room, ignoring the TV; if you ask them why, they may tell you that they cannot follow what is going on, or they may try to cover up their defect by saying they are tired. One of my patients was an avid New York Yankees baseball fan prior to his illness, but he refuses to watch the game now even when the Yankees are on and he is in the room at the time, because he cannot understand what is happening. As a practical aside, the favorite TV programs and movies of many persons with schizophrenia are cartoons and travelogues; both are simple and can be followed visually without the necessity of integrating auditory input at the same time.

But the job of the switchboard operator in our brain does not end with sorting and interpreting the incoming stimuli. The job also includes hooking up the stimuli with proper responses to be sent back outside. For example, if somebody asks me, "Would you like to have lunch with me today?" my brain focuses immediately on the overall content of the question and starts calculating: Do I have time? Do I want to? What excuses do I have? What will other people think who see me with this person? What will be the effect on this person if I say no? Out of these calculations emerges a response which, in a normal brain, is appropriate to the situation. Similarly, news of a friend's death gets hooked up with grief, visual and auditory stimuli from a Woody Allen movie are hooked up with mirth, and a new idea regarding the creation of the universe is hooked up with logic and with previous knowledge in this area. It is an orderly, ongoing process, and the switchboard operator goes on, day after day, making relatively few mistakes.

The inability of schizophrenic patients not only to sort and interpret stimuli but to select out appropriate responses is one of the hallmarks of the disease. It led Swiss psychiatrist Eugen Bleuler in 1911 to introduce the term "schizophrenia," meaning in German a splitting of the various parts of the thought process. Bleuler was impressed by the inappropriate responses frequently given by persons with this disease; for example, when told that a close friend has died, a schizophrenic may giggle. It is as if the switchboard operator not only gets bored and stops sorting and interpreting but becomes actively malicious and begins hooking the incoming stimuli up to random, usually inappropriate, responses.

The inability to interpret and respond appropriately is also at the core of schizophrenics' difficulties in relating to other people. Not being able to put the auditory and visual stimuli together makes it difficult to understand others; if in addition you cannot respond appropriately, then interpersonal relations become impossible. One patient described such difficulties:

> During the visit I tried to establish contact with her, to feel that she was actually there, alive and sensitive. But it was futile. Though I certainly recognized her, she became part of the unreal world. I knew her name and everything about her, yet she appeared strange, unreal, like a statue. I saw her eyes, her nose, her lips moving, heard her voice and understood what she said perfectly, yet I was in the presence of a stranger. To restore contact between us I made desperate efforts to break through the invisible dividing wall but the harder I tried, the less successful I was, and the uneasiness grew apace.

It is for this reason that many persons with schizophrenia prefer to spend time by themselves, withdrawn, communicating with others as little as possible. The process is too difficult and too painful to undertake except when absolutely necessary.

Just as auditory and visual stimuli may not be sorted or interpreted by the schizophrenic brain and may elicit inappropriate responses, so too may actions be fragmented and lead to inappropriate responses. This will be discussed in greater detail in a subsequent section, but it is worth noting that the same kind of brain deficit is probably involved. For example, compare the difficulties this patient has in the simple action of getting a drink of water with the difficulties in responding to auditory and visual stimuli described above:

> If I do something like going for a drink of water, I've got to go over each detail—find cup, walk over, turn tap, fill cup, turn tap off, drink it. I keep building up a picture. I have to change the picture each time. I've got to make the old picture move. I can't concentrate. I can't hold things. Something else comes in, various things. It's easier if I stay still.

It suggests that there may be relatively few underlying brain deficits leading to the broad range of symptoms which comprise the schizophrenic disease.

When schizophrenic thought patterns are looked at from outside, as when they are being described by a psychiatrist, such terms as "disconnectedness," "loosening of associations," "concreteness," "impairment of logic," "thought blocking" and "ambivalence" are used. To begin with disconnectedness: one of my patients used to come into the office each morning and ask my secretary to write a sentence on paper for him. One request was "Write all kinds of black snakes looking like raw onion, high strung, deep down, long winded, all kinds of sizes." This patient had put together several apparently disconnected ideas which a normally functioning brain would not join. Another patient wrote:

> My thoughts get all jumbled up, I start thinking or talking about something but I never get there. Instead I wander off in the wrong direction and get caught up with all sorts of different things that may be connected with the things I want to say but in a way I can't explain. People listening to me get more lost than I do.

Sometimes there may be a vague connection between the jumbled thoughts in schizophrenic thinking; such instances are referred to as loose associations. For example, in the sentence about black snakes above, it may be that the patient juxtaposed onions to black snakes because of the onionlike pattern on the skin of some snakes. On another occasion I was drawing blood from a patient's arm and she said, "Look at my blue veins. I asked the Russian women to make them red," loosely connecting the color of blood with the "Reds" of the Soviet Union. Other examples of loose associations are:

> "Sun," I intoned. "From the Sun to Son to Son of God to Jesus Christ. From Christ to Christmas, Christmas to Mass. Mass to solid mass. Solid mass to earth. Earth to element. Element for four elements to earth, air, fire, water, the four elements. Four elements to Universe. Universe to everything."

And the great Russian dancer Nijinsky wrote the following as he was becoming schizophrenic, jumping from the round shape of a stage to his eye to people's criticism of him:

> I am not artificial. I am life. The theatre is not life. I know the customs of the theatre. The theatre becomes a habit. Life does not. I do not like the theatre with a square stage. I like a round stage. I will build a theatre which will have a round shape, like an eye. I like to look closely in the mirror and I see only one eye in my forehead. Often I make drawings of one eye. I dislike polemics and therefore people can say what they like about my book; I will be silent. I have come to the conclusion that it is better to be silent than to speak.

Occasionally the loose association will rest not upon some tenuous logical connection between the words but merely upon their similar sound. For example, one young man presented me with a written poem one morning.

> *I believe we will soon*
> *achieve world peace. But*
> *I'm still on the lamb.*

He had confused the lamb associated with peace with the expression "on the lam," the correct spelling of which he apparently did not know. There is no logical association between "lamb" and "lam" except for their similar sound; such associations are referred to as clang associations.

Another characteristic of schizophrenic thinking is concreteness. This can be tested by asking the person to give the meaning of proverbs, which require an ability to abstract, to move from the specific to the general. When most people are asked what "People who live in glass houses shouldn't throw stones" means, they will answer something like:

"If you're not perfect yourself, don't criticize others." They move from the specific glass house and stones to the general concept without difficulty.

But the person with schizophrenia frequently loses this ability to abstract. I asked one hundred schizophrenic patients to explain the proverb above; less than one-third were able to think abstractly about it. The majority answered simply something like "It might break the windows." In many instances the concrete answer also demonstrated some disconnected thinking.

> Well, it could mean exactly like it says 'cause the windows may well be broken. They do grow flowers in glass houses.
>
> Because if they did they'd break the environment.
>
> Because they might be put out for the winter.

A few patients personalized it:

> People should always keep their decency about their living arrangements. I remember living in a glass house but all I did was wave.
>
> Because it might bust the wall and people could see you.

Others responded with totally irrelevant answers that illustrated many facets of the schizophrenic thinking disorder.

> Don't hit until you go—coming or going.
>
> Some people are up in the air and some in society and some up in the air.

A few patients were able to think abstractly about the proverb, but in formulating their reply incorporated other aspects of schizophrenic thinking.

> People who live in glass houses shouldn't forget people who live in stone houses and shouldn't throw glass.
>
> If you suffer from complexities, don't talk about people. Don't be agile.

The most succinct answer came from a quiet, chronically schizophrenic young man who pondered it solemnly, looked up and said, "Caution."

Concrete thinking can also occur during the everyday life of some schizophrenic persons. For example, one day I was taking a picture of my schizophrenic sister. When I said, "Look at the birdie," she immediately looked up to the sky. Another patient, passing a newspaper stand, noticed a headline announcing that a star had fallen from a window. "How could a big thing like a star get into a window?" he wondered, until he realized it referred to a movie star. *Death of a Salesman,* read the movie marquee, and a patient "speculated vaguely that a salesman might be a native of some country named Sales, probably in Asia."

An impairment of the ability to think logically is another facet of schizophrenic thinking, as illustrated in several of the previous examples. Another example was a patient under my care who, in psychological testing, was asked, "What would you do if you were lost in a forest?" He replied, "Go to the back of the forest, not the front." Similarly, many schizophrenic patients lose the ability to reason causally about events. One, for example, set his home on fire with his wheelchair-confined mother in it; when questioned carefully he did not seem to understand the fact that he was endangering her life.

In this kind of impaired thinking, opposites can coexist.

I was extremely unhappy, I felt myself getting younger; the system wanted to reduce me to nothing. Even as I diminished in body and in age, I discovered that I was nine centuries old. For to be nine centuries old actually meant being not yet born. That is why the nine centuries did not make me feel at all old; quite the contrary.

I had no time to go to sleep. Instantly the board of judges appeared. I could not see them clearly and was unable to identify any of them since there were no features on any of the faces . . . hardly faces at all, just blank oval spaces, poised on shoulders. They were seated behind a raised wooden platform, peering over at me. How could they peer without eyes? Perhaps they had eyes but I could not see them? Of course, I didn't have my glasses. In any case, they were definitely peering.

In the first instance no attempt is made to resolve the disparity between being very old and not yet born; in the second the person realizes that a face cannot peer yet have no eyes, but is unable to resolve the discrepancy. Given this impairment of causal and logical thinking in many persons with this disease, it is not surprising that they frequently have difficulty with daily activities, such as taking a bus, following directions, or planning meals. It also explains the fantastic ideas that some schizophrenic patients offer as facts. One of my patients, for example, wrote me a note about "a spider that weighs over a ton" and "a bird which weighs 178 pounds and makes 200 tracks in the winter and has only one foot." The writer was college-educated.

In addition to disconnectedness, loosening of associations, concreteness, and impairment of logic, there are other features of schizophrenic thinking. Neologisms—made-up words—are occasionally heard. They may sound like gibberish to the listener, but to those saying them they are a response to their inability to find the words they want.

> The worst thing has been my face and my speech. The words wouldn't come out right. I know how to explain myself but the way it comes out of my mouth isn't right. My thoughts run too fast and I can't stop the train at the right point to make them go the right way. Big magnified thoughts come into my head when I am speaking and put away words I wanted to say and make me stray away from what was in my mind. Things I am speaking just fade away and my head gets very heavy and I can't place what I wanted to say. I've got a lot to say but I can't focus the words to come out so they come out jumbled up. A barrier inside my head stops me from speaking properly and the mind goes blank. I try to concentrate but nothing comes out. Sometimes I find a word to replace what I wanted to say.

Another uncommon but dramatic form of schizophrenic thinking is called a word salad; the person just strings together a series of totally unrelated words and pronounces them as a sentence. One of my patients once turned to me solemnly and asked, "Bloodworm Baltimore frenchfry?" It's difficult to answer a question like that!

Generally it is not necessary to analyze a schizophrenic's thought pattern in detail to know that something is wrong with it. The overall effect on the listener is both predictable and indicative. In its most common forms, it makes the listener feel that something is fuzzy about the thinking, as if the words have been slightly mixed up. John Bartlow Martin wrote a book about mental illness called *A Pane of Glass,* and Ingmar Bergman portrayed a schizophrenic onset in his *Through a Glass Darkly.* Both were referring to this opaque quality in schizophrenic speech and thinking. The listener hears all the words, which may be almost correct, but at the end of the sentence or paragraph realizes that it doesn't "make sense." It is the feeling evoked when, puzzled by something, we squint our eyes, wrinkle our forehead, and smile slightly. Usually we exclaim "What?" as we do this. It is a reaction evoked often when we listen to people with a schizophrenic thinking disorder.

> I am glad as well as sorry not to have heard from you for a long time. I begin to confirm my suspicions along a totally different aspect of the nature of religions, nationalism or imperialism. I admit I never even dreamt that it centered around the laziness, imperfection, or improper understanding of the tendencies in the nature of human fight and struggle against this religious approach which was partially forced on me.

> I feel that everything is sort of related to everybody and that some people are far more susceptible to this theory of relativity than others because of either having previous ancestors connected in some way or other with places or things, or because of believing, or by leaving a trail behind when you walk through a room you know. Some people might leave a different trail and all sorts of things go like that.

There can, of course, be all degrees of these thinking disorders in schizophrenic patients. Especially in the early stages of illness there may be only a vagueness or evasiveness that defies precise labeling, but in the full-blown illness the impairment usually is quite clear. It is an unusual patient who does not have some form of thinking disorder. Some psychiatrists even question whether schizophrenia is the correct diagnosis if the person's thinking pattern is completely normal: they would say that schizophrenia, by definition, must include some disordered thinking. Others claim that it is possible, though unusual, to have genuine schizophrenia with other symptoms but without a thinking disorder.

A totally different type of thinking disorder is also commonly found in persons with schizophrenia: blocking of thoughts. To return to the metaphor of the telephone operator at the switchboard, it is as if she suddenly dozes off for a few moments and the system goes dead. The person is thinking or starting to respond and then stops, often in midsentence, and looks blank for a brief period. John Perceval described this as long ago as 1840:

> For instance, I have been often desired to open my mouth, and to address persons in different manners, and I have begun without premeditation a very rational and consecutive speech . . . but in the midst of my sentence, the power has either left me, or words have been suggested contradictory of those that went before: and I have been deserted, gaping, speechless, or stuttering in great confusion.

Other people have given these accounts:

> I may be thinking quite clearly and telling someone something and suddenly I get stuck. You have seen me do this and you may think I am just lost for words or that I have gone into a trance, but that is not what happens. What happens is that I suddenly stick on a word or an idea in my head and I just can't move past it. It seems to fill my mind and there's no room for anything else. This might go on for a while and suddenly it's over. Afterwards I get a feeling that I have been thinking very deeply about whatever it was but often I can't remember what it was that has filled my mind so completely.

> If I am reading I may suddenly get bogged down at a word. It may be any word, even a simple word that I know well. When this happens I can't get past it. It's as if I am being hypnotized by it. It's as if I am seeing the word for the first time and in a different way from anyone else. It's not so much that I absorb it, it's more like it is absorbing me.

> I would start a thought and then couldn't remember what I was thinking. Trains of thought were left in mid-air.

> Sometimes I commit brief disappearances—my mind pauses and closes down for a short while, like falling asleep suddenly.

Everyone who has spent time with persons with schizophrenia has observed this phenomenon. James Chapman claims it occurs in 95 percent of all patients. Some of the patients explain it by saying the thoughts are being taken out of their head. This symptom—called thought withdrawal—is considered by many psychiatrists to be strongly suggestive of a diagnosis of schizophrenia when it is present.

Ambivalence is another common symptom of schizophrenic thinking. Although now a fashionable term used very broadly, it was originally used in a narrower sense to describe schizophrenic patients who were unable to resolve contradictory thoughts or feelings, holding opposites in their minds simultaneously. A person with schizophrenia might think: "Yes, they are going to kill me and I love them." One woman described the contradictory thoughts as follows:

> I am so ambivalent that my mind can divide on a subject, and those two parts subdivide over and over until my mind feels like it is in pieces and I am totally disorganized.

Sometimes the ambivalence gets translated into actions as well. For example, one of my patients frequently leaves the front door of the building, turns right, then stops, takes three steps back to the left and stops, turns back and starts right, and may continue in this way for a full five minutes. It is not found as dramatically in most patients, but is of sufficient frequency and severity for Bleuler to have named it as one of the cardinal symptoms of schizophrenia. It is as if the ability to make a decision has been impaired. Normally our brain assesses the incoming thoughts and stimuli, makes a decision and then initiates a response. The brains of some schizophrenic persons are apparently impaired in this respect, initiating a response but then immediately countermanding it with its opposite, then repeating the process. It is a truly painful spectacle to observe.

DELUSIONS AND HALLUCINATIONS

Delusions and hallucinations are probably the best-known symptoms of schizophrenia. They are dramatic and are therefore the behaviors usually focused on when schizophrenia is being represented in popular literature or movies. The person observed talking to himself or to inanimate objects is almost a *sine qua non* for schizophrenia; it is the image evoked in our minds when the term "crazy" or "mad" is used.

And certainly delusions and hallucinations are very important and common symptoms of this disease. However, it should be remembered that they are not essential to it; indeed no *single* symptom is essential for the diagnosis of schizophrenia. There are many true schizophrenics who have a combination of other symptoms, such as a thought disorder, disturbances of affect, and disturbances of behavior, who have never had delusions or hallucinations. It should also be remembered that delusions and hallucinations are found in brain diseases other than schizophrenia, so their presence does not automatically mean that schizophrenia is present. Finally, it is important to realize that most delusions and hallucinations, as well as distortions of the body boundaries, are a direct outgrowth of overacuteness of the senses and the brain's inability to interpret and respond appropriately to stimuli. In other words, most delusions and hallucinations are logical outgrowths of what the brain is experiencing. They are "crazy" only to the outsider;

to the person experiencing them they form part of a logical and coherent pattern.

Delusions are simply false ideas believed by the patient but not by other people in his/her culture and which cannot be corrected by reason. One simple form of a delusion is the conviction that random events going on around the person all relate in a direct way to him or her. If you are walking down the street and a man on the opposite sidewalk coughs, you don't think anything of it and may not even consciously hear the cough. The person with schizophrenia, however, not only hears the cough but may immediately decide it must be a signal of some kind, perhaps directed to someone else down the street to warn him that the schizophrenic person is coming. The schizophrenia sufferer *knows* this is true with a certainty that few people experience. If you are walking with such a person and try to reason him/her past these delusions your efforts will probably be futile. Even if you cross the street, and in the presence of the same person question the man about his cough, the individual will probably just decide that you are part of the plot. Reasoning with schizophrenic people about their delusions is like trying to bail out the ocean with a bucket. If, shortly after the cough incident, a helicopter flies overhead, the delusion may enlarge. Obviously the helicopter is watching the person, which further confirms suspicions about the cough. And if in addition to these happenings, the person arrives at the bus stop just too late to catch the bus, the delusional system is confirmed yet again; obviously the person who coughed or the helicopter pilot radioed the bus driver to leave. It all fits together into a logical, coherent whole.

Normal persons would experience these events and simply curse their bad luck at missing the bus. The person with schizophrenia, however, is experiencing different things so the events take on a different meaning. The cough and the helicopter noise may be very loud to him/her and even the sound of the bus may be perceived to be strange. While the normal person responds correctly to these as separate and unrelated events, similar to the stimuli and events of everyday life, the schizophrenic patient puts them together into a pattern. Thus both overacuteness of the senses and impaired ability to logically interpret incoming stimuli and thoughts may lie behind many of the delusions experienced by afflicted minds. To them the person who *cannot* put these special events together must be crazy, not the other way around.

There are many excellent examples of delusional thinking in litera-

ture. From Rilke's *The Notebooks of Malte Laurids Brigge* there is this
example:

> Why did she keep walking beside me and watching me? As if she were
> trying to recognize me with her bleared eyes, that looked as though some
> diseased person had spat slime into the bloody lids? And how came that
> little grey woman to stand that time for a whole quarter of an hour by my
> side before a shopwindow, showing me an old, long pencil, that came
> pushing infinitely slowly out of her miserable, clenched hands? I pretended
> to look at the display in the window and not notice anything. But she knew
> I had seen her, she knew I stood there wondering what she was really
> doing. For I understood quite well that the pencil in itself was of no
> consequence; I felt it was a sign, a sign for the initiated, a sign the outcast
> knew; I guessed she was indicating to me that I should go somewhere or
> do something.

Chekhov, in his well-known "Ward No. 6," described it as follows:

> In the morning Ivan Dmitritch got up from his bed in a state of horror,
> with cold perspiration on his forehead, completely convinced that he
> might be arrested any minute. Since his gloomy thoughts of yesterday had
> haunted him so long, he thought, it must be that there was some truth in
> them. They could not, indeed, have come into his mind without any
> grounds whatever.
>
> A policeman walking slowly passed by the windows: that was not for
> nothing. Here were two men standing still and silent near the house. Why?
> Why were they silent? And agonizing days and nights followed for Ivan
> Dmitritch. Everyone who passed by the windows or came into the yard
> seemed to him a spy or a detective.

Another good example was written by a patient:

> I got up at seven A.M., dressed and drove to the hospital. I felt my
> breathing trouble might be due to an old heart lesion. I had been told when
> I was young that I had a small ventricular septal defect. I decided that I
> was in heart failure and that people felt I wasn't strong enough to accept
> this, so they weren't telling me. I thought about all the things that had
> happened recently that could be interpreted in that light. I looked up heart
> failure in a textbook and found that the section had been removed, so I
> concluded someone had removed it to protect me. I remembered other
> comments. A friend had talked about a "walkie-talkie," and the thought
> occurred to me that I might be getting medicine without my knowledge,

perhaps by radio. I remembered someone talking about a one-way plane ticket; to me that meant a trip to Houston and a heart operation. I remembered an unusual smell in the lab and thought that might be due to the medicine they were giving me in secret. I began to think I might have a machine inside me which secreted medicine into my bloodstream. Again I reasoned that I had a disease no one could tell me about and was getting medicine for it secretly. At this point, I panicked and tried to run away, but the attendant in the parking lot seemed to be making a sign to motion me back. I thought I caught brief glimpses of a friend and my wife so I decided to go back into the hospital. A custodian's eyes attracted my attention; they were especially large and piercing. He looked very power-ful. He had to be "in on it," maybe he was giving medicine in some way. Then I began to have the feeling that other people were watching me. And, as periodically happened throughout the early stages, I said to myself that the whole thing was absurd, but when I looked again the people really were watching me.

A young man with paranoid schizophrenia expressed the anguish of his own delusions in a poem:

> *Anxiety:*
> *like metal on metal in my brain*
> *Paranoia: it is*
> *making me run*
> *away, away, away*
> *and back again quickly*
> *to see if I've been caught*
> *Or lied to*
> *Or laughed at*
> *Ha ha ha. The ferris wheel*
> *in Looney Land is not so funny.*

Even as innocuous an incoming stimulus as the sound of the wind can trigger off delusional thinking in some persons.

I should emphasize that the unreality had grown greater and the wind had taken on a specific meaning. On windy days in bad weather I was horribly upset. At night I could not sleep, listening to the wind, sharing its howls, its complaints and despairing cries, and my soul wept and groaned with it. More and more I imagined the wind bore a message for me to divine.

In many cases the delusions become more complex and integrated. Rather than simply being watched, the schizophrenic person becomes convinced that he/she is being controlled by other persons, manipulated, or even hypnotized. Such persons are constantly on the alert for confirmatory evidence to support their beliefs; needless to say, they always find it from among the myriad visual and auditory stimuli perceived by all of us each day. A good example of this was a kind, elderly Irish lady who was a patient on my ward. She believed that she had been wired by some mysterious foreign agents in her sleep and that through the wires her thoughts and actions could be controlled. In particular she pointed to the ceiling as the place from which the control took place. One morning I was dismayed to come onto the ward and discover workmen installing a new fire alarm system; wires were hanging down in all colors and in all directions. The lady looked at me, pointed to the ceiling, and just smiled; her delusions had been confirmed forever!

Delusions of being wired or radio controlled are relatively common. Often it is the FBI or the CIA which is the suspected perpetrator of the scheme. One patient was convinced that a radio had been sewn into his skull when he had had a minor scalp wound sutured and had tried to bring legal suit against the FBI innumerable times. Another man, at one time a highly successful superintendent of schools, became convinced that a radio had been implanted in his nose. He went to dozens of major medical centers, even to Europe, seeking a surgeon who would remove it. He even had an X ray of his nose showing a tiny white speck which he was convinced was the radio.

Friends of the unfortunate people often try to reason them out of their delusions. Rarely is this successful. Questions about why the FBI would want to control them are deftly brushed aside as irrelevant; the important point is that they do, and the person is experiencing sensations (such as strange noises) which confirm the fact. Reasoning a schizophrenic person out of a delusion is hampered by the distorted stimuli he/she is perceiving and also by the fact that the thinking processes may not be logical or connected. A further impediment is the fact that delusions frequently become self-fulfilling. Thus someone who believes others are spying on him/her finds it logical to act furtively, perhaps running from shelter to shelter and peering anxiously into the faces of passersby. Such behavior inevitably invites attention and leads to the delusional person's actually being watched by other people. As the saying goes, "I used to be paranoid but now people really *are* watching me."

Delusions in which the person is being watched, persecuted, or attacked are commonly called paranoid delusions. Paranoia is a relative concept; everybody experiences bits and pieces of it from time to time. In some places a little paranoia even has survival value; the fellow who works across the hall may really be stealing your memos, because he wants your job. Paranoid thinking by itself is not schizophrenia; it is only when it becomes a frank delusion (unaffected by reason) that it *may* be. Even then, however, it must be remembered that paranoid delusions can occur in brain diseases other than schizophrenia.

Paranoid delusions may on occasion be dangerous. "During the paranoid period I thought I was being persecuted for my beliefs, that my enemies were actively trying to interfere with my activities, were trying to harm me, and at times even to kill me." The paranoid person may try to strike first when the threat is perceived as too close. Facilities for the criminally insane in every state include among their inmates a large number of schizophrenic persons who have committed a crime in what they believed to be self-defense. It is this subgroup of the schizophrenic that has produced the general belief that people with schizophrenia as a whole are dangerous. In fact, when we take into consideration all persons with schizophrenia, this subgroup is very small. Most persons with schizophrenia are not dangerous at all, and I would far rather walk the halls of any mental hospital than walk the streets of any inner city.

Delusions may be of many types other than paranoid; grandiose delusions are quite common: "I felt that I had power to determine the weather, which responded to my inner moods, and even to control the movement of the sun in relation to other astronomical bodies." This often leads to a belief by the person that he/she is Jesus Christ, the Virgin Mary, the President, or some other exalted or important person. One admission to our hospital believed himself to be Mao Zedong. We began him on medication and, by the next day, knew he was getting better because he had become only the brother of Mao Zedong. Other individuals with grandiose delusions may believe that they are starring in a movie:

> I once believed that I was in the process of making a gigantic film of which I was the star. Everywhere I went in London there was a hidden camera and microphone and everything that I said and did was being recorded.

Grandiose delusions can on occasion be dangerous. People who believe that they can fly, or stop bullets with their chest may place themselves in a position to demonstrate the truth of their belief with predictably tragic consequences.

There is one particular type of grandiose delusion which, although not seen commonly, is so distinctive that it has acquired its own name. It is the delusion that another person, usually famous, is deeply in love with the patient. Such cases, originally called *psychoses passionnelles* by Dr. de Clerembault, a French psychiatrist, now often bear the designation of de Clerembault syndrome, or erotomania. One of my patients, who believed that Senator Edward Kennedy was in love with her, spent all her time and money following him around but always staying at a distance; she produced a multitude of incredible reasons why he could not acknowledge her presence. Another patient believed she was engaged to a man whom she had met once casually several years before, and spent all day walking the city streets looking for him. Most patients with such delusions have schizophrenia, although a few may have bipolar disorder. These patients have a pathos to their lives which is unusually evocative.

A relatively common delusion is that a person can control other people's minds. One young woman I saw had spent five years at home because each time she went into the street she believed that her mind compelled other people to turn and look at her. She described the effect of her mind as "like a magnet—they have no choice but to turn and look." Another patient believed he could change people's moods by "telepathic force": "I eventually felt I could go into a crowded restaurant and while just sitting there quietly, I could change everyone's mood to happiness and laughter." Here is a variant on this delusion:

> I like talking to a person but not in audible words. I try to force my thoughts into someone. I concentrate on how they move. I think of a message and concentrate in my head. It's thought you're passing over. I send the messages by visual indication. Sometimes the shoulder, sometimes my whole body.

Another variant is the delusional belief that one's thoughts are radiating out of one's head and being broadcast over radio or television; this is called thought broadcasting and is considered to be an almost certain indication of schizophrenia.

In evaluating delusions it is very important to keep in mind that their content is culture-bound. It is not the belief *per se* that is delusional, but how far the belief differs from the beliefs shared by others in the same culture or subculture. A man who believes he is being influenced by others who have "worked roots" (put a hex) on him may be completely normal if he grew up in lowland South Carolina where "working roots" is a widespread cultural belief. If he grew up in Scarsdale, on the other hand, his belief in being influenced by "worked roots" is more likely to suggest schizophrenia. Minority groups in particular may have a culturally induced high level of paranoid belief, and this belief may be based upon real discrimination and real persecution. In two other subcultural groups it may be difficult to assess the pathological nature of delusional thinking, for instance regarding grandiose delusions among the deeply religious and paranoid delusions among employees of the intelligence community. Imagine, for example, the dilemma of a Mother Superior in evaluating a novitiate who claims to have a special relationship with the Virgin Mary, or a supervisor at the CIA who is told by one of his undercover employees that he is being watched all the time. Beliefs of persons suspected of having schizophrenia must *always* be placed within a cultural context and regarded as only one facet of the disease.

Occasionally individuals come to attention who have odd thoughts, but it may be very difficult to decide whether these thoughts constitute true delusions. Such an individual, apparently, is John Hinckley, who in 1981 attempted to assassinate President Ronald Reagan. According to court testimony, Hinckley had a fantasy relationship with Jodi Foster, a young movie actress, and spent much of his time and energy trying to engage her attention; the assassination attempt was said to be Hinckley's ultimate effort to prove his love for Jodi Foster. At his trial, psychiatrists for the defense and the prosecution differed sharply on whether such thinking constituted a true delusion.

Hallucinations are very common in schizophrenia and are the end of that spectrum which begins with overacuteness of the senses. To take vision as an example: the spectrum has overacuteness of vision at one end of it, that is, lights are too bright, colors take on a more brilliant hue. In the middle of the spectrum are gross distortions of visual stimuli (also called illusions), such as a dog which takes on the appearance of a tiger. And at the far end of the spectrum are things which are seen by the schizophrenic person when there is nothing there; this is a true hallucination. The experiences described by schizophrenics are usually a mixture of different points on the spectrum.

Gross distortions of visual or auditory stimuli are not uncommon experiences in schizophrenia.

I was sitting listening to another person and suddenly the other person became smaller and then larger and then he seemed to get smaller again. He did not become a complete miniature. Then today with another person, I felt he was getting taller and taller. There is brightness and clarity of outline of things around me. Last week I was with a girl and suddenly she seemed to get bigger and bigger, like a monster coming nearer and nearer. The situation becomes threatening and I shrink back and back.

One day we were jumping rope at recess. Two little girls were turning a long rope while two others jumped in from either side to meet and cross over. When it came my turn and I saw my partner jump toward me where we were to meet and cross over, I was seized with panic; I did not recognize her. Though I saw her as she was, still it was not she. Standing at the other end of the rope she seemed smaller, but the nearer we approached each other, the taller she grew, the more she swelled in size.

I cried out, "Stop, Alice, you look like a lion; you frighten me!" At the sound of the fear in my voice which I tried to dissemble under the guise of fooling, the game came to an abrupt halt. The girls looked at me, amazed, and said, "You're silly—Alice, a lion? You don't know what you are talking about."

This phenomenon can perhaps best be depicted by a description of the first time I experienced it. I was one of four men at a bridge table. On one of the deals, my partner bid three clubs. I looked at my hand: I had only one small club. Though my hand was weak, I had to bid to take him out. My bid won. When my partner laid down his cards, he showed only two small clubs in his hand. I immediately questioned why he had bid three clubs. He denied having made such a bid. The other two men at the table supported him. There was no opportunity and no reason for the three clubs despite the fact that I had distinctly heard him do so. Not only had the hallucination included a spatial component synchronized with the man's position, but it had also duplicated exactly the vocal tones of the man. Furthermore, the man had actually declared a different bid at the time I had heard him bidding three clubs. This bid I had not heard. Somewhere along the line of my nervous system the words which he had actually spoken were blocked and the hallucinatory words substituted.

In all three instances there was a stimulus of some kind, but the person saw or heard it in a grossly distorted way. It is as if the schizophrenic person's brain is playing tricks.

Even worse tricks are played in forming true hallucinations, in which there is no initial stimulus at all. The brain makes up what it hears, sees, feels, smells, or tastes. Such experiences may be very real for the person. A person who hallucinates voices talking to him may hear the voices just as clearly as, or even more clearly than, the voices of real people talking to him. There is a tendency for people close to patients to scoff at the "imaginary" voices, to minimize them and not believe the persons really hear them. But they do, and in the sense that the brain hears them, they are real. The voices are but an extreme example of the malfunctioning of the sufferer's sensory apparatus.

Auditory hallucinations are by far the most common form of hallucination in schizophrenia. They are so characteristic of the disease that a person with true auditory hallucinations should be assumed to have schizophrenia until proven otherwise. They may take a variety of forms. They may be a simple swishing or thumping sound, such as the beating of the heart in Poe's famous short story:

> No doubt I now grew very pale;—but I talked fluently, and with a heightened voice. Yet the sound increased and what could I do? It was a low, dull, quick sound—much such a sound as a watch makes when enveloped in cotton. I gasped for breath—and yet the officers heard it not. I talked more quickly—more vehemently; but the noise steadily increased. Why would they not be gone? I paced the floor to and fro with heavy strides, as if excited to fury by the observation of the men—but the noise steadily increased. Oh, God; what could I do? I foamed—I raved—I swore! I swung the chair upon which I had been sitting, and grated it upon the boards, but the noise arose over all and continually increased. It grew louder—louder—louder! And still the men chatted pleasantly, and smiled. Was it possible they heard not? Almighty God!—no, no! They heard!—they suspected—they knew!—they were making a mockery of my horror!

They may be a single voice: "Thus for years I have heard daily in hundredfold repetition incoherent words spoken into my nerves without any context, such as 'Why not?' 'Why, if,' 'Why, because I,' 'Be it,' 'With respect to him.' "

Or they may be multiple voices:

The voices . . . were mostly heard in my head, though I often heard them in the air, or in different parts of the room. Every voice was different, and each beautiful, and generally, speaking or singing in a different tone and measure, and resembling those of relations or friends. There appeared to be many in my head, I should say upwards of fourteen. I divide them, as they styled themselves, or one another, into voices of contrition and voices of joy and honour.

Or they may even be choirs:

There was music everywhere and rhythm and beauty. But the plans were always thwarted. I heard what seemed to be a choir of angels. I thought it the most beautiful music I had ever heard. Two of the airs I kept repeating over and over until the delirium ended. One of them I can remember imperfectly even now. This choir of angels kept hovering around the hospital and shortly afterward I heard something about a little lamb being born upstairs in the room just above mine.

The hallucinations may be heard only occasionally or they may be continuous. When occasional, the most common time for them, in my clinical experience, is at night when going to sleep.

For about almost seven years—except during sleep—I have never had a single moment in which I did not hear voices. They accompany me to every place and at all times; they continue to sound even when I am in conversation with other people, they persist undeterred even when I concentrate on other things, for instance read a book or a newspaper, play the piano, etc.; only when I am talking aloud to other people or to myself are they of course drowned by the stronger sound of the spoken word and therefore inaudible to me. But the well-known phrases recommence at once, sometimes in the middle of a sentence, which tells me that the conversation had continued during the interval, that is to say that those nervous stimuli or vibrations responsible for the weaker sounds of the voices continue even while I talk aloud.

I have taken care of people with similar manifestations. One unfortunate woman had heard voices continuously for twenty years. They became especially loud whenever she tried to watch television, so she couldn't watch it at all.

In the vast majority of cases, the voices are unpleasant. They are often accusatory, reviling the victims for past misdeeds, either real or imagined. Often they curse them, and I have had many people refuse to tell me what the voices say to them because they were embarrassed by it. In a minority of cases the voices may be pleasant, as in the example with lovely music cited above. Occasionally they are even helpful, as with a woman who announced to me one day that she was getting well: "I know I am, because my voices told me so."

The precise mechanism of auditory hallucinations is not well understood and has received remarkably little attention from researchers. The most plausible explanation is that the schizophrenic disease process selectively affects the auditory tract or auditory centers in the brain, thereby producing auditory hallucinations. There are several different auditory centers in the brain, some immediately adjacent to the limbic system, which is thought to be the area affected in schizophrenia. There is supporting evidence of this theory in that schizophrenic patients show other evidences of auditory tract pathology (see chapter 6). It is also of interest that individuals who are born deaf and who later develop schizophrenia can experience auditory hallucinations. Another possible explanation was put forth by Julian Jaynes, who suggested that auditory hallucinations are simply historical holdovers from the function of the right side of the brain in ancient man. His theories, although interesting, are inconsistent with other data, including the fact that schizophrenia is probably a disease primarily of the left side of the brain (see chapter 6).

Visual hallucinations also occur but much less frequently. One schizophrenic patient described the variety of these hallucinations:

At an early stage the appearance of colored flashes of light was common. These took the form either of distant streaks or of near-by round glowing patches about a foot in diameter. Another type, which took place five or six times, was the appearance of words or symbols on blank surfaces. Closely connected with this was the occasional substitution of hallucinatory matter for the actual printed matter in books which I have been reading. On these occasions, the passage which I have been seeing has dissolved while I have been looking at it and another and sometimes wholly different passage has appeared in its place. . . . A further form of visual hallucinations that happened on two occasions was the appearance on a wall of the pictures of the heads of young women as though projected from a projection machine. These pictures were of women whom to the best of my knowledge I had never met.

Visual hallucinations usually appear in conjunction with auditory hallucinations. When only visual hallucinations appear, it is unlikely that schizophrenia is the cause. Many other brain diseases, notably drug intoxications and alcohol withdrawal, cause purely visual hallucinations and are the more likely diagnosis in such cases.

Like delusions, hallucinations must always be evaluated within their cultural context. In medieval times and today among some religious groups, visual hallucinations are not uncommon and do not necessarily suggest mental illness. Dr. Silvano Arieti has attempted to distinguish the hallucinations of the profoundly religious from those of schizophrenia by proposing the following criteria:

a. Religious hallucinations are usually visual, while those in schizophrenia are predominantly auditory.
b. Religious hallucinations usually involve benevolent guides or advisers who issue orders to the person.
c. Religious hallucinations are usually pleasant.

Hallucinations of smell or taste are very unusual but do occur. One patient gave this description of hallucinations of smell:

On a few occasions, I have experienced olfactory hallucinations. These have consisted of the seeming smelling of an odor as though originating from a source just outside the nose. Sometimes this odor has had a symbolical relationship with the thoughts-out-loud, as for instance, the appearance of an odor of sulphur in connection with a threat of damnation to hell by the thoughts-out-loud.

Another patient illustrated the same phenomenon of associating a smell with a thought:

During the time I was getting sick again, I began to think about the abortions I had before I was married. I was feeling guilty about them again. In those days you always tried to abort yourself first by taking quinine. When I was taking a shower and thinking about the past, I suddenly noticed the unmistakable smell of quinine. Soon after that, my mother and I were talking and she said something about oranges. I immediately began to smell oranges.

Hallucinations of taste usually consist of familiar food tasting differently. I have had two patients with paranoid schizophrenia, for example, who decided that they were being poisoned when their food began tasting "funny." Certainly if one's food suddenly starts changing in taste, it is logical to suspect that somebody is adding something to it.

Hallucinations of touch are also found among schizophrenic patients, although not commonly. I have provided care for one woman who feels small insects crawling under the skin on her face; it is an understatement to say that this is very upsetting to her. Another patient experienced hallucinatory pain.

> To the person who experiences hallucinatory pains, the pains feel identical with actual pains. There is no difference between the sensation of hallucinatory and the sensation of actual pain. The person who experiences it can distinguish it only by its lack of normal cause and its interrelations with other hallucinatory phenomena. The person who feels it undergoes real suffering. The fact that the cause of the pain is obscure and abnormal does not reduce the actuality of the suffering. Rather, insofar as it makes more difficult the correction of the causative factor and the removal of the pain, it tends to add depressive factors which increase the suffering caused by the sensation itself.

> To give some specific data concerning hallucinatory pains that I have experienced, it may be stated that they have varied considerably in intensity, in duration, and in locus. In intensity, they have ranged from a fraction of a second up to ten minutes or so. In locus, they have ranged over all parts of the body. In type, they have included smarting, burning, aching.

ALTERED SENSE OF SELF

Closely allied with delusions and hallucinations is another complex of symptoms which is characteristic of many schizophrenic patients. Normal individuals have a clear sense of self; they know where their bodies stop and where inanimate objects begin. They know that their hand, when they look at it, belongs to them. Even to make a statement like this strikes most normal persons as absurd because they cannot imagine its being otherwise.

But many persons with schizophrenia can imagine it, for alterations in their sense of self are not uncommon in this condition. Renée, in Marguerite Sechehaye's poignant biography, describes how she began to confuse herself with a doll:

I was present when Mamma first held a doll in her arms, a baby doll whom I named Ezekiel. She covered him, kissed him affectionately, put him to bed in his cradle. In the beginning it was enough for me to watch him avidly. All at once I experienced profound amazement that Ezekiel should receive Mamma's love and affection without the occurrence of anything untoward. At any moment I expected Mamma to cast Ezekiel off because I did not deserve to live. In my mind reigned utter confusion concerning Ezekiel and me. When Mamma held him in her arms, I trembled lest she drop him precipitously in his cradle, and if she did, I had the uncanny impression that it was I who had been so treated.

At another time she was unable to clearly distinguish herself from Mamma.

Sometimes I did not know clearly whether it was she or I who needed something. For instance if I asked for another cup of tea and Mamma answered teasingly, "But why do you want more tea; don't you see that I have just finished my cup and so you don't need any?" Then I replied, "Yes, that's true, I don't need any more," confusing her with myself. But at bottom I did desire a second cup of tea, and I said, "But I still want some more tea," and suddenly, in a flash, I realized the fact that Mamma's satiety did not make me sated too. And I was ashamed to let myself be thus trapped and to watch her laugh at my discomfiture.

Renée also describes how much more comfortable she felt when she was referred to in the third person ("Renée do this") rather than in the second person as "you."

Another patient described a similar experience in which

I saw myself in different bodies. . . . The night nurse came in and sat under the shaded lamp in the quiet ward. I recognized her as me, and I watched for some time quite fascinated; I had never had an outside view of myself before. In the morning several of the patients having breakfast were me. I recognized them by the way they held their knives and forks.

A schizophrenic patient's body parts may develop lives of their own, as if they have become disassociated and detached. One patient described this feeling:

I get shaky in the knees and my chest is like a mountain in front of me, and my body actions are different. The arms and legs are apart and away from me and they go on their own. That's when I feel I am the other person and copy their movements, or else stop and stand like a statue. I have to

> stop to find out whether my hand is in my pocket or not. I'm frightened
> to move or turn my head. Sometimes I let my arms roll to see where they
> will land. After I sit down my head clears again but I don't remember what
> happened when I was in the daze.

Renée describes confusion regarding where her body stopped and the
rest of the world began: "This was equally true in body functions. When
I urinated and it was raining torrents outside, I was not at all certain
whether it was not my own urine bedewing the world, and I was
gripped by fear."

Confusion about one's sexual characteristics is also not uncommonly found among schizophrenics, as in this man who believed his
body was acquiring a feminine appearance:

> My breast gives the impression of a pretty well-developed female bosom;
> this phenomenon can be *seen* by anybody who wants to observe me *with
> his own eyes*. . . . A brief glance would not suffice. The observer would have
> to go to the trouble of spending ten or fifteen minutes near me. In that way
> anybody would notice the periodic swelling and diminution of my bosom.

The altered sense of self may be further aggravated if hallucinations of touch or delusions about the body are also present. Rilke
described the horror of such feelings very graphically:

> Now it was there. Now it grew out of me like a tumor, like a second head,
> and was a part of me, though it could not belong to me at all, because it
> was so big. It was there like a huge, dead beast, that had once, when it
> was still alive, been my hand or my arm. And my blood flowed both
> through me and through it, as if through one and the same body. And my
> heart had to make a great effort to drive the blood into the Big Thing; there
> was hardly enough blood. And the blood entered the Big Thing unwill-
> ingly and came back sick and tainted. But the Big Thing swelled and grew
> over my face like a warm bluish boil and grew over my mouth, and already
> the shadow of its edge lay upon my remaining eye.

Another possible example of this is Kafka's famous story "The Meta-
morphosis," in which Gregor awakens in the morning and slowly
realizes that he has been transformed into a huge beetle. Such passages
in Kafka have led some scholars to speculate that Kafka himself may
have been schizophrenic at times.

The origin of this altered sense of self in schizophrenic persons is
unknown. Normally our sense of self is formed by a complex set of

tactile and visual stimuli through which we can feel and see the limits of our body and by which we differentiate it from the objects around us. It is likely that the same disease process which alters the senses and the thinking process is also responsible for the altered sense of self.

CHANGES IN EMOTIONS

Changes in emotions—or affect, as it is often called by professionals—are one of the most common and characteristic changes in schizophrenia. These changes are especially prominent in the later stages of the disease. They are probably the most tragic of its symptoms, for they often result in individuals who appear to be unable to feel emotion at all. This in turn makes it difficult for us to relate to them, so we tend to shun them more and more.

Very early in the course of illness the schizophrenic patient may feel widely varying and rapidly fluctuating emotions. Exaggerated feelings of all kinds are not unusual, especially in connection with the peak experiences described previously.

> During the first two weeks of my psychosis, religious experience provided that dominant factor of the psychotic phenomena. The most important form of religious experience in that period was religious ecstasy. The attempts of the thoughts-out-loud to persuade myself to adopt a messianic fixation formed the hallucinary background. In affective aspects, a pervasive feeling of well-being dominated the complex. I felt as though all my worries were gone and all my problems solved. I had the assurance that all my needs would be satisfied. Connected with this euphoric state, I experienced a gentle sensation of warmth over my whole body, particularly on my back, and a sensation of my body having lost its weight and gently floating.

Guilt is another commonly felt emotion in these early stages:

> Later, considering them appropriate, I no longer felt guilty about these fantasies, nor did the guilt have an actual object. It was too pervasive, too enormous, to be founded on anything definite, and it demanded punishment. The punishment was indeed horrible, sadistic—it consisted, fittingly enough, of being guilty. For to feel oneself guilty is the worst that can happen, it is the punishment of punishments. Consequently, I could never

be relieved of it as though I had been truly punished. Quite the reverse, I felt more and more guilty, immeasurably guilty. Constantly, I sought to discover what was punishing me so dreadfully, what was making me so guilty.

And fear is frequently described by patients, often a pervasive and nameless fear that exists without any specific object. Rilke captured this feeling skillfully:

> I am lying in my bed, five flights up, and my day, which nothing interrupts, is like a dial without hands. As a thing long lost lies one morning in its old place, safe and well, fresher almost than at the time of its loss, quite as though someone had cared for it—so here and there on my coverlet lie lost things out of my childhood and are as new. All forgotten fears are there again. The fear that a small, woollen thread that sticks out of the hem of my blanket may be hard, hard and sharp like a steel needle; the fear that this little button on my night shirt may be bigger than my head, big and heavy; the fear that this crumb of bread now falling from my bed may arrive glassy and shattered on the floor, and the burdensome worry lest at that really everything will be broken, everything for ever; the fear that the torn border of an opened letter may be something forbidden that no one ought to see, something indescribably precious for which no place in the room is secure enough; the fear that if I fell asleep I might swallow the piece of coal lying in front of the stove; the fear that some number may begin to grow in my brain until there is no more room for it inside me; the fear that it may be granite I am lying on, grey granite; the fear that I may shout, and that people may come running to my door and finally break it open; the fear that I may betray myself and tell all that I dread; and the fear that I might not be able to say anything, because everything is beyond utterance—and the other fears . . . the fears.

It is also well described by a young man with schizophrenia:

> I sat in my basement with a fear that I could not control. I was totally afraid—just from watching my cat look out the window.

Exaggerated feelings usually are not found in schizophrenic patients beyond the early stages of the disease. If they are, they should raise questions as to whether schizophrenia is the correct diagnosis. It is the *retention* of such feelings and emotions which is the single sharpest dividing line between schizophrenia and manic-depressive illness (see chapter 4). If the person retains exaggerated feelings to a prominent degree beyond the early stages of the disease, it is much more likely that the correct diagnosis will turn out to be manic-depressive illness.

The most characteristic changes in emotions in schizophrenia are inappropriate emotions or flattened emotions. It is an unusual patient who does not have one or the other—and sometimes both—by the time the disease is full-blown.

Inappropriate emotions are to be expected in light of the previous analogy of the telephone operator at the switchboard. Just as he/she hooks up the wrong thoughts with incoming stimuli, so she also hooks up wrong emotions. The incoming call may carry sad news but she hooks it up with mirth and the patient laughs. In other instances a patient responds with an inappropriate emotion because of the other things going on in his/her head which cause laughter.

> Half the time I am talking about one thing and thinking about half a dozen other things at the same time. It must look queer to people when I laugh about something that has got nothing to do with what I am talking about, but they don't know what's going on inside and how much of it is running round in my head. You see I might be talking about something quite serious to you and other things come into my head at the same time that are funny and this makes me laugh. If I could only concentrate on the one thing at the one time I wouldn't look half so silly.

These inappropriate emotions produce one of the most dramatic aspects of the disease—the victim suddenly breaking out in cackling laughter for no apparent reason. It is a common sight in mental hospitals, and one familiar to those who have worked or lived with people with this disease.

The flattening of emotions may be subtle in the earlier stages of the disease. Chapman claims that "one of the earliest changes in schizophrenic experience involves impairment in the process of empathy with other people." The schizophrenic person loses the ability to put him/herself in the other person's place or to feel what the other person is feeling. As the disease progresses this flattening or blunting of the emotions may become more prominent: "During my first illness I did not feel the emotions of anger, rage, or indignation to nearly as great an extent as I would have normally. Attitudes of dislike, estrangement, and fear predominated."

Emotions may become detached altogether from specific objects, leaving the victim with a void, as poignantly described by this patient:

Instead of wishing to do things, they are done by something that seems mechanical and frightening, because it is able to do things and yet unable to want to or not to want to. All the constructive healing parts that could be used healthily and slowly to mend an aching torment have left, and the feeling that should dwell within a person is outside, longing to come back and yet having taken with it the power to return. Out and in are probably not good terms, though, for they are too black and white and it is more like gray. It is like a constant sliding and shifting that slips away in a jelly-like fashion, leaving nothing substantial and yet enough to be tasted.

And Michael Wechsler summarized it neatly in a statement to his father: "I wish I could wake up feeling really bad—it would be better than feeling nothing."

In the advanced stage of flattening of the emotions there appear to be none left at all. This does not happen frequently, but when it does it is an unforgettable experience for those who interact with the victims. I have two such patients in whom I am unable to elicit *any* emotion whatsoever under any circumstances. They are polite, at times stubborn, but never happy or sad. It is uncannily like interacting with a robot. One of these patients set fire to his house, then sat down placidly to watch TV. When it was called to his attention that the house was on fire he got up calmly and went outside. Clearly the brain damage in these cases has seriously affected the centers mediating emotional response. Fortunately most persons with schizophrenia do not have such complete damage to this area of the brain.

Often associated with a flattening of emotions are apathy, slowness of movement, underactivity, lack of drive, and a paucity (usually called poverty) of thought and speech. The composite picture is frequently seen in schizophrenic patients who have been sick for many years. They appear to be desireless, apathetic, seeking nothing, wanting nothing. It is as if their will had eroded: and indeed something like that probably does happen as part of the disease process.

It is fashionable nowadays to believe that much of the flattening of emotions and apathy common in patients with schizophrenia are side effects of the drugs used to treat the disease. In fact there is only a little truth to this. Many of the drugs used to treat schizophrenia do have a calming or sedative effect (see chapter 7). Most of the flattening of emotions and weakening of motivation, however, are products of the disease itself and not of the drug effects. This can easily be proved by reviewing descriptions of schizophrenic patients in the literature prior to the introduction of these drugs. Emotional flattening and apathy are just as prominent in those early descriptions as they are today.

CHANGES IN MOVEMENTS

In recent years changes in movements have been closely linked in people's minds with the side effects of drugs used to treat schizophrenia. And indeed the antipsychotic drugs and lithium may cause changes in movements, varying from a fine tremor of the fingers to gross jerky movements of the arms or trunk.

But it is important to keep in mind that the schizophrenic disease process can also cause changes in movements, and that these were clearly described in accounts of the disease for many years before modern drugs became available. One study of changes of movements in schizophrenia found that they occur "in virtually all cases of conservatively defined schizophrenia" and concluded that they were consequences of the disease process and not of the medication being taken by the patients. In another study half the patients in remission remembered changes in their movements. In some cases their movements appeared to speed up while in others they slowed down. A feeling of awkwardness or clumsiness is relatively common, and persons with this disease may spill things, or stumble while walking, much more commonly than before they became sick.

Another change in movement is decreased spontaneity and the person may be aware of this. One recalled: "I became the opposite of spontaneous, as a result of which I became very diffident, very labored." Some patients with schizophrenia have decreased spontaneous swinging of their arms when they walk, a finding which has led some researchers to theorize that the cerebellum or basal ganglia portions of the brain may be affected in this disease.

Repetitious movements such as tics, tremors, tongue movements and sucking movements are also seen. In the majority of patients in whom they occur they are side effects of the medication being given the patient, but in a minority they will not be due to the medication but rather to the schizophrenic disease process. Even subtle body movements like eye blinking may be affected in schizophrenia. Some patients with the disease blink much less often than normal people. Drugs can account for some of this decrease but not for all of it. Balzac noted it in a patient in the early years of the nineteenth century: "[He] stood, just as I now saw him, day and night, with fixed eyes, never raising or lowering the lids, as others do."

The most dramatic change of movements in schizophrenia, of course, is catatonic behavior. A patient may remain motionless for hours, and if the person's arm is passively moved the arm will often remain in its new position for an hour or longer. Catatonic forms of schizophrenia were seen more commonly in the earlier years of this century but have become much less common; the availability of anti-psychotic medication may be one reason for this as catatonic symptoms usually respond promptly to medication.

CHANGES IN BEHAVIOR

Changes in behavior are usually secondary rather than primary symptoms of schizophrenia; that is, the behaviors shown by persons with this illness are most often a response to other things occurring in their brains. For example, if the person with schizophrenia is beset by overacuteness of the senses and an inability to synthesize incoming stimuli, it makes perfect sense for him/her to withdraw into a corner. Many of the other behaviors seen in this disease can be similarly and logically explained.

Withdrawing, remaining quietly in one place for long periods, and immobility are all common behaviors in this illness. The extreme versions of such behaviors are catatonia, where the person remains rigidly fixed in one position for long periods of time, and mutism, where the person does not speak at all. Catatonia and mutism are part of a continuum that includes the less blatant forms of withdrawal and immobility so commonly seen in schizophrenic persons.

A schizophrenia patient may withdraw and remain silent for any one of a number of reasons. Sometimes this occurs when the person becomes lost in deep thought:

> When I am walking along the street it comes on me. I start to think deeply and I start to go into a sort of trance. I think so deeply that I almost get out of this world. Then you get frightened that you are going to get into a jam and lose yourself. That's when I get worried and excited.

Or it may be adopted in order to slow down the incoming sensory stimuli so the brain can sort them out:

> I don't like moving fast. I feel there would be a breakup if I went too quick. I can only stand that a short time and then I have to stop. If I carried on I wouldn't be aware of things as they really are. I would just be aware of the sound and noise and the movements. Everything would be a jumbled mass. I have found that I can stop this happening by going completely still and motionless. When I do that, things are easier to take in.

> Everything is all right when I stop. If I move, everything I see keeps changing, everything I'm looking at gets broken up and I stop to put it together again.

Unexpected sensory stimuli can also result in a slowing.

> I get stuck, almost as if I am paralysed at times. It may only last for a minute or two but it's a bit frightening. It seems to happen even when something unexpected takes place, especially if there's a lot of noise that comes on suddenly. Say I am walking across the floor and someone suddenly switches on the wireless: the music seems to stop me in my tracks, and sometimes I freeze like that for a minute or two.

> My responses are too slow. Things happen too quickly. There's too much to take in and I try to take in everything. Things happen but I don't respond. When something happens quickly or unexpectedly it stuns me like a shock. I just get stuck. I've got to be prepared and ready for such things. Nothing must come upon me too quickly.

The movements may also be slowed so as to allow them to be integrated into a whole in exactly the same way that visual and auditory stimuli may need to be integrated.

> I am not sure of my own movements any more. It's very hard to describe this but at times I am not sure about even simple actions like sitting down. It's not so much thinking out what to do, it's the doing of it that sticks me. . . . I found recently that I was thinking of myself doing things before I would do them. If I am going to sit down, for example, I have got to think of myself and almost see myself sitting down before I do it. It's the same with other things like washing, eating, and even dressing—things that I have done at one time without even bothering or thinking about at all. . . . All this makes me move much slower now. I take more time to do things because I am always

conscious of what I am doing. If I could just stop noticing what I am doing, I would get things done a lot faster.

Withdrawal and mutism may also be a defense the individual assumes to get away from the horrors of other symptoms, as is illustrated by Renée:

As a matter of fact, these "things" weren't doing anything special; they didn't speak, nor attack me directly. It was their very presence that made me complain. I saw things, smooth as metal, so cut off, so detached from each other, so illuminated and tense that they filled me with terror. When, for example, I looked at a chair or a jug, I thought not of their use or function—a jug not as something to hold water and milk, a chair not as something to sit in—but as having lost their names, their functions and meanings; they became "things" and began to take on life, to exist. . . . When I protested, "Things are tricking me; I am afraid," and people asked specifically, "Do you see the jug and the chair as alive?" I answered, "Yes, they are alive." And they, the doctors too, thought I saw these things as humans whom I heard speak. But it was not that. Their life consisted uniquely in the fact that they were there, in their existence itself. To flee from them I hid my head in my hands or stood in a corner. I lived through a period of intense suffering. Everything was alive, defied me. Outside in the street people were struck mad, moved around without reason, encountered each other and things which had become more real than they.

Other unusual behaviors are also found in persons with schizophrenia. Ritualistic behaviors are not uncommon. Some patients repeatedly walk in circles, and I have one who walks through all doors backwards. There are reasons why they do such things, as explained by this woman who felt compelled to beat eggs a certain way when making a cake:

As the work progressed, a change came. The ingredients of the cake began to have a special meaning. The process became a ritual. At certain stages the stirring must be counter-clockwise; at another time it was necessary to stand up and beat the batter toward the east; the egg whites must be folded in from the left to the right; for each thing that had to be done there were complicated reasons. I recognized that these were new, unfamiliar, and unexpected, but did not question them. They carried a finality that was effective. Each compelling impulse was accompanied by an equally compelling explanation.

Another example of ritualistic behavior is the following:

> The state of indifference reigning until now was abruptly replaced by inner and outer agitation. At first I felt obliged to get up and walk; it was impossible to stay in bed. Singing a requiem without pause, I marched three steps forward and three steps back, an automatism that wearied me exceedingly and which I wished someone would help me break. I could not do it alone, for I felt forced to make these steps and if I stopped from exhaustion, even for a moment, I felt guilty again. Moreover, when any behavior became automatic, I felt guilty in interrupting it. But no one could believe that I wanted to stop, for as soon as they made me give up some stereotyped procedure, I began anew.

Certain gestures may be repeated often, for reasons which are quite logical to the person doing them but appear bizarre to the onlooker. One patient shook his head rhythmically from side to side to try and shake the excess thoughts out of his mind. Another massaged his head "to help to clear it" of unwanted thoughts.

Specific postures may also be adopted by persons with schizophrenia. One of my patients marches endlessly up and down the sidewalk with his left hand placed awkwardly on his left shoulder. It appears to be uncomfortable but he invariably returns to it for reasons I have not been able to ascertain. Another posture was described by Perceval:

> There were two or three other delusions I laboured under of which I hardly recollect how I was cured—one in particular, that I was to lean on the back of my head and on my feet in bed, and twist my neck by throwing my body with a jerk from side to side. I fancy that I never attempted this with sincerity, because I feared to break my neck.

Occasionally a person with schizophrenia will repeat like a parrot whatever is said to him/her. In psychiatric language this is called echolalia. Chapman believes that repeating the words probably is useful to the patient because it allows time to absorb and synthesize what was said. Much rarer is the occurrence of behavior which is parroted, called echopraxia. When it occurs it may be the consequence of a dissolution of boundaries of the self so that the schizophrenic person does not know where his/her body leaves off and where the body of the other person begins.

Most worrisome to friends and relatives of schizophrenic patients, for obvious reasons, are socially inappropriate behaviors. Fortunately most schizophrenic patients who act inappropriately on hospital wards usually act quite appropriately when taken out of the hospital on trips. It is always impressive to see patients from even the most regressed hospital wards go to public places; they are usually more distinguishable by their dress (characteristically poorly fitting) than by their behavior. A small number of schizophrenic patients are so ill that they continue inappropriate behaviors (such as random urination, open masturbation, spitting on others) even in public, but such patients are comparatively rare. Some—but not all—of them can be improved by proper medication or conditioning techniques.

It should always be remembered that the behavior of schizophrenic persons is internally logical and rational; they do things for reasons which, given their disordered senses and thinking, make sense *to them*. To the outside observer the behavior may appear irrational, "crazy," "mad," the very hallmark of the disease. To the schizophrenic person, however, there is nothing "crazy" or "mad" about it at all. Here, for example, is an account of a schizophrenic woman who broke two pairs of glasses worn by her nurses, an action which must have seemed inexplicable ("crazy") to those who observed it.

> My feelings about excessive light and truth were shown in ideas I had about glasses. I was afraid of people who wore glasses, and thought that I was being deliberately persecuted by doctors and nurses who refracted an excessive amount of light into my eyes by wearing glasses. At the same time glasses symbolized false or literary vision, a barrier between the individual and the direct apprehension of life. I myself normally wear glasses (slightly tinted, as my eyes are normally somewhat oversensitive to light). I grabbed and broke two pairs of glasses worn by nurses.

Similarly Daniel P. Schreber, in the autobiographical account of his illness, describes sleeping with his feet out the window and clinging to icy trees with his hands until they were almost frozen in order to accomplish an important goal—such exposure to cold was the only way he could successfully divert the "rays" that afflicted him away from his head. Even bizarre behavior like taking one's clothes off in public may be done for logical reasons. One man with schizophrenia wrote me that he did so in an effort to be pure, like Adam and Eve when they first entered the Garden of Eden.

This same point can be made about everything a schizophrenic person says and does. It is "crazy" only to the outsider who sits on the sidelines and observes from afar. To someone who will take the time to listen, a person with schizophrenia is not "crazy" at all if by "crazy" one means irrational. The "craziness" has its roots in the disordered brain function that produces erroneous sensory data and disordered thinking.

FROM ENCHANTED LOOM TO WARING BLENDER

Schizophrenia, then, is a disorder of the brain. The distinguished neurologist C. S. Sherrington once referred to a normal brain as "an enchanted loom," taking the threads of experience and weaving them into the fabric of life. For persons whose brains are afflicted with schizophrenia the loom is broken, and in some cases appears to have been replaced by a Waring blender which produces jumbled thoughts and loose associations. Given the resulting cerebral cacophony, is it any wonder that patients with this disease often describe their life as like being in the Twilight Zone?

Some people with schizophrenia are aware of the misfunctioning of their brain; this is what is called insight. A few of them even tell those around them in the early stages of illness that something is going wrong with their head. One mother remembered her son holding his head and pleading: "Help me, Mom, something is wrong in my head." John Hinckley wrote a letter to his parents (but never sent it), in which he said: "I don't know what's the matter. Things are not going well. I think there's something wrong with my head." One of the most poignant stories I have ever heard concerned a very bright teenage boy who realized that something was going wrong with his brain in the earliest stages of the disease and then spent months in the local medical libraries researching the illness before his symptoms became too severe. In another instance a parent told me that her son "had diagnosed himself as having schizophrenia" before anyone in the family fully realized that he was sick.

Such insight is usually lost as the disease becomes fully manifest. This is not surprising since it is the brain which is malfunctioning and it is also the brain which we use to think about ourselves. In fact I am always surprised at the many patients with schizophrenia who have insight. Even in the stage of chronic illness an occasional person with schizophrenia will exhibit surprising insight. One woman, afflicted by schizophrenia for many years, wrote me that she would gladly "sacrifice my right arm to make my brain work." Another woman who has had severe schizophrenia for seven years, when I asked her what she was asking for at Christmas, looked at me sadly, paused for a moment, and then replied: "A mind."

Imagine what it would be like to have the alterations of the senses, the inability to interpret incoming stimuli, the delusions and hallucinations, changes in bodily boundaries, emotions, and movements that are described above. Imagine what it would be like to no longer be able to trust your brain when it told you something. As one very articulate woman with schizophrenia explained to me, the problem is one of "a self-measuring ruler"—that is you must use your malfunctioning brain to assess the malfunction of your brain. Is it any wonder that people with this disease get depressed? Is it any wonder that they frequently feel humiliated by their own behavior? If a worse disease than schizophrenia exists, it has not come to light. One young man with the disease captured its essence in a poem entitled "Lost":

> Gigantic tides have overwhelmed me
> I don't see anymore
> Swept to the bottom of the
> oceans floor.
>
> The great pull has drawn me beneath
> to the bottom
> I can't hear anymore
> What had he said?
> I may never see home again
> It feels that way
> down here
> Dead on the oceans floor
>
> I'm so sad
> I can't pull against the tow
> I'm trapped
> I'm gone
> I'll never relive again
> Somebody has pressed a pillow
> against my face and
> I can't breathe

How can family and friends of persons with schizophrenia understand what they are going through? Taking mind-altering drugs will produce alterations of the senses and even delusions that may resemble schizophrenia briefly, but it is not recommended that families use these drugs. A better way to understand the experience of having schizophrenia is to take a walk by yourself through an art museum and pretend that you are inside some of the pictures. (It is better not to tell your friends that you are doing this; they may worry about *your* mental status.) Some of the works described below are reproduced on the following pages.

Begin with works by Vincent van Gogh painted in late 1888 and 1889 when he was undergoing a psychosis; "Starry Night" and "Olive Grove with White Cloud" especially illustrate van Gogh's distorted perception of light, colors, and texture. Many other artists, although they themselves were not psychotic, included in their artistic creations elements that are reminiscent of the perceptions of schizophrenics. Joan Miró, for example, in paintings such as "Portrait IV, 1938," "Head of a Woman, 1938," and "Head of a Catalan Peasant," shows facial features as grossly distorted and disjointed. The viewer of a painting such as "Nude Woman" by Pablo Picasso is faced with the perplexing task of synthesizing the individual pieces into a whole, a task not unlike that faced every day by some individuals with schizophrenia. Marcel Duchamp's "Nude Descending a Staircase" suggests the jerky movements, lack of coordination, and clumsiness complained of frequently by persons with schizophrenia; this painting was specifically cited by one woman with schizophrenialike symptoms from viral encephalitis to illustrate to the doctor how she felt.

Distorted emotions are evoked in several paintings of Henri Rousseau. Imagine yourself in "The Dream," for example, with eyes staring at you and unnamed terrors lurking behind every bush. Move on to lithographs or paintings by Edvard Munch, such as "The Scream," which mirrors the depression, despair, and loneliness of schizophrenia; the woman in the picture is covering her ears just as some schizophrenic patients do to try and shut out the auditory hallucinations. Finally end your tour of the art museum at Hieronymus Bosch's "Garden of Earthly Delights." Study the tortures designed by Bosch for the "Hell" portion of the triptych, and think about the fact that the experience of having schizophrenia is much worse than anything Bosch ever imagined.

Given the disordered brain function as a starting point, many persons with schizophrenia are heroic in their attempts to keep a mental equilibrium. And the proper response of those who care about the unfortunate persons with this disease is patience and understanding.

Vincent van Gogh's "Starry Night," painted in 1889 while he was intermittently psychotic, shows distortions of textures, light, and color as perceived by some individuals with schizophrenia. (Collection, The Museum of Modern Art, New York. Acquired through the Lillie P. Bliss Bequest. Oil on canvas, 29" × 36¼".)

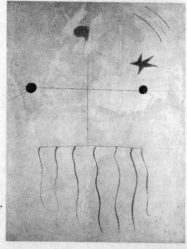

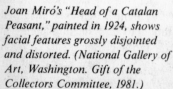

Joan Miró's "Head of a Catalan Peasant," painted in 1924, shows facial features grossly disjointed and distorted. (National Gallery of Art, Washington. Gift of the Collectors Committee, 1981.)

Marcel Duchamp's "Nude Descending a Staircase," painted in 1912, illustrates the disjointed perceptions and lack of coordination that often accompany schizophrenia. (Philadelphia Museum of Art. Louise and Walter Arensberg Collection. Oil on canvas, 58" × 35".)

Pablo Picasso's "Nude Woman," a work from 1910, presents the viewer with the perplexing task of synthesizing the pieces into a coherent whole; this is not unlike the task faced every day by some persons with schizophrenia. (National Gallery of Art, Washington. Ailsa Mellon Bruce Fund.)

Henri Rousseau's "The Dream," painted in 1910, evokes the dreamlike, other-worldly quality of life expressed by some patients, as well as the unnamed terrors of watching eyes described in paranoid schizophrenia. (Collection, The Museum of Modern Art, New York. Gift of Nelson A. Rockefeller. Oil on canvas, 6'8½" × 9'9½".)

Edvard Munch's lithograph "The Scream" was created in 1895 as an expression of anxiety and fear. It also mirrors the despair, depression, and bewilderment of auditory hallucinations experienced so often in schizophrenia. (National Gallery of Art, Washington. Rosenwald Collection.)

Perhaps nowhere is this better illustrated than by Balzac's heroine in "Louis Lambert," a young woman who married a man who developed schizophrenia. She then dedicates her life to caring for him:

> "No doubt Louis appears to be 'insane,'" she said, "but he is not so, if the word insanity is applied only to those whose brain, from unknown causes, becomes vitiated, and who are, therefore, unable to give a reason for their acts. The equilibrium of my husband's mind is perfect. If he does not recognize you corporeally, do not think that he has not seen you. He is able to disengage his body and to see us under another form, I know not of what nature. When he speaks, he says marvellous things. Only, in fact often, he completes in speech an idea begun in the silence of his mind, or else he begins a proposition in words and finishes it mentally. To other men he must appear insane; to me, who lives in his thought, all his ideas are lucid. I follow the path of his mind; and though I cannot understand many of its turnings and digressions, I nevertheless reach the end with him. Does it not often happen that while thinking of some trifling matter, we are drawn into serious thought by the gradual unfolding of ideas and recollections? Often, after speaking of some frivolous thing, the accidental point of departure for rapid meditation, a thinker forgets, or neglects to mention the abstract links which have led him to his conclusions, and takes up in speech only the last rings in the chain of reflections. Common minds to whom this quickness of mental vision is unknown, and who are ignorant of the inward travail of the soul, laugh at dreamers and call them madmen if they are given to such forgetfulness of connecting thoughts. Louis is always so; he wings his way through the spaces of thought with the agility of a swallow; yet I can follow him in all his circlings. That is the history of his so-called madness."

Such dedication and understanding, unachievable except in fiction, is a worthy ideal. It exists to some degree in many families with schizophrenic members and among some nursing staff who must care for such individuals on the wards of mental hospitals. As Louis Lambert's wife illustrates, compassion follows understanding. It is therefore incumbent on us to understand as best we can; the burden of disease will become lighter for all.

RECOMMENDED FURTHER READING

Chapman, J. "The Early Symptoms of Schizophrenia." *British Journal of Psychiatry* 112 (1966): 225–51. This article contains a useful description of the early symptoms frequently encountered in schizophrenia.

Cutting, J., and F. Dunne. "Subjective Experience of Schizophrenia." *Schizophrenia Bulletin* 13 (1987).

Kaplan, B., ed. *The Inner World of Mental Illness.* New York: Harper & Row, 1964. Like all such collections, the quality of the excerpts from many personal accounts of madness is varied, but many of the accounts are excellent.

McGhie, A., and J. Chapman. "Disorders of Attention and Perception in Early Schizophrenia." *British Journal of Medical Psychology* 34 (1961): 103–16. The symptoms experienced by many schizophrenic patients are analyzed in a succinct and clear manner.

North, C. *Welcome Silence: My Triumph Over Schizophrenia.* New York: Simon and Schuster, 1987. This is the account of a young woman's courageous eight-year struggle with the symptoms of schizophrenia, which clearly depicts the hell those afflicted must suffer.

Sechehaye, M. *Autobiography of a Schizophrenic Girl.* New York: Grune & Stratton, 1951. Paperback by New American Library. Even in translation from the French, this is the single best account of what it is like to be schizophrenic. But Part 2 of the book, a psychoanalytic interpretation of the woman's symptoms, should be skipped.

3

THE DIAGNOSIS OF SCHIZOPHRENIA: VIEW FROM THE OUTSIDE

Insanity is a chronic disease of the brain, producing either derangement of the intellectual faculties, or prolonged change of the feelings, affections and habits of an individual.

Dr. Amariah Brigham, 1845

The definition of most diseases of mankind has been accomplished. We can define typhoid fever by the presence of the bacteria which cause it, kidney failure by a rise in certain chemicals in the blood, and cancers by the appearance of the cells under the microscope. In almost all diseases there is something which can be seen or measured, and this can be used to define the disease and separate it from nondisease states.

Not so with schizophrenia! To date we have no single thing which can be measured and from which we can then say: Yes, that is schizophrenia. Because of this, the definition of the disease is a source of great confusion and debate. This confusion is exacerbated because of the likelihood that schizophrenia is more than one disease entity.

Since we do not yet have anything which can be reliably measured to help define schizophrenia, we are left only with its symptoms. These may be misleading, however, for different diseases may cause the same symptoms. For example, a pain in the abdomen is a symptom, but the diseases which may cause this symptom number well over one hundred. Thus to use symptoms to define diseases is risky. Such is the state of the art with schizophrenia; yet precise diagnosis is of utmost importance. It will both determine the appropriate treatment for the patient and provide the patient and family with an informed prognosis. It also makes research on the disease easier because it will allow researchers to be certain that they are talking about the same thing.

DEFINING SCHIZOPHRENIA

Although there is no single symptom that is found only in schizophrenia, there are several that are found very uncommonly in diseases other than schizophrenia. When these are present they should elevate the index of suspicion considerably. Bleuler, for example, believed that loosening of associations in the thinking process was central to the disease. More recently, Kurt Schneider, a German psychiatrist, proposed a list of symptoms which he called "first rank" symptoms, meaning that when one or more of them are present they point strongly toward schizophrenia as the diagnosis. This is his list:

1. Auditory hallucinations in which the voices speak one's thoughts aloud
2. Auditory hallucinations with two voices arguing
3. Auditory hallucinations with the voices commenting on one's actions
4. Hallucinations of touch when the bodily sensation is imposed by some external agency
5. Withdrawal of thoughts from one's mind
6. Insertion of thoughts into one's mind by others
7. Believing one's thoughts are being broadcast to others, as by radio or television
8. Insertion by others of feelings into one's mind
9. Insertion by others of irresistible impulses into one's mind
10. Feeling that all one's actions are under the control of others, like an automaton
11. Delusions of perception, as when one is certain that a normal remark has a secret meaning for oneself

These symptoms are commonly used in European countries as grounds for the diagnosis of schizophrenia, although less so in the United States. Studies have shown that at least three-quarters of schizophrenic patients have one or more of these symptoms. However, they cannot be considered as definitive for the disease because they are also found in at least one-quarter of patients with manic-depressive illness.

Until recently, the term "schizophrenia" was used much more loosely and broadly in the United States than in most European countries. In fact the only other country in the world where schizophrenia was diagnosed just as loosely was in the Soviet Union, where it has been abused as a label to discredit and stigmatize opponents of the government.

American psychiatry took a major step forward in 1980 when it adopted a revised system of diagnosis and nomenclature and issued it in the third edition of the *Diagnostic and Statistical Manual of Mental Disorders,* usually referred to as *DSM-III.* (A further revised edition published in 1987 is known as *DSM-III-R.*) Under this system a diagnosis of schizophrenia should be made only when the following criteria have been fulfilled:

1. Symptoms of illness have been present for at least six months.
2. There has been some deterioration of functioning from previous levels in such areas as work skills, social relations, and self-care.
3. The disease symptoms do not suggest organic mental disorders or mental retardation.
4. The disease symptoms do not suggest manic-depressive illness (see pages 91–94).
5. Either a), b), or c) must be present:
   a) Two of the following:
      i. delusions
      ii. prominent auditory hallucinations
      iii. incoherence or marked loosening of associations
      iv. catatonic behavior
      v. flat or grossly inappropriate affect, *or*
   b) Bizarre delusions which other people in the individual's subculture regard as totally implausible, e.g., the belief that your thoughts are being taken out of your head and broadcast over the radio, *or*
   c) Prominent auditory hallucinations consisting of voices keeping up a running commentary on the person's behavior, or two or more voices conversing with each other. The content of the voices should not be explainable by the person's depression or elation.

These criteria for diagnosing schizophrenia have achieved wide acceptance in the United States and may be utilized by families who are seeking a definition of the disease. If these criteria are not met, the diagnosis of schizophrenia should not be made.

Requiring that symptoms be present for at least six months before schizophrenia can be diagnosed is a sharp departure from traditional American practice. It is a useful advance, however, for schizophrenia is a serious diagnosis and should not be applied indiscriminately to someone with any schizophrenialike symptom, however brief, as happened frequently in the past. For persons with schizophrenialike symptoms of less than six months' duration, the *DSM-III* recommends the use of schizophreniform disorder as a diagnosis. If the duration is less than one month, the diagnosis of brief reactive psychosis should be used.

Although the *DSM-III* criteria have been valuable in clarifying the diagnosis of schizophrenia, problems persist. Diagnosis remains based on the psychiatrist's subjective evaluation of patients' behavior and what patients say they are experiencing. What is clearly needed, and may be available before many years, are objective measures for diagnosis, such as laboratory tests of blood and cerebrospinal fluid. Until that time the diagnosis of schizophrenia will remain a complicated matter requiring skilled clinical judgment.

A highly publicized experiment carried out by Dr. David L. Rosenhan, a psychologist at Stanford University, in 1973 illustrates some of the ongoing diagnostic problems. Rosenhan had volunteers go to psychiatric hospitals seeking admission and claiming to be hearing voices which had lasted for three weeks. Auditory hallucinations of any kind are unquestionably important and common symptoms of schizophrenia, with the majority of patients experiencing them at some point in the course of their illness. They are so important as symptoms that most psychiatrists take their presence as an indication of schizophrenia until proven otherwise. Thus it should not have been surprising that all the volunteers were admitted as genuine patients. Rosenhan used this study to mock psychiatrists and their ability to diagnose patients, but this is erroneous. It would have been much *more* disturbing if these volunteers, who said they were being greatly troubled by the voices, had *not* been admitted for further investigation. Auditory hallucinations are to schizophrenia what abdominal pain is to appendicitis or vomiting blood is to a peptic ulcer. They are all danger signs suggesting that more definitive studies need to be done. Dr. Seymour Kety illustrates the fallacy of the Rosenhan study nicely:

> If I were to drink a quart of blood and, concealing what I had done, come to the emergency room of any hospital vomiting blood, the behavior of the staff would be quite predictable. If they labeled and treated me as having a bleeding ulcer, I doubt that I could argue convincingly that medical science does not know how to diagnose that condition.

SCHIZOPHRENIA SUBTYPES AND PARANOID DISORDERS

During the last half of the nineteenth century different subtypes of what we now call schizophrenia were described as separate diseases. Thus paranoid psychosis was characterized in 1868, hebephrenia in 1871, and catatonia in 1874. These three were grouped together in 1896 by Emil Kraepelin and called dementia praecox (dementia of early life). Bleuler changed the name to schizophrenia in 1911 and added the simple schizophrenia subtype as well.

Since that time these subtypes of schizophrenia have continued to be widely used. Their differentiation is based exclusively on the symptoms of the illness. Thus paranoid schizophrenia is characterized by delusions and/or hallucinations with a predominantly persecutory or, less commonly, a grandiose content. Hebephrenic schizophrenia, called the "disorganized type" in the *DSM-III* nomenclature, has as its predominant symptoms inappropriate emotions, extreme social impairment, and frequently disorganized thinking; well-developed delusions are usually absent. Catatonic schizophrenia is diagnosed when the outstanding features of the disease are behavioral disturbances, such as posturing, rigidity, stupor, and often mutism. And simple schizophrenia, no longer included as a separate entity under *DSM-III*, is characterized by an insidious loss of interest and initiative, withdrawal, blunting of emotions, and the absence of delusions or hallucinations.

The validity and utility of these subtypes are very questionable despite their widespread usage. Few patients fall cleanly into one subtype or another, with most having some mix of symptoms. Of greater concern is the fact that persons with schizophrenia often show a shift in their symptoms over time, so that initially the person may appear to be a catatonic subtype but a few years later may have symptoms of a hebephrenic nature. Even the old psychiatric axiom "Once a paranoid always a paranoid" has been found not to hold up; I have seen many patients who present initially classic paranoid schizophrenia symptoms and five years later may have a quite different constellation of symptoms. For these reasons there has been an increasing tendency among psychiatrists in recent years to diagnose most patients as having the "undifferentiated type," which simply means that their symptoms are mixed, and to rely less on the traditional four-part division.

Paranoid schizophrenia presents special diagnostic problems because it is one end of the spectrum of a common personality type. Paranoid personalities are found in all walks of life and are known for being suspicious, mistrusting, guarded, quick to take offense, and emotionally distant. The other end of the spectrum is the full-blown paranoid schizophrenic with delusions and hallucinations of persecution. Between these two poles, however, can be found a continuum of individuals with more or less disabling paranoid personality traits. The architects of *DSM-III* chose to restrict the diagnosis of paranoid schizophrenia only to those individuals who had the fully developed disease and to classify less severely disabled paranoid individuals as a paranoid disorder or a paranoid personality disorder. Thus a patient with fixed delusions of persecution or jealousy without other symptoms of schizophrenia should not technically be classified as schizophrenic under the new criteria.

There is also a belief among some researchers that paranoid schizophrenia and its related disorders are a separate disease entity altogether and probably have causes different from the larger group of schizophrenias. Such researchers point to genetic studies suggesting that paranoid schizophrenics are more likely to occur within the same family than are other types of schizophrenics and to biochemical studies which found an increase in some brain chemicals in paranoid schizophrenics but not in other types. This research area remains completely unresolved, and for the time being paranoid schizophrenia should continue to be viewed as a legitimate variant of schizophrenia.

Another method of classifying schizophrenia is that which is in use in the Soviet Union. Rather than utilizing the symptoms of the disease, this classification focuses on its course. Thus Soviet psychiatrists divide schizophrenia into a periodic type in which the person has attacks of the disease but recovers from each one; a "shiftlike" type in which the person recovers some but not complete function; and a continuous type in which the person has a steady downhill course. Each of these types is in turn divided into subtypes. Because this method of classification can only be utilized retrospectively with any accuracy, it has not proven any more useful than the traditional classification based on symptoms and its use has not become widespread elsewhere.

The most recent method of subtyping schizophrenia, which is gaining acceptance in the research community, divides patients into those with predominantly "positive" symptoms and those with predominantly "negative" symptoms. Although the use of "positive" as an adjective for any schizophrenic symptoms seems like a contradiction of terms, it denotes those symptoms which are present but should be absent (e.g., delusions, hallucinations, thinking disorders such as loose associations). "Negative" symptoms, on the other hand, indicate symptoms which are absent but should be present (e.g., apathy, social withdrawal, poverty of thoughts, blunting of emotions, slowness of movement, lack of drive).

This subtyping of schizophrenia, found in writings on the subject for over one hundred years, has become the subject of much recent attention. Dr. Timothy Crow and his colleagues at the Northwick Park Clinical Research Center in London, one of the best research units for schizophrenia in the world, have argued that patients with predominantly "positive" symptoms (called type I) have less structural damage to the brain, a better response to antipsychotic drugs, and a better prognosis. Those with predominantly "negative" symptoms (type II) have more structural brain damage as visualized on CT scans, a poorer response to drugs, and a worse prognosis. Although there is still considerable controversy about "positive" and "negative" subtyping, it appears to be useful at least for research purposes. Whether the two types represent two different causes of schizophrenia, however, is still unknown.

SCHIZOAFFECTIVE DISORDER

As will be discussed in chapter 4, there is another brain disease called manic-depressive psychosis, which is distinct from schizophrenia and on which there is widespread agreement regarding symptoms. Textbooks of psychiatry and psychology usually imply that patients with psychosis fall neatly into either the schizophrenia or the manic-depressive category and that the two can be readily distinguished. Unfortunately that is not always the case, as a large percentage of patients have symptoms of both diseases. Furthermore it is not rare to find patients whose symptoms change over time, appearing initially as a textbook case of schizophrenia or manic-depressive psychosis, and a year or two later clearly exhibiting symptoms of the other disease. It has been facetiously suggested that either we need to insist that patients read the books and choose the disease they wish to have or we must become more flexible in our psychiatric thinking. I personally have seen patients with virtually every possible combination of schizophrenic and manic-depressive symptoms.

The resolution of the problem within the psychiatric establishment has been the creation of an intermediate disease category called schizoaffective disorder. Prior to *DSM-III* it was officially included as a subtype of schizophrenia. *DSM-III* classified it independently and noted that " at the present time there is no consensus on how this category should be defined." It is further discussed in chapter 4 with manic-depressive psychosis.

ONSET AND EARLY SYMPTOMS

One of the questions most frequently asked by families is how to identify the early symptoms of schizophrenia. This question is different from that of relapse of the disease, which is discussed in chapter 7. The question is asked by families who are raising difficult teenage children and are wondering if they might be developing schizophrenia. It is also asked by families in which an older child has been diagnosed with schizophrenia and the parents are worried about the younger children.

In thinking about the early symptoms of schizophrenia it is helpful to remember that this disease has a strikingly narrow age of onset. In the United States three-quarters of those who get schizophrenia do so between ages 17 and 25. Having an initial onset before age 14 or after age 30 is unusual; the former will be discussed below under childhood schizophrenia.

Why the onset of schizophrenia occurs in this particular age group is unknown. It should be pointed out, however, that other chronic brain diseases, such as multiple sclerosis and Alzheimer's disease, have particular age ranges of onset and we do not understand the reasons in these diseases either. There are also suggestions that the average age of onset of schizophrenia may be younger in the United States than it is in Europe, that the age of onset for paranoid schizophrenia is older than for the other subtypes, and other suggestions that the average age of onset in the United States is younger now than it was twenty years ago. It is hoped that the current World Health Organization multi-nation study of the incidence of schizophrenia will provide harder data on these intriguing but unanswered questions.

There are some patients for whom it is impossible to date the onset of the disease. The family says things like "She was always different from the other children" or "Throughout childhood his teachers noticed he was eccentric and told us to get him evaluated." The suggestion in such cases is that the schizophrenic disease process began early in life despite the fact that the full-blown thinking disorder, delusions, and hallucinations did not begin until the late teens or early twenties. Such individuals with an insidious onset probably comprise no more than a quarter of patients with schizophrenia; whether they represent a different causal group or not is unknown.

This raises the question of when families with an eccentric child should worry. It is known that the great majority of individuals who develop schizophrenia have normal childhoods and are not identifiable in their early years. And it is also known that the vast majority of eccentric children will not develop schizophrenia; many, in fact, grow up to be leaders. The problem of separating the eccentricities of normal childhood from the early symptoms of schizophrenia is especially difficult in adolescence, approximately ages 11 to 13, when the norms of behavior are very strange indeed. Overacuteness of the senses is a common symptom of schizophrenia, yet how many adolescents have not had some such experiences? Moodiness, withdrawal, apathy, loss of interest in personal appearance, perplexity, the belief that people are watching one, preoccupation with one's body, and vagueness in thoughts may all be harbingers of impending schizophrenia, but they may also be just normal manifestations of early adulthood and its accompanying problems. For this reason families should *not* worry about every quirk in their children, but rather should assume they are normal until proven otherwise. This can be particularly difficult for a parent who has already had one child diagnosed with schizophrenia and who is expecting the worst for the younger children, but it is important. A 15-year-old has enough to worry about without being told things like "Don't daydream. That's what your brother did and it got him sick and into the hospital."

At what point *should* parents begin to worry that something may be wrong? When do the normal psychological vicissitudes of early adulthood cross the line and enter the realm of early symptoms of schizophrenia?

Alterations of the senses or in body image are common early symptoms as might be surmised from the discussion in chapter 2. Often the patient will be aware of them but will not confide in others. Perhaps more common early complaints are somatic symptoms, especially weakness, pains, and bizarre bodily sensations. Researchers in Canada asked newly diagnosed schizophrenic patients how frequently such symptoms occur in the early stages of illness and found that 86 percent complained of weakness, 38 percent of bodily pains or aches, 23 percent of headaches, 22 percent of poor coordination, and 47 percent of "bizarre symptoms."

Changes in the sleep pattern occur very commonly in early schizophrenia. The person may sleep less, or more, or simply begin sleeping at unusual times (e.g., up all night, sleeps all day). The important thing to notice is that the pattern has changed, sometimes dramatically. I have also found this to be one of the most reliable harbingers of relapse in schizophrenia, and I routinely ask patients about it whenever I have reduced their medication.

Disorders of thinking, including delusions, are occasionally the earliest signs of schizophrenia. Patients may have ideas of reference in which they think everyone is talking about them. Or their thinking may take a bizarre turn, and they come out with off-the-wall ideas at the dinner table that startle everyone. Some patients simply begin talking in a vague way in the early stages of their illness, with tangential thoughts that sound almost, but not quite, logical.

Changes in behavior are one of the commonest signs of early schizophrenia. The patients' personal habits may slowly change: for example, they stop taking showers, or they may no longer straighten up their room when previously they had been compulsively neat. Another common behavior change is social withdrawal; previously outgoing and socially adroit young adults are noticed to withdraw and spend increasingly long periods in their room by themselves. The emphasis in evaluating all these symptoms is on *change* in a young adult. Parents may say things such as: "John has become a different person over the last six months," or "None of Jennifer's friends come around anymore, and she doesn't seem to want to see anyone." Such changes may of course be caused by things other than schizophrenia; the use of street drugs must always be considered as a possibility in this age group.

MALE-FEMALE DIFFERENCES

Although textbooks say that schizophrenia occurs equally in men and women, that generalization neglects some important gender differences in this disease. Most striking is the earlier age of onset for men, which in the United States occurs two to three years earlier than in women. An analysis of a group of 17- or 18-year-old individuals with schizophrenia will reveal four or five males for every female.

Schizophrenia is also a more serious disease in men than it is in women. Men do not respond as well to antipsychotic drugs, they require higher doses of the drugs, they have a higher relapse rate, and their long-term adjustment—measured by such indices as social life, marriage, work record, suicide rate, and level of function—is not nearly so good as women's. There are, of course, many women with schizophrenia who have had a severe course and many men who have done well, but statistics clearly establish that schizophrenia occurs earlier and in more severe form in the male.

The reasons for such gender differences, still unknown, provide one of the many questions about schizophrenia needing to be researched. It should be noted that both infantile autism and childhood schizophrenia also have a strong predominance for males, and that male fetuses generally are known to be more susceptible to environmentally caused problems such as infections. The fact that males get schizophrenia both younger and more severely, then, may simply be another reflection of Mother Nature's dictum that in many ways men are the weaker sex. Another speculation about why schizophrenia might be more severe in males is the possibility that female sex hormones (estrogens) may exert an antipsychotic effect and be protective. It is also possible, although unlikely, that schizophrenia resembles diabetes in having two major subgroups: an early-onset, more severe variety that affects mostly men, and a later-onset, less severe variety more apt to afflict women.

Another facet of male-female differences in schizophrenia is the effect of the menstrual cycle on the disease in some women. Although it has not been adequately studied, clinicians and families have noted for many years that some women with schizophrenia have a worsening of their symptoms in the days immediately preceding their menstrual period. This is almost certainly caused by the ebb and flow of hormones during the cycle, and lends further support to theories linking male-female differences in schizophrenia to hormonal differences.

THE IDEAL DIAGNOSTIC WORKUP

In its full-blown stages, most cases of schizophrenia are not difficult to diagnose. Auditory hallucinations and/or delusional thinking are among the commonest and most prominent symptoms, and more than three-quarters of all patients will have one or the other. Various kinds of thinking disorders become evident on simple conversation (e.g., thought blocking) or on asking the patient to give the meaning of proverbs (e.g., inability to think abstractly). Emotions may be blunted or inappropriate, and the individual's behavior may vary from unusual to catatonic to bizarre.

For a person with the symptoms of schizophrenia who has become ill for the first time, what kind of diagnostic tests and procedures are appropriate? Most public psychiatric hospitals, and many private ones as well, offer cursory diagnostic workups, and there is no question that some patients are diagnosed with schizophrenia who have the diseases described in chapter 4. Given this fact, what should be done diagnostically to maximize the chances of uncovering all potentially reversible diseases masquerading as schizophrenia? Although I recognize that some of my psychiatric colleagues may disagree, the following diagnostic workup is what I would personally want to happen to me if I or a member of my family was admitted to a hospital with symptoms of schizophrenia for the first time.

History and Mental Status Examination. These are routinely done for all psychiatric admissions but often incompletely so. Visual hallucinations, headaches, and recent head injury should be specifically asked about. A general review of organ systems other than the central nervous system may turn up diseases masquerading as schizophrenia (e.g., abdominal pains suggesting acute intermittent porphyria, urinary incontinence suggesting normal pressure hydrocephalus). Perhaps the single most important question which the examining physician can ask is: "What drugs are you using?" It is a two-pronged question intended to elicit information about street drug use, which may be producing or exacerbating the psychiatric symptoms, as well as prescription drug use which may be producing psychiatric symptoms as a side effect (see chapter 4). Since acutely psychotic patients often cannot give a coherent history, family members and friends play an essential role in providing the needed information.

Physical and Neurological Examinations. These are also often done superficially with the consequence that many medical and neurological diseases are missed. A careful neurological examination of patients with schizophrenia will elicit abnormal findings in a significant number of them (see chapter 6). A useful part of the neurological exam, which can be taught to nonphysicians who must screen psychiatric patients, is a series of pencil-and-paper tests such as write-a-sentence and draw-a-clock; as Dr. Robert Taylor describes in *Mind or Body,* such tests can help identify patients with other brain diseases, such as brain tumors or Huntington's disease, who may initially present with schizophrenialike symptoms.

Basic Laboratory Work: Blood Count, Blood Chemical Screen, and Urinalysis. These are also routine everywhere, but abnormal results are sometimes not noticed or followed up. The blood count may elicit unexpected findings suggesting such diseases as pernicious anemia or lead intoxication. Blood chemical screens have become widespread and do as many as thirty-four different tests on a single sample of blood. These normally include tests which may screen endocrine or metabolic imbalances. If a thyroid function test is not included in the routine blood chemical screen, it should be ordered separately. A routine test to screen for syphilis should also be included. Urinalysis should include screening tests to detect street drugs in the urine.

Psychological Tests. The choice of psychological tests varies from hospital to hospital and depends on the psychologist. Such tests can be extremely useful in making the diagnosis of schizophrenia in early or borderline cases, and can also point the examiner away from schizophrenia and toward other brain diseases. Acutely agitated patients with the full-blown schizophrenic syndrome frequently are unable to concentrate long enough to do psychological tests.

CT Scan. Computerized tomography (CT) scanning has become widely available in recent years. It will show brain abnormalities in approximately 20 percent of individuals with schizophrenia. Dr. Daniel Weinberger, one of the pioneer investigators of CT scans in schizophrenia, recommends that all patients with an initial psychotic episode should have a CT scan. Some diseases that mimic schizophrenia may be detected by CT scans, including brain tumors, Huntington's disease, Wilson's disease, metachromatic leukodystrophy, sarcoidosis, subdural hematomas, Kuf's disease, viral encephalitis, and aqueductal stenosis. For a person who has had symptoms of schizophrenia for many years, a CT scan probably is not justified diagnostically, for the diseases which the procedure is capable of detecting would have become evident over the years because of other signs or symptoms.

Lumbar Puncture. Despite the stereotype to the contrary, lumbar punctures are simple procedures producing little more discomfort than the drawing of blood. Cerebrospinal fluid is withdrawn by a needle from a sac in the lower back; since the sac is connected to fluid channels in the brain, examination of the cerebrospinal fluid often provides clues (e.g., antibodies to viruses) about events in the brain. They are routinely used in the diagnosis of brain diseases, such as multiple sclerosis, and probably will become routine for schizophrenia in the future. They are capable of detecting a variety of diseases, especially viral diseases of the central nervous system. Indications for their use in patients admitted for a first episode of schizophrenia include the following:

a. Patient complains of headache (20 percent do) or stiff neck with nausea or a fever
b. Rapid onset of psychotic symptoms
c. Fluctuations in patient's orientation (e.g., patient knows where he is one day but does not know the next day)
d. Visual or olfactory (smell) hallucinations
e. Neurological signs or symptoms suggesting central nervous system disease other than schizophrenia (e.g., nystagmus of the eyes in which the gaze moves rapidly from side to side)
f. Concurrent or recent history of flu or fever.

Lumbar punctures in patients with schizophrenia are relatively free of side effects, persons with schizophrenia being especially immune to getting post-lumbar-puncture headaches; up to one-third of non-schizophrenic patients may get such a headache.

Electroencephalogram (EEG). The indications for an EEG are virtually identical to those for lumbar puncture, and in fact the two are often ordered together. I personally believe that both the lumbar puncture and EEG should be routinely included in the diagnostic workup of any young adult presenting with symptoms of psychosis for the first time. An EEG should always be ordered if there is a history of meningitis or encephalitis, birth complications, or severe head injury; it should be mandatory for any patient who has had episodic attacks of psychosis with a sudden onset. An EEG may detect temporal-lobe epilepsy, which sometimes mimics schizophrenia.

To be most useful an EEG should be done using nasopharyngeal leads (electrodes are put into the mouth as well as on the scalp) and be done after the person has been kept up all night (sleep-deprived); the diagnostic rewards for doing this more sophisticated type of EEG are appreciable. EEGs are completely harmless procedures which simply measure electrical impulses in the brain; there are no known side effects or harmful effects of any kind.

Other. Other diagnostic tests may be indicated by specific findings but are not routine. Newer brain scans can be done in a variety of ways (e.g., xenon scans, PET scans) but their use is still experimental. The dexamethasone suppression test (DST) was originally thought to be useful to differentiate certain kinds of schizophrenic patients, but it has not proven to be so. Magnetic resonance imaging (MRI) and newer methods of measuring brain structure and function will undoubtedly become widespread within the next few years and will replace CT scans. As technology improves, the ideal diagnostic workup of schizophrenia will become increasingly complex and sophisticated.

CHILDHOOD SCHIZOPHRENIA

It is generally believed that childhood schizophrenia is simply an early version of the adult disease, although much rarer. Approximately four males are affected for every female. Only about 2 percent of individuals with schizophrenia have the onset of their disease in childhood al-though that percentage varies, depending on where one fixes the child-hood-adult line. Schizophrenia beginning before age 5 is exceedingly rare (see section on infantile autism, chapter 5), and between ages 5 and 10 it increases only slightly. From age 10, schizophrenia slowly in-creases in incidence until age 15, when it begins its sharp upward peak as the adult disease.

The symptoms of childhood schizophrenia are identical to those of adult schizophrenia with a major addition. In the childhood ver-sion other evidence of brain damage is much more prominent, con-current with the symptoms of schizophrenia. Thus seizures, neuro-logical disabilities, dyslexia, hyperactivity, and retardation may all be found among some children with schizophrenia. The mix of symp-toms leads to a semantic quagmire. Is the child mentally retarded with secondary schizophrenia or vice versa? Is the child's schizo-phrenia secondary to his seizures or are both due to generalized brain damage? To resolve this confusion, the American Psychiatric Association in *DSM-III* discarded the term "childhood schizophre-nia" altogether and suggested instead "childhood-onset pervasive de-velopmental disorder."

It is known that mothers of children with childhood-onset schizo-phrenia have had more complications of pregnancy and birth. Further evidence of brain damage in many of these children can be seen in their abnormal electroencephalograms. Most geneticists believe that child-hood schizophrenia can be found in the same families as adult schizo-phrenia, although little is firmly established about this disease because so little research work has been done on it.

Childhood schizophrenia is treated with the same antipsychotic medication used for adult schizophrenia. A recent follow-up of ten children with this disease from fourteen to thirty-four years after its onset found them still diagnosed with schizophrenia but with relatively few delusions or hallucinations. Instead they tended to be quiet and withdrawn with poverty of thought and lack of drive. A minority of children with schizophrenia will recover and do quite well as adults, but what percentage this constitutes is uncertain. In general it is thought that the earlier the age of onset of schizophrenia, the worse the outcome is likely to be, but there are major exceptions to this rule. A good description of childhood schizophrenia is provided by Louise Wilson in *This Stranger, My Son*.

DUAL DIAGNOSES

The term "dual diagnoses" usually signifies that the individual under consideration has both a severe psychiatric disability and a congenital or developmental disability such as mental retardation, cerebral palsy, blindness, or deafness. Most often this is schizophrenia and retardation, although all combinations are possible. The two conditions may occur quite separately in an individual (the twice-cursed), or the two may arise from the same original brain condition which caused damage to two different parts of the brain. Diagnosing such individuals is made even more complex by the fact that someone with mental retardation, blindness, etc., may have psychiatric problems as a reaction to his/her disability.

The problems engendered by an individual with schizophrenia, who also has one of these other disabilities, are legion. Facilities and services for someone with schizophrenia are poor enough, but for the dually diagnosed they are abysmal. Psychiatric hospitals are not equipped to handle the disabilities, while facilities for the disabled deny admission because of the person's psychiatric problems. Dually diagnosed individuals in most states are passed back and forth from one institution to another, each institution disclaiming ultimate responsibility, with the individual made to feel like a leper's leper. Families of such individuals often achieve heroic heights providing services at home with little or no assistance from public health officials.

Rarely one finds a facility trying to provide humane services for the dually diagnosed. St. Elizabeths Hospital in Washington, D.C., has for many years had an exemplary program for individuals with schizophrenia and deafness. And one of the most moving experiences I had in my early days of training was spending a morning in a New York facility trying to train blind children who also had schizophrenia. Such examples demonstrate that good services are possible if we can only find the will to provide them.

RECOMMENDED FURTHER READING

Cadet, J. L., K. C. Rickler, and D. R. Weinberger. "The Clinical Neurologic Examination in Schizophrenia." In *The Neurology of Schizophrenia,* edited by H. M. Nasrallah and D. R. Weinberger. Amsterdam: Elsevier, 1986. This is the best description of neurological exams in schizophrenia available. The book contains several other chapters which include the latest findings in neurological aspects of this disease.

Diagnostic and Statistical Manual of Mental Disorders (DSM-III-R). Washington, D.C.: American Psychiatric Association, 1987. This is the official diagnostic manual in the United States for all psychiatric disorders.

Seeman, M. V. "Gender Differences in Schizophrenia." *Canadian Journal of Psychiatry* 27 (1982): 107–11. A concise synopsis of the many differences between schizophrenia in men and women.

Slater, E., and M. Roth. *Clinical Psychiatry.* Baltimore: Williams & Wilkins, 1969. This is the best textbook description of schizophrenia by a wide margin. From England, the book was originally published in 1954, with Dr. Willy Mayer-Gross as chief author, and it is still known informally by his name.

Taylor, R. L. *Mind or Body: Distinguishing Psychological from Organic Disorders.* New York: McGraw-Hill, 1982. This useful manual for distinguishing brain diseases which may mimic schizophrenia is especially recommended for mental health workers, psychologists, social workers, and psychiatric nurses.

Wilson, L. *This Stranger, My Son.* New York: Putnam, 1968. Paperback by New American Library. A mother's account of raising a schizophrenic son who becomes sick in early childhood, it is especially good in describing the guilt and shame of a parent who is told by the mental health professionals that she is to blame.

4

WHAT SCHIZOPHRENIA IS NOT

What consoles me is that I am beginning to consider madness as an illness like any other, and that I accept it as such.

Vincent van Gogh, 1889, in a letter to his brother, Theo

One way to understand a disease is to describe what it is, which has been the task of the past two chapters. The alternative is to describe what it is not. In the case of schizophrenia this is especially important to do, for the term has been used very broadly and imprecisely in both popular culture and in medicine. If we hope to move forward in our understanding of this disease, then we must first be clear what we are talking about.

MANIC-DEPRESSIVE PSYCHOSIS

The fundamental division of the psychoses into dementia praecox (now called schizophrenia) and manic-depressive psychosis was proposed by Emil Kraepelin in 1896 and has continued to be widely accepted in psychiatry. In 1980 the American Psychiatric Association under *DSM-III* proposed changing the name of manic-depressive psychosis to bipolar disorder, but the new term offers no significant advantages.

Manic-depressive psychosis is approximately one-third as prevalent as schizophrenia. It has a modest predilection for women over men and is thought to be disproportionately common in higher socioeconomic groups for unknown reasons. It usually begins before age 30 but, unlike schizophrenia, later onsets are not unusual. Research on the causes of the disease is proceeding along the same lines as that for schizophrenia. A genetic predisposition is clearly established, with some researchers arguing that it is an inherited disease. In 1987 a study of the Pennsylvania Amish found that the transmission of manic-depressive psychosis was associated with a gene on chromosome number 11; other researchers, however, claimed that the location of the putative gene was on other chromosomes. Biochemical dysfunction in the brain of individuals with manic-depressive psychosis is also suspected, with interest centered on serotonin and its metabolites rather than on dopamine. Most biological abnormalities found in schizophrenia (e.g., ventricular enlargement on CT scans, neurological abnormalities) are also found in manic-depressive psychosis, although they are not as marked.

The major clinical characteristic of manic-depressive psychosis is episodes of mania, depression, or some combination thereof. Manic episodes consist of elevated (or occasionally irritated) mood, during which time the person is excessively cheerful, talkative, sociable, expansive, grandiose, energetic, and hypersexual, and apparently needs little sleep. The person's speech may be rapid (pressured), with ideas thrown out faster than the listener can sort through them (flights of ideas). Grandiosity may proceed to a delusional state (e.g., belief that one is the President), dress may turn flamboyant, and behavior may become dangerous and inappropriate (e.g., buying sprees, foolish investments). Depressive episodes consist of sad ("dysphoric") mood with hopelessness, poor appetite, sleep disturbances (either insomnia or excessive sleeping), loss of interest in usual activities, hyposexuality, loss of energy, slowed thinking, feelings of guilt or worthlessness, and often suicidal ideas. To qualify for these diagnoses under current *DSM-III* diagnostic standards, a manic episode must last at least one week (or require hospitalization) and a depressive episode must last at least two weeks.

Although the public stereotype of manic-depressive illness is a person who swings from one extreme to the other and back again, this is found only rarely. Some affected persons have a series of manic episodes, some have a series of depressive episodes, while others have the two in every conceivable combination. Many months or even years may separate episodes; between episodes the person is characteristically normal. There are of course all gradations of mood swings in either direction within the general population; some people have great energy and cheerfulness as part of their personality, others are chronically self-deprecating and depressed. A person who falls just short of being fully manic is referred to as hypomanic. If a person has numerous mood swings that fail to meet the full criteria for manic-depressive psychosis, the psychiatric diagnosis used is cyclothymic disorder. Approximately 10 percent of persons with manic-depressive psychosis commit suicide, similar to the suicide rate in schizophrenia (see chapter 5).

In its typical form, then, manic-depressive psychosis is easy to differentiate from schizophrenia. The onset of manic-depressive psychosis is not centered in the late teens and early twenties but spread over a much wider age range; males are not affected earlier or more severely; and the predominant clinical symptoms involve disorders of *mood* rather than disorders of *thought*. Patients with manic-depressive psychosis may have delusions or hallucinations, but when they occur they accompany and are congruent with the elevated or depressed mood. Most important, manic-depressive psychosis occurs in discrete episodes with a return to normal functioning between episodes being the rule; schizophrenia rarely occurs in such discrete episodes and residual disability is the rule. Because of their recovery, it is common to find people with manic-depressive psychosis holding important jobs in government, industry, and the entertainment field, and some traits of the hypomanic (e.g., high energy, inflated self-esteem, decreased need for sleep) lead to greater productivity and success in such fields.

The treatment of manic-depressive psychosis is hospitalization when necessary, until the episodes can be controlled. Manic episodes respond to antipsychotic medication, and depressive episodes respond to antidepressants and occasionally electroconvulsive therapy (ECT). Lithium has become an exceedingly useful drug in treating this condition, especially when used between episodes to reduce both the number of episodes and their severity.

John, a resident in psychiatry who came from a wealthy family, became gradually more energetic, talkative, and grandiose over one week's time. He then proceeded to buy three new cars in a 48-hour period, invest the remainder of his savings in a highly questionable venture, and begin new relationships with several women simultaneously. His family had him involuntarily hospitalized, where he was successfully treated with antipsychotics and lithium. He has remained on lithium for ten years with only modest mood swings and has become a successful practicing psychiatrist.

However, in many cases patients with psychoses cannot be divided neatly into those with schizophrenia and those with manic-depressive psychosis. The majority of psychotic patients have a mélange of thinking and mood disorders, and many patients change symptoms over time. These patients are diagnosed with schizoaffective disorder, a catchall category for everyone who cannot be easily placed into the two ends of the diagnostic spectrum. Debate within psychiatry never ends regarding the boundaries of these categories, with some theoreticians (including myself) inclined to place most psychotic patients into the schizophrenia category, while others see most psychotic patients as variants of the manic-depressive category. Although these diagnostic differences are often confusing for patients and their families (e.g., "Three different doctors have given my son three different diagnoses"), in terms of approaches to treatment the different diagnoses are not very important (see chapter 7).

In recent years suggestions have increased that perhaps Kraepelin was wrong, with schizophrenia and manic-depressive psychosis simply being two ends of the spectrum of a single disease. Perhaps the specifically affected part of the brain determines symptoms, or the period in brain development when the damage occurs. The genetics of the two disorders suggests that schizophrenia and manic-depressive psychosis should occur in separate families (and this usually is the case), yet occasionally both are found in families predisposed to only one. Also of interest are examples such as a pair of identical twins, in which both became psychotic at age 20, one with classical schizophrenia and the other with manic-depressive psychosis, or a set of identical triplets, two of whom were diagnosed with schizophrenia and the third with manic-depressive psychosis. Despite the assumptions of textbooks and the utilization of Kraepelin's dichotomy for almost a century, in fact no conclusive evidence exists for dividing patients with psychosis into separate disease entities.

SCHIZOID, SCHIZOTYPAL, PARANOID, AND BORDERLINE PERSONALITY DISORDERS

If attempts to set the boundary between schizophrenia and manic-depressive psychosis will keep psychiatrists up arguing half the night, discussions about personality disorders will keep them up for the other half. There are few murkier lands to enter in medicine than the shadowy terrain lying at the edge of schizophrenia; travelers to this region must have a high tolerance for ambiguity.

The current diagnostic divisions of this area, as proposed by *DSM-III* and widely used in the United States, concern various personality disorders. Such disorders are said to be collections of personality traits which "are inflexible and maladaptive and cause either significant impairment in social or occupational functioning or subjective distress." These personality disorders, then, are not categorized under *DSM-III* as diseases like schizophrenia and manic-depressive psychosis, but rather are considered to be maladaptive lifestyles. Let us consider each in turn and then discuss them as a group.

Schizoid Personality Disorder.   These individuals are loners and have virtually no friends. They avoid social situations and seek employment in which they do not have to interact with others (e.g., forest ranger, computer programmer). Schizoid men rarely marry. Such individuals appear incapable of experiencing feelings for others, either those of affection or those of hostility, and are relatively indifferent to praise or criticism. Some also appear to be detached from their environment as if in a perpetual fog.

Schizotypal Personality Disorder.   These individuals were in the past said to have such things as borderline schizophrenia, ambulatory schizophrenia, pseudoneurotic schizophrenia, latent schizophrenia, subclinical schizophrenia, and schizophrenic character. They have oddities and eccentricities of perception, thinking, speech, and behavior, including some combination of the following:

a. Ideas of reference, hypersensitivity, suspiciousness, and paranoid ideation
b. Magical thinking, such as clairvoyance and mental telepathy
c. Illusions in which they "feel" the presence of others who are not actually present
d. Feelings of unreality
e. Odd speech with vagueness and unusual usage of words
f. Social withdrawal and isolation, often as severe as that described for the schizoid personality disorder

Paranoid Personality Disorder. These individuals are known for their hypersensitivity, mistrust, and suspiciousness of other people's motivations. They are always on guard, easily slighted, and quick to take offense. They believe that others are trying to trick or harm them, and will go to great lengths to prove it. They question the loyalty of others and often see plots where nobody else can see them. They are often rigid, argumentative, and litigious. Many are interested in electronics and mechanical devices that can be used for spying. They appear to have few tender feelings, disdain weak people, and lack any sense of humor.

Borderline Personality Disorder. This is a most unfortunate term adopted by *DSM-III,* since it is invariably confused with the older term borderline schizophrenia, now categorized as schizotypal personality disorder. Individuals with borderline personality disorder are unstable in their behavior, relationships, and moods. Their behavior is often impulsive and unpredictable in such areas as money management, sex, alcohol and drug abuse, gambling, shoplifting, fights, reckless driving, and suicide gestures. Their relationships are intense but shift markedly over short periods of time. Their mood also shifts unpredictably and often includes temper tantrums or outbursts.

Since *DSM-III* was published in 1980, there has been continuing controversy about the validity of these personality disorders and their relationship to schizophrenia and manic-depressive psychosis. It is widely acknowledged that the four personality disorders overlap and that many individuals have combinations of these traits. Studies of families of individuals with schizophrenia have found more relatives with schizotypal and paranoid personality disorders, suggesting that they may be genetically related to schizophrenia. They can, in a theoretical sense, be considered a mild form of the disease. This possibility, generally referred to as the "spectrum concept" of schizophrenia, implies that there may be individuals at all points on the spectrum between mild personality disorder and severe schizophrenia. The concept has received support from the finding that many individuals with schizotypal and borderline personality disorders feel better and function better on low doses of antipsychotic drugs.

At the same time it should be pointed out that the concept of "mild schizophrenia" without biological markers to clearly delineate the disease poses potential danger. This concept is widely used in the Soviet

Union, where political dissidents and other undesirables may be so labeled and involuntarily hospitalized. Until we have clear biological and laboratory markers of "mild schizophrenia," it is preferable to maintain it as a personality disorder.

An example of a schizotypal personality disorder with schizoid features follows:

> Samuel had always been a shy, withdrawn child who avoided other people. As an adult he became a bookkeeper who was known to do good work as long as he was left alone. Colleagues at work regarded him as eccentric and strange, saying he misinterpreted their remarks in a paranoid fashion and remarking that his replies were sometimes off-target to their questions. On one occasion Samuel implied that he had known what they were going to say by means of mental telepathy.

BRIEF REACTIVE PSYCHOSIS

Brief episodes of schizophrenialike symptoms occur occasionally among individuals who are otherwise normal. Characteristically the illness begins suddenly, lasts a few days, and then remits suddenly. The causes of these illnesses are unknown but probably include brief viral infections of the brain (encephalitis), as well as other brain diseases which may mimic schizophrenia. Such illnesses may apparently also be precipitated by overwhelming stress and are seen in some soldiers undergoing enemy fire, inmates in prisons or concentration camps, and in individuals in extreme sensory deprivation situations (e.g., alone in a lifeboat for several days at sea).

The symptoms displayed by such patients may mimic schizophrenia closely, with delusions and hallucinations being prominent; disorders of thinking are much less common. Here is an example of such a patient:

> Frank, a 21-year-old Peace Corps volunteer, had only been in Africa for a month. Assigned to a small village with two coworkers, he was having difficulty mastering the language and complained of feeling isolated. One evening he began complaining that the Africans were spying on him. Within

twenty-four hours his illness had developed into a full-blown
psychosis with delusions of persecution and hallucinations.
When seen by a physician, he was hiding under the bed saying
that he could hear the army marching down the road to take
him and hang him.

At this stage of his illness, based on symptoms alone, Frank looked very
much like a schizophrenic. He was removed from his village and hospitalized, treated with drugs, and within one week he was completely well
again. Such patients will usually recover whether they are treated with
drugs or not and usually do not get sick again.

These patients should not be diagnosed with schizophrenia but
rather with brief reactive psychosis. If the illness persists for longer
than one month but less than six months, it should then be called a
schizophreniform disorder. The more rapid the onset and the shorter
the duration of illness, the more likely the person is to return to full
normality and not experience recurrence.

STREET DRUG PSYCHOSIS

It is a well-recognized fact that many drugs which are abused for their
psychic effects may produce symptoms similar to schizophrenia. Even
after ingesting a comparatively mild drug like marijuana the user may
experience strange bodily sensations, loss of body boundaries, and paranoid delusions. There is even a subgroup of people who give up using
marijuana because it leads to an unpleasant paranoid state after each
usage. Stronger drugs, such as LSD and PCP, regularly produce hallucinations (although these are more likely to be visual than auditory),
delusions, and disorders of thinking. Occasionally these symptoms become so severe that the person must be hospitalized and, if the history
of drug abuse is not known, the person may be diagnosed with schizophrenia by mistake. Amphetamines (speed) in particular are well
known for producing symptoms which may look identical to those of
schizophrenia.

Becky, a 17-year-old high school senior, was brought to the
emergency room by friends. She was confused, anxious, believed
that people were following her, that she was "losing" her body,
and was experiencing visual hallucinations of threatening faces.

On physical examination her skin was flushed, and she had an elevated temperature and dilated pupils. Her friends finally acknowledged that they had smoked marijuana which had been mixed with "angel dust" (PCP). Over the following three days, Becky's psychiatric symptoms completely resolved.

The question naturally arises whether drug abuse can *cause* schizophrenia. It is a question asked frequently by families and relatives of schizophrenic patients. There is now abundant evidence that chronic and repeated usage of many of the mind-altering drugs can damage the brain, impairing intellectual functions and memory. Whether these drugs can cause schizophrenia, however, remains unresolved; my own guess is that if it occurs, it does so only rarely.

Why, then, is it so common to see schizophrenia begin after a person has used mind-altering drugs? The answer is probably twofold. First, both drug abuse and the onset of schizophrenia occur in the same age range of the late teens and early twenties. The percentage of people in this age range who have at least smoked a few "joints" is very high. Assuming there is no connection whatsoever between drug abuse and schizophrenia, it would still be expected that a considerable number of people developing schizophrenia would also have tried mind-altering drugs.

Second, and more important, is the common sequence of people developing the early symptoms of schizophrenia and then turning to mind-altering drugs to provide a rationalization for what they are experiencing. Hearing voices for the first time in your life, for example, is a very frightening experience; if you then begin using hashish, PCP, or some similar drug, it provides you with a persuasive reason for hearing the voices. Drug use can put off the uncomfortable confrontation with yourself that tells you something is going wrong—very wrong—with your mind. You are, quite literally, losing it. Drugs, and alcohol as well, may also partially relieve the symptoms. In these cases persons can be said to be medicating themselves.

The families of schizophrenic persons are usually not aware of the earliest symptoms of the disease. Not knowing what their relative is experiencing, all they see is him/her turning to increasingly heavy drug abuse. Three to six months later the person is diagnosed with schizophrenia and the family immediately concludes that it was caused by the drug abuse. Such reasoning also relieves any burden of guilt on their part by making it clear that they had nothing to do with causing it. This may be especially attractive to relatives if they are faced with a psychiatrist who implies that problems of child rearing or problems of family communication contributed to the genesis of the disease. In these cases relatives will often seize on drug-abuse-causes-schizophrenia as a defense against the psychiatrist.

> Ted was a promising college student who had his life well planned. Midway through his sophomore year he began having episodes of euphoria, strange bodily sensations, and ideas that he had been sent to save the world. His grades dropped sharply, he began going to church every day, and then began using LSD. Prior to that time he had only used marijuana occasionally at parties. His roommate, college authorities, and finally his parents became alarmed about his turn to drugs. Within one month he was admitted to the local hospital with overt schizophrenic symptomatology. His parents believe it was caused by his drug use and have never been persuaded otherwise.

In most such instances, a careful questioning of the schizophrenic patient will establish the existence of early symptoms of the disease prior to his or her turning to significant drug abuse.

PRESCRIPTION DRUG PSYCHOSIS

Our society is a drug-using society; young adults abuse street drugs, while older adults use extraordinary numbers of prescription drugs. One only has to randomly open a medicine cabinet in any American home to realize the number of prescription drugs available for ingestion.

Many of these drugs can cause psychiatric symptoms as side effects, ranging from confusion to depression to paranoid delusions or hallucinations. In the majority of cases the hallucinations will be visual, suggesting that the symptoms are due to drugs or other organic medical conditions. Occasionally the hallucinations may be auditory and the patient may appear to have a sudden onset of classical schizophrenia. For any first episode of psychosis, therefore, the physician should always ask the question: "What drugs are you taking?"

Prescription drugs that cause symptoms of psychosis as a side effect almost always do so when they are first started. The psychotic symptoms will go away, sometimes immediately and in other cases more slowly, as soon as the drug is stopped. The following is a list of prescription drugs which have been reported as causing symptoms that might be confused with schizophrenia. There are undoubtedly others, and just because a specific drug is not listed here does not mean that it cannot cause such symptoms. The interaction of two or more drugs can also produce such symptoms. This list is taken mostly from *The Medical Letter* (volume 26, August 17, 1984, and volume 28, August 29, 1986) and lists drugs generically with a common trade name in parenthesis.

acyclovir (Zovirax)

albuterol (Ventolin)

amantadine (Symmetrel)

aminocaproic acid (Amicar)

amphetamines and other
   drugs taken for weight
   reduction

asparaginase (Elspar)

atropine and anticholinergics

baclofen (Lioresal)

bromocriptine (Parlodel)

chloroquine (Aralen)

cimetidine (Tagamet)

clomiphene citrate (Clomid)

clonazepam (Klonopin)

clonidine (Catapres)

corticosteroids (prednisone,
   cortisone, ACTH, others)

cyclobenzaprine (Flexeril)

cycloserine (Seromycin)

cyclosporine (Sandimmune)

dapsone (Avlosulfon)

diazepam (Valium)

diethylproprion (Tenuate)

digitalis glycosides

disopyramide (Norpace)

disulfiram (Antabuse)

ephedrine

ethchlorvynol (Placidyl)

ethosuximide (Zarontin)

fenfluramine (Pondimin)

gentamycin (Garamycin)

ibuprofen (Motrin)

indomethacin (Indocin)

isoniazid (INH)

ketamine (Ketalar, Ketaject)

levodopa (Dopar, others)

lidocaine (Xylocaine)

maprotiline (Ludiomil)

methyldopa (Aldomet)

methysergide (Sansert)

metrizamide (Amipaque)

metronidazole (Flagyl)

naproxen (Naprosyn)

niridazole (Ambilhar)

oxymetazoline (Afrin, others)

pentazocine (Talwin)

phenelzine (Nardil)

phenmetrazine (Preludin)

phenteramine (Fastin, others)

phenylephrine
   (Neo-Synephrine)

phenylpropanolamine
   (Dexatrim, others)

phenytoin (Dilantin, others)

podophyllin

primidone (Mysoline)
procainamide (Pronestyl)
propoxyphene (Darvon)
propranolol (Inderal)
pseudoephedrine
quinacrine (Atabrine)
sulindac (Clinoril)

theophylline
thiabendazole (Mintezol)
thyroid hormones
tocainide (Tonocard)
trazodone (Desyrel)
triazolam (Halcion)
vincristine (Oncovin)

> Christopher, a 29-year-old lawyer with a severe alcohol problem, was noted to become increasingly paranoid over four days and to then begin responding to auditory hallucinations. He was initially diagnosed as possible schizophrenia, but questioning by an emergency room doctor revealed that a psychiatrist had started Christopher on disulfiram (Antabuse) one week previously. The disulfiram was stopped and the symptoms went away within 48 hours. When disulfiram was again resumed the symptoms recurred. Subsequent withdrawal from alcohol without disulfiram produced no psychotic symptoms, suggesting that it had been the disulfiram and not alcohol withdrawal which had been the cause of the paranoia and hallucinations.

PSYCHOSIS DUE TO OTHER DISEASES

There are several diseases of the body that can produce symptoms similar to schizophrenia. In most cases there is no ambiguity because the disease is clearly diagnosable; in a few cases, however, there may be some confusion, especially in the early stages of the disease.

There is considerable dispute about how often other diseases mimic schizophrenia and go undetected. In a widely quoted study, Hall and his associates in Texas examined 38 hospitalized patients with schizophrenia and found 39 percent of them had a medical illness which "caused or exacerbated" the schizophrenia. A larger study of 318 hospital admissions with a diagnosis of schizophrenia found 8 percent "with antecedent organic cerebral disorders." A postmortem study of 200 patients with schizophrenia "found organic cerebral disease thought to be causally related in 11 percent." What is clear is that there is a subgroup of patients hospitalized with schizophrenia who have other medical diseases which are causing their schizophrenic symptoms, and that some of these other diseases are treatable.

The most important diseases that may produce symptoms of schizophrenia are:

Brain Tumors. Tumors of the pituitary gland are especially likely to cause symptoms of schizophrenia, but other tumors (e.g., a meningioma of the temporal lobe) may also do so. These are usually detectable on CT scan and often curable by surgery in their early stages.

Viral Encephalitis. It has been known for many years that viral encephalitis can produce schizophrenialike symptoms following the encephalitis. What is becoming increasingly clear is that encephalitis occasionally mimics schizophrenia in the early stages of illness, before other signs and symptoms of encephalitis become apparent; how often this occurs is unknown. A recent review of twenty-two such cases identified a variety of viruses as capable of doing this, including herpes simplex, Epstein-Barr virus, cytomegalovirus, measles, coxsackie, and equine encephalitis. An example of such a case follows:

> Ruth was an 18-year-old navy nursing aide. Following a flulike illness she developed headaches, began hearing voices talking to her, had feelings of unreality and loss of body boundaries, and became depressed. She slashed her wrists on instruction from the voices and was hospitalized. Her emotions were then noted to be inappropriate, and she had mild disorders in her thinking. She was alternately treated as a depressive reaction and as a schizophrenic, although neurologists were also asked to see her because of the continuing headaches. She improved slowly over a three-month period and was discharged to be followed as an outpatient. Three months after discharge she died suddenly and without warning during an all-night prayer service. Autopsy revealed a viral infection of the brain which appeared to have been present for several months.

If suspected, most such cases can be diagnosed by lumbar puncture and EEG.

Temporal Lobe Epilepsy. The relationship between epilepsy and schizophrenia has been a controversial issue for many years. There is agreement, however, that one type of epilepsy—that of the temporal lobe—frequently produces symptoms like schizophrenia. One study found that 17 percent of patients with temporal lobe epilepsy had some symptoms of schizophrenia.

Cerebral Syphilis. Although not seen so much as in the past, syphilis should never be forgotten as a possible cause of schizophrenia-like symptoms. A routine blood test will alert one to its possibility, and a lumbar puncture will confirm the diagnosis.

Multiple Sclerosis. Depression and intellectual deterioration are commonly found in the early stages of multiple sclerosis. Occasionally symptoms of schizophrenia may also occur, with one recent report of a woman with "paranoid schizophrenia" for ten years before her multiple sclerosis became fully manifest.

Huntington's Disease. Schizophrenia is said to be "a common initial diagnosis" and "the most frequent persisting mis-diagnosis" in Huntington's disease, a genetic disease beginning in midlife. Once choreiform movements begin in the patient, the correct diagnosis becomes clear.

Other Diseases. A large number of other diseases have been recorded as occasionally presenting with symptoms similar to schizophrenia. They include the following:

Wilson's disease
acute intermittent porphyria
metachromatic leukodystrophy
lupus erythematosus
congenital calcification of
   basal ganglia
progressive supranuclear palsy
aqueductal stenosis
normal pressure
   hydrocephalus
cerebral vascular accident
   (stroke)
narcolepsy
thyroid disease

adrenal disease
hepatic encephalopathy
pellagra
pernicious anemia
metal poisoning (e.g., lead,
   mercury)
insecticide poisoning (e.g.,
   organophosphorus
   compounds)
sarcoidosis
leptospirosis
tropical infections (e.g.,
   trypanosomiasis, cerebral
   malaria)

The best means of detecting these diseases are a competent physician and a complete diagnostic workup, as outlined in chapter 3.

PSYCHOSIS FOLLOWING CHILDBIRTH

Some degree of depression in mothers following childbirth is relatively common and on occasion may be severe. Much less common, occurring approximately once in every thousand births, are schizophrenialike symptoms which develop in the mother. These usually begin between three and seven days postpartum and may include delusions (e.g., believing her baby is defective or has been kidnapped) or hallucinations (voices telling her to kill the baby). Depression may occur as well, and a schizoaffective diagnosis is frequent. Because of the unpredictability of such patients, the baby is usually separated from the mother until she improves. Treatment with medication usually produces rapid improvement, with resolution of the symptoms in most cases within two weeks. A small percentage of such cases persist and proceed to become a full-blown schizophrenic disorder.

The cause of this disorder is not known. Formerly it was believed that psychological factors, such as the mother's ambivalent feelings toward the baby, were primary. In recent years more attention has been focused on possible biochemical factors, especially the massive hormonal changes which take place following childbirth. Such theories receive added impetus from the observation that some female schizophrenic patients regularly become more symptomatic just prior to or at the time of their menstrual period. Those cases which go on to true schizophrenia may be women who would have become schizophrenic even if they had not become pregnant. Since the onset of schizophrenia occurs most often during the same years in which most childbearing takes place, such a coincidence is occasionally inevitable.

Mary had just returned from the hospital after delivering her first child, a girl. Within the next three days her husband noted that she was talking strangely and appeared confused. She acknowledged that voices were telling her to kill the baby. Mary was hospitalized, treated with drugs, and completely returned to normal within ten days.

The use of the term "schizophrenia" is not appropriate for illnesses such as this.

PSYCHOSIS FOLLOWING TRAUMA

The fact that psychosis can occasionally follow severe head injuries has been well established since studies on soldiers during the Franco-Prussian War of 1870. Still very controversial, however, is how often this occurs and what kinds of head trauma can produce psychosis. Localized injury to the temporal or frontal lobe is seen more often in individuals who develop post-traumatic psychosis, as is a history of coma for more than 24 hours. It has also been claimed that thinking disorders are uncommon in these psychoses but that paranoid delusions are common.

The problem arises in trying to assess whether the head trauma is related to the onset of the psychosis. Head trauma and schizophrenia are both common in young adults and so will occur coincidentally from time to time. Most young adults can recall some instance of head trauma, and associating the trauma with the schizophrenia has an appeal to relatives who may be looking for an explanation for the sickness. Further complicating this assessment is the fact that individuals developing early symptoms of schizophrenia may do irrational things which produce head trauma; the family may not have been aware of the early symptoms, and so may associate the onset of the schizophrenia with the trauma. Finally there is the confounding issue of whether the trauma produces the psychosis by direct injury to the brain or by acting as a severe stressor, the straw that broke the camel's back.

> John, a 22-year-old college student with no history of psychiatric symptoms, was struck by a car while riding his bicycle. He was semicomatose for 16 days, had signs of neurological damage, and seizures. Emerging from his semicomatose state, he told his mother that voices on the radio had accused him of being a homosexual. No further symptoms were noted over the following year except insomnia and headaches, until he became suicidal and was hospitalized.

At that time paranoid delusions were noted and these became more severe. He had seven more admissions over the next five years. His delusions responded to antipsychotic medication, which he stopped taking each time he left the hospital.

INFANTILE AUTISM

Infantile autism, a brain disease of infancy, appears unrelated to schizophrenia. This syndrome, beginning within the child's first two-and-one-half years, is characterized by severe social withdrawal (e.g., child resists being held or touched), retarded language development, abnormal responses to sensory stimuli (e.g., sounds may overwhelm the child), and a fascination with inanimate objects (e.g., a faucet, the child's own shadow) or repetitive routines (e.g., spinning). It occurs in approximately 4 children per 10,000 and thus is one twenty-fifth as common as schizophrenia. At one time it was said that autism was more common in higher socioeconomic groups but that has been disproven. It occurs four times more in males than in females.

Autism is almost certainly a collection of diseases rather than a single disease. Autistimlike behavior may also be observed in children with the fragile X syndrome, phenylketonuria, viral encephalitis, and other diseases. Epilepsy commonly accompanies autism; approximately one-half of autistic children may have some degree of mental retardation; and a higher than expected percentage of autistic children also have blindness or deafness.

Like schizophrenia, the evidence that autism has biological causes has become overwhelming in recent years; older psychogenic theories such as Kanner's "refrigerator mother" now are completely discredited. There definitely appears to be a genetic component to autism: neuropathological and EEG abnormalities occur in the brains of these children, and several abnormalities in endocrine function and blood chemistry have also been found. One of the most interesting findings which may relate to the causes of autism is that mothers who give birth to autistic children report having had an unusually high frequency of bleeding during pregnancy, compared with controls. In addition to being found in retrospective studies, the increased bleeding has also been found it in a prospective study in which information was collected

on a large group of mothers, and only later was the data analyzed on
those who gave birth to autistic children.

Drugs such as haloperidol, fenfluramine, and pyridoxine are being
used to treat autism but so far with only modest success. As the autistic
child gets older, a small percentage improve and function well. The
majority, however, take on the characteristics of adult schizophrenia
with an emphasis on "negative" symptoms (e.g., withdrawal, flattened
emotions, poverty of thoughts), rather than "positive" symptoms (e.g.,
delusions, hallucinations).

Differentiation of infantile autism from childhood schizophrenia
is in most cases not too difficult. Autism almost always begins before
age two-and-one-half, while schizophrenia is rare before 5 and very
uncommon before age 10. The autistic child will have prominent withdrawal, language retardation, and repetitive routines, while the schizophrenic child will have delusions, hallucinations, and thinking disorders. Half the autistic children will be retarded but far fewer of the
schizophrenic children will be. Finally schizophrenic children may
have a family history of schizophrenia, but autistic children almost
never have a family history of schizophrenia.

CULTURALLY INDUCED OR HYSTERICAL PSYCHOSIS

Occasionally confusion will arise between schizophrenia and culturally
induced or hysterical psychosis. This is an altered state of consciousness
usually entered into voluntarily by an individual; while in this altered
state of consciousness the person may exhibit symptoms which look
superficially like schizophrenia. For example, the person may complain
of altered bodily sensations and hallucinations and may behave in an
excited and irrational manner. In the United States these conditions are
seen most commonly in connection with fundamentalistic religious
services. In other cultural groups and in other countries these conditions are known by such names as moth craziness (Navajo Indians),
windigo (Cree and Ojibwa Indians), zar (Middle East), koro (China),
susto (Latin America), latah (Southeast Asia), and amok (worldwide).

Cecelia led a perfectly normal life except for the monthly
all-night worship service at her fundamentalist church. During

the service she claimed to hear voices talking to her, often spoke in tongues, and occasionally behaved in a wild and irrational way so that others had to restrain her. Other members of the congregation regarded her with both fear and awe, suspecting that she was possessed by spirits.

People like Cecelia should not be labeled as schizophrenic unless there are other symptoms of the disease. Occasionally persons who have schizophrenia will be attracted to fundamentalist religious groups or religious cults, however, since such groups often value hearing voices or "speaking in tongues." This will be discussed at greater length in chapter 10.

MULTIPLE PERSONALITY

Like "Sybil" and "The Three Faces of Eve," the person with multiple personality is the true "split personality" that so many people confuse with schizophrenia. This extremely rare condition occurs mostly in women and is usually diagnosed in early adulthood. The two or more personalities emerge at different times, often changing abruptly from one to another, and may have quite different personality characteristics. A quiet, hard-working, withdrawn young woman, for example, may alternate with an irresponsible and promiscuous other self. One personality may have no knowledge of another. Most persons with multiple personality have been sexually and/or physically abused as children and the condition is thought to be a reaction to such abuse.

Multiple personality is officially classified as a dissociative reaction, along with such conditions as psychogenic amnesia and fugue states. It should not be confused with schizophrenia, since none of the symptoms of schizophrenia are normally found in such patients except for feelings of depersonalization. A person with multiple personality has no thinking disorder, delusions, or auditory hallucinations, other than one personality occasionally being able to overhear the other personality speaking.

CREATIVITY AND SCHIZOPHRENIA

An oft-debated question around firesides and pubs is whether there is a relationship between creativity and schizophrenia. John Dryden reflected the views of many people when he wrote three hundred years ago, "Great wits are sure to madmen near allied." Since then we have moved a little closer to a definitive answer to this question.

It is known that the creative person and the schizophrenic person share many cognitive traits. Both use words and language in unusual ways (the hallmark of a great poet or novelist), both have unusual views of reality (as great artists do), both often utilize unusual thought processes in their deliberations, and both tend to prefer solitude to the company of others. When creative persons are given traditional psychological tests, they manifest more psychopathology than noncreative persons, and creative persons are often viewed as eccentric by their friends. Conversely, when nonparanoid schizophrenics are given traditional tests of creativity they score very high (paranoid schizophrenics do not).

Several surveys have shown that highly creative persons are not themselves more susceptible to schizophrenia. However, one study has suggested that the immediate relatives of creative persons may be more susceptible to schizophrenia. As a case in point one thinks of Robert Frost, whose aunt, son, and perhaps daughter all developed schizophrenia. Looking at the problem from the other side, the same study found that the immediate relatives of schizophrenic patients scored higher on tests of creativity than would be expected by chance. Such studies need to be replicated before one can seriously suggest a link between schizophrenia and creativity. If such a link exists, it would most likely be a genetic predisposition to both conditions.

There is one fundamental difference between the creative person and the schizophrenic person, of course. The creative person has his/her unusual thought processes under control and can harness them in the creation of a product. The person with schizophrenia, on the other hand, is at the mercy of disconnected thinking and loose associations which tumble about in cacophonic disarray. The creative person has choices whereas the schizophrenia sufferer does not.

The list of creative individuals who have been suspected of having schizophrenia is remarkably short; this is not surprising when one considers how thinking disorders interfere with a person's ability to work. Those whose names are mentioned most often include Nietzsche, Strindberg, Wittgenstein, Hölderlin, Blake, Kafka, Nijinsky, Joyce, and van Gogh; the last two will be discussed below.

Manic-depressive psychosis, on the other hand, lends itself to creativity because of a high energy level and for much of the time the absence of thinking disorders. The list of people suspected of having manic-depressive psychosis among creative individuals includes Handel, Berlioz, Schumann, Gluck, Byron, Shelley, Coleridge, Poe, Balzac, Hemingway, Fitzgerald, Eugene O'Neill and Virginia Woolf. Alcoholism is also common among creative individuals; the first five Americans who won a Nobel Prize for literature were all alcoholics or nearly so (Sinclair Lewis, O'Neill, Faulkner, Hemingway, and Steinbeck).

James Joyce is a particularly interesting study in psychopathology. A biography on him noted his "keen pleasure in sounds," his periods of depression, intermittent alcohol abuse, and at least one episode of mania during which "he could not sleep for six or seven nights . . . he felt as if he were wound up and then suddenly shooting out of water like a fish. During the day he was troubled by auditory hallucinations." A psychiatrist who studied Joyce's writings concluded that he was a schizoid personality with paranoid traits and claimed that *"Finnegans Wake* must ultimately be diagnosed as psychotic." Joyce's only daughter, Lucia, was diagnosed with classical schizophrenia at age 22, treated by Jung, and spent the rest of her life in mental hospitals. It was noted that "Joyce had a remarkable capacity to follow her swift jumps of thought, which baffled other people completely."

Vincent van Gogh was also troubled by episodes of depression, intermittent alcohol abuse, and periods of great energy. At Arles, while being "assailed by auditory hallucinations," he "suddenly cut off his left ear," then presented it to a prostitute as a gift. Hospitalized in Arles twice in the next two months, he displayed paranoid delusions, visual and auditory hallucinations, and mutism. He then was involuntarily committed to an asylum in St.-Rémy for a year, during which time he had to be periodically placed in isolation and complained of hearing "sounds and strange voices." Various diagnoses of van Gogh's illness have been offered, including schizophrenia, schizoaffective disorder, manic-depressive psychosis, temporal lobe epilepsy, and cerebral syphilis. Although there is a tendency to romanticize his psychosis and view it as partially responsible for his great art, van Gogh's own letters make explicit how painful and unpleasant it was. He ultimately committed suicide after painting for just ten years. From St.-Rémy he wrote to his brother, Theo: "Oh, if I could have worked without this accursed disease—what things I might have done."

RECOMMENDED FURTHER READING

Coleman, M., and C. Gillberg. *The Biology of the Autistic Syndromes.* New York: Praeger Publishers, 1985. The best book on autism, with a good summary of the evidence for biological causes.

Davison, K. "Schizophrenia-like Psychoses Associated with Organic Cerebral Disorders: A Review." *Psychiatric Developments* 1 (1983): 1–34. This is an excellent review of psychosis due to medical conditions. An earlier version of the paper, widely referenced, was published by Davison and C. R. Bagley as "Schizophrenia-like Psychoses Associated with Organic Disorders of the Central Nervous System" in *Current Problems in Neuropsychiatry,* edited by R. N. Herrington, Ashford, England: Headley Brothers, 1969.

Fieve, R. *Moodswing: The Third Revolution in Psychiatry.* New York: Bantam Books, 1976. One of the standard references on manic-depressive psychosis directed at a lay audience.

Lishman, W. A. *Organic Psychiatry: The Psychological Consequences of Cerebral Disorder.* Oxford: Blackwell Scientific Publications, 1978. This is an excellent textbook on psychiatric symptoms caused by medical diseases. If it is on your psychiatrist's shelf, you are probably in good hands.

Papolos, D. F., and J. Papolos. *Overcoming Depression.* New York: Harper & Row, 1987. A concise and current manual on depression and manic-depressive illness for afflicted individuals and their families.

Torrey, E. F. "Functional Psychoses and Viral Encephalitis." *Integrative Psychiatry* 4 (1986): 224–36. This paper demonstrates how patients with viral encephalitis can present with symptoms of schizophrenia.

5

PROGNOSIS AND POSSIBLE COURSES

Such a disease, which disorders the senses, perverts the reason and breaks up the passions in wild confusion—which assails man in his essential nature—brings down so much misery on the head of its victims, and is productive of so much social evil—deserves investigation on its own merits, by statistical as well as other methods. . . . We may discover the causes of insanity, the laws which regulate its course, the circumstances by which it is influenced, and either avert its visitations, or mitigate their severity; perhaps in a later age, save mankind from its inflictions, or if this cannot be, at any rate ensure the sufferers early treatment.

Dr. William Farr, 1841

When diagnosed with schizophrenia for the first time, the person and his/her family want to know what is likely to happen next. What are the chances for complete recovery? How independent is the person likely to be ten years later, or thirty years later? What are the chances for little recovery or for spending most of the person's life in a mental hospital? What is the risk of suicide? These are important questions, for the answers to them will determine how the family of a person with schizophrenia plans for the future.

PREDICTORS OF OUTCOME

Over the years it has been noted that some persons afflicted with schizophrenia recover completely, others recover partially, and some do not recover at all. This observation led many professionals to review the clinical data at the time of the original hospital admission to determine what factors might predict a good outcome and which might predict a poor outcome. The result of these efforts has been a series of predictive factors, each of which taken by itself has limited usefulness, but which taken together may be very useful. From this a subtyping of schizophrenia into good outcome (good prognosis) and poor outcome (poor prognosis) has emerged and is becoming widely used. It is probably the most valid way to classify the disease which has been found to date.

The factors which are included in determining whether the person fits the good outcome or the poor outcome group are:

History of Adjustment Prior to Onset of Illness. Schizophrenic patients who are more likely to have a good outcome are those who were considered to be relatively normal prior to getting sick. Thus, if as children they were able to make friends with others, did not have major problems with delinquency and achieved success levels in school reasonable for their intelligence level, their outcome is likely to be good. Conversely, if they are described by relatives as "always a strange child," had major problems in school or with their peers, were considered delinquent, or were very withdrawn, they are more likely to fall into the poor outcome group.

Gender. It has now been clearly established that women with schizophrenia have a much more favorable outcome than men (see chapter 3).

Family History. Patients with the best outcome are those with no history of schizophrenic relatives. The more close relatives who have schizophrenia, the poorer the outcome becomes. If there is a history of depression or manic-depressive psychosis in the family, the person is likely to have a good outcome. Thus a good outcome is suggested by a family history with no mental disease or only depression and/or manic-depressive illness. A poor outcome is suggested by a family history of schizophrenia.

Age of Onset. In general, the younger the age at which schizophrenia develops, the poorer the outcome. A person who is first diagnosed with schizophrenia at age 15 is likely to have a poorer outcome than a person with the onset at age 25. Persons who are first diagnosed with schizophrenia in older age groups, especially over age 30, are likely to fall into the good outcome group.

Suddenness of Onset.   This is an important predictor of recovery, with the best outcomes occurring in those patients whose onset is most sudden. A relative who describes the gradual onset of the person's symptoms over a period of many months is painting a bleak picture, for it is much more likely that the person will fall into the poor outcome group. Conversely, as a practicing psychiatrist I am very happy when a relative tells me that "John was completely normal up until about a month ago," for I know that such a history bodes well for the future.

Precipitating Events.   These are very difficult to evaluate and therefore less reliable as predictors. The reason is that during the time of life when most schizophrenic persons become ill for the first time (ages 15 to 25), there is a great deal—much of it stressful—happening in their lives. Changing girlfriends and boyfriends, separations and divorces, school failures and new jobs, vocational plans, the death of parents, and existential crises all flow naturally through these years. Ask anyone in the 15-to-25 age range on any given day what is going on in his/her life that is important and you will probably get a long list in answer. If, however, there have been major life events immediately preceding the schizophrenic breakdown, this points toward a good outcome. The absence of such precipitating factors signals the greater likelihood of a poor outcome.

Clinical Symptoms.   The symptoms during the initial breakdown are often suggestive of the outcome of the disease and can be used as predictive factors. Some of the more important of these are:

a. Catatonic symptoms are a good sign.
b. Paranoid symptoms are a good sign.
c. The presence of depression or other emotions is a good sign. If the person is diagnosed as schizoaffective (see chapter 3), that is also a good sign.
d. The predominance of "negative" symptoms such as flattening of emotions, poverty of thoughts, apathy, and social withdrawal is a sign of a poor outcome.
e. Obsessive (compelled to think about a certain thing) and com-

pulsive (repeated ritualistic behavior) symptoms are bad signs.

f. Symptoms which are atypical—which do not fit the established clinical patterns for schizophrenia—are a good sign.

g. The presence of confusion (e.g., "I don't understand what is happening to me") is a good sign.

CT Scan Findings. If a diagnostic CT scan is done and it is normal, that is a good sign. If it shows enlargement of the ventricles in the brain and/or atrophy of brain tissue, that is a bad sign.

Response to Medication. The initial response of the person to antipsychotic medication is a strong indicator of prognosis: the better the response, the better the outcome is likely to be.

It should be emphasized again that each of these factors *by itself* has limited predictive value. It is only when they are all put together that an overall prognosis can be assigned. Many patients will, of course, have a mixture of good and poor outcome signs, whereas others will fall quite clearly into one category or the other.

It should also be remembered that all predictions are only statistical assertions of likelihood. There is nothing in the least binding about them. All of us who regularly care for patients with schizophrenia have seen enough exceptions to these guidelines to make us humble about any predictions. Thus I have seen a schizophrenic patient with a normal childhood, no family history of the disease, a rapid onset at age 22, clear precipitating events, and initial catatonic symptoms who never recovered from even his initial illness and whose outcome is poor. More optimistically, I have seen patients with virtually every poor prognostic sign go on to almost complete recovery.

POSSIBLE COURSES: TEN YEARS LATER

From the early years of this century it has been said that there is a rule of thirds determining the possible courses in schizophrenia: a third recover, a third are improved, and a third are unimproved. Recent long-term follow-up studies of persons with schizophrenia both in Europe and in the United States suggest that this rule is simplistic and out-of-date. It is clear, for example, that the course of the disease over thirty years is better than it is over ten years. The use of medications has probably improved the long-term course for many patients, while the positive effect of deinstitutionalization has been to decrease dependency on the hospital and increase the number of patients able to live in the community. On the other hand, it is also clear that the mortality rate, especially by suicide, for persons with schizophrenia is very high and apparently increasing.

The best summary of possible courses of schizophrenia was done by J. H. Stephens, who analyzed twenty-five studies in which follow-up was for at least ten years. The percentage of patients "recovered," "improved," or "unimproved" varied widely from study to study depending on the initial selection of patients, e.g., inclusion of large numbers with acute reactive psychosis increased the percentage of fully recovered. Utilizing all studies done to date, the ten-year course of schizophrenia can be seen in the chart below and more nearly approximates a rule of "quarters," rather than a rule of "thirds":

THE COURSE OF SCHIZOPHRENIA

10 Years Later

25% Completely recovered	25% Much improved, relatively independent	25% Improved, but require extensive support network	15% Hospitalized, unimproved	10% Dead (mostly suicide)

30 Years Later

25% Completely recovered	35% Much improved, relatively independent	15% Improved, but require extensive support network	10% Hospital- ized, unim- proved	15% Dead

Twenty-five Percent Recover Completely. This assumes that all patients with symptoms of schizophrenia are part of the analysis, including those who have been sick for less than six months with schizophreniform disorders. If only patients with *DSM-III* schizophrenia are included (i.e., "continuous signs of the illness for at least six months"), then the percentage of completely recovered will be under 25 percent. Patients who recover completely do so whether they are treated with antipsychotic medication, wheat germ oil, Tibetan psychic healing, psychoanalysis, or yellow jellybeans, and all treatments for schizophrenia must show results better than this spontaneous recovery rate if they are to be accepted as truly effective. Those who recover also do so within the first two years of illness and usually have had no more than two discrete episodes of illness.

> Andrea became acutely psychotic during her second year of college and was hospitalized for six weeks. She recovered slowly, with medication and supportive psychotherapy over the following six months while living at home, and was able to resume college the following year. She has never had a recurrence. She believes she got sick because of a failed romance and her family, when they refer to the illness at all, talk vaguely of a "nervous breakdown."

Such families often deny that their family member had schizophrenia and rarely join family support groups such as the National Alliance for the Mentally Ill (NAMI).

Twenty-five Percent Are Much Improved.   These patients usually have a good response to antipsychotic medication, and as long as they take it continue to do well. They can live relatively independently, have a social life, may marry, and often are capable of working part- or full-time.

> Peter had a normal childhood and successful high school career. He then married and joined the army to get training and travel. There was no family history of mental illness. At age 21, while assigned to Germany, he began to have strange feelings in his body and later to hear voices. He started drinking heavily, which seemed to relieve the voices, then turned to the use of hashish and cocaine. His condition deteriorated rapidly, and he was arrested for hitting an officer who he believed was trying to poison him. He was hospitalized and eventually discharged from the army with a full service-connected disability. Over the next three years he was hospitalized three more times with schizophrenic symptoms. On the final admission he was extremely hostile and paranoid, sitting suspiciously in the corner wearing sunglasses and threatening staff members with a pool cue. He believed he had

the body of a woman, and also had bizarre delusions about being the king of a group of people who were half-human and half-fish. He acknowledged continuous auditory hallucinations, occasional visual hallucinations (e.g., presidential portraits), and occasional hallucinations of smell.

Peter responded slowly to very high doses of medication and was released from the hospital two months later almost completely well. He returned faithfully for an injection of medicine every week, lived in his own apartment, and visited his family (including his divorced wife and children) and friends during the day. He clearly was capable of holding a job, but declined to do so for fear that it would jeopardize his monthly army disability check. His only remaining symptoms were voices which he heard late in the day but which he was able to ignore. After two years he insisted on trying to continue without medicine, and stopped it under close psychiatric supervision. His schizophrenic symptoms returned almost immediately and he resumed his medication. He continues to get an injection every week.

Twenty-five Percent Are Modestly Improved. These patients respond less well to medication, often have "negative" symptoms, and have a history of poorer adjustment prior to the onset of their illness. They require an extensive support network; in communities where this is available they may lead satisfactory lives, but where it is not they may be victimized and end up living on the streets or in public shelters.

Frank was a loner as a child but had considerable musical ability and received a college scholarship. In his third year of college his grades slowly dropped as he complained of continuous auditory hallucinations. Hospitalization and medication produced a modest improvement so that he could eventually be placed in a halfway house in the community. He is supposed to attend a day program but usually walks the street talking to himself or composing music on scraps of paper. He stays completely to himself and needs to be reminded to change his clothes, brush his teeth, and take his medicine.

Fifteen Percent Are Unimproved. These are the treatment-resistant patients for whom we have little to offer except humane care. They are candidates for long-term asylum care in a sheltered setting (see chapter 8). When released into the community, often against their will, the results are frequently disastrous.

> Dorothy was known as a quiet child who attained straight A's in school. Her mother was hospitalized for schizophrenia for two years during Dorothy's childhood, and a brother was in an institution for the mentally retarded. She was first hospitalized at age 15 for one month; information on this hospitalization was not obtainable except for a diagnosis of "transient situational reaction of adolescence." Following this, Dorothy dropped out of school, went to work as a domestic, married, and had three children. She remained apparently well until age 22, at which time she believed people were trying to kill her, believed people were talking about her, and heard airplanes flying overhead all day. She neglected her children and housework and simply sat in a corner with a fearful expression on her face. On examination she had a marked thinking disorder and catatonic rigidity and was noted to be very shy and withdrawn.
>
> Over the ensuing fifteen years Dorothy has been hospitalized most of the time and has responded minimally to medication. During the earlier years she was returned to her home for brief periods, with homemaker services; and in more recent years she lived for several months in a halfway house. There she was invariably victimized by men and was judged not to be capable of defending herself. She remains in the hospital, sitting quietly in a chair day after day. She answers politely but with absolutely no emotion and shows marked poverty of thought and of speech.

Ten Percent Are Dead. Almost all of these die by suicide or accident, and other factors will be discussed at greater length below.

POSSIBLE COURSES: THIRTY YEARS LATER

It has been clearly established in recent years that the thirty-year course of schizophrenia is more favorable for the average patient than is the ten-year course. This directly contradicts a widespread stereotype about the disease which dates to Kraepelin's pessimistic belief that most patients slowly deteriorate.

The definitive work on the long-term course of schizophrenia has come from studies carried out by Dr. Manfred Bleuler, in Zurich, on patients diagnosed by his father, by Dr. Luc Ciompi and his colleagues in Lausanne, by Dr. Gerd Huber and his colleagues in Bonn, and by Dr. Courtenay Harding and her colleagues in New Haven on patients deinstitutionalized from the Vermont State Hospital. Some patients followed up by these groups were as much as forty years older than when they became ill, and the agreement between the results of the different studies is impressive. As summarized by Ciompi for patients followed for an average of thirty-six years: "About three-fifths of the schizophrenic probands have a favorable outcome; that is, they recover or show definite improvement." And for patients with chronic schizophrenia in Vermont, followed up by Harding, et al., twenty to twenty-five years after leaving the hospital, "the current picture of the functioning of these subjects is a startling contrast to their previous levels described during their index hospitalization." Approximately three-quarters of the Vermont patients required little or no help in meeting their basic daily needs.

In most patients with schizophrenia, the "positive" symptoms of hallucinations, delusions, and thinking disorders decrease over the years. A person who was severely incapacitated at age 25 by these symptoms may have only residual traces of them at age 50. It is almost as if the disease process has burned itself out over time and left behind only scars from its earlier activity. Patients also learn how to live with their symptoms, ignoring the voices and not responding to them in public.

The residual phases of schizophrenia are often referred to in psychiatric literature as a chronic defect state and are described as follows in a standard textbook:

The patient, living in an institution or outside, has come to an *arrangement with his illness*. He has adapted himself to the world of his morbid ideas with more or less success, from his own point of view and from that of his environment. Compared with the experiences during the acute psychosis, his positive symptoms, such as delusions or hallucinations, have become colorless, repetitive, and formalized. They still have power over him but nothing is added and nothing new or unexpected happens. Negative symptoms, thought disorder, passivity, catatonic mannerisms and flattening of affect rule the picture, but even they grow habitual with the patient and appear always in the same inveterate pattern in the individual case. There is a robotlike fixity and petrification of attitude and reactions which are not only due to poverty of ideas but also to a very small choice of modes of behavior.

As with all rules, there are exceptions, so this final course can vary. Occasional patients retain their more florid symptoms all their lives. For example, I had under my care a 75-year-old man who hallucinated all day every day and had been doing so for fifty years. His illness was virtually unaffected by medications. These kinds of patients are certainly exceptional, but they do exist.

It is currently popular to attribute the late symptoms of schizophrenia to drug effects. The truth is that exactly the same picture was described for fifty years before the drugs were introduced. Drugs used in schizophrenia may certainly produce some sedation, especially in older patients, but such effects account for a minuscule portion of the total picture on a properly run hospital ward. Similarly these late schizophrenic symptoms are often blamed on the effects of chronic institutionalization; this also accounts for only a small portion of the picture. The late symptoms may be attributed to depression and hopelessness in a patient who is chronically ill and sees no possibility of leaving the hospital; this too may account for a small portion. The vast majority of the late clinical symptoms seen in schizophrenic patients, however, has been shown to be a direct consequence of the disease and its probable effects on the brain.

As seen in the chart on page 117, only 10 percent of patients with schizophrenia will require hospitalization (or a similar total-care facility) thirty years later. The vast majority are able to live in the community, with only about 15 percent requiring an extensive support network.

One of the mysteries which has perplexed mental health professionals in recent years is where all the persons with schizophrenia have gone. Comparisons of past hospitalization rates with the number of patients receiving care as outpatients invariably find that approximately half of the expected number of patients are missing. The answer is that the missing patients are living in the community, most taking no medication, with varying degrees of adjustment. A recent community survey in Baltimore, for example, found that half the persons with schizophrenia in the community were receiving no ongoing care or medication from any psychiatric clinic. An example of such a patient follows:

> A 72-year-old recluse was forcibly evicted from his rural decaying house by the police. He had been hospitalized for schizophrenia twice in his twenties, worked briefly as a clerk, then returned to live with his aging parents. After they died he had continued to live in the house for thirty years on Social Security disability checks. The house had no electricity or running water and the rooms were packed to the ceiling with piles of newspapers. He cooked over a sterno stove, did not bother anybody, and asked nothing except to be left alone.

The fierce independence and ability to live with his disease in such cases is commendable. The sad aspect, however, is how much better a life he might have led had well-organized rehabilitation services been available.

Many questions about the long-term course of schizophrenia are as yet unanswered. Do more episodes of schizophrenia cause progressively more damage to the brain? Does early treatment with antipsychotic medications decrease the brain damage and thereby improve functioning in later years? How much can the long-term course be affected by rehabilitation programs which provide jobs and social interaction? As basic as these questions are, there is remarkably little research in progress to find the answers.

SUICIDE AND MORTALITY RATES

For an increasing number of young adults it is becoming apparent that schizophrenia may be a fatal disease. Forty years ago, when most patients were kept on locked hospital wards for most of their lives, suicide was not a major problem, in large part because so few opportunities occurred to carry it out successfully. That has all changed with the release of most patients into the community, and now suicide is a more common sequel to schizophrenia. Dr. Charles Miles, reviewing all studies on suicide in schizophrenia, estimated that 10 percent of all patients kill themselves, approximately 3,800 per year in the United States. Among some groups, such as poor inner-city residents with very inadequate psychiatric services, it is probably higher than that.

Depression represents the single most important cause of suicide among persons with schizophrenia, just as it does among persons without schizophrenia. The majority of schizophrenic patients will experience significant depression at some point during the course of their illness; this realization should lead psychiatrists to remain alert for depression and to treat it more aggressively with antidepressant medication (see chapter 7). Depression may arise from the disease process itself (i.e., the schizophrenia affects the brain chemistry so as to cause depression), from the patients' realization of the severity of their illness (i.e., as a reaction to the disease), or occasionally as a side effect of medications used to treat schizophrenia. Depression must also be differentiated in schizophrenia from the slowed movements (akinesia) and slowed thought processes which may be symptoms of the disease.

Most persons with schizophrenia who commit suicide do so within the first ten years of their illness. As might be expected, approximately three-quarters of them are men. Those at highest risk have a remitting and relapsing course, good insight (i.e., they know they are sick), a poor response to medication, are socially isolated, hopeless about the future, and have a gross discrepancy between their earlier achievements in life and their current level of function. Any patient with these characteristics *and* associated depression should be considered a high risk for suicide. The most common time for suicide is during a remission of the illness immediately following a relapse.

Occasionally persons with schizophrenia will commit suicide accidentally in a stage of acute psychosis, e.g., they may jump off a building because they think they can fly or because voices tell them to do so. Most suicides in schizophrenia are intended, however, and are often carefully planned by the person. Like all clinicians who have taken care of large numbers of patients with schizophrenia, I have known several who eventually committed suicide. It is always a tragic event, but in a young patient who does not respond to medication and whose symptoms are extremely unpleasant it is sometimes understandable. Such deaths evoke sadness, but at the same time I am forced to ask myself whether I would want to live with such symptoms. There are other suicides, however, which evoke not only sadness but anger. These are the preventable ones—the patient who is treated inadequately with medications and then told that nothing more can be done, or the patient who is doing nicely on medication until another doctor reduces it and begins insight-oriented psychotherapy. I wish I could say that these suicides were rare occurrences but they are not. The high suicide rate in schizophrenia is in part due to our inadequate care system (or, more accurately, nonsystem) on which these patients are forced to rely.

In addition to suicide, most other causes of death are higher among persons with schizophrenia than among the general public. In 1981 a follow-up was done on 1,190 patients with schizophrenia who had been discharged from psychiatric hospitals in Sweden ten years earlier. Rates were compared with those of the general population for the same age groups, and the mortality for persons with schizophrenia was found to be twice the national average. Suicide was 10 times higher in men and 18 times higher in women, fatal injuries 8 times higher, deaths from infections 4 times higher, and deaths from other diseases approximately 2 times higher. There has been speculation in the past that death due to cancer might be lower among persons with schizophrenia than among the general population, but recent studies have shown that this is not true.

Why should mortality rates for conditions other than suicide be so high for persons with schizophrenia? There are probably several reasons. Schizophrenia certainly predisposes people to fatal accidents because of the confusion and disability consequent on their brain dysfunction; one of my patients, who had great difficulty concentrating, for example, inadvertently walked in front of a bus with fatal consequences. Diseases generally tend to be more serious in persons with schizophrenia because they often are less able to explain their symptoms to medical personnel. At the same time medical personnel tend to pay less attention to their complaints, assuming that the complaints are merely part of their psychiatric illness. There is also evidence that some persons with schizophrenia have an elevated pain threshold so that they may not complain of symptoms until the disease has progressed too far to be treatable.

WHO ARE THE "YOUNG ADULT CHRONICS"?

In recent years there has been an outpouring of literature on the "young adult chronic." Some of it has implied that there is a new breed of persons with schizophrenia and that persons with this disease are different now from those in the past. This is only partially true. Schizophrenia today is remarkably similar to the disease twenty and forty years ago, and the characteristics attributed to the "young adult chronics" which make them different are entirely predictable. The "young adult chronics" are simply young graduates of the era of deinstitutionalization.

Forty years ago young adults with schizophrenia were hospitalized, usually for many years, during which time they were "socialized" to their disease. They learned to expect little from life, and they were taught (often brutally) to respect mental health care personnel. Thus when these patients were finally released into the community, they were usually docile when they returned to the clinic for their follow-up.

As deinstitutionalization moved from a slow walk to a full gallop, young adults with schizophrenia were no longer hospitalized for more than two or three weeks at a time. They were treated in the community and therefore not "socialized" to the mental health care system, as the older generation had been. Thus when these patients come to the clinic for follow-up, they are less likely to wait for three hours without complaining, and when they encounter a psychiatrist who cannot speak intelligible English, they are likely to tell him/her to learn English rather than quietly nodding and pretending to understand.

In addition their expectations are higher—they want to be rid of their symptoms and to lead a normal life. Because they are living in the community most of the time, they have access to alcohol and street drugs, which they use just as their nonschizophrenic peers do. Finally they have been defended by patients' rights advocates and lawyers during their brief admissions and have been taught that they need not accept medication if they do not want to. Given these life experiences, it is not surprising that "young adult chronics" evoke consternation and negative feelings in many mental health professionals. They are reminders to us of the inadequacies of the care system we have created and of our laws, which often make it difficult to treat those who need it most.

COURSES OF SCHIZOPHRENIA
IN CROSS-CULTURAL PERSPECTIVE

Since schizophrenia occurs in all parts of the world (although with varying prevalence), it is of interest to learn whether the courses of the disease are similar in other countries. There is unfortunately little hard information with which to answer this question. The major impediment to cross-cultural inquiries of this kind is the dissimilar diagnostic practices and various meanings of the term "schizophrenia." Since the term has been used more strictly in European countries than in the United States, the patients who were used for follow-up studies there were usually sicker. Thus their recovery rate appeared to be lower. Allowing for these differences, however, it appears that the courses of schizophrenia in western European countries are quite similar to those in the United States.

When we turn to developing countries the answer is different. In several preliminary studies it appears that the courses of schizophrenia in these countries are more likely to be favorable. The percentage of patients who recover completely is specifically higher (about 40 percent, compared with 25 percent in the United States) for reasons which are not understood. The percentage of patients in the unimproved category, on the other hand, is virtually identical in developing countries as in the United States, suggesting that the core group of treatment-resistant patients is the same all over the world.

This observation is not a new one. In work done more than thirty years ago among the aborigines on Taiwan, it was noted that "the prognosis in the aboriginal patients was also fairly good. They do not seem to deteriorate into the chronic schizophrenic state that we see in many Chinese and Western communities." And on Mauritius a twelve-year follow-up study found more schizophrenics who had fully recovered (59 percent) than in Britain (34 percent). Finally data from the World Health Organization nine-nation schizophrenia study showed that patients in developing countries (especially Colombia and Nigeria) had considerably better courses than patients in developed countries (Denmark, England, United States, Czechoslovakia, and USSR).

There is also some international discussion on the question of whether the courses of schizophrenia are becoming more benign in western countries. Manfred Bleuler in Switzerland believes that they are and that this is related to the introduction of medications. E. H. Hare in England claims that the improvement began before the drugs were introduced. K. A. Achte has also noted an improvement in the courses of schizophrenic patients in Scandinavia. Whatever the cause, they appear to be going in the right direction.

RECOMMENDED FURTHER READING

Ciompi, L. "Aging and Schizophrenic Psychosis." *Acta Psychiatrica Scandinavica,* Supplementum no. 319, 71 (1985): 93–105. This is a summary of the work of Ciompi et al. on the long-term course of schizophrenia.

Hare, E. "The Changing Content of Psychiatric Illness." *Journal of Psychosomatic Research* 18 (1974): 283–89. In his usual lucid and challenging style, Hare makes a persuasive case that schizophrenia is becoming a milder disease.

Miles, C. P. "Conditions Predisposing to Suicide: A Review." *Journal of Nervous and Mental Disease* 164 (1977): 231–46. This is the best summary to date of suicide rates in schizophrenia.

Test, M. A., W. H. Knoedler, D. J. Allness, et al. "Characteristics of Young Adults with Schizophrenic Disorders Treated in the Community." *Hospital and Community Psychiatry* 36 (1985): 853–58. This is a balanced view of the "young adult chronic" patient.

The Information Exchange on Young Adult Chronic Patients. A newsletter edited by Dr. Bert Pepper, available from Box 278, Spring Valley, NY 10977.

Wrobeleski, A. "Suicide: Your Child Has Died"; "Suicide: Questions and Answers"; and "Suicide: The Danger Signs." Three pamphlets, useful for families concerned about suicide, are available from Ms. Wrobeleski, 5124 Grove Street, Minneapolis, MN.

6

THE CAUSES OF SCHIZOPHRENIA

Something has happened to me—I do not know what. All that was my former self has crumbled and fallen together and a creature has emerged of whom I know nothing. She is a stranger to me—and has an egotism that makes the egotism that I had look like skimmed milk; and she thinks thoughts that are—heresies. Her name is insanity. She is the daughter of madness—and according to the doctor, they each had their genesis in my own brain.

Lara Jefferson, *These Are My Sisters*

We are in the midst of an explosion of knowledge in the neurosciences, and its effects are spilling over to schizophrenia. With each passing year we know more about how the brain functions, both normally and abnormally. The brains of individuals with schizophrenia are slowly beginning to yield their secrets to researchers. If schizophrenia research were funded at a level commensurate with the importance of this disease, then major breakthroughs on the causes of schizophrenia could reasonably be hoped for in the next decade.

Despite the lack of research support, however, considerable knowledge has accumulated about the causes of schizophrenia. It includes four established facts:

1. It is a brain disease.
2. The limbic system and its connections are primarily affected.
3. It often runs in families.
4. The brain damage may occur very early in life.

Each of these facts relating to the causes of schizophrenia will be discussed. Then the various theories regarding specific causes will be

THE LOCATION OF THE LIMBIC SYSTEM
IN THE BRAIN

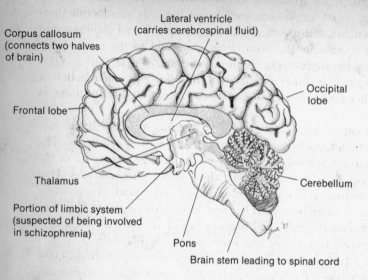

Corpus callosum
(connects two halves
of brain)

Lateral ventricle
(carries cerebrospinal fluid)

Occipital
lobe

Frontal lobe

Thalamus

Cerebellum

Portion of limbic system
(suspected of being involved
in schizophrenia)

Pons

Brain stem leading to spinal cord

reviewed: genetic, biochemical, nutritional, viral, immunological, developmental, and stress. The problem of inadequate research funding for schizophrenia will be touched upon and, finally, discarded theories about schizophrenia's causes (psychoanalytic, family interaction, Szaszian, Laingian) will be summarized.

Before proceeding to a discussion of abnormalities in the brains of persons with schizophrenia, however, let us consider the normal brain—a mushroomlike organ with a stem narrowing into the spinal cord, which runs down the back. The bulk of the brain consists of four lobes (frontal, parietal, temporal, and occipital), which are divided in two by a deep vertical cleft. At the bottom of the cleft is the corpus callosum, a thick band carrying nerve fibers back and forth between the two halves of the brain. The four major lobes perform functions such as muscle coordination, thinking, memory, language, hearing, and vision. It is now established that the two halves of the brain are not identical; in most persons the left half controls language skills and conceptual thinking, whereas the right half is in charge of spatial skills and intuitive thinking.

The four lobes come together at the base of the brain beneath the corpus callosum. There lie the thalamus, hypothalamus, pituitary gland, limbic system, basal ganglia, midbrain, and brain stem tapering into the spinal cord. It is this area which controls all vital functions (e.g., heart, respiration, eating, and the body's endocrine [hormone] system), and which acts as a gatekeeper for all incoming and outgoing stimuli for the major lobes. Attached to the back of this area, as if by afterthought, is the cerebellum, which until recently was thought to function exclusively to coordinate muscle function; it is now thought to interact with the brain stem on other functions as well.

The entire brain is housed in the vaultlike bony skull and surrounded by a layer of cerebrospinal fluid for further protection. The fluid circulates around the brain and goes through the center of the major lobes by a series of canals which widen into ventricles. It is because the brain is so well protected that we understand comparatively little about it or its diseases. It has been facetiously suggested that if we could persuade the brain to change places with the liver we might then understand its functioning and what causes schizophrenia.

The actual work of the brain is performed by approximately fifty billion nerve cells. Each has branches with which it can transmit and receive messages from other cells; one cell can receive messages from as many as ten thousand other cells. The branches do not physically touch each other but rather release chemical messengers, called neurotransmitters, which carry the messages from the end of one nerve branch to the end of an adjacent branch. We already know of over sixty different kinds of neurotransmitters, and it is likely that there are many more. Some of these neurotransmitters, such as dopamine, norepinephrine, serotonin, GABA, and the endorphins, are of great interest to schizophrenia researchers.

WHAT IS KNOWN

It Is a Brain Disease

The evidence is now overwhelming that brains of persons who have schizophrenia are, as a group, different from brains of persons who do not have this disease. Mental health professionals who are unaware of this fact have either been on an extended trek in Nepal or restricted their professional reading to the *National Geographic* for the last ten years. The differences can be measured by gross pathology, microscopic pathology, neurochemistry, cerebral blood flow and metabolism, electrically, neurologically, and neuropsychologically.

Gross Pathology. Sporadic reports of gross pathological differences in the brains of persons with schizophrenia have appeared since the early years of this century. Until recently, however, such findings were mostly restricted to measurements carried out postmortem, since technology was lacking to make measurements on living subjects.

Since 1976 that has changed dramatically with the advent of computerized tomography (CT) and nuclear magnetic resonance imaging (MRI) scans. These technologies provide noninvasive and painless methods of visualizing and measuring the structures of the brain in living subjects. Since the initial CT scan findings were reported in 1976, there have been over a hundred such studies on schizophrenia with the following abnormalities reported: enlargement of the lateral ventricles or the third ventricles (which carry fluid throughout the brain), increased markings on the surface of the brain suggesting loss of brain tissue, atrophy of a portion of the cerebellum, abnormalities in brain density, and abnormalities in brain asymmetry. A recent review of eighty such studies concluded that "the most robust finding is that suggestive of cerebral atrophy, as revealed by enlarged lateral and third ventricles and an increase of cortical surface markings, perhaps clearest in the prefrontal cortex." Schizophrenics with enlarged lateral ventricles are more likely than other schizophrenics to have impaired thinking, "negative" symptoms, a poorer adjustment before becoming psychotic, a poorer response to medication, and a poorer outcome. The brain changes are apparently not due to medication, having been found in patients never previously treated. Nor are they specific for schizophrenia, occurring in some patients with manic-depressive psychosis and other brain diseases, so they cannot be used as a diagnostic marker for schizophrenia.

MRI, which measures magnetic properties of brain tissue, promises to yield data on brain structure even more precise than that obtainable from CT scans. The initial MRI studies on schizophrenia were reported in 1984 and reports have multiplied each year. Among the more interesting early studies was one showing that individuals with schizophrenia have smaller brains and specifically smaller frontal lobes (see developmental theory, below). Other MRI studies in schizophrenics have reported increased thickening of the corpus callosum, which carries messages between the right and left halves of the brain,

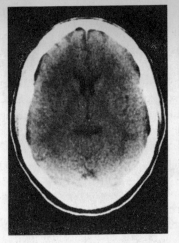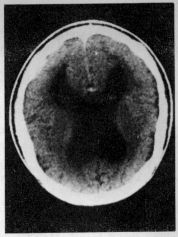

CT scans from two patients with schizophrenia. The one on the left is normal; the one on the right is very abnormal. Approximately 20 percent of those with schizophrenia have abnormal CT scans although not usually to this extent.

and abnormalities in an area called the globus pallidus in patients who had never received medication. Even as these preliminary MRI studies of schizophrenia are being published, rumors circulate in the research community of new technologies being developed, which will permit the visualization of brain structures several times more precisely than even the MRI.

Microscopic Pathology. Claims that the brains of individuals with schizophrenia differ microscopically from those of normal individuals date back to the early twentieth century. Over the years these claims gradually fell into disrepute because the differences turned up in some schizophrenic brains but not in others. Since it was widely believed until recently that schizophrenia was a single disease, the structual differences were assumed not to be important because they could not be found in all cases.

On the other hand, if one begins with the assumption that schizophrenia is not a single disease but rather consists of several different diseases, then the structural differences look much more impressive in these earlier studies. Furthermore, in recent years there has been a resurgence of interest in microscopic studies of schizophrenia; since 1980 at least nine separate studies have been published showing patho-

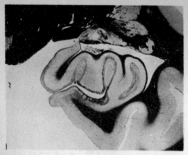

Identical sections from normal and schizophrenic brains, showing impaired development of hippocampus.

logical changes in the brains of individuals with this disease.

The work of Dr. Janice Stevens at St. Elizabeths Hospital in Washington, D.C., is an example of this kind of work. Dr. Stevens studied twenty-five brains from persons with schizophrenia and compared them with twenty-eight nonschizophrenic controls; the brains of the schizophrenic patients showed significantly more gliosis, indicative of brain damage, in parts of the limbic system. Of the twenty-five brains from sufferers of schizophrenia, nine of them had never been treated with medications and these were just as severely affected as those who had been treated; the findings, then, were clearly not a drug effect.

Another example of such work is that being done by Dr. Bernhardt Bogerts and his colleagues in West Germany. Utilizing brains collected from thirteen patients who died before the introduction of antipsychotic medication, Dr. Bogerts has shown "a considerable shrinkage of the limbic temporal structures (hippocampal formation, amygdala, and parahippocampal gyrus) and a moderate shrinkage of the inner pallidal segment in the schizophrenic group" compared with controls. Microscopic studies of brains from schizophrenics is thus a very promising research area, especially since newer technologies make such work both easier and more accurate to do.

Neurochemistry. Studying the chemistry of the postmortem brain is one of the newest and most exciting areas of schizophrenia research, but also technically one of the most difficult. The problems are that chemicals in the brain change after death and also that antipsychotic medications can have an effect on these chemicals. Research studies, therefore, must control for both these factors. In the last decade there has been an outpouring of research in this field. Perhaps the single most impressive finding to date is the excessive number of dopamine receptors found in the limbic system and basal ganglia in brains from patients with schizophrenia compared with control brains. Initially it was not certain whether or not this increase in dopamine receptors was due to schizophrenia or was merely an artifact due to the antipsychotic medication the patients had been taking; this question was definitively answered in 1986 when Wong and his colleagues at Johns Hopkins University demonstrated increased dopamine receptors in individuals with schizophrenia who had never been treated with medication.

Cerebral Blood Flow and Metabolism. The study of regional blood flow in the brain and regional metabolism (e.g., glucose or oxygen uptake) has received wide publicity in recent years, especially the type of studies known as positron emission tomography (PET) scans. As summarized by one reviewer, however: "Although the beautiful pictures generated are works of both art and science, the data can be overwhelming and their interpretation difficult." Controlling for the effects of medication on the brain is especially important in such studies.

Despite the technological problems with this research, which is still in its infancy, there have already been several reported findings suggestive of significant differences between persons with schizophrenia and controls. Studies of regional cerebral blood flow by Drs. Berman and Weinberger and their colleagues in Washington, utilizing the uptake of xenon (a slightly radioactive gas), showed changes in a portion of the frontal lobe (dorsolateral prefrontal cortex) in schizophrenia; these changes do not appear to be due to medication. Other studies utilizing the uptake of xenon, by Dr. Raquel Gur and her colleagues in Philadelphia, showed that patients with schizophrenia have overactivation of their left hemisphere and that these differences were observable whether or not the patients were taking medications. There have also been differences reported in preliminary PET scans done on patients with schizophrenia, especially the decreased uptake of glucose in regions of the frontal lobe.

Electrical. One method the brain uses to send information from one area to another is by electrical impulses, and these have been shown to be abnormal in many schizophrenic patients. This is true when the electrical impulses are measured as evoked potentials, a special electrical impulse elicited by auditory, visual, or sensory input, and abnormal evoked potentials (especially the P-300 component) have been reported in schizophrenia since the early 1970s. It is also true when electrical activity is recorded on electroencephalograms (EEGs); approximately one-third of persons with schizophrenia have abnormal EEGs. Abnormal EEGs among schizophrenics are twice as common as among persons with mania, and four times as common as among persons with depression. A recent review article summarizing electrical abnormalities in schizophrenia concluded that "a broad interpretation of the EEG and EP [evoked potential] findings supports the presence of brain disease in many patients with this disorder."

Recent advances in technology promise to make electrical studies of the brain even more useful. EEGs and evoked potentials have been computerized and can yield their findings as topographic maps of the brain, thereby localizing the abnormalities to specific areas. These are usually referred to as BEAM (brain electrical activity mapping) or CEAM (computerized electrical activity mapping). Preliminary studies utilizing these techniques on patients with schizophrenia have appeared since 1982 and suggest abnormalities in the frontal lobe as well as left-hemisphere dysfunction. It is likely that these promising techniques will help to further localize the lesions in schizophrenia.

Neurological. Neurological abnormalities in patients with schizophrenia are very common, were observed for many years prior to the introduction of antipsychotic medication, and strongly suggest abnormal brain function. The neurological abnormalities include some "hard" neurological signs such as a transient grasp reflex (a reflex found in infants who automatically close their hand around any object they feel, found in 6 percent of patients with schizophrenia) and an impaired gag reflex (in 26 percent of patients, not related to medication), but many more "soft" neurological signs—such as double simultaneous stimulation (being unable to feel two simultaneous touches), agraphesthesia (being unable to identify numbers traced on the palm of the hand), and confusion about the right and left sides of the body.

In a 1983 review of eight neurological studies of schizophrenic patients, Seidman concluded: "The frequency of abnormal neurological examinations using soft signs is consistently between 36 percent and 75 percent for those studies providing frequency data. . . . A second clear-cut finding is that schizophrenics have more frequent neurologic abnormalities than other psychiatric patients (e.g., affective disorder) and normal controls. . . . The data are very consistent from study to study and consequently are rather convincing." Since then three additional studies have reported abnormal neurological findings in 50, 62, and 92 percent of the schizophrenic subjects. One researcher noted that subtle neurological signs such as "clumsiness and repetitive movements . . . are frequent, occurring in virtually all conservatively diagnosed cases." Whether or not the patient is taking medication seems to make little difference in the neurological findings.

Neurological dysfunction is also suggested by the multiple abnormal eye movements that occur commonly in schizophrenia. Increased or decreased blink rates, abnormal eye reflexes, inequality in pupil size, and abnormal eye movements have all been well documented. Abnormalities in the auditory tract controlling balance have also been reported in schizophrenia; one such abnormality has been found in twenty-three separate studies since it was first described in 1921. The auditory tract and auditory part of the brain are of special interest in schizophrenia research; since approximately three-quarters of all patients have auditory hallucinations sometime during the course of their illness it is probable that this part of the brain is involved. The altered pain threshold sometimes observed in individuals with schizophrenia can also be considered evidence of neurological dysfunction.

Neuropsychological.   Neuropsychological abnormalities in schizophrenia can be regarded as yet another way to quantitatively document impaired functioning of the brain. Neuropsychological tests measure functions such as intelligence, visual-spatial ability, attention span, memory, problem-solving ability and concept formation; the best-known such test is the Halstead-Reitan battery, which is especially sensitive to cerebral dysfunction. The literature is voluminous on these tests used on patients with schizophrenia and the results are remarkably consistent. As summarized by a recent review of over a hundred such studies: "Chronic or process schizophrenics may have a cerebral deficit because they performed much as did many of the diffusely brain-damaged patients and could not be statistically differentiated from them. . . . Neuropsychological impairment appears to be mild to moderate in severity and more likely to be diffuse or bilateral than focal." Or, as succinctly summarized in another review of these tests: "Schizophrenic patients perform like organic patients because they too have brain disease."

In summary, based on studies of gross pathology, microscopic pathology, neurochemistry, cerebral blood flow, and metabolism, as well as electrical, neurological, and neuropsychological measures, schizophrenia has been clearly established to be a brain disease just as surely as multiple sclerosis, Parkinson's disease, and Alzheimer's disease are established as brain diseases. The dichotomy used in the past, whereby schizophrenia was classified as a "functional" disorder as distinct from an "organic" disorder, is now known to be inaccurate; schizophrenia has impeccable credentials for admission to the organic category. As noted by Dr. Daniel Rogers at the Institute of Neurology in London: "The more severe a psychiatric illness, the more neurological it appears."

The Limbic System and Its Connections
Are Primarily Affected

In the early part of this century, when scientists began looking at autopsies for abnormalities in the brains of schizophrenics, they looked mostly in the outer layer of the brain. At that time it was believed that most of the important functions of the brain were closest to the surface. The limbic system, which lies deep below the surface in the center of the brain, was thought to be merely an ancestral remnant of the primitive system for smelling.

All this has changed radically. The limbic system is now known to be the gate through which most incoming stimuli must pass. It has "selective, integrative, and unifying functions by which raw experience is harmonized into reality and coherent activity is organized." According to Dr. Paul MacLean, the modern father of the limbic system, it is "able to correlate every form of internal and external perception."

All of this takes place in an area which is anatomically very small. It is composed of contiguous portions of the frontal and temporal lobes, and its main structures include the amygdala, hippocampus, hypothalamus, nucleus accumbens, ventral septum, mammillary bodies, stria terminalis, and olfactory area. However, its size is deceptive, for the limbic system has direct connections to all areas of the brain, including the upper brain stem and the cerebellum. Increasingly it has been realized that the brain works as a functionally interdependent and intricate system and an abnormality anywhere within it can throw the whole system off. It is analogous to an electrical system with a short circuit in it; the short circuit may occur at any one of several places, but the result will be the same.

Evidence that the limbic system is the site of pathology for some, if not most, cases of schizophrenia is strong. Abnormalities in this system in animals may produce profound changes in emotion, inappropriate behavior, and an impairment in the animal's ability to screen out multiple visual stimuli. Abnormalities in the limbic system in human beings may produce, in addition to the above effects, distortions of perception, illusions, hallucinations, feelings of depersonalization, paranoia, and catatoniclike behavior. In short, the symptoms of schizophrenia described in chapter 2 are a logical consequence of impaired limbic system dysfunction, given what we know about it.

Diseases of the brain which affect the limbic system are also more likely to produce schizophrenialike symptoms. This is seen, for example, with brain tumors located in the limbic system. Cases of encephalitis which produce schizophrenialike symptoms have been found in several studies to involve the limbic system, and epilepsy, when it originates in the limbic area, is more likely to be accompanied by schizophrenialike symptoms.

The strongest evidence linking the limbic system to schizophrenia has come from studies of electrical activity in this area. Robert Heath and his coworker in New Orleans found abnormal limbic electrical activity in schizophrenic patients; these findings have been replicated by at least three other groups of researchers. One group found abnormal electrical impulses in the limbic area of sixty-one out of sixty-two schizophrenic patients tested, and as the electrodes were moved away from the limbic area, the abnormalities became less frequent. Another group was able to correlate the occurrence of abnormal electrical activity and bizarre behavior in a patient.

Also significant in this regard is the discovery that many of the structural changes described in the brains of schizophrenic persons have been found in the limbic area, or in nearby areas with which it is closely connected. The widening of the corpus callosum, the abnormalities in the upper brain stem, and the dopamine and norepinephrine neurochemical changes are all specifically linked to the limbic system. It seems incontrovertible that the limbic system is the part of the brain which is primarily affected in many, if not most, cases of schizophrenia.

There is one other curious fact about the anatomical location of schizophrenia, which should be mentioned. In recent years there have been several studies suggesting that the left side of the brain is primarily affected in schizophrenia much more often than the right side of the brain. Patients with temporal lobe epilepsy, for example, will be more likely to have schizophrenialike symptoms if the epilepsy is in the left temporal lobe. Similarly, studies of visual evoked potentials, abnormal EEGs, lateral eye movements, auditory discrimination, galvanic skin response, information processing, and neurological signs, all suggest that the major problem may lie in the left hemisphere.

Research findings in this field have proliferated greatly in recent years and have been summarized by Dr. Henry A. Nasrallah, a leading schizophrenia researcher, as follows: "The evidence for a lateralized hemispheric dysfunction or an interhemispheric integration defect in schizophrenia is strongly suggestive but certainly not definitive."

As both gross and microscopic pathological lesions have continued to be described in the brains of individuals with schizophrenia, a subject of great controversy has lately arisen among researchers in this field. Where precisely is the primary lesion (or lesions) which gives rise to schizophrenia? Each researcher has his or her favorite area to bet on and long hours are spent in debate on the merits of each choice. Most researchers believe that the limbic system is the site of the primary lesion(s), although a few are betting on a portion of the frontal lobe immediately adjacent to the limbic system (the dorsolateral prefrontal cortex). Scattered here and there can also be found proponents for other portions of the brain with intimate connections to the limbic system, such as the midbrain or the cerebellum.

To translate the research discussions into geographical terms, imagine that the brain is the equivalent of the United States. Most researchers are convinced that schizophrenia is caused by dysfunction in the greater New York area, although a few believe it is in Baltimore and occasional proponents can be found arguing for Cleveland or Detroit. Within the New York area many researchers have favorite sites which they are researching; these may be as large as Queens, Bergen, or Suffolk counties or the size of towns like Hicksville, New Rochelle, or Paterson. Although the area under investigation is still relatively large, many other areas of the country (e.g., the northwest and southwest) have been effectively eliminated from consideration. In schizophrenia research, as in geography, it is obvious that the more researchers you have looking, the greater the chances are of finding it. To date, only a handful of researchers have been looking, because of the general neglect of schizophrenia research.

It Often Runs in Families

Ever since schizophrenia was first described in the early years of the nineteenth century, it has been noted that the disease sometimes runs in families. The brothers, sisters, and children of a person with schizophrenia, for example, have approximately a 10 percent chance of getting the disease. If it did not run in families, these close relatives would have only a 1 percent chance, the same proportion as in the general population. And all of us who work in the schizophrenia research area have encountered families in which there are three, four, or even five family members affected.

Thus the fact that schizophrenia may run in families has been established beyond any doubt. Less clear is how often this is true. Estimates vary widely, depending on the population group studied, the size of the families, and the definition used for schizophrenia. In my own work with large, inner-city families, I find that in almost half of all cases someone else in the family (mother, father, brother, sister, aunts, uncles, or grandparents) also has had schizophrenia. That means, of course, that in half of the cases there is no family history of the disease.

That schizophrenia runs in families means to most people that it is inherited. This may be but is not necessarily true. Genetic theories could explain why schizophrenia runs in families (these will be discussed below); however, other theories involving no genetic mechanisms could also explain it. For example, if some cases of schizophrenia were caused by an infectious agent, such as a virus, it may run in families because of transmission of the virus from mother or father to child either before or after birth; in this case the disease would run in families but would not be inherited in the genetic sense of the word.

The Brain Damage May Occur Very Early

Evidence has also accumulated that some cases of schizophrenia begin with damage to the brain in early childhood, perhaps even while the child is still growing in the uterus. This may be true even in persons who show no symptoms of schizophrenia until they are in their late teens or twenties.

Five separate types of studies point toward brain damage early in life in some cases of schizophrenia. First, it is known that minor physical anomalies (e.g., low-set ears, a single transverse palmar crease, greater distance between the eyes) may arise from subtle damage to the fetus in the first three months of pregnancy. In 1983 a study was published showing that patients with schizophrenia had a greater incidence of such minor physical anomalies than normal controls. It is also known that subtle damage to the fetus can cause minor deviations of a person's fingerprint pattern, the study of which is known as dermatoglyphics. Since 1935 there have been reports that persons with schizophrenia have an excessive number of unusual fingerprint (and palmprint) patterns. Such reports now cover more than 4,000 schizophrenics and come from England, Denmark, Sweden, Germany, Italy, Spain, Chile, Mexico, Australia, and the United States. It is not possible to say yet exactly what causes these unusual patterns. It does imply, however, that something significant is occurring before birth in some people who later develop schizophrenia.

Many studies have also been done on the incidence of pregnancy and birth complications (e.g., bleeding during pregnancy, anoxia at birth) on people who are later diagnosed with schizophrenia. Although no single pregnancy or birth complication occurred in high frequency, the complications as a group occurred statistically more often in individuals who later developed schizophrenia, compared with controls. As summarized by Dr. Thomas F. McNeil of Sweden, a leading schizophrenia researcher, "substantial evidence exists that obstetrical complications are associated with the development of schizophrenia." Another group of studies pointing toward brain damage early in life are those on the neuropathology of schizophrenia, many of which suggest that the brain abnormalities began either *in utero* or shortly thereafter.

The most impressive evidence suggesting brain damage early in life in schizophrenia is the seasonal excess of schizophrenic births in the late winter and early spring months. The excess varies from 5 to 15 percent and has been shown to occur using carefully controlled studies in England and Wales, Ireland, Denmark, Norway, Sweden, Japan, and the Philippines. Studies in southern-hemisphere countries have been less conclusive but have pointed in the same direction (i.e., a disproportionate number of schizophrenics are born during the winter and spring there). There is also evidence that the peak months for schizophrenic births have shifted over time, at least in Japan and the United States.

There are, of course, several possible explanations for the seasonality of schizophrenic births, including nutritional factors, infectious agents, and other environmental variables which differ by season. At one time it was speculated that peculiar conception patterns among parents more likely to give birth to schizophrenic offspring might account for the seasonal birth pattern, but this has subsequently been ruled out by examining the birth pattern of the siblings of the person with schizophrenia. The precise explanation for the seasonal excess of schizophrenic births is unknown; the important point is that *something* is going on during the conception, pregnancy, or birth of these children which makes them more susceptible to schizophrenia later in their lives, and that this something has a seasonal occurrence.

WHAT IS SPECULATED: THEORIES

We now leave the world of facts (things known about schizophrenia) and enter the realm of theories, where researchers may speculate about the ultimate causes of the disease. As knowledge accumulates, some theories lose favor and drop by the wayside, while others gain adherents. Adequate research funding for schizophrenia could speed this process substantially.

We say that schizophrenia is a heterogeneous condition, which means that it has more than one subgroup and more than one cause. Virtually everything written about schizophrenia today includes that caveat, and it may well be true but it is not established as fact. A case can be made for the opposite approach—that schizophrenia may turn out to have a single major cause. Dr. Lewis Thomas has pointed out that syphilis, tuberculosis, and pernicious anemia were all conditions with a bewildering variety of manifestations that few scientists thought could constitute a single illness, yet in each case a single cause (spirochete, tubercle bacillus, and vitamin deficiency) was eventually found to be the primary cause. That this may be true for schizophrenia (and possibly for manic-depressive psychosis as well) is not beyond the realm of possibility.

Keep in mind that the theories of causation discussed below are not mutually exclusive. The cause or causes of schizophrenia may well turn out to be an amalgam of these components, such as a genetic predisposition to immunological and biochemical dysfunction, or a developmental anomaly triggered by a virus *in utero*.

144   SURVIVING SCHIZOPHRENIA

Genetic Theories

Genetic theories of the disease are probably the oldest and the most
tested. Basically, these say that schizophrenia is an inherited disorder,
passed on by the genes from generation to generation. The genes, of
which we each have six million, are carried on chromosomes in the
nuclei of all our body cells, and we receive half of them from our mother
and half from our father. Recent research has suggested that the defect
causing Huntington's disease is carried on a gene on chromosome
number 4 and the defect causing Alzheimer's disease is carried on a
gene on chromosome number 21. There have been some indications
that manic-depressive psychosis is associated with a gene carried on
chromosome number 11, but other researchers have been unable to
confirm this.

In years past, genetic theories were relatively simple. Either the
disease was inherited as a dominant gene (and would be activated
whether inherited from either the mother *or* the father) or as a recessive
gene (and would not be activated unless inherited from both parents).
Inbreeding among families has long been discouraged because it tends
to elicit otherwise recessive diseases even when the parents are only
distantly related. Neither dominant nor recessive inheritance patterns
fit the facts of schizophrenia, however. Areas where schizophrenia is
more prevalent do not necessarily have more inbreeding, and areas with
more inbreeding do not necessarily have more schizophrenia.

There continues to be a general consensus among schizophrenia
experts that genetics plays some role in the disease—the fact that
schizophrenia runs in families suggests it—but its precise role is unclear. The offspring of nonschizophrenic parents has a 1 percent chance
of developing the disease, of one schizophrenic parent a 13 percent
chance, and of two schizophrenic parents a 46 percent chance. Twin
studies also suggest it; the twin of a nonidentical (dizygotic) schizophrenic twin has only a 10 to 15 percent chance of developing schizophrenia (only slightly higher than for other brothers and sisters),
whereas the twin of an identical (monozygotic) schizophrenic twin has
a 35 to 50 percent chance. It is important to note, however, that not
all identical twins develop schizophrenia when one does. In fact, since
these twins have identical genes, such studies prove conclusively that
genetic inheritance cannot be the only cause of schizophrenia.

Genetic influences on schizophrenia are also suggested by the
work on abnormal eye movements carried out by Philip Holzman and

his colleagues. Not only were schizophrenics found to have the abnormal eye movements, but a study of nonschizophrenic relatives of these patients found that 45 percent of them *also* had abnormal eye movements, suggesting that something had been inherited in the family that produced schizophrenia in some family members but not in others. Such abnormal eye movements have been proposed as a "genetic marker" for the putative gene thought to carry schizophrenia from generation to generation. Other biological traits have also been proposed as possible genetic markers, including neurological abnormalities, neuropsychological tests (e.g., continuous performance test), and the reaction of blood lymphocytes (e.g., their binding to spiperone). It is an area of considerable research interest, but whether in fact any of these turn out to be true genetic markers remains to be determined.

Studies done in Denmark on children of schizophrenic parents who were adopted by other families at birth have added immeasurably to our knowledge of schizophrenia. The children were followed up after they had become adults, and it was found that children of schizophrenic parents retained their increased predisposition toward developing the disease despite the fact that they had been raised by nonschizophrenic parents. The conclusion drawn from these studies is that "something necessary but not sufficient for the development of a schizophrenic disorder is transmitted genetically." Or as summarized by Seymour Kety in a wry response to Thomas Szasz, "If schizophrenia is a myth, it is a myth with a strong genetic component."

Increasingly, it is suspected that the disease schizophrenia is not itself inherited; rather, what is inherited is a predisposition of some people to react to environmental influences in a particular way which leads to schizophrenia. This is similar to current theories for many other chronic diseases of humankind, including diabetes, hypertension, heart disease, and some cancers. For diabetes, for example, Abner Notkins and his colleagues at the National Institutes of Health have developed a strain of mice which, when injected with a particular virus, develop diabetes. Another strain of mice is completely resistant and never develops diabetes. It is clear that the first strain has a genetic predisposition toward reacting with the virus in such a way as to produce diabetes. The mice do not inherit the diabetes but rather the predisposition. This model may well be operant for schizophrenia as well. One may hypothesize any one—or more—of many possible precipitating causes in addition to viruses, including specific dietary factors, stress, or environmental contaminants such as insecticides.

Other genetic theories of schizophrenia encompass the idea that what is inherited is a specific defect in the brain that causes it to malfunction and thereby produce the symptoms of schizophrenia. For example, an inherited defect in the sensory-processing mechanism of the limbic system, or of the brain centers which integrate communication, could theoretically lead to schizophrenialike symptoms. A variant of this theory says that what is inherited is an abnormal or unusual blood supply to the limbic areas, thereby making them particularly liable to damage (e.g., too little oxygen at birth) or environmental insults (susceptibility to infections). Finally, it is possible to invoke complex models of genetic transmission, such as the disease's being carried on more than one gene, to explain why schizophrenia is sometimes passed from generation to generation and sometimes is not.

It is clear, then, that genetic theories of schizophrenia fit comfortably with the facts known about the disease. The one major criticism which can be leveled at these theories is that persons with schizophrenia themselves have a very low rate of reproduction. This was especially true in the past, for obvious reasons, when patients spent their lives in asylums on single-sex wards; it is less true now with large numbers of schizophrenic sufferers living in the community. Given the low reproductivity rate, schizophrenia should have died out, or at least become markedly less prevalent, if it is transmitted from affected individuals to their offspring.

The geneticists' response to this criticism is that schizophrenia could be simply one manifestation of a genetically related spectrum of personality disorders. If the spectrum also included individuals, such as antisocial personality types, these individuals might have a higher-than-average reproductivity rate and so transmit the disorder. In other words the schizophrenia-producing genes would be passed on not only through persons with schizophrenia, but through a range of schizophrenia-spectrum individuals.

Biochemical Theories

Many biochemical theories of schizophrenia assume a genetic basis as well. The biochemical mechanisms describe what is wrong in the brain but not how it got to be wrong. The ultimate cause is usually assumed to be genetic, such as an inherited error of brain metabolism leading to the biochemical defect.

Biochemical theories date back to the early years of this century, although they have become much more sophisticated in recent years as the technology for measuring the body's chemistry has improved. The center of attention throughout the last decade has been the neurotransmitter dopamine, one of the brain chemicals in the class called catecholamines, which transmit information between nerve cells. Dopamine has come under suspicion because amphetamines, when given in high doses, cause a rise in the dopamine level at the same time that they produce symptoms which resemble schizophrenia. Similarly, when L-dopa, a drug which the body may turn into dopamine, is given to persons with schizophrenia, it often makes them worse. Finally, it is now known that drugs which are effective in schizophrenia block dopamine action. For all of these reasons many researchers suspect that an excess of dopamine is one of the causes of schizophrenia.

Dopamine is broken down in the body to other compounds through the action of certain enzymes. One such enzyme is monoamine oxidase, known as MAO, and this enzyme has been the object of intensive research studies over the past decade. It has been reported, for example, that blood platelets of schizophrenic patients have a lower concentration of MAO than expected; recent findings suggest that this may be a drug effect, however, and the status of MAO research is being reevaluated.

Other neurotransmitters under investigation in schizophrenia are serotonin and norepinephrine; the latter is suspected of playing a role in the causation of some depressions as well. Naturally occurring chemicals of the body, such as endorphins, prostaglandins, and prolactin (a hormone of the pituitary gland), have generated intense interest among some researchers. Perhaps all such efforts can be summed up by Joseph J. Schildkraut, a psychiatric researcher, who claims that we "have crossed the threshold into the era that I like to call psychiatric chemistry. . . . We are at a point in psychiatry today that is analogous to where our internist colleagues were in the 1950s. . . . I suspect that ten years from now we will probably view what we were doing here in the early 1980s as being as crude and primitive as what the endocrinologist was doing in his laboratory in the 1950s."

Just as there are different chemicals under investigation, so too there are different theories about how these chemicals may cause the symptoms of schizophrenia. These include the possibility of there being an excess (as is believed true for dopamine) or a deficit (as is believed true for MAO) of the chemical. It is also possible that there are too many or too few receptors in the brain for these neurotransmitters, and much recent interest has focused on the D-2 receptors for dopamine as possibly being present in excessive numbers in the brains of people with schizophrenia.

Another theory suggests that the chemical may get changed into a toxic product and act as an internal brain poison; for example, it was widely believed for many years that chemicals such as dopamine might be changed to a mescalinelike compound and thus cause hallucinations. In recent years attention has been directed toward the branches of the nerve cells which send and receive neurotransmitters, and there has been speculation that blockage of the neurotransmitter may occur at that juncture.

How well do such biochemical theories fit the known facts of schizophrenia? They fit very well, especially when combined with the possibility of a genetically transmitted defect. Much of the structural and functional evidence of brain dysfunction is compatible with postulated biochemical defects. The limbic system would be a likely site for such defects since many of the neurotransmitters are concentrated there. The tendency for schizophrenia to run in families could be explained by a genetic transmission of the biochemical abnormality. And if there were biochemical abnormalities which were genetically inherited, it is possible that they might manifest themselves in childhood as altered personality traits even if the full disease did not develop until many years later.

Nutritional Theories

Nutritional theories of schizophrenia are really just a subset of biochemical theories. They have developed an identity of their own, however, under the name of orthomolecular psychiatry.

Nutritional theories have had adherents ever since it was discovered that some B vitamin deficiency diseases (e.g., beriberi, pellagra, and pernicious anemia) may be accompanied by psychiatric symptoms. Then in the early 1950s, Drs. Humphrey Osmond and Abram Hoffer began treating schizophrenic patients with high doses of niacin (a generic name for vitamin B-3, which includes nicotinic acid and nicotinamide) along with electroconvulsive therapy (ECT), in an attempt to block the formation of adrenochrome, a toxic metabolite of the neurotransmitter epinephrine which they believed to be causing the symptoms of schizophrenia. They claimed remarkable therapeutic success, and orthomolecular psychiatry was born.

Since that time its theories have expanded and become more complex. Other scientists joined their ranks, most notably Dr. Linus Pauling, who had previously won a Nobel Prize in another area of research. They postulated that a genetically determined biochemical defect leads to subtle changes in brain chemistry. This in turn leads to altered subjective experiences (such as those described in chapter 2) which are called "metabolic dysperception" in orthomolecular terms. The original treatment with niacin has expanded to include large doses of many other vitamins (thiamine, pyridoxine, folic acid, vitamin B-12, vitamin C, vitamin E) and minerals (e.g., zinc, manganese). Control of the diet has also been incorporated into therapeutic regimens, especially restricting the intake of carbohydrates, caffeine, and alcohol. Smoking is discouraged, and the person is urged to exercise regularly. The theories and combinations of these orthomolecular therapeutic elements have proliferated rapidly and now fill a textbook.

As this was occurring, orthomolecular psychiatry became separated from the mainstream of American psychiatry. No further evidence to support the adrenochrome theory was found, and attempts to replicate the original Osmond-Hoffer work with niacin were unsuccessful. Increasingly the orthomolecular adherents were regarded as cultists or food faddists by most American psychiatrists, and their claims were not taken seriously. Nonetheless, the orthomolecular group continued to grow, formed a network of patients and their families (the American Schizophrenia Association), and ridiculed the prevailing psychoanalytic and family interaction theories of schizophrenia which were prevalent in American psychiatry.

In retrospect, it appears that much of the controversy surrounding orthomolecular psychiatry has been not about the use of vitamins to treat schizophrenia but rather about the medical model of the disease. The orthomolecular followers have staunchly and loudly championed the view that schizophrenia is a *real* disease; this has probably been the main source of their appeal to schizophrenics and their families. Traditional American psychiatry, meanwhile, was pursuing the psychoanalytic and family interaction theories of schizophrenia.

This view apart, when the specific theories of orthomolecular psychiatry are examined in a critical light, they are found to be lacking in supporting evidence. There are no studies comparable to the biochemical research referred to in the previous section, and the theories of

vitamins, minerals, and dietary deficiencies remain completely unproven by generally accepted scientific standards. Since over thirty
years have passed since the original Osmond-Hoffer report, it is possible
that proof for these theories never will eventuate. If this turns out to
be the case, then orthomolecular psychiatry will be remembered as
having been right on the big issue (the validity of the medical model
of schizophrenia) long before the rest of American psychiatry, but
wrong on the smaller issue (vitamin deficiency as the specific cause).
They will have been in the right church but the wrong pew.

In addition to orthomolecular psychiatry's theories of vitamin
deficiency, there are other nutritional theories of schizophrenia's causation. Gluten, for example, has been proposed by Dr. Curtis Dohan of
Philadelphia as a likely dietary cause of the disease, and he pointed out
that the lower schizophrenia rate in Scandinavian countries during
World War II closely paralleled the decrease in glutens in the diet.
Some observers have claimed that maintaining schizophrenic patients
on a gluten-free and milk-free diet improves their clinical condition, but
other studies have found that it has no effect.

How well do nutritional theories fit what is known about schizophrenia? They could certainly account for structural and functional
abnormalities in the brain. Furthermore, it is theoretically possible that
specific dietary deficiencies or excesses might selectively affect the limbic system. Nutritional deficiencies, such as pellagra, run in families,
and it is also possible to invoke genetic mechanisms to explain an
inborn error of metabolism which would be passed down over several
generations. Nutritional deficiencies or excesses would also be compatible with the beginnings of the disease prenatally or early in childhood
and could theoretically be used to explain facts such as the seasonality
of schizophrenic births (e.g., a dietary deficiency might be more common during certain months and affect the developing brain in the
unborn child).

The problem with nutritional theories is the lack of data to support
them. A recent search for food allergies among schizophrenic patients
yielded negative results, and the analysis of schizophrenic spinal fluid
for evidence of zinc or copper deficiency has been similarly unreward-
ing. Since the list of possible dietary substances is enormous, however,
it is still possible that such a substance will prove to be causal of
schizophrenia for at least a subgroup of patients. The serendipitous
finding that lithium, a trace mineral in the body, improves some persons
with schizophrenia (as well as persons with mania) suggests that we still

know very little about the nutritional requirements of the brain. And one cannot help but be impressed by the stories of individual patients who claim to have an exacerbation of their schizophrenic symptoms whenever they ingest certain foods.

Viral Theories

During the early years of this century, there was considerable interest in infectious agents as the possible cause of schizophrenia. This interest was especially stimulated by the finding of a spirochete as the cause of brain syphilis, a disease which can closely resemble schizophrenia. Most of this early research centered on bacteria, as viruses were not well known at the time.

In the last thirty years there has been sporadic interest in viruses as a possible cause of schizophrenia. Viral particles in the spinal fluid of schizophrenic patients were first reported by several researchers in the 1950s. Many observers also noted the occurrence of schizophrenia-like symptoms in known viral infections of the brain, especially in cases of encephalitis caused by the influenza virus, herpes viruses, and encephalitis lethargica. As far back as 1928 it had been noted that "encephalitis and schizophrenia are different diseases, but it seems that some factor common to both is sometimes present and accounts for the coincidence of identical symptoms."

Current infectious disease theories of schizophrenia claim that the "factor common to both" is a virus. Viruses are known to attack very specific areas of the brain while leaving other areas untouched; for example, the rabies virus and the herpes zoster virus will attack only one kind of cell in one part of the central nervous system. Viruses may also alter the function of brain cells without altering their structure; cell enzymes, for example, may be permanently disrupted by a viral infection yet the cell itself will continue to live and show no evident damage. This means that viruses could conceivably cause schizophrenia and leave no trace of their damage visible under a microscope.

Another intriguing fact about viruses as a possible cause of schizophrenia is that they may remain latent for many years at a time. This is true for some well-known viruses, such as those in the herpes family, but it is also true for a group of viruses called "slow" viruses, which may not cause disease for twenty years or more after they originally infect the person. Thus persons with schizophrenia could theoretically become infected while still in the uterus or shortly after birth and yet not show symptoms of the disease until their twenties or thirties.

If viruses are involved in the causation of schizophrenia, it may be that the timing of the original infection is critical. There are known viral diseases which cause brain damage if introduced at one stage of fetal brain development but not at another stage. German measles (rubella) is the best-known example of this, causing mental retardation and heart and other defects if it infects the baby in the first three months of pregnancy but often causing no damage if infection takes place a few months later.

Is there any evidence that schizophrenia might be caused by a virus? Within recent years such evidence has begun to accumulate but it is still far from definitive. The evidence is of three types. First, Dr. Timothy Crow and his colleagues in England found that the cerebrospinal fluid of one-third of patients with schizophrenia has a viral-like activity suggesting the presence of a virus; attempts to ascertain the identity of this agent have been unsuccessful. Second, there have been reports from several laboratories of abnormal antibody levels against different viruses in the blood and/or cerebrospinal fluid of patients with schizophrenia. The involved viruses include herpes simplex virus–I (which causes cold sores on the lips), Epstein-Barr virus (which causes mononucleosis), cytomegalovirus, mumps virus, and measles virus. Unfortunately, however, the results of these tests have not been consistent from laboratory to laboratory, and it is unclear whether the results are due to the virus identified, to cross-reactivity with other viruses, or to immunological abnormalities in the patients.

Third, it has been found in three studies that during periods in which more individuals who eventually developed schizophrenia were *in utero*, viral illnesses were especially prevalent. The most interesting of these reports followed up a 1957 influenza epidemic in Finland and found that a disproportionate number of individuals who eventually developed schizophrenia were in the fourth through sixth months *in utero* at the time of the influenza epidemic.

In summary, evidence for viral theories of schizophrenia can perhaps best be compared with similar theories for multiple sclerosis. In both diseases a variety of viruses have been implicated but results have been inconsistent from laboratory to laboratory. Clearly much more work needs to be done. Viral theories of schizophrenia continue to be appealing because they fit the known facts nicely. They can explain the minor physical anomalies and fingerprint changes *in utero*, the microscopic and CT-scan changes in the brains, the seasonality of births, and the involvement of the limbic system since several viruses have an affinity for that part of the brain. The fact that schizophrenia runs in families can be explained either by a genetic predisposition to the virus, by transmission of a virus on the gene itself (such as is known to occur in the mouse leukemia virus), or by transmission of the virus across the placenta from the mother (or the father, via the semen) during pregnancy. It should also be noted that some viruses have been shown to cause changes in neurotransmitters, such as dopamine in the brain, and so could theoretically account for some of the biochemical changes described in schizophrenia.

Immunological Theories

Immunological theories of schizophrenia, like viral theories, have been of greatest interest to Russian researchers, while being comparatively neglected in the United States. Evidence that many persons with schizophrenia have abnormalities in their immune system dates back to Russian studies in the early years of this century and precedes the introduction of antipsychotic medications by fifty years. Early work on immune dysfunction in schizophrenics in the United States was carried out by Dr. John Whitehorn at Johns Hopkins University, who demonstrated that the patients have a less-than-normal reaction to histamine when injected beneath the skin; this study has been confirmed many times.

Modern research on the immune system of persons with schizophrenia has encompassed a wide variety of immune components, including antibrain antibodies (the best known being Dr. Robert Heath's "taraxein"), antinuclear antibodies, lymphocytotoxic antibodies, myelin basic protein, nerve growth factor, C-reactive protein, oligoclonal bands, and immune complexes. The majority of immunological research on schizophrenia, however, has focused on lymphocytes and immunoglobulins. Some researchers have claimed that atypical lymphocytes (similar to those found in mononucleosis) are found in the blood of persons with schizophrenia. Other researchers have zeroed in on particular types of lymphocytes—B type, T type, and NK type—and reported evidence of their overabundance (B lymphocytes) or underabundance (T lymphocytes). Immunoglobulins have been studied in schizophrenia in both the blood and the cerebrospinal fluid (CSF), with many, but contradictory, reports of overabundance or underabundance of the immunoglobulin A, G, and M fractions (IgA, IgG, and IgM).

Perhaps the easiest way to summarize the scattered and conflicting immunological research results to date is to assert that *something* is wrong with the immune system in schizophrenia but that researchers cannot yet agree on what that is. The questions raised by the research far outnumber the answers. Is schizophrenia an autoimmune disease (in which the body makes antibodies against itself), like the disease lupus erythematosus? Is there evidence that schizophrenics as a group have more allergies than nonschizophrenics? Are viral infections in schizophrenia the cause of the immunological abnormalities or do immunological abnormalities make the patient more susceptible to viral infections? And all of this is further complicated by the fact that both lithium and antipsychotic drugs have their own effect on the immune system and thus compound research results.

Nevertheless there is no question that immunological theories of schizophrenia remain attractive if underresearched. They fit many of the known facts about the disease, and are especially compatible with genetic theories of inherited immune dysfunction. Biochemical, nutritional, and viral theories of schizophrenia can also be easily fitted into an immunological frame.

Developmental Theories

These theories are in a sense an extension of the data discussed above: that brain damage in schizophrenia may occur very early in life. Developmental theories postulate that the specific causative agent in schizophrenia is not the important factor but rather *where* the insult occurs in the brain and *when* it occurs. It is known that the brain is the only organ in humans that develops over a prolonged period from conception until the end of the second year of life; all other organs have completed their basic development by the time a child is born. The brain, therefore, is vulnerable to developmental insults and injuries for a longer period than any other organ. It is also known that the timing of brain injuries is critical, with serious disturbances in function the consequence of an injury at one specific period, but no disturbance the consequence of a similar injury two months earlier or later.

Theoretically any one of numerous factors might cause brain injury at a specific time, thereby leading to schizophrenia later in life.

These include hereditary factors, infection, exposure to particular medications or immunizations, environmental toxins such as lead or pesticides, anoxia, birth trauma causing specific injuries, deprivation of specific nutritional elements needed for normal development, maternal alcohol consumption or street drug use, immunological disorders, or metabolic disorders. Developmental theories suggest that any or all of these may cause schizophrenia and that the common denominator of the disease is the site and timing of the injury in the brain. As summarized by Dr. Daniel Weinberger, who has published an extensive review of developmental theories: "Schizophrenia is a neurodevelopmental disorder in which a fixed lesion from early in life interferes with brain maturational events that occur much later."

Developmental theories of schizophrenia are attractive because they explain so many of the emerging research findings. CT-scan findings, for example, appear to have been present long before the person's schizophrenia began. Similarly, many of the microscopic abnormalities in brains from persons with schizophrenia can be most easily explained as having begun in early stages of the brain's development. In recent findings by Dr. Nancy Andreason and her colleagues, using magnetic resonance imaging (MRI) scans, it was found that individuals with schizophrenia have slightly smaller heads, brains, and frontal lobes. "These findings," they conclude, "are consistent with the hypothesis that some schizophrenics may have a type of early developmental abnormality."

Stress Theories

Stress theories of schizophrenia are included as a separate category only because they are prominently mentioned in all standard textbooks and because many researchers of other theories (e.g., biochemical, genetic) invoke stress to complement their own theory. Personally I am unimpressed with the role that stress plays in the causation of schizophrenia and doubt that it is any more important in this disease than in multiple sclerosis, Parkinson's disease, Alzheimer's disease, polio, or any other chronic disease of the central nervous system. In this section stress will be considered as a cause of schizophrenia; in chapter 10 stress will be discussed as a precipitant of relapses in schizophrenia.

Stress is widely believed by the general public to cause schizophrenia. Overwork, too much pressure, family problems, and similar formulations are commonly heard as causal explanations by friends and relatives of persons who develop this disease. Stress is also commonly invoked by people who become ill with schizophrenia as an explanation for their illness. Judi Chamberlain, a leader of ex-patient organizations, wrote, "We believe that the kinds of behavior labeled 'mental illness' have far more to do with the day-to-day conditions of people's lives than with disorders in their brain chemistry." The invoking of stress to explain schizophrenia has been common since the nineteenth century; a prominent theory regarding the increase of insanity in England in the 1850s was the stress of train travel.

The reasons why stress theories are so widely believed are multiple. It is known that stress can be a major cause of diseases such as ulcers, so it seems logical to suspect it of causing schizophrenia. More important, it is known that subjecting individuals to very large amounts of stress can produce bizarre behavior which may mimic schizophrenia. This is seen, for example, in wartime, when "combat neurosis" may produce a soldier with a sudden hysterical paralysis or an acute paranoid reaction; or in persons subjected to severe sensory deprivation that causes them to experience hallucinations. These kinds of reactions—usually called brief reactive psychosis—were discussed in chapter 4; they are not the same as schizophrenia, but may look very similar to it for a short period of time. Given these facts, it is not surprising that stress has been linked to schizophrenia in the minds of many people.

In recent years stress theories have been popular among schizophrenia researchers as well. Usually they assume a genetic predisposition (diathesis) in addition to stress, the so-called diathesis-stress theory. For example, one can postulate that some brains are genetically unable to handle stress and that, because of this inherited inability, such people develop schizophrenia under an amount of stress which others would find easy to handle. Alternatively, some brains may be genetically unable to process sensory input, thereby producing much stress when subjected to such input and eventually leading to schizophrenia. By mixing various genetic predispositions with childhood experiences and learning, one can create dozens of possible scenarios producing stress and, hypothetically, schizophrenia as well.

Attempts to determine whether individuals who develop schizophrenia have more stress in their lives have produced contradictory results. The oft-quoted 1968 study by Brown and Birley in London concluded that people developing schizophrenia had a significant increase in stressful life events immediately preceding the illness and that the stress acted as a trigger. Dohrenwend and Egri reviewed this and other studies and concluded that "stressful life events whose occurrences are outside the control of the subject play a part in the causation of schizophrenic episodes." Rabkin, however, reviewing many of the same studies, concluded: "No study found more [stressful life] events reported by schizophrenics than by other patient groups. Findings are inconsistent regarding event frequency reported by schizophrenics and normals. . . . Overall the research evidence indicates a weaker relationship between life events and schizophrenia than the clinical literature suggests." Tennant's excellent 1985 review is even more emphatic in its conclusions: "There is no good evidence that life stress is causally related to episodes of schizophrenia." The most recent major study of stressful life events and schizophrenia found "only 15.4 percent of the patients had severe or extreme premorbid stress . . . half of the patients had either no or minimal premorbid stress . . . This is consistent with previous data on the relatively minor role of stressful life events prior to illness onset."

How well do stress theories fit what is known about schizophrenia? They are consistent with some genetic, biochemical, and immunological findings (e.g., severe stress may cause alterations in the immune system). There are major problems with stress theories, however. One of the largest is the problem of sorting out the chicken from the egg in the weeks immediately preceding the onset of schizophrenia: Did stressful life events cause the schizophrenia, or was the person in the process of becoming sick and thereby acted in such a way that life crises were precipitated? Stress theories of schizophrenia also fail to explain the epidemiology of the disease. Why does schizophrenia occur in postadolescence rather than during adolescence? Why are men affected earlier and more severely than women? Why do epidemics of schizophrenia not occur in prison and concentration camps? Why was the schizophrenia rate not high during the Renaissance, the Inquisition, or the French Revolution? Why did the schizophrenia rate go down in many countries during World War II, rather than up? Why is the schizophrenia rate low in places like warring Northern Ireland, yet much higher in the relatively peaceful western part of Ireland? Why would stress produce increased strength of character in many people, yet produce schizophrenia in others?

It is commonly said that contemporary mankind is subject to great stress. Yet how does this compare with our forefathers' lives? An English researcher summarizes the contemporary situation as follows:

Today, of course, every niggling inconvenience and frustration of urban
life is hailed as "stress," but this is merely the characteristic hyperbole of
self-pity. I would contend that, by any objective criteria, the generation
that is now entering middle age in this country has suffered less real stress
than any in recorded history. Cosseted from birth by a welfare state, the
only obvious stresses they suffer are the physical ones arising from life-long
overconsumption of food, drink, and tobacco.

It is not a question of whether stress can cause mental distress; that is
known. Rather it is a question of whether stress is in any way causative
of schizophrenia. And if so, is the stress an important cause, or merely
the straw that breaks the camel's back, and of little consequence in the
larger picture?

THE FAILURE TO FUND SCHIZOPHRENIA RESEARCH

Research funds for studying diseases come from one of three sources:
(a) the public, via general tax dollars which are allocated by Congress
to government agencies such as the National Institute of Mental
Health; these funds can then be used to support research by government scientists (intramural research) or given as research grants to
universities and medical centers (extramural research); (b) the public,
via donations to public drives such as those sponsored for cancer,
leukemia, and muscular dystrophy; and (c) foundations, whose money
usually comes from the estates of wealthy individuals or corporations.

For all intents and purposes the support of schizophrenia research
in the United States derives almost exclusively from the first source.
There has never been a public drive for schizophrenia research, although
the research fund recently set up by the National Alliance for the
Mentally Ill (National Alliance for Research on Schizophrenia and
Depression, or NARSAD; see chapter 14) may change that situation in
the future. Nor has there ever been a foundation which became interested in schizophrenia research, with two exceptions. Since 1934 the
Scottish Rite of Freemasonry, headquartered in Boston, has supported a
modest but high-quality schizophrenia research program which presently spends approximately half a million dollars a year. Since the
current annual federal government expenditures on schizophrenia research are only about $21 million, the Scottish Rite support has been

very important over the years. Second, in 1958 a foundation to support schizophrenia research (Research in Schizophrenia Endowment, or RISE) was begun by Dr. Stanley R. Dean and others. It was subsequently placed under the National Mental Health Association, where it withered and died.

Most schizophrenia research funds, then, derive from the general tax dollars which go to the National Institute of Mental Health (NIMH). This agency was created by Congress in 1946 in reaction to the large number of American men who were rejected for service in World War II because of their serious mental illnesses. NIMH was explicitly created as a research institute whose major focus was supposed to be serious mental illnesses such as schizophrenia.

NIMH, however, has until recently evinced little interest in schizophrenia research over the four decades of its existence. It evolved from being primarily a research institute to one that supported the training of mental health professionals and then mental health services through Community Mental Health Centers (see chapter 8). Research became proportionately a smaller and smaller part of its total budget, and the research it supported became less focused on serious mental illnesses such as schizophrenia. Between 1980 and 1986 NIMH spent only 9 to 10 percent of its research budget each year targeted on schizophrenia research. At the same time it continued to fund many projects in social psychology (e.g., "Television's Role in Affecting Socializations"), labor relations (e.g., "How Vietnam Vets Can Cope with Job Loss"), child development (e.g., "Friendship Foundation Among Children"), sociology (e.g., "Factors Regulating Family-Kin Relationships"), and other aspects of human behavior. In the 1970s it became interested in poverty, racial discrimination, violence on city streets, rape, women's rights, and many other social causes—worthy projects, to be sure, all of which diverted more energy and resources *away* from research on serious mental illnesses. Schizophrenia, once the cornerstone of NIMH, became increasingly just another pebble in a stone quarry as NIMH ventured ever farther afield with each passing year.

The consequences of this trend for schizophrenia research have been tragic. There is no major disease in the western world which has been as underresearched as schizophrenia, no disease which has had fewer champions, no disease which has had a less visible advocacy group fighting for it. For every patient with multiple sclerosis, $161 is spent on research. For every patient with cancer, it is $300. For every patient with muscular dystrophy, it is over $1,000. Yet for every patient with schizophrenia, just $14 is spent on research.

There is no question that we should know more about the causes of schizophrenia than we do. It is also clear that schizophrenia lags far behind research on other brain diseases because of four decades of neglect. Research on the brain—the neurosciences—is probably the single most exciting and promising research area in medicine at this time, with great advances likely in the next decade because of improving research technology. Yet schizophrenia may not benefit from these advances because there is so little research support compared with that for other diseases.

What can be done? As will be discussed in chapter 14, the advocacy of organized groups such as the National Alliance for the Mentally Ill can be exceedingly important in correcting the decades of neglect. Federal research dollars are tax dollars, public dollars, and the allocation of these dollars is determined by Congress. NIMH can rediscover schizophrenia as a research priority if encouraged to do so. In 1986 the Director of NIMH at that time, Dr. Shervert Frazier, reorganized NIMH to give more visibility to schizophrenia research, and the new Schizophrenia Research Branch is carrying out its mandate. Later the same year Senator Lowell P. Weicker held hearings of the Committee on Appropriations to determine why research on schizophrenia had been so neglected, and in 1987 research funds for schizophrenia research were increased modestly.

These changes are significant steps in the right direction to correct the decades of neglect in schizophrenia research. What is needed, however, are increases in funding not merely from $20 million to $30 million per year, but increases from $20 million to $100 million or $200 million per year. That is the kind of effort which is needed to achieve breakthroughs on causes and treatment.

If NIMH is unable or unwilling to continue moving vigorously forward on schizophrenia research, then alternatives are available. One is to take schizophrenia research out of NIMH and instead to place that responsibility upon the National Institute of Neurological and Communicative Disorders and Stroke (NINCDS), which conducts research on many other brain diseases (e.g., multiple sclerosis). Still another alternative is to encourage Congress to set up a National Institute of Brain Research, which would incorporate portions of both NIMH and NINCDS, including schizophrenia research. Drastic measures clearly are needed to get research on this disease back on track. What is needed is a major thrust such as was organized for cancer research, a Manhattan

Project for schizophrenia. What we have had so far is a drop in a bucket off the lower tip of Manhattan.

DISCARDED THEORIES

As knowledge evolves in every field of scientific enquiry, new theories arise to explain the observations. At the same time, older theories which no longer fit the facts are set aside and eventually discarded. All areas of science have dusty shelves full of discarded theories and schizophrenia research is no exception. They include psychoanalytic theories, family interaction theories, and the theories of Thomas Szasz and Ronald Laing.

Psychoanalytic Theories. In 1911 Sigmund Freud published his analysis of a paranoid schizophrenic, the Schreber case. Working from the memoirs which Daniel Schreber had published in 1903 and never actually examining the patient, Freud concluded that Schreber suffered from "conflict over unconscious homosexuality" which led to an inverted Oedipus complex. Schreber had become attached to his father instead of his mother, as occurs in a normal childhood Oedipal situation, and that in turn had produced schizophrenia. Prior to this, Freud had acknowledged very limited experience with schizophrenics; in 1907 he wrote to Karl Abraham that "I seldom see dements [dementia] and hardly ever see other severe types of psychosis."

In the ensuing years Freud's followers began a lively debate about the cause of schizophrenia. Carl Jung and Karl Abraham made the debate public, with Jung favoring a chemical toxin and Abraham arguing for a massive blockage of libido. Freud sided with Abraham, ironically attributing Jung's views to his mystical tendencies. Much of the debate focused on when the psychic damage causing schizophrenia occurred. On one end of the spectrum were psychoanalysts who argued that the trauma may even have preceded birth and be related to "the unceasing terror and tension of the fetal night" while in the womb. Melanie Klein, an influential protégée of Freud, fixed the critical schizophrenia-producing period at 3 to 6 months of age, while others focused on later parts of the oral, genital, or Oedipal periods of development. Related to this were differences of opinion as to whether schizophrenia was primarily due to disorders of libido development (e.g., drives, such as sex), or due to disorders of ego development (the inability to differentiate the self from others). The one thing on which all psychoanalysts could agree was that the ultimate cause of schizophrenia was the psychic trauma inflicted on the patient by his mother and father early in life. Psychoanalysts such as Frieda Fromm-Reichmann and Harry Stack Sullivan, who attempted to treat patients with schizophrenia, therefore tried to correct the deviant parental experience by giving the patient a "relationship of security beyond what they have ever had."

Psychoanalytic theories of schizophrenia, it should be noted, were never based upon any scientific evidence but merely on the ideas of Freud and his followers. Most psychoanalysts, including Freud, had little experience with schizophrenic patients. No studies were conducted using controls. In some cases the psychoanalysts had clear personal biases. Sullivan, for example, was enamored with Freud's theory that failure of attachment to the mother in childhood led to unconscious homosexuality and paranoid schizophrenia; Sullivan himself was "dominated by an unhappy, indulgent mother," was "a homosexual who wished to be a heterosexual," and almost certainly experienced multiple episodes of schizophrenia.

Psychoanalytic theories were discarded when they were found not to fit any of the emerging data on schizophrenia. Genetic data, gross and microscopic structural changes in the brain, cerebral blood flow, EEG findings, the seasonality of schizophrenic births—none could be accounted for by theories which postulated that patients' mothers or fathers acted toward them in a particular way. Psychoanalytic theories also predicted things which turned out not to be true. For example, on the basis of psychoanalytic theories one would expect birth order to be a determinant of schizophrenia (e.g., more firstborn sons affected), yet several studies have shown birth order to be irrelevant in determining which child becomes ill. Similarly, psychoanalytic theories predicted that psychoanalysis would be effective therapy for schizophrenia, yet such therapy has been such an utter failure (see chapter 7) that to practice it today on a patient with schizophrenia could be considered malpractice.

Ultimately, however, psychoanalytic theories were discarded on the basis of common sense alone. Any parent who has raised a child knows that parents are not powerful enough to cause a disease like schizophrenia simply by favoring one child over another or giving the child inconsistent messages. Furthermore, families in which one child had become schizophrenic usually contained one or more other children who were perfectly normal; they stood as the final refutation of psychoanalytic theories.

For all these reasons psychoanalytic theories of schizophrenia have been discarded by almost all psychiatrists. When a new book on the psychoanalytic treatment of schizophrenia appeared in 1981, it was overtly ridiculed in the *American Journal of Psychiatry:*

> This book is anomalous, atavistic. While others demonstrate the cerebral pathology of schizophrenia with computerized tomography, Boyer and Giovacchini employ dream analysis to uncover preoedipal symbiotic fusions. Do schizophrenia patients have cerebral atrophy, dilated ventricles, neurological deficits, dementia? No matter, just interpret the transference regression and everything will be set right again. In this netherworld of science fantasy the brains of schizophrenic patients are haunted by partially cathected psychotic introjects that loom menacingly out of the murky darkness, while a hideous throng of primitive, internalized, preoedipal dyads rush out forever and laugh but smile no more.

Family Interaction Theories. Following World War II, traditional psychoanalytic theories of schizophrenia were slowly replaced by family interaction theories. The latter were direct offspring of the psychoanalysts, but in place of what-mother-did-to-baby-at-six-months were introduced concepts about what-mother-*said-to*-son-at-age-12. Mothers were focused upon as the primary pathogenic agents and were said to be "schizophrenogenic." Dr. Trude Tietze, for example, published in 1949 her study of twenty-five mothers of schizophrenic patients. No controls were used. "All mothers," she concluded, "were overanxious and obsessive, all were domineering." She noted that "the majority of mothers were reluctant to discuss their sex life with the psychiatrist" but then went on to conclude: "The mothers' own warped psychosexual development and their own distorted ideas about sex were reflected in their attitude toward their children's sexual development." Ten years later in a standard textbook of psychiatry, psychoanalyst Silvano Arieti estimated that "the majority" of cases of schizophrenia were caused by such mothers.

In 1952 Dr. Theodore Lidz and his colleagues at Yale University began an intensive study of sixteen families of schizophrenic patients. Like Tietze's study, it appears that no controls of any kind were used. Lidz differed from many of his colleagues in claiming that, like mothers, fathers could also be pathogenic cause agents of schizophrenia.

Approximately half the mothers of the patients, said Lidz, are "strange, near-psychotic or overtly schizophrenic," but fathers could exert as well "an extremely noxious or pathogenic influence upon the family and the patient."

In 1956 the "double-bind" was born, destined to become the cornerstone of family interaction theorists. Basically it postulated that schizophrenia arises when parents give their children heads-I-win-tails-you-lose messages. The lead author of the original paper describing this theory was Gregory Bateson, an anthropologist who had undergone Jungian psychoanalysis; Don Jackson, Jay Haley, and John Weakland were also authors. According to a later essay by Bateson, the inspiration for the "double-bind" came from his studies of communications theory, cybernetics, rituals among natives in Papua New Guinea, the communications of dolphins, and Lewis Carroll's *Through the Looking Glass*. No control studies were done and Bateson freely acknowledged that "this hypothesis has not been statistically tested." In fact it never was, and in retrospect the single most important antecedent of the theory appears to have been the thinking of Lewis Carroll.

Family interaction theories of schizophrenia, like psychoanalytic theories, have by now been discarded and for many of the same reasons. Not only did they lack a scientific base, but when controlled studies were done on families of schizophrenic patients by other researchers the family interaction theories failed to hold up. As early as 1951, for example, Prout and White compared the mothers of twenty-five schizophrenic men with the mothers of twenty-five normal men and reported no significant differences; several subsequent studies found the same results. The other major problem with family interaction theories is that they fail to distinguish family interactions which cause schizophrenia from those *caused by* schizophrenia. Clinicians experienced in dealing with schizophrenia are acutely aware of the disruptions to normal family life, including family communications, which can result from having a schizophrenic family member at home.

For all these reasons family interaction theories were set aside by mental health professionals except for a hopelessly out-of-date few who continue to espouse them. Even professionals devoted to the psychotherapy of families have concluded that "a single-minded, family-etiological theory of schizophrenia is now out of the question. . . . The idea that unique family processes cause schizophrenia has been all but discarded by most thoughtful figures in the field." Dr. Steven Hirsch, who has done extensive research on families of schizophrenics in London, similarly concluded that "there is as yet no evidence to support the view that parents bring about, in the formative years, the tendency for their children to become schizophrenic in later life." Family interaction theories have not been *disproved,* of course; as Hirsch notes, "Neither has anyone ever proved that there are no unicorns; one could turn up at any time."

Thomas Szasz. Dr. Szasz, a psychoanalyst in Syracuse, New York, has become well known not for his theory of schizophrenia but rather for his theory of nonschizophrenia. According to Szasz, schizophrenia and other mental disorders are simply semantic artifacts and do not really exist. This will certainly be welcome news to the more than one million individuals afflicted with this disease and to their families. Schizophrenics, says Szasz, have a "fake disease," which is simply "the sacred symbol of psychiatry." To be a true disease, Szasz claims, "it must somehow be capable of being approached, measured, or tested in a scientific fashion."

Szasz' theories deserve refutation only because they have been so widely circulated. Szasz himself conducts a traditional psychoanalytic practice for individuals with problems of living; there is nothing in his writings to suggest that he has any experience with or ever treats patients with schizophrenia. Moreover, schizophrenia is now regularly "approached, measured, or tested in a scientific fashion" and the evidence that schizophrenia is a brain disease is overwhelming. The theories of Thomas Szasz about schizophrenia, therefore, have been relegated to the shelf of quirks of medical history.

Ronald Laing. Dr. R. D. Laing, a British psychoanalyst, achieved considerable fame in the 1960s for his suggestion that schizophrenia may be a healthy response to an insane world and in fact may be a growth experience. His theory was a direct consequence of family interaction theories as explained by Dr. Joseph Berke, one of Laing's followers:

> Long before I ever heard of Mary Barnes, I had begun to realize that what is commonly called "mental illness" is not an "illness" or "sickness" (according to the prevailing medical-psychiatric use of the term), but an example of emotional suffering brought about by a disturbance in a whole field of social relationships, in the first place, the family. In other words, "mental illness" reflects what is happening in a disturbed and disturbing

group of people, especially when internalized in and by a single person. More often than not, a person diagnosed as "mentally ill" is the emotional scapegoat for the turmoil in his or her family or associates, and may, in fact, be the "sanest" member of this group.

The person with schizophrenia is not really sick, but merely acting in a crazy way to ensure his/her survival because of the pressures of the family and/or society.

Laing's theories are romantic nonsense devoid of any scientific basis. Initially several houses were set up in London to allow individuals to experience their psychosis in an atmosphere of love and understanding, but these have gradually closed down from disuse. Laing himself has become uncertain of his theories and in a 1982 interview commented: "I don't think I could pass an exam question on what is R. D. Laing's theory. I was looked to as one who had the answers but I never had them." As far as schizophrenia's being a growth experience for those who must suffer from it, the last word on that theory was provided by Dory Previn, a song-writer and singer who herself had undergone a psychosis: "Insanity is terrific on the 'Late Show' . . . but in the real world it's shit."

THE TRIAL

Theories without a scientific basis are merely statements of belief and therefore enjoy the same scientific plane as philosophies or religions. Mental health professionals often make the mistake of confusing theories with scientific facts, harmless in many instances, but concerning the psychoanalytic, family interaction, and Laingian theories of schizophrenia, not harmless at all. These theories postulated that mothers and fathers cause the disease. When these theories were presented to families of schizophrenic patients as facts, they caused guilt, blame, and all the interfamilial consequences which follow. Nobody will ever know how many marriages dissolved because of this guilt and blame, how much depression resulted, how many suicides took place. My deduction from listening to families is that the costs of these theories-reified-as-facts have been incalculable. It was with this in mind that in 1977 I published "A Fantasy Trial About a Real Issue," and it is here reproduced as originally written.

No trial since Nuremberg had stirred so much public interest. And when the names of the accused were finally made public—more than 100 psychoanalysts, psychiatrists, psychologists, social workers, and others—the crowds became so large that the proceedings had to be switched to JFK Stadium.

The main charge was a serious one—iatrogenic ("induced by medical treatment") anguish. As intoned by the federal prosecutor: "Over a period of more than two decades, the accused did willfully and with forethought but no scientific evidence blame the parents of patients with schizophrenia and autism for their children's condition, thereby causing great anguish, guilt, pain, and suffering by these parents. As healers you broke the cardinal rule; you *caused* suffering when you should have been relieving suffering." It was a class-action suit for the parents of over 1.2 million schizophrenic and autistic patients, and it seemed as if all the parents wanted to attend the trial.

According to the charges, the defendants had blamed the parents for being overprotective, hostile, rejecting, cold, unfit, domineering, irrational, indifferent, schizophrenogenic—in short, malevolent, inhuman mothers and fathers. Charges against Bruno Bettelheim took several hours to read. He was accused of blaming mothers for being inept, and thereby causing autism in some children. The ineptness, Bettelheim said, may begin with the mother's first attempts to feed her child.

R. D. Laing had been extradited from England and was additionally charged with willful obfuscation. As evidence the prosecutor read into the court records passages such as the following:

"In those families of schizophrenics that have been studied in detail, a consistent finding appears to be that there is minimal genuine confirmation of the parents by each other and of the child by each parent, separately or together, but there may not be obvious disconfirmation. One finds, rather, interactions marked by pseudoconfirmations, by acts which masquerade as confirming actions but are counterfeit." The defense maintained that Laing was really a poet, and that his writings should be taken the way we read Lewis Carroll's "Jabberwocky."

The views of Theodore Lidz evoked cries of outrage from the assembled crowd, especially his contentions that parents of schizophrenic children are "narcissistic" and "egocentric."

And so it went, day after day, defendant after defendant. Harry Stack Sullivan, Melanie Klein, Fromm-Reichmann, Jackson, Bateson, Haley, Wynne, Bowen, Searles, Stierlin, Burnham, on and on. Those who had died were tried in absentia. It was rumored that several hundred more, who had told parents they were responsible though they had not published papers on it, were going to be brought to trial at a later date.

The prosecutor made a devastating case. "Why did you extrapolate your theories from so few case histories? Why didn't you use controls? Didn't you know your sample was biased? Why didn't you do prospective studies? Why didn't you take into consideration genetic, biochemical, and neurophysiological research? Weren't you reading your professional journals? Isn't it true that you personally gained prestige and an associate professorship from the promulgation of your theories? Wasn't this all at the expense of the parents?"

The defense based its whole case on ignorance, but ignorance is no defense even for the well-educated.

The jury's verdict was swift and certain: guilty on all counts as charged. In the days before sentencing there was much speculation on what would be appropriate punishment. Some advocated life imprisonment. Others thought that the defendants themselves should have to raise autistic or schizophrenic children. Finally, the sentence was read: "The convicted, for a period of 10 years, shall be forced to read and reread continuously their own writings." Everyone was stunned. Relatives wept openly. Nobody had expected that harsh a sentence.

RECOMMENDED FURTHER READING

Andreasen, N. *The Broken Brain: The Biological Revolution in Psychiatry.* New York: Harper & Row, 1984. Written at a nontechnical level, this is an excellent overview of the neuroscience revolution under way.

Gottesman, I. I., and J. Shields. *Schizophrenia: The Epigenetic Puzzle.* New York: Cambridge University Press, 1982. A summary of genetic theories and data, it assumes some background in biology and genetics.

Helmchen, H., and F. Henn, eds. *Biological Perspectives of Schizophrenia.* Chichester, England: John Wiley and Sons, 1987. These are the collected papers from the Dahlem Conference held in Berlin in late 1986. Many of the papers are valuable overviews of schizophrenia research areas, but they assume some scientific background.

Nasrallah, H. A., and D. R. Weinberger, eds. *The Neurology of Schizophrenia.* Amsterdam: Elsevier, 1986. This is an up-to-date textbook with excellent summaries of the evidence proving that schizophrenia is a brain disease.

Siegler, M., and H. Osmond. *Models of Madness, Models of Medicine.* New York: Macmillan, 1974. The authors of this lucid analysis of the theoretical models for schizophrenia and other mental diseases deal specifically with the psychoanalytic, social, family interaction, conspiratorial, moral and medical models of schizophrenia and show how the medical model best fits both the facts and common sense.

7

THE TREATMENT OF SCHIZOPHRENIA

> To lighten the affliction of insanity by all human means is not to
> restore the greatest of the divine gifts; and those who devote them-
> selves to the task do not pretend that it is. They find their sustainment
> and reward in the substitution of humanity for brutality, kindness for
> maltreatment, peace for raging fury; in the acquisition of love instead
> of hatred; and in the acknowledgment that, from such treatment
> improvement, and hope of final restoration, will come if hope be
> possible.
>
> Charles Dickens, *Household Words*

Contrary to the popular stereotype, schizophrenia is an eminently
treatable disease. That is not to say it is a curable disease, and the
two should not be confused. Successful treatment means the control
of symptoms, whereas cure means the permanent removal of their
causes. Curing schizophrenia will not become possible until we understand its causes; in the meantime we must continue improving its
treatment.

The best disease model to explain schizophrenia is diabetes, a
disease which has many similarities. Both schizophrenia and diabetes
have childhood and adult forms, both almost certainly have more
than one cause, both have relapses and remissions in a course which
often lasts over many years, and both can usually be well controlled,
but not cured, by drugs. Just as we don't talk of curing diabetes but
rather of controlling its symptoms and allowing the diabetic to lead
a comparatively normal life, so we should also do with schizophrenia.

HOW TO FIND A GOOD DOCTOR

There is no easy solution to this problem, one which is most frequently faced by friends and relatives of persons with schizophrenia. There are few doctors in the United States who either know anything about, or have any interest in, schizophrenia. This is both shocking and sad, since it is one of the most important chronic diseases in the world. In Europe, especially the British Isles and Scandinavia, it is somewhat easier to find a good doctor.

Since schizophrenia is a true biological disease, and since drugs are the mainstay of treatment, there is no avoiding the doctor-finding issue. If schizophrenia is to be properly treated, sooner or later a doctor will need to be involved. He or she will be needed not only to prescribe the proper drugs but also to do an initial diagnostic workup, including laboratory tests, in order to rule out other diseases which may be masquerading as schizophrenia. Before the schizophrenia is treated, one had better be certain that it is not really a brain tumor or herpes encephalitis in disguise. Only a doctor can do this.

The best way to find a good doctor for schizophrenia or any other disease is to ask others in the medical profession whom they would send their own family to if they had a similar problem. Doctors and nurses know who the good doctors are and pass the information freely among themselves; often they will tell you if you ask. If your brother-in-law has a sister who is a nurse, all the better. Use every contact and every relative you have, however distant, to locate and identify competent doctors who may know something about schizophrenia. It is an appropriate time to cash in all your IOUs, for the information is invaluable and may save you months of searching.

Another way to find a good doctor is through other families who have a schizophrenic family member. They can often provide a quick rundown of the local resources and save weeks of hunting and false starts. Sharing this information is one of the most valuable assets of organizations of relatives of schizophrenics. These support organizations, which are proliferating rapidly, provide bewildered relatives ready access to others who have faced identical problems and who may have invaluable ideas (see chapter 14 for a detailed account of these organizations and appendix D for a contact person in each state). Without such help one must flounder through the local mental health labyrinth until, by chance, the right resources are identified. The frustrations of such searches are well described by James Wechsler in *In a Darkness* and the Gotkins in *Too Much Anger, Too Many Tears.*

Distinctly *un*helpful in searching for a good doctor are referral lists maintained by local medical societies or the local chapters of the American Psychiatric Association. Anyone can call these organizations and obtain three names. The names, however, are taken from a rotating list of those doctors who are looking for additional patients. Since any doctor who wishes to pay the annual dues can belong to these organizations, there is no screening or ascertainment of quality of any kind. Even those doctors who are under investigation for malpractice will continue to be listed by such organizations until they are specifically removed from membership, which is an all-too-rare occurrence. Thus referral lists from medical and psychiatric societies are really no better than picking a name at random from the physicians' list in the Yellow Pages.

What should one look for in a good doctor who can treat schizophrenia? Ideally he/she should combine technical competence with an interest in the disease and empathy with its sufferers. Training in psychiatry or neurology is helpful but not mandatory; there are some internists and family practitioners who have an interest in schizophrenia and can treat it very competently. As a general rule younger physicians who have been trained recently are more likely to view schizophrenia as a biological disease. However, there are major exceptions to this rule: some older practitioners who will tell you, "I've said all along it was a real disease" and some younger practitioners who still believe that what is needed is psychoanalysis of the mother-child relationship.

In trying to find a good doctor it is perfectly legitimate to ask questions such as "What do you think causes schizophrenia?" and "Do you believe in drugs to treat it?" Such questions will usually elicit the relative biological orientation of the practitioner—or its absence—quite rapidly and save both time and money. The goal is to find a physician who views the schizophrenic, in the words of one psychiatrist, "as a suffering patient, not a defective creation of abstruse, mystical, psychic body parts."

How important is it for the physician to be "board eligible" or "board certified" in his/her specialty? "Board eligible" means that the physician has completed an approved residency program in that specialty. "Board certified" means that the physician has taken and passed an examination in the specialty. Such board examinations are completely optional and are not required for licensure or for membership in any professional organization. They are simply a badge indicating that, at the time the boards were taken, the physician knew the theoretical knowledge required to be competent in that specialty area.

Whether or not the physician has kept up with professional developments since he/she took the board exam is another question. The sciences of neurophysiology, neurochemistry, and neuropharmacology are moving rapidly and physicians who do not read their scientific journals are soon out-of-date; a psychiatrist, for example, who thinks a "free radical" is a released Abbie Hoffman or Daniel Berrigan may be perfectly adequate to do psychotherapy but incompetent to medicate a person with schizophrenia.

Unfortunately, there is relatively little relationship between success in passing board examinations and being a good physician capable of treating any disease, including schizophrenia. I have known many board-certified psychiatrists who were woefully incompetent to treat anyone with schizophrenia, and I have known some physicians—psychiatrists and otherwise—who have never taken board examinations who were excellent. Some physicians have refused to take the board examinations because of the belief that they are irrelevant; others (including me) have refused to take them on the grounds that they should be made mandatory in order to provide consumers with a guaranteed minimal level of knowledge. Until that time comes, it is probably wise for families to seek out "board eligible" (i.e., fully trained) physicians and to further favor those who are "board certified," but not to let this factor be an overriding consideration.

What about nonphysicians for treating schizophrenia? These include psychologists, psychiatric social workers, nurses (especially psychiatric or public health nurses), and mental health counselors of various kinds. These people may be perfectly appropriate for ongoing care of patients with schizophrenia *once* the person has been properly diagnosed by a physician and *if* a physician is overseeing the patient's medications. Such nonphysicians often do a better job of continuing contact and psychiatric assessment since they are usually more available and less hurried than physicians. You do need a medical degree to diagnose persons with schizophrenia and to prescribe drugs for them, but you do not need a medical degree to provide ongoing care. This has been demonstrated many times.

To those looking for a good doctor to treat schizophrenia, one final word of caution. Doctors are human beings and, as such, run a wide range of personality types. Throughout the medical profession can be found occasional physicians who are dishonest, mentally ill, addicted to alcohol or drugs, sociopathic, or who have some combination of the above. I have a sense that psychiatry attracts more than its share of such physicians, often because the physician has become interested in his/her own mental aberrations. Thus one should not make an absolute assumption that physicians who treat persons with schizophrenia are themselves beyond question. If the physician seems strange to you, move on quickly to another. There *are* occasional strange birds in the psychiatric aviary.

SHOULD THE PERSON BE HOSPITALIZED?

In most cases persons *acutely* ill with schizophrenia need to be hospitalized. Such hospitalization accomplishes several things. Most important, it enables mental health professionals to observe the person in a controlled setting. Laboratory tests can be undergone to rule out other medical illnesses which may be causing the symptoms, psychological testing can be done, and medication can be started in an environment in which trained staff can watch for side effects. In addition, the hospitalization often provides the family with a respite from what have often been harrowing days and nights leading up to the acute illness.

Hospitalization is frequently necessary to protect such patients. Some will try to injure themselves or others because of their illness (e.g., their voices tell them to do so). For this reason most hospitals utilize a locked ward for acutely agitated schizophrenics, and its use is often needed. Even in a locked setting the person occasionally may be dangerous and require additional restraints. These may include wrist or ankle restraints (usually made of leather), a special jacket which keeps the arms next to the body (the famous straitjacket of popular lore), or a seclusion room. None of these measures should be necessary for more than a few hours if the person is being properly medicated. It is currently chic in some circles to condemn locked wards and all use of restraints as "barbaric" and antiquated; the people who make such statements have usually never been faced with the task of providing care for persons with acute schizophrenia. It certainly will be nice when we arrive at the point where medications are instantly effective in acutely disturbed patients and restraint is not necessary, but we have not reached that nirvana yet.

There are ancillary benefits of hospitalization for persons with schizophrenia. Well-functioning psychiatric units have group meetings for the patients; this often allows each of them to see that his or her experience is not unique. Occupational therapy, recreational activities, psychodrama, and other forms of group interaction often accomplish the same thing. For someone who has been acutely schizophrenic and who has experienced many of the disturbances described in chapter 2, it is usually a relief to learn that other people have experienced them too. None of the above activities are likely to be of much benefit, however, unless the person is also being properly medicated to relieve the acute symptoms.

There are several different types of hospitals available in which people can be treated for schizophrenia. Psychiatric wards in community hospitals have become increasingly common in recent years and are often satisfactory. Psychiatric wards in university (teaching) hospitals generally have good reputations. Private psychiatric hospitals run a wide gamut from those of excellent reputation to fly-by-night operations in which making a profit is the main incentive and quality of care is often sacrificed. Of special concern are private hospitals which are owned by the psychiatrists themselves; in these instances there is an inherent conflict of interest between the needs of the patient and the need of the psychiatrist to make money. This may be seen, vividly, in the frequent instances in which the length of hospitalization in such hospitals coincides with suspicious closeness with the maximum period covered by the patient's hospitalization insurance. When the insurance runs out, the patient is declared well and discharged.

In addition to community, university, and private hospitals, there are also state and Veterans Administration (VA) hospitals. The VA hospitals are very similar to state hospitals except that only those who have served in the armed forces are eligible for admission to them. State hospitals, by contrast, are open to everyone and run as wide a range in quality as do the private psychiatric hospitals.

In selecting a hospital for treatment, the most important factor by far is the competence of the treating psychiatrist. The type of hospital is relatively insignificant compared with this factor. Thus, in some state hospitals there are well-run wards with a competent psychiatrist offering excellent treatment for schizophrenia; and there are other wards in state hospitals which are still proverbial snake pits. The same can be said for private psychiatric hospitals and VA hospitals. As a general rule, community hospitals and university hospitals offer a more predictably high level of care than state, VA, or private hospitals, but this is not always so. I have treated patients who have received abysmal care in both community and university hospitals.

A measure of hospital quality which has become increasingly useful in recent years is accreditation by the Joint Commission on Accreditation of Hospitals (JCAH) in Chicago. At the invitation of a hospital, JCAH sends a survey team to evaluate it, as well as provide consultation and education. The survey is very thorough, focusing especially on patient care and services but also including such related issues as the therapeutic environment, safety of the patient, quality of staffing, and administration of the hospital. The survey team then recommends that the hospital receive full three-year accreditation, full accreditation with a contingency (which may necessitate a follow-up inspection to ensure that the contingency has been corrected), or no accreditation. Full accreditation by JCAH probably means that the hospital is a good one although, since the accreditation is for the hospital as a whole, there may be individual wards in an accredited hospital which are below standard. The JCAH certification of accreditation is usually displayed by hospitals in the entryway or lobby; alternatively, anyone in the hospital administrator's office can tell you, or you can find out by writing to JCAH, 875 North Michigan Avenue, Chicago, IL 60611. Currently, approximately one-half of the state psychiatric hospitals and three-quarters of the private psychiatric hospitals and general hospitals are accredited.

A yardstick for measuring hospital quality which is *not* very useful is the fees charged. People throughout the world have a strong inclination to equate higher cost with higher quality of medical care, but this is erroneous; in psychiatry, as in the rest of medicine, that which costs more is not necessarily better. Far more important is the JCAH accreditation status.

How, then, should a hospital be chosen? The answer is, again, first to identify a good doctor. Since doctors have admitting privileges in a limited number of hospitals, you will probably have to hospitalize the person where the doctor you choose has access. If you have a choice, because the doctor has more than one hospital affiliation, always opt for a JCAH-accredited facility.

ALTERNATIVES TO HOSPITALIZATION

Hospitalization is usually necessary for schizophrenic patients who are sick for the first time, for the reasons described above. For those who have already been clearly diagnosed and who have relapsed (often because they have stopped taking their medicine), hospitalization can sometimes be avoided. There are several possible alternatives.

One such alternative is the use of drugs given by injection in an emergency room or clinic. A skilled physician can dramatically reduce the psychotic symptoms in approximately half of schizophrenic patients within six to eight hours, thereby allowing the person to return home. One problem with this technique, however, is that frequently the family members are so worn out by the person's recent behavior that *they* need the rest and understandably are not prepared to accept the schizophrenic home again immediately.

Another alternative is the treatment of the schizophrenic patient at home, using public health nurses or, rarely, physicians to make home visits. This technique is used much more often in England, with apparent success. It was also demonstrated to be feasible in a study done in Louisville by Benjamin Pasamanick and his colleagues, who concluded that "the combination of drug therapy and public health nurses' home visitation is *effective* in preventing hospitalization, and that home care is at least as good a method of treatment as hospitalization by any or all criteria, and probably superior by most." It has also been used successfully in the model treatment program in Dane County, Wisconsin, described in chapter 8.

I utilized it once when practicing in a rural village, when the family expressed a wish to keep the person at home if possible; it required home visits for injections twice a day for a week, but it was successful.

The use of partial hospitalization is another good alternative. Day hospitals, in which the patient goes to the hospital for the day and returns home at night, and night hospitals, in which the patient goes to the hospital only to sleep, can both be effective in selected cases. Since both cost less than full hospitalization they may be useful in communities in which they are available. They are usually affiliated with a full-time institution. Unfortunately both are much less available than they should be in the United States. When present, they are inspected by the JCAH accreditation team at the same time as the parent institution is surveyed.

178 SURVIVING SCHIZOPHRENIA

Another theoretical alternative to hospitalization is the use of homes or hostels set up to provide care for acutely psychiatrically disturbed individuals in the community. There are only a handful of such institutions in the United States, but when used they have been shown to be extremely cost-effective compared to hospitalization. A well-known example of this is the southwest Denver program involving "crisis homes" in place of hospitalization; by employing such facilities the use of psychiatric hospital beds in southwest Denver was at one time lower than anywhere in the United States.

A STITCH IN TIME GATHERS NO MOSS

The infusion of foreign medical graduates into American psychiatry cuts across the quest for both a good doctor and the optimum hospital for a patient with schizophrenia. Following World War II, when American-trained psychiatrists abandoned public mental hospitals to go into private practice, states and counties filled the vacuum by importing large numbers of foreign medical graduates. By the late 1970s, when Congress passed a bill restricting the number of foreign medical graduates who could enter the United States, it was estimated that half of all state hospital psychiatrists were foreign medical graduates from developing countries, and in twelve states they comprised over 70 percent of the psychiatric staff. This was a description of Ohio's state institutions in 1979:

Three-fourths of all full-time physicians in the department were foreign-born graduates of foreign medical colleges. Between 1970 and 1975 only four of 29 institutions had been able to recruit and retain a full-time psychiatrist who graduated from an American medical college. Only five of the 29 institutions had full-time physicians who had graduated from an American medical college within the past 14 years. Eighty-eight of 94 psychiatric residents in training were foreign-born graduates of foreign medical colleges.

Only one of the full-time U.S. medical college graduates in the department was under age 40, and 35 percent of all full-time physicians were older than 60. Two institutions had no physician under the age of 65. Forty-one physicians practicing in the department had no Ohio license. Thus the department for years had been almost totally unable to recruit graduates of U.S. medical colleges. It was surviving almost entirely with foreign graduates and U.S. graduates recruited many years ago.

Fortunately, since that time the Ohio state psychiatric system has improved dramatically, but in many states the number of foreign medical graduates in psychiatry remains high and problems have been well documented.

Some excellent foreign medical graduates are making major contributions to the care of schizophrenic patients. I have worked with such doctors and been in many communities where psychiatrists who were foreign medical graduates were the most competent and respected for treating schizophrenia. There is evidence, however, that others are mediocre at best and in some cases incompetent. Some have had no training whatsoever in psychiatry yet are allowed to practice as psychiatrists by the state. The two foreign medical schools which contributed the greatest number of psychiatrists to American state hospitals both had very low pass rates on the Education Council for Foreign Medical Graduates (ECFMG) examination. Some of the foreign graduates who cannot pass basic licensing exams are given special exemptions by the state to practice only in the state institutions. In essence the state is saying that it does not consider them competent to treat the "worried well" in private practice but will accept them if they treat the truly sick in the state hospitals.

The most disturbing aspect of utilizing large numbers of foreign medical graduates to treat America's schizophrenic patients is the inevitable difficulties in communication. Verbal language skill is only one part of this; beyond it are many other levels of communication which involve nonverbal language, shared ideals and values, and other components of what is called culture. Communication between a psychiatrist and a schizophrenic is difficult enough even when they share a common language and culture; when they do not share these things, communication becomes virtually impossible. Delusions must be assessed in the context of the patient's culture. Affect which may appear appropriate within one culture context may be inappropriate within another. The evaluation of subtle disorders of thinking assumes a complete command of the idioms and metaphors of a language. One psychiatrist, for example, argued for an increase in medication for a patient who complained about "butterflies in her stomach." Another used as evidence of a patient's delusions the fact that she had talked of "babies coming from birds." "Do you mean storks?" asked the psychologist present. "Yes, that's the one," exclaimed the psychiatrist. "Isn't that crazy!" Still another foreign-trained psychiatrist was observed asking a schizophrenic patient the following proverb during a diagnostic interview: "What does mean, a stitch in time gathers no moss?" That kind of question inspires neither confidence nor clarity of thought in a person with schizophrenia.

COMMITMENT PROCEDURES: HOW TO GET
SOMEONE INTO A HOSPITAL

It is ideal when people with schizophrenia recognize that they are becoming sick and voluntarily seek treatment for their sickness. Unfortunately, however, this is often not the case. Schizophrenia is a disease of the brain, the body organ charged with the responsibility of recognizing sickness and the need for treatment—the same organ which is sick. Out of this unfortunate coincidence arises the frequent need for schizophrenic persons to be committed to psychiatric treatment settings against their will.

How does the commitment process work? All laws governing commitment of psychiatric patients are state laws, not federal laws. Therefore commitment laws vary from state to state, especially those governing long-term commitment. In addition, commitment is a legal area very much in flux, and the laws are currently being amended in several states. To keep up with developments in this field it is recommended that the *Mental Disability Law Reporter* be consulted; this is a bimonthly publication of the American Bar Association (see appendix B).

Legally there are two rationales for the commitment of mental patients. The first is referred to as *parens patriae* and is the right of the state to act as parent and protect a disabled person; it arose in early English law from the belief that the king was the father of all his subjects. The second is the right of the state to protect other people from a person who is dangerous. The first right may be invoked when persons are so disabled that they do not recognize their own need for treatment or cannot provide for their own basic needs and therefore may be dangerous to themselves. The second may be invoked when persons, because of their mental illness, are dangerous to other people.

The legal and ethical ramifications of commitment procedures are manifold and complex. Some of the ethical issues will be covered in chapter 11; this chapter will focus more on the actual mechanics of getting a person committed to a hospital and getting him or her out again. It should be noted, however, that there was a broad swing from 1970 to 1980 toward changes in state laws that made the commitment of mental patients more difficult. In particular there was a move to narrow the use of *parens patriae* in many states and a reliance on stricter "dangerousness" criteria instead. Since it is well known that the ability of psychiatrists to accurately predict dangerousness is very poor, this swing, in effect, ensured that fewer psychiatric patients would be committable. The move to narrow commitment criteria was spearheaded by lawyers concerned about individual civil liberties. Given past abuses of commitment procedures, the changes were brought about relatively easily in most states. What nobody pointed out in the process, however, was that the changes would also make it impossible to get many sick individuals back into treatment before they had demonstrated their dangerousness to self or others. Because of this there has been the beginning of a shift back toward reliberalizing commitment criteria in some states, with the State of Washington leading the way in 1979. The struggle over commitment criteria continues to be an important issue and is not likely to be resolved to the satisfaction of all in the near future.

There are two kinds of commitment—emergency and long-term. The basic purpose of commitment laws is to enable persons who are psychiatrically ill to be put forcibly into hospitals so that they will not harm themselves or others and can be treated. This can be done as follows:

1. A petition for commitment of the person thought to be psychiatrically ill must be initiated. In most states this can be done by one of several persons; for example, Tennessee allows petitions to be filed by "the parent, guardian, spouse, or a responsible adult relative of the individual or by any licensed physician or licensed psychologist or by any health or public welfare officer, or by the head of any institution in which the individual may be, or by any officer authorized to make arrests in Tennessee."

2. The person initiating the petition asks a physician (not necessarily a psychiatrist) to examine the person for whom commitment is sought. Some states require two physicians to be exam-

iners while others allow psychologists. If the examiner(s) conclude that the person is mentally ill and meets the grounds for commitment in that state, then the examiners' report is attached to the petition and it is filed.

3. The examination may take place anywhere, including in the person's home.

4. If the person for whom commitment is sought refuses to be examined, many states have a provision for the petitioner to file a sworn written statement. In, for example, Nevada, this says, "such person is mentally ill and, because of such illness, is likely to harm himself or others, or is gravely disabled."

5. Once the petition has been filed, a police officer can bring the person to the hospital for examination by a psychiatrist.

6. Alternatively, if any person is acting strangely in public, a police officer can bring the person to the hospital for examination by a psychiatrist.

7. The examining psychiatrist at the hospital decides on the basis of his/her examination whether the person meets the criteria for commitment in that state. If the person does, emergency commitment is effected and the person is kept at the hospital. If not, the person is released.

8. An emergency commitment lasts for seventy-two hours in most states, not including weekends and holidays. At the end of that period the person must be released unless either the director of the hospital or the family has filed a petition with the court asking for long-term commitment. If this has been filed, then the person can be held until the hearing.

9. The hearing for long-term commitment may be held in a room in the hospital or in a courtroom. The person alleged to be mentally ill is expected to be present unless a psychiatrist testifies that the person's presence would be detrimental to his/her mental state. The person is represented by a lawyer appointed by the state if necessary, and normal judicial rules of evidence and due process apply. Testimony may be taken from the examining psychiatrist, from family members, and from the person alleged to be mentally ill.

10. The hearing is held before a mental health commission, judge, or similar judicial authority depending on the state. In nineteen states the person has the right to a jury trial if he/she so wishes.

The major differences in commitment procedures among states are the grounds which are used for commitment and the standard of proof. In states that utilize only dangerousness to self or others and define dangerousness stringently, it is generally more difficult to get a commitment than in states which define dangerousness vaguely (for example, Texas laws say a mentally ill person can be committed "for his own welfare and protection or the protection of others"). Similarly, in states in which "gravely disabled" or "in need of treatment" are grounds for commitment by themselves, it may be easier to get a commitment.

The standard of proof utilized by states is also a major source of variation. The most stringent level of proof is "beyond a reasonable doubt," the same standard used to judge persons charged with crimes. Currently eight states utilize this (California, Hawaii, Kansas, Kentucky, Massachusetts, New Hampshire, Oklahoma, and Oregon). If all other things are equal (see below), then it should be theoretically more difficult to commit a mentally ill person in these states. A lesser level of proof is "clear and convincing evidence," which is utilized in the rest of the states. In 1979 the United States Supreme Court ruled that the use of "clear and convincing evidence" was an acceptable level of proof under the Constitution and that "beyond a reasonable doubt" could be utilized by individual states if desired but was not required. The ruling in effect says that the same level of proof is not required to commit a person to a mental hospital as is required to convict a person of a crime and commit him/her to jail. Civil rights lawyers interested in the mentally ill continue to fight for more stringent standards of proof, whereas many psychiatrists and families of schizophrenics would prefer to see the standard of proof remain more flexible.

In the past some states utilized standards of proof more lenient than "clear and convincing evidence." Texas, New Jersey, and Mississippi, for example, required only "a mere preponderance of the evidence" for a person to be involuntarily committed; this was generally interpreted to mean that the evidence on each side was added up and the side with the "preponderance of the evidence" won. Since the 1979 Supreme Court ruling, however, these states have had to adopt stricter criteria.

Probably the most important variables in determining how easy or difficult it is to commit psychiatric patients to hospitals are the specific judge involved and the local community standards. As lawyers well know, laws are written one way but can be interpreted in many ways, and this is certainly true for those concerned with psychiatric commitment. Thus in the same state one judge may interpret dangerousness much more stringently than another, and what for one judge is "clear and convincing evidence" is for another judge not at all persuasive. The standards of the community vary as well, with some localities more inclined to "lock up all those crazies" whereas another part of the same state may be reluctant to commit people unless absolutely necessary. Also important is the current local milieu. For example, if a former psychiatric patient has recently been accused of murder in the local newspaper, the tendency may be to commit everyone with acute symptoms. If, on the other hand, the local newspaper is doing an exposé on the poor conditions in the state hospital, the tendency may be to commit nobody unless absolutely necessary.

What does all this mean for a family with a schizophrenic member who is in need of treatment and who refuses to go to the hospital? It means that the family must first learn the commitment procedures and criteria which apply in that state. The quickest way to do this is to telephone or visit the admission unit of the nearest state psychiatric hospital, whose personnel are usually experts in this area. Other potential resources for this information are the local or state Department of Mental Health, public defenders, psychiatrists, or policemen. The family must also know what kinds of evidence are necessary and admissible to prove dangerousness. Are threats to other people sufficient, or does the person actually have to have injured someone? Families who wish to can usually testify at the commitment hearing, and their knowledge of what proof is necessary will often determine whether the person with schizophrenia is or is not committed. Indeed, many persons with schizophrenic family members have become amateur lawyers in order to survive!

COMMITMENT PROCEDURES: HOW TO GET SOMEONE OUT OF A HOSPITAL

The other side of the commitment coin is protection of people's rights and getting those who have been committed out of the hospital. There is no question that commitment laws were too liberal prior to 1960 and that they were abused. Popular psychiatric literature abounded with horror stories of people committed indefinitely to mental hospitals on the strength of one person's signature.

Thanks to reformers in this field, especially Bruce Ennis of the American Civil Liberties Union and Paul Friedman and Charles Halpern of the Mental Health Law Project, all this changed. Psychiatric patients increasingly have the rights to counsel, the rights to a jury trial, and the rights to appeal which are guaranteed to other people before they are involuntarily incarcerated. This is the way it should be. The current push and pull between those fighting for more commitments and those fighting for fewer is a healthy struggle and a sign that the democratic process is well. For those who wish to keep up with the blow-by-blow account of this struggle, subscriptions to *Mental Disability Law Reporter* will be more than sufficient.

Psychiatric patients who are being, or have been, committed have several safeguards. Initially they can demand a "probable cause" hearing in some states, which is a preliminary assessment of whether the person should be held beyond the seventy-two-hour provision of the emergency commitment. This hearing can be conducted before a judge. The actual legal proceedings determining commitment are usually held before a mental health commission (a mixture of lawyers and psychiatrists) or a judge. In many states the patient now has the right to a jury trial, a right which should be extended to all states. Other basic legal safeguards, such as written advance notice of proceedings, prompt hearings, the right to be present at all proceedings, the right to call witnesses, the right to appeal, and the right to periodic review of all commitments, should also become incorporated into the laws of all states. Persons who have been committed, or relatives or friends on their behalf, may also petition for a writ of habeas corpus to question the legality of detention and request the court for release.

Most important is the right to be represented and defended by a lawyer at all commitment hearings. In the past this was often a sham, with the patient's lawyer not defending him/her at all. In recent years, with the growth of legal advocacy for the poor and of public defenders, this has improved dramatically. There now exist in many parts of the United States legal organizations specializing in defending the rights of mental patients. Some of these are public defender units funded by the local government or the Department of Justice. Others are local units of the National Legal Services Corporation, an independent federal corporation which underwent some reduction in funding during the Reagan administration but which continues to provide legal services for the poor. Still others are small groups of independent lawyers who have developed a special interest in the legal problems of psychiatric patients. For a patient with schizophrenia, or a relative or friend interested in the legal defense of such patients, the best way to identify the local resources is to telephone the local bar association. In addition, lists of these organizations on a state-by-state basis can be ordered from the National Legal Aid and Defender Association, 1625 K Street, N.W., Washington, D.C. 20006.

ANTIPSYCHOTIC DRUGS

Once a competent doctor has been located and the intricacies of hospitalization have been mastered, then the treatment of schizophrenia becomes comparatively simple. Drugs are the most important treatment for schizophrenia, just as they are the most important treatment for many physical diseases of the human body. Drugs do not *cure,* but rather *control,* the symptoms of schizophrenia—as they do those of diabetes. The drugs we now have to treat schizophrenia are far from perfect, but they work most of the time for most of the people with the disease if they are used correctly.

The main drugs used to treat schizophrenia are usually called antipsychotics. They have also been called neuroleptics and major tranquilizers, but the best term is "antipsychotic" because that is what they are. They frequently do not produce tranquilization, so that term is a misnomer. We do not know precisely how they work, but we suspect it is through their ability to block dopamine receptors in the brain. They also block receptors for norepinephrine, acetylcholine, and probably other neurotransmitters as well. The antipsychotic drugs were discovered in 1952 in France; chlorpromazine (Thorazine) was the first such drug discovered.

Five different chemical families of antipsychotic drugs are used in the United States—phenothiazines, thioxanthines, butyrophenones, dibenzoxazepines, and dihydroindolones (tables 1 and 2). The drugs in each family are listed by their generic name (the official name for that chemical compound), and their trade names (the brand names used by drug companies for that product; e.g., Thorazine and Largactil are both chlorpromazine, exactly the same drug chemically, though marketed by two different drug companies under their own registered trade names).

Antipsychotic drugs are usually given as tablets or liquid. Tablets

Table 1

Types of Antipsychotic Drugs

Type	Generic Name	Trade (Brand) Names
Aliphatic phenothiazines	chlorpromazine	Thorazine, Largactil, and others
	triflupromazine	Vesprin
Piperidine phenothiazines	thioridazine	Mellaril
	mesoridazine	Serentil
Piperazine phenothiazines	fluphenazine	Prolixin, Permitil
	trifluoperazine	Stelazine and others
	perphenazine	Trilafon, Phenazine
	prochlorperazine	Compazine
	acetophenazine	Tindal
Thioxanthines	thiothixene	Navane
	chlorprothixene	Taractan
Butyrophenones	haloperidol	Haldol
	pimozide	Orap
	droperidol	Inapsine
Dibenzoxazepines	loxapine	Loxitane, Daxolin
Dihydroindolones	molindone	Moban

can be taken once a day and are more effective if taken on an empty stomach. If ingested at the same time as antacids containing aluminum or magnesium (information that appears on the lists of ingredients on their labels), their effectiveness is reduced. Some people believe that washing them down with tea or coffee also reduces their effectiveness, but recent studies have not supported this idea. Tablets may usually be crushed for ease of administration. In addition, a liquid form of many of the antipsychotic drugs can be mixed with juice and may be useful if there is doubt whether the patient is really swallowing the tablets; the liquid form is usually more expensive. Many of these drugs can also be given as a short-acting intramuscular injection, and two (fluphenazine and haloperidol) can be given as long-acting injections which need be given only every one to four weeks. Such long-acting injections are extremely useful for individuals who find it difficult (or refuse) to take pills; they have to return to the clinic for another injection only once every few weeks in order to stay well. Injections are usually given in the buttocks, although they may be given in the arm if preferred.

The efficacy of antipsychotic drugs is well-established. Studies show that approximately 70 percent of patients with schizophrenia clearly improve on these drugs, 25 percent improve minimally or not

Table 2

Equivalent Doses of Antipsychotic Drugs

The following list of antipsychotic drugs by drug equivalency is only approximate. Fluphenazine and haloperidol, the most potent (and among the most used), are taken as the baseline. To find out what an equivalent dose of another drug is, multiply by the number indicated. Thus 10 milligrams of fluphenazine is approximately equivalent to 20 milligrams of thiothixene (× 2), 50 milligrams of molindone (× 5), 100 milligrams of acetophenazine (× 10), 150 milligrams of mesoridazine (× 15), and 200 milligrams of chlorpromazine (× 20).

Generic Name	Trade (Brand) Names
Baseline	
fluphenazine	Prolixin, Permitil
haloperidol	Haldol
Multiply × 2	
thiothixene	Navane
trifluoperazine	Stelazine and others
Multiply × 5	
perphenazine	Trilafon, Phenazine
molindone	Moban
loxapine	Loxitane, Daxolin
Multiply × 10	
prochlorperazine	Compazine
triflupromazine	Vesprin
acetophenazine	Tindal
Multiply × 15	
mesoridazine	Serentil
chlorprothixene	Taractan
Multiply × 20	
thioridazine	Mellaril
chlorpromazine	Thorazine and others

NOTE: Adapted from R. I. Shader, ed., *Manual of Psychiatric Therapeutics* (Boston: Little, Brown & Co., 1975); J. M. Davis, "Comparative Doses and Costs of Antipsychotic Medication," *Archives of General Psychiatry* 33 (1976): 858–61; and R. J. Baldessarini, "The Neuroleptic Antipsychotic Drugs," *Postgraduate Medicine* 65 (1979): 108–19. Differences among the authors were averaged.

at all, and 5 percent get worse. This is approximately the same level of effectiveness that penicillin exerts in pneumonia or streptomycin in tuberculosis. Antipsychotic drugs reduce symptoms of the disease, shorten the stay in the hospital, and reduce the chances of rehospitalization dramatically. Whereas persons with schizophrenia entering a psychiatric hospital used to stay for several weeks or months, the average stay with these drugs is now reduced to days. And the data on their preventing rehospitalization are even more impressive. John Davis, for example, reviewed twenty-four scientifically controlled studies testing whether antipsychotic drugs were effective. All twenty-four studies found that schizophrenic persons who took antipsychotic drugs were less likely to have to return to the hospital than those who did not take these drugs. The differences between the two groups were highly significant, especially for persons with chronic schizophrenia. On the average, a person who takes the drugs has a 3-out-of-5 chance (60 percent) of not being rehospitalized, whereas the person who does not take the drugs has only a 1-out-of-5 chance (20 percent) of not being rehospitalized.

When studies have been done on the long-acting, injectable form of antipsychotics (where compliance in taking the drug is assured), the results are even more impressive. In one study of chronic schizophrenic patients, only 8 percent of the patients who were taking the drug relapsed within one year, but 68 percent of those not taking the drug relapsed. In another study of schizophrenic patients taking injectable antipsychotics, 80 percent relapsed within two years when the drug was stopped. What all this means is that though taking the drugs does not guarantee you will *not* get sick again, and not taking the drugs does not guarantee you *will* get sick again, their use improves the odds toward staying out of the hospital tremendously. The data on the effectiveness of drugs are so clear that any physician or psychiatrist who fails to try them on a person with schizophrenia is probably incompetent. It is not that drugs are the *only* ingredient necessary to treat schizophrenia successfully; they are just the most essential ingredient.

Antipsychotic drugs are not equally effective for all the symptoms of schizophrenia. They are most effective at reducing delusions, hallucinations, aggressive or bizarre behavior, thinking disorders, and the symptoms having to do with the overacuteness of the senses—the so-called "positive" symptoms. For example, against auditory hallucinations, one of the most common and disabling symptoms of schizophrenia, antipsychotic drugs are 80 to 90 percent effective in being able to relieve the hallucinations, usually making them disappear altogether. The drugs have less efficacy (sometimes none) against symptoms such as apathy, ambivalence, poverty of thought, and flattening of the emotions—the "negative" symptoms.

In using antipsychotic drugs to treat schizophrenia, several factors must be kept in mind. These may be grouped under the following headings.

General Principles

Dose Variability.   It has become clear in recent years that people require widely varying doses for these drugs to be effective. This is probably a genetic trait and is not surprising in view of how differently our bodies handle other chemical compounds. One ounce of alcohol will make one person intoxicated and will not even be felt by another. Similarly, when 20 milligrams a day of fluphenazine was given to a group of schizophrenic patients and then the blood level of the drug was measured, the difference between the lowest and highest blood level was *fortyfold*. The absorption and excretion of antipsychotic drugs varies widely from person to person, so that one patient requires 10 milligrams and another patient 400 milligrams to achieve identical blood levels. In another experiment into the same phenomenon, some patients with schizophrenia proved to need *thirty-two times* more fluphenazine than other patients to produce a similar blood level of the drug.

The practical implications of this dose variability is that both physicians and patients must be flexible in thinking about dosage. Minidoses may suffice for some patients, with as little as 1 mg. a day of fluphenazine, haloperidol, or thiothixene keeping them well. And long-acting injectable fluphenazine doses as low as 1.25 mg. every two weeks have proved effective in some patients. On the other end of the spectrum, some patients with schizophrenia require megadoses of antipsychotic drugs in order to achieve a blood level which will be effective. Daily megadoses of haloperidol 270 mg., thiothixene 480 mg., and loxapine 500 mg. are described in the psychiatric literature, and I personally have had patients who failed to respond at daily doses of less than fluphenazine 150 mg. or chlorpromazine 3,000 mg. One well-known psychiatric researcher in New York claims to have had a patient take as much as 1,200 mg. a day of fluphenazine by mouth—and the patient continued working as a taxi driver! For long-acting injectable fluphenazine, Dr. Sven Dencker in Sweden has used weekly injectable doses of 900 mg. on rare treatment-resistant patients with good results; he has followed such patients for over ten years and reports no more side effects from the megadoses than from standard doses. Dr. Dencker's top dose is *over 1,400 times* the minidoses found to be effective in other patients. The findings on dose variability also suggest that many patients who received drugs failed to respond because the drug was administered in too low a dosage. This information conflicts with a presently popular stereotype of mental hospitals which portrays all the patients as being overmedicated. The truth is quite the opposite, and in every state hospital I have been in I find at least five *under-medicated* patients with schizophrenia for every one who is overmedicated.

But stereotypes die slow deaths, and the image of the overmedicated, "zonked-out," "zombied" schizophrenic patient is a very strong one. It has its principal origin in the fact that the *symptoms* of schizophrenia are often confused with the *effects* of the drugs used in its treatment. Thus when families see their schizophrenic relatives sitting lethargically, apathetic, ambivalent, and suffering poverty of thought, they assume that the drugs made them that way. All one has to do to prove this is not so is to talk with anyone who had to care for schizophrenic patients *before* antipsychotic drugs were introduced in the 1950s; you will invariably be told that *more* patients were "zonked-out" in the old days.

This is not to say that antipsychotic drugs are never abused or that patients are not sometimes overmedicated for the convenience of the hospital staff who want to calm them down. These things certainly do happen. But stereotypes to the contrary, this problem is relatively minor in the treatment of schizophrenia, compared with the number of patients who have never been given an adequate trial of available medications.

Trial and Error. There is currently no way to predict which drug is best for which person with schizophrenia, and the only way to find out is by trial and error. Three clues to predicting response should be noted, however. First, if a person responds well to a certain drug one time, then he/she is likely always to respond well to that drug. Second, if another person in the same family has been psychiatrically ill and responded well to a certain drug, then other members of the same family who become ill will probably respond well to that drug. This suggests that there is a genetic predisposition to how well one responds to these drugs. Third, at least two groups of investigators have shown that if the person with schizophrenia has a very unpleasant subjective reaction (called a dysphoric effect) to the first dose of the medication, then the chances of the person's ultimately responding favorably to this medication are low.

At a practical level, every person with schizophrenia or the family members should keep a list of which drugs they have been tried on, what dosage level (i.e., how many milligrams), and what the response was. This can be extremely helpful and save weeks of trial-and-error medications in future treatment.

Persons with schizophrenia who do not respond to one type of drug at all may respond well to another type of drug, a very important fact. This is true even of those schizophrenic patients who have been sick for many years. I have treated patients who have been given chlorpromazine for twenty years with poor results and who, once they were switched to another type of drug such as haloperidol, improved dramatically. It is one of the major tragedies of schizophrenia that in the state hospitals the newer types of antipsychotic drugs have not been tried on many patients; some of them would certainly respond and some could then be released from the hospital. Patients and families of patients with this disease should insist that the treating physician or psychiatrist try each of the major types of antipsychotic agents. And if the doctor switches the patient from one drug to another drug of the same family (e.g., from fluphenazine to trifluoperazine), then he/she probably doesn't know what he is doing because, with rare exceptions, switching to different drugs within the same drug family makes no sense at all. Such treatment suggests that it is time to look for a new physician.

Continuous vs. Intermittent Medication.   Until recent years it was assumed that most individuals with schizophrenia needed to take antipsychotic medication continuously for many years. Several groups of researchers, however, are now exploring the possibility that some patients can stop medication and resume it only when signs and symptoms of the disease begin to recur. It is not yet clear what percentage of patients can do this without serious relapses; they must be motivated to seek care and a well-organized system of psychiatric services must be in place. Preliminary studies suggest that at least half of all patients with schizophrenia might be able to go on intermittent medication if such services were available. This would be especially useful to patients for whom the medication's side effects had proved troublesome.

How Long Drugs Should Be Continued.   If a person has had an initial episode of schizophrenia and recovered, it is known that one-quarter of such individuals will not get sick again and will not need medication. There is currently no way to identify for certain which patients fall into that group. Within a few weeks following recovery, therefore, medication should be slowly decreased and then discontinued.

The three-quarters who eventually relapse will again be treated with medication. For this group, medication should probably be continued for several months after recovery. If patients relapse a third time, then it is known that they will need the medication, continuously or intermittently, for several years, and I encourage them to think of themselves as similar to a diabetic who needs insulin. In summary, then: first episode, continue medications for several weeks; second episode, for several months; and third episode, for several years.

As persons with schizophrenia age, can they reduce and eventually discontinue their medication? Many can do so in their forties or fifties, and most can do so by their sixties. Usually the older a person gets, the lower the required dose of antipsychotic medication.

Abuse and Addiction to Antipsychotic Drugs. The abuse of antipsychotic drugs to achieve a "high" is extremely rare and has been reported only for loxapine. Antipsychotic drugs do not produce a pleasant or euphoric effect on normal people. I have had street-wise patients try to sell them and I always tell them: "If you can find somebody who will buy these from you, tell them I'll gladly give them an additional supply free because they undoubtedly need them."

In terms of addiction to antipsychotic drugs, this is unknown. The person's body does not slowly get used to them and therefore require higher and higher doses, and the stopping of these drugs does not usually cause withdrawal symptoms. Antipsychotic drugs for schizophrenia are exactly the same as insulin for diabetes or digitalis for heart failure—they are drugs needed by the body to restore the functioning of the respective organs (brain, pancreas, and heart) to more normal levels.

Patients Who Get Worse. Despite the fact that antipsychotic drugs are extremely useful for the majority of people afflicted with schizophrenia, it must be remembered that a small percentage of patients—approximately 1 in 20—will have their symptoms made worse by these drugs. In such cases it is worth trying other drugs such as lithium and carbamazepine (see pages 210–13).

Polypharmacy. Until recent years it was considered bad medicine to give more than one medication to a person with schizophrenia.

Called polypharmacy, it was regarded with derision by most mental health professionals; this attitude disappeared with the realization that some patients with schizophrenia do best on combinations of medications. Examples of combinations now frequently employed include an antipsychotic plus an anticholinergic plus lithium, or an antipsychotic plus lithium plus an antidepressant, or an antipsychotic plus lithium plus propranolol (to counteract akathisia—see pages 196–97).

Side Effects

"The antipsychotic agents," says Dr. Ross J. Baldessarini, "are among the safest drugs available in medicine." As one of the foremost experts on these drugs, Dr. Baldessarini should know, yet his claim is at variance with popular stereotypes of the drugs. It is widely believed that antipsychotic drugs have terrible side effects, are dangerous, and almost invariably produce tardive dyskinesia (involuntary muscle movements) and other irreversible conditions which may be worse than the original schizophrenia.

Dr. Baldessarini is in fact correct, and the popular stereotype is wrong. Antipsychotic drugs are among the safest group of drugs known. It is almost impossible to commit suicide with them by overdosing, and their serious side effects are comparatively rare.

Then why is there such a strong misperception and fear of these drugs? Much of the reason can be traced to theories of causation of the disease. As we have noted, it is only in the past few years that the evidence for schizophrenia's being a real biological disease has become clear. The resistance to this idea among mental health professionals trained in the psychoanalytic or other psychogenic belief systems has been impressive. And one of the ways this resistance is shown is by strongly opposing the use of drugs; implicitly, if the drugs are too dangerous to be used, then schizophrenic patients will again have to rely on psychotherapy and other nondrug modes of treatment. For this reason it is not uncommon to find psychiatrists—who should be better informed—warning schizophrenic patients about all kinds of terrible calamities which will befall them if they take antipsychotic drugs.

This is *not* to say that antipsychotic drugs are perfectly safe and have no side effects whatsoever. They do have side effects, sometimes so severe that the drug must be stopped. The side effects have on occasion even been fatal, but this is very rare. One of the main goals of the current search for newer antipsychotic drugs is to find effective compounds which will continue to suppress psychotic symptoms while producing minimal undesirable side effects. But it is important to repeat that the point to be remembered is that antipsychotic drugs, as a group, are one of the safest groups of drugs in common use and are the greatest advance in the treatment of schizophrenia which has occurred to date.

The side effects of antipsychotic drugs can be discussed as a group. Some side effects are more common with particular drugs, but the differences are not great. And, like side effects to all drugs used in medicine, it is not possible to predict with any accuracy which person is likely to get which side effect. The side effects can be divided into five types: common and less serious; uncommon and less serious; common and more serious; uncommon and serious; and tardive dyskinesia.

Common and Less Serious. In this category are many side effects which people complain of when first starting to use these drugs. The most common are dry mouth, constipation, and blurring of vision. Drowsiness occurs commonly with the aliphatic and piperidine phenothiazines (see table 1, page 187) but much less commonly with the other types. These side effects usually diminish or go away altogether after the first few weeks of use.

More frightening to the patient and his/her family is a side effect called a dystonic reaction. It usually occurs within the first few days after beginning antipsychotic drug therapy, is more common in younger people and in men, and consists of the stiffening of muscles on one side of the neck and jaw. Usually the neck becomes rigid so it cannot turn, talking becomes difficult because of stiffening of the tongue, and occasionally it also affects the eye muscles, causing the eyes to look upward. This side effect can be reversed within minutes by giving the patient an anticholinergic drug such as benztropine (Cogentin), biperiden (Akineton), procyclidine (Kemadrin), or trihexyphenidyl (Artane), or by giving diphenhydramine or diazepam (Valium). Dystonic reactions can also be prevented by giving anticholinergic drugs prophylactically (see pages 209–10).

Uncommon and Less Serious. Side effects in this category are seen less often than the above. Menstrual changes in women can be caused by antipsychotic drugs; discharge from the breasts can also occur. Both are caused by the effect of the drugs on the pituitary gland and may be annoying, but they are rarely so serious that the drugs must be stopped. Loss of appetite and increased salivation are other uncommon and nonserious side effects.

Changes in sexual functioning definitely occur as a side effect of antipsychotic drugs, but both their frequency and their seriousness are matters of dispute. Decreased sexual desire may be found in both sexes and impotence or retrograde ejaculation may occur in men; the latter occurs especially with thioridazine (Mellaril). It is difficult to evaluate how many of these effects are due to the drugs, how many are due to the schizophrenia, and how many antedated the disease altogether. For example, impotence is a common condition among men, and it is obviously inaccurate to blame all impotence in men who take antipsychotic drugs on these medications. There is a general consensus among clinicians that thioridazine (Mellaril) is most likely to cause sexual problems as a side effect, and some belief (although unproven) that molindone (Moban) and loxapine (Loxitane) are least likely to do so.

It is similarly difficult to evaluate the seriousness of these symptoms since sexual functioning varies so widely in people who do not have schizophrenia. For some people with comparatively little interest in sex, the decreased libido from antipsychotic drugs may not even be noticed. For others it may be a disaster of monumental proportions and they may insist on stopping the drugs for that reason. I had one patient, for example, who definitely was impotent when he took antipsychotic drugs and who became acutely psychotic whenever he did not. He was faced with a painful dilemma; the role of the physician in such cases should be to outline the choices and consequences as clearly as possible and then support the person's choice. This kind of dilemma is fortunately not common.

Common and More Serious. The most common serious side effects of antipsychotic drugs are restlessness (called akathisia), stiffness and diminished spontaneity (called akinesia), slurring of speech, and tremors of the hands or feet. Although they are in no way life-threatening to the patient, they may be subjectively very unpleasant. Psychiatrists and other mental health professionals often minimize these symptoms but it is important to recognize how unpleasant they may be for the patient. Akathisia may be so uncomfortable that the patient considers suicide, tremors may interfere with simple acts such as brushing teeth or writing a letter, and akinesia may rob life of its spontaneity. Akinesia is especially difficult to evaluate because it includes not only stiffness but also diminished spontaneity of physical movements, gestures, and speech. As such it may be indistinguishable from residual schizophrenic symptoms in the patient or demoralization and depression as a reaction to illness. It takes an experienced clinician to evaluate such side effects, and the relationship between the patient and the physician is critical in this evaluation; the better the physician knows the patient, the easier and more accurate such evaluations become. These symptoms are often the reason that patients with schizophrenia discontinue antipsychotic medications despite the fact that to an outsider they seem much better on the medications. Mental health professionals must ask about such side effects and listen carefully to patients such as the following:

> I am unfortunate in feeling quite seriously affected, with symptoms ranging from a dry mouth and blurred vision to a terrible tension and restlessness and fears of "losing myself" completely and being entirely controlled by the drugs. These feelings are often hard to appreciate, and therefore doctors are inclined to prescribe medication without really being aware of the implications for the patient. . . . Somehow I think I prefer to be a little bit "mad" than overdosed by major tranquilizers.

Another patient felt the antipsychotic drugs had inhibited her thinking:

> Whereas I lived in a fascinating ocean of imagination, I now exist in a mere puddle of it. I used to write poetry and prose because it released and satisfied something deep inside myself; now I find reading and writing an effort and my world inside is a desert.

In some cases akathisia, akinesia, and tremors can be successfully treated by giving another medication simultaneously with the antipsychotic. The medications used for this most commonly are anticholinergics such as are used to treat acute dystonic reactions, diphenhydramine or amantadine (Symmetrel). Akathisia has also been reversed with a benzodiazepine like diazepam (Valium), beta blockers in low dosages such as propranolol (Inderal) or naldolol (Corgard) 40 to 80 mg. per day, and clonidine (Catapres). If none of these work, then switching to another antipsychotic may be useful; one study showed that haloperidol causes more akathisia than thiothixene, and the aliphatic or piperidine phenothiazines cause less tremor than other antipsychotics. These side effects may also be reasons to try intermittent medication (see page 192) or to switch from antipsychotics to some of the other drugs used to treat schizophrenia (see pages 209–18).

There are three other side effects of antipsychotic drugs which are relatively common and potentially serious. One is oversensitivity to the sun (called photosensitivity) in which the person may become sunburned much more easily; it occurs most commonly with the aliphatic phenothiazines. Such people must wear wide-brimmed hats and be very careful when they are outside on sunny days; strong sunscreens also provide effective protection. Another potentially serious side effect is fainting whenever the person goes from a lying to a standing position; this is called orthostatic hypotension and is also seen most commonly with aliphatic and piperazine phenothiazines but rarely with the other drugs (see table 1, page 187).

Weight gain is another potentially serious side effect and may sometimes involve the gain of one hundred pounds or more. A large gain is always serious, for it can often be life-shortening and may lead to other diseases. Antipsychotic drugs definitely cause weight gain in some people. In others it is less clear whether the weight gain is a direct consequence of taking the drugs or whether it is a consequence of inactivity due to the disease itself. Some schizophrenic patients may have symptoms, such as auditory hallucinations and delusions, which are relieved by the antipsychotic drugs, but continue to show apathy, withdrawal, and inactivity, which then lead to weight gain. For patients taking antipsychotics who gain large amounts of weight, it may be worthwhile switching to another antipsychotic, using intermittent medication, or trying other drugs such as lithium. Molindone has reportedly caused less weight gain, though this has been disputed by others.

Uncommon and Serious. Antipsychotic drugs can have serious and, rarely, even fatal side effects, but fortunately these are uncommon. Liver damage was seen more often in the past, especially with chlorpromazine, but is rarely observed now even when chlorpromazine is used; the reasons for this decline are not known. Damage to the blood-forming organs, thus decreasing the number of white cells, may occur, making the person very susceptible to infections. Damage to the eye lens or the retina has been reported, especially with thioridazine (Mellaril), and for this reason it is strongly recommended that thioridazine should never be given in a dose of more than 800 mg. per day; thioridazine is the only antipsychotic drug with a clearly defined upper limit for its maximum dose. Thioridazine is also thought to cause more heart abnormalities, especially in older patients, and these can rarely produce sudden death. Other serious but uncommon side effects of antipsychotic drugs are urinary tract obstruction in men with large prostate glands, intestinal obstruction, worsening of glaucoma, and convulsions.

Tardive Dyskinesia. Much of the fear of using antipsychotic drugs is linked to a fear of tardive dyskinesia. This syndrome has received much publicity in recent years, and most persons with schizophrenia, and their families, have been warned about it. The condition usually develops in schizophrenics who are older and who have been on antipsychotic drugs for many years. It consists of involuntary movements of the tongue and mouth, such as chewing movements, sucking movements, pushing the cheek out with the tongue, and smacking of the lips. Occasionally these are accompanied by jerky, purposeless movements of the arms or legs or, rarely, even the whole body. It usually begins while the patient is taking the drug, but rarely may begin shortly after the drug has been stopped. Occasionally it persists indefinitely, and no effective treatment has been found to date.

The frequency and seriousness of tardive dyskinesia are one of the most hotly debated topics in current psychiatry. Estimates of frequency are confounded by the fact that the movements of tardive dyskinesia can be caused by schizophrenia, as well as by the drugs used to treat it. Kraepelin described such movements in patients as early as 1904; more recently researchers found involuntary movements in half of all chronic schizophrenics who had never been treated with antipsychotic medications. Thus to say what portion of tardive dyskinesia is drug-caused and what portion is disease-caused is not yet possible. The most informed estimate to date is that 13 percent of chronic schizophrenic patients suffer from some degree of drug-induced tardive dyskinesia. This also falls within the 10 to 20 percent range estimated by the American Psychiatric Association's 1980 task force on the subject.

Much current research takes place in an attempt to identify which persons with schizophrenia are most likely to get tardive dyskinesia. It is clear that the older the person, the more susceptible he or she is. There are also suggestions that tardive dyskinesia occurs more commonly in women, in Jews, in schizophrenics who have affective symptoms (e.g., depression, mania, pressure of speech), in those with blunted affect or mutism, in those with more akathisia or tremor, and in those with more pathological changes on CT scans. None of these associations are firmly established yet, and thus our ability to predict who is more likely to get tardive dyskinesia is very limited. There exists no firm evidence to date that any one antipsychotic is more likely to cause tardive dyskinesia than another.

The earliest signs of tardive dyskinesia are muscle twitching beneath the surface of the tongue (visible when the tongue is stuck out) and chewing movements. If antipsychotic drugs are stopped in these early stages, the movements will go away in the majority of cases. If the patient is taking anticholinergic drugs (see pages 209–10) these should be stopped, if possible, as some researchers believe that they worsen symptoms of tardive dyskinesia. The real problem in tardive dyskinesia consists not in its early signs, which are usually reversible, but rather in the dilemma faced when the patient clearly needs the antipsychotic drugs to stay well but displays early signs of tardive dyskinesia on the drug. Some alternatives to consider in such cases are intermittent medication or the use of drugs which do not seem to cause dyskinesia symptoms (e.g., lithium, clozapine, reserpine). There is also some preliminary evidence from long-term follow-up of patients with tardive dyskinesia that leaving them on the antipsychotic medication does not necessarily worsen their dyskinesia symptoms, as previously assumed. In any case the problem and options should be fully discussed with the patient and family. Tardive dyskinesia is a serious problem but one not meriting the hysteria prevalent among some people. As an American Psychatric Association task force concluded, "While the problem is serious, an alarmist view is unwarranted."

Neuroleptic Malignant Syndrome. While rare, this side effect of antipsychotic medication merits serious study. Its prevalence appears to be less than 1 in 250 patients; men are affected twice as often as women. It may occur at any time while taking antipsychotic drugs, even in a person who has been taking them for several years, but in most cases it begins within ten days of starting medication. The symptoms come on slowly over a period of one to three days and consist of rigidity of the muscles, fever, confusion or coma, pallor, sweating, and rapid heart rate. Laboratory tests show elevations of the white blood cell count and of the blood creatine phosphokinase level.

The precise mechanism causing the neuroleptic malignant syndrome is unknown, other than being a kind of toxic reaction to the drug. There is no evidence that one type of antipsychotic drug causes it more than another. Between 15 and 20 percent of its victims die of it, although this may now be reduced because there are specific drugs for treating it (dantrolene, bromocriptine), which appear to be effective. It is not yet clear what relationship the neuroleptic malignant syndrome has to malignant hyperthermia, a rare but potentially fatal allergic reaction to anesthetic agents used in medicine. The neuroleptic malignant syndrome may also appear similar to lethal catatonia, a very rare but often fatal development in some patients with schizophrenia, in which the person's temperature becomes extremely high. Lethal catatonia was clearly described before antipsychotic medications began to be used and is presumably a complication of the schizophrenia itself on the brain center controlling temperature regulation.

Interactions with Other Drugs. Drugs not only may cause side effects by themselves but may interact with other drugs in the body as well. Physicians prescribing antipsychotic medications and individuals taking them should be aware of interactions which have been reported to occur between antipsychotics and other drugs. Many of these are rare. They do not necessarily mean that the two drugs should not be given at the same time, but only that caution should be used. The majority of interactions reported to date are for the phenothiazines, which have been in use the longest; it should be assumed that any antipsychotic drug may cause such reactions until proven otherwise.

Antipsychotic drug may interact with	Causing
alcohol	impaired motor coordination
anesthetics	severe hypotension
antidepressants	severe drowsiness
barbiturates	severe drowsiness
bethanidine	bethanidine to be ineffective
debrisoquine	debrisoquine to be ineffective
guanadrel	guanadrel to be ineffective
guanethidine	guanethidine to be ineffective
insulin	increased need for insulin
levodopa	levodopa to be ineffective
narcotics (e.g., codeine)	severe drowsiness
phenytoin (Dilantin)	antipsychotic to be less effective

There are also a few reactions which appear to be specific to certain antipsychotics:

Antipsychotic	May interact with	Causing
perphenazine (Trilafon)	disulfiram (Antabuse)	perphenazine to be less effective
haloperidol	indomethacin (Indocin)	severe drowsiness
haloperidol	methyldopa (Aldomet)	mental changes

Use in Pregnancy

The safest advice regarding medications to give any pregnant woman is not to take anything. That may be impossible for women with schizophrenia. The antipsychotic drugs have been used by thousands of women while pregnant and appear to be safe compared to many other drugs used in medicine. Recent studies, however, have shown that these drugs occasionally cause malformations or congenital anomalies to the growing fetus, so they should not be considered completely safe and should be taken only when absolutely necessary. The most critical time for such damage appears to be the first three months of pregnancy.

Given what is currently known, a reasonable plan for pregnant women with schizophrenia is the following:

a) Stop antipsychotic medication for the first three months of pregnancy if she can do so without a serious relapse.

b) Remain off medication for as much of the pregnancy as possible beyond three months unless symptoms start to recur.

c) If it is necessary to restart the medication, use whichever medication she has responded to in the past. There is insufficient data yet to say that one type of antipsychotic medication is more dangerous than another during pregnancy.

d) Do not be heroic by avoiding medications at all costs. If the woman needs medication, use it. Having a pregnant woman who is acutely psychotic has risks of its own to both the woman and the fetus.

e) Discuss the issue of medication in detail before the pregnancy or as early in the pregnancy as possible. Be certain that the woman's family and all concerned understand the options. If the decision is made to stop medication, draw up a contract that specifies that the woman will resume medication if the doctor deems it advisable. The contract must be binding on the woman, even if she changes her mind because of her psychosis, so that she can be medicated involuntarily if necessary; this is sometimes referred to as a "Ulysses contract" after the Greek hero who ordered his sailors to tie him to the mast and not to change course even if he ordered them to do so in response to the Sirens' song.

Regarding the taking of antipsychotic drugs while breastfeeding, this should not be done. The drugs are transmitted in the breast milk in small amounts but because the baby's liver and kidneys are not mature the drugs may accumulate in the baby's body. Since a woman who needs medication has the option of bottle feeding, it seems an unnecessary risk to take.

Signs of Relapse

Signs of relapse in schizophrenia are closely watched for by patients, their families, and the mental health professionals providing care. As mentioned in chapter 3, the symptoms experienced by the patient and signs of illness observed by others tend to be characteristic for any given patient; once a person has relapsed once or twice, the symptoms and signs each succeeding time are likely to be similar.

The best study of relapse in schizophrenia was done by Drs. Marvin Herz and Charles Melville. They questioned 145 patients who had relapsed and 80 family members. The following symptoms and signs were the most frequently reported:

Patients reported	*Percent*
being tense and nervous	80
eating less	72
trouble concentrating	70
trouble sleeping	67
enjoy things less	65
restlessness	63
not able to remember things	63
depression	61
being preoccupied with one or two things	60
seeing friends less	60
being laughed at, talked about	60

Families reported	*Percent*
being tense and nervous	83
restlessness	79
trouble concentrating	76
depression	76
talking in nonsensical way	76
loss of interest in things	76
trouble sleeping	69
enjoy things less	68
being preoccupied with one or two things	65
not able to remember things	60
hearing voices, seeing things	60

The remarkable thing about this study is the similarity of symptoms and signs reported by the patients and their families. In a later paper, Herz concluded that "it is extremely important to educate both patients and families" about the symptoms and signs of relapse, and that "family involvement is a crucial component in the treatment of schizophrenia."

In many cases the patient and/or family has learned over time which symptoms and signs herald relapse. One woman who had had multiple episodes of schizophrenia described to me the things she looks for: "My main prodromal symptoms are quick irritability and anger and, when out-of-doors, thinking that everyone I see looks familiar although I do not know *whom* they remind me of." Another woman described her relapse as occurring in four stages:

> In the first stage, I feel just a bit estranged from myself. From my eyes the world seems brighter and more sharply defined, and my voice seems to echo a bit. I start to feel uncomfortable being around people, and also uncomfortable in sharing my changing feelings.
>
> In the second stage, everything appears a bit clouded. This cloudiness increases as does my confusion and fear, especially fear of letting others know what is happening to me. I try to make logical excuses and to get control over the details of my life, and often make frantic efforts to organize everything; cleaning, cataloging, and self-involved activity is high. Songs on the radio begin to have greater meaning, and people seem to be looking at me strangely and laughing, giving me subtle messages I can't understand. I start to misinterpret people's actions toward me, which increases my fear of losing control.
>
> In the third stage, I believe I am beginning to understand why terrible things are happening to me: others are the cause of it. This belief comes with a clearing of sight, an increasing level of sound, and an increasing sensitivity to the looks of others. I carry on an argument with myself as to whether these things are true: "Is the FBI or the devil causing this? . . . No, that's crazy thinking. I wonder why people are making me crazy."
>
> In the fourth and last stage, I become chaotic and see, hear, and believe all manner of things. I no longer question my beliefs, but act on them.

When the Patient Refuses to Take Medicine

One of the most common yet most difficult problems faced by families and mental health professionals centers on the person with schizophrenia who refuses to take medication. Sometimes the person refuses out-

right, but more often noncompliance with medication takes place sur-
reptitiously, so that for weeks or months the family and mental health
professionals believe the person is taking it. Noncompliance with medication is the single greatest cause of relapse among individuals with
schizophrenia.

Although the reasons for noncompliance may be varied, it is
vital to ascertain the correct one. The most common reason why persons with schizophrenia refuse to take medication is because they
have no insight into their illness and do not believe there is anything
wrong with them. Alternatively they may refuse medication as a
means of denying their illness, with reasoning such as the following:
if I take medicine, then I must be ill, but if I do not take medicine,
then I am not ill. Some persons with schizophrenia refuse medication
for delusional reasons, believing that it is intended to poison them or
alter their body in some way. Individuals with manic-depressive psychosis will sometimes refuse to take medication because they prefer
the highs of their mania to the reality of a medicated state; this rarely
occurs in schizophrenia because almost nobody with schizophrenia
finds psychosis to be pleasurable. Still another reason for noncompliance with medication is the person's wish to "take a chance" that he
or she will not get sick again. Risk-taking behavior is a strong personality trait of many persons, especially males, and can be seen in such
everyday decisions as driving without a seat belt. It should also be
noted that noncompliance with medication is a much greater problem
in men than women, apparently because men feel that taking medication impinges upon their autonomy or masculinity, plus the male
stereotype of being strong.

Another frequent reason for medication noncompliance in schizophrenia concerns the side effects of the drugs. Mental health professionals and family members can see side effects like tremor and akathisia
described above. What they cannot see are side effects which may be
experienced by the patient but which are invisible, for example, depression, loss of spontaneity, slowing of movements and thoughts, and loss
of creativity. The assessment of such symptoms in a patient is extraor-
dinarily difficult because the symptoms may be caused by the schizophrenic disease process, by the medication, or by both. Furthermore,
depression may cause loss of spontaneity, and loss of spontaneity may
bring on depression. These complex relationships can be illustrated
schematically:

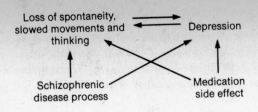

The important point is that some persons with schizophrenia experience unintended and invisible side effects of their medication which may not be apparent to others, and these side effects can lead to the person's decision to stop taking medication. This dilemma is described by Dr. Ronald Diamond in a lucid paper in which he discusses "the effect of antipsychotic medications on the patient's quality of life" and concludes: "It is still important to listen to what patients say and to take seriously their experience with their medication. It may well be that they have something to teach us about what these drugs do and how they make patients feel, apart from their effect on the illness."

Once the reason for a patient's noncompliance with medication has been ascertained, what can be done? If the reason is a rational one (e.g., visible or undetected side effects), then the mental health professional needs to enter into a partnership with the patient to explore lower doses or alternative medications. Having the patient maintain a daily diary of side effects is often effective. The patient and physician make joint decisions about medication and continue to explore other options, such as those described under New and Experimental Drugs on pages 214–18. An alternative is the use of intermittent or targeted medication, described previously, in which the person uses medications only when symptoms of schizophrenia start to recur.

If, on the other hand, the reason for noncompliance is an irrational one such as lack of insight or denial and if medication has been shown to be effective, then the family and mental health professionals have an obligation to do whatever they can to ensure that the patient takes medication. This may include pleading and having everyone who knows the person urge him or her to take it. Many persons with schizophrenia do not remember how sick they were during psychotic episodes and do not believe it when you describe it to them. I have often wished I had a videotape of their psychotic behavior which I could show them in hopes of frightening them into taking the medication.

Bribery is another, often effective approach if the family can figure out what the person with schizophrenia really wants. Threats may also be effective, especially if they can be carried out. Threats to evict the person from the house or return her or him to the hospital are so readily verbalized that both the patient and the family may know that they are mere bluff.

In unusual circumstances it may occasionally be justified to persuade individuals that taking antipsychotic medication will improve physical symptoms that are bothering them. This is especially true for people with schizophrenia who have no insight into their illness and no understanding of their need for medication. Using this strategy I have persuaded patients to take antipsychotic medication for every conceivable physical complaint from chronic sinusitis to hemorrhoids. In fact, the antipsychotic medication often does relieve the symptoms, both because the person feels better generally and because some of the physical symptoms are delusional. Although some professionals may be surprised that I would advocate such a strategy for a patient with schizophrenia in selected circumstances, there is precedent for this approach in the work of Avicenna, a Persian physician who lived from A.D. 980 to 1037 and who is generally acknowledged as one of the greatest physicians in history. Avicenna was called upon to treat a young prince who had become psychotic, believing himself to be a cow and imploring everyone to kill him "so that a good stew may be made from my flesh." The prince had become completely anorexic, was losing weight, and refused to eat food or take medication. Avicenna sent word to the prince that "the butcher is going to come to slaughter him."

Then Avicenna with his court staff went to the house of the patient. Avicenna with two staff went to the courtyard. He had a butcher knife in his hand and said aloud, "Where is this cow so I can slaughter it?" The patient lowed like a cow as if to say "Here I am." Avicenna said, "Bring it to the middle of the court and tie its hands and its feet and throw it on the ground." When the patient heard that, he ran to the middle of the courtyard. He lay down on the ground on his right side. They tied his feet tightly. Then Avicenna came rubbing butcher knives against each other. He sat down and put his hand by the side of the patient as was the custom of the butchers. Then he said, "Ah! What a thin cow! It is not worth killing! Give it grass to be fattened." Then Avicenna got up and left and told the people, "Untie him and any food [and medicine] I prescribe, take to him and tell him—eat so that you will be fattened soon."

They did as he said. They took all the food, drink, and medication that Avicenna prescribed. They told him, "Eat heartily, this will fatten the cow very well." The young prince listened and ate with the hope of getting fat and being killed.

The physicians continued to treat him according to Avicenna's regular advice. It took him a month to regain his health.

If none of the above strategies are effective in persuading the noncompliant individual to take medication, then legal measures may be needed. Especially important is a conditional hospital release or outpatient commitment which specifies that the person must take medication as a condition of being out of the hospital. Outpatient commitments are legally available in the majority of states but very little used; they can be very effective. To ensure that the person actually takes the medication it can be given in injectable form (e.g., as long-acting injections of fluphenazine or haloperidol) or in liquid form where it can be mixed with juice and the person cannot hide it under his or her tongue, as is often done with tablets. For some medications, such as lithium (see pages 210–12), blood levels can also be tested to ensure that the person is really taking the medication.

Costs of Medications

The cost of antipsychotic medication can vary tremendously for a patient, with equivalent dosages of different antipsychotic drugs ranging from approximately $5 per month to $40 per month or higher. Even the same medication prescribed and filled in exactly the same dose in one pharmacy may cost more than twice as much if obtained from another pharmacy in the same town.

Whether the family, the county, or the state is paying the bill, it is incumbent on us all to keep drug costs under control. Some means for controlling antipsychotic drug costs are the following:

a) Use generic drugs when available. Although drug companies often claim that generics are not as effective as brand-name drugs, there is little evidence for this assertion except in a few rare instances (e.g., digoxin). The prestigious *Medical Letter,* in a recent review of the issue of generics, concluded: "The newly approved generic drug products now being marketed will probably prove to be as reliable as brand-name drugs. Whether using brand-name products or generics, the possibility of product failure should always be kept in mind." The majority of antipsychotic drugs are available as generics, including chlorpromazine, thioridazine, fluphenazine and haloperidol. The Food and Drug Administration publishes a listing of approved generic drugs called *Approved Drug Products With Therapeutic Equivalence Evaluations.*

b) Use the largest-size tablet available, consistent with the dose needed. For example a 20 mg. tablet of Haldol costs only slightly more than a 10 mg. tablet. A patient on Haldol 20 mg. per day who takes the daily dosage as two 10 mg. tablets will be paying almost twice as much as the patient taking a single 20 mg. tablet.

c) Consistent with the above, give all antipsychotic medication at a single dose at bedtime. Except in unusual instances it is not necessary to take antipsychotic medication more than once a day; for example, it is just as effective to take fluphenazine 30 mg. at bedtime, as it is to take 10 mg. three times a day. It used to be thought that lithium had to be given in divided doses two or three times a day but recent research suggests that lithium, like the antipsychotics, can be given once a day. Once-a-day dosing makes it easier for the patient and family and so improves compliance.

d) Shop around for the best price, since pharmacies vary so widely. Buy the largest quantity of drugs possible at one time since they are less expensive in larger numbers. Families using the same medication may even want to band together and negotiate a joint price with one pharmacy such as is done by food-buying cooperatives.

OTHER DRUGS FOR SCHIZOPHRENIA

Anticholinergics. The anticholinergics are a class of drugs which include benztropine (Cogentin), biperiden (Akineton), procyclidine (Kemadrin), and trihexyphenidyl (Artane) among others. They have been used in schizophrenia since shortly after the antipsychotic drugs were introduced, because of the known ability of anticholinergics to block dystonic reactions. They are also used to treat tremors and akathisia caused by antipsychotic drugs.

For many years it was considered good practice to withhold anticholinergic drugs until side effects actually appeared. More recently it has become accepted practice to use them prophylactically, especially in patients who are younger and/or male (in whom dystonic reactions are more common) or who are paranoid (and in whom a dystonic reaction would be construed as "proof" that the doctor was trying to poison him or her). One recent study suggests that giving anticholinergics for seven days to all patients being started on antipsychotic drugs has many more benefits than risks.

The use of long-term anticholinergics in schizophrenia, concurrent with antipsychotics, continues to be controversial. On the one hand, certain psychiatrists claim that anticholinergics do more than simply block side effects and may *enhance* the effect of antipsychotic medication in many patients. On the other hand, some psychiatrists are convinced that the anticholinergics *decrease* the effect of antipsychotic medication but may increase the chances of getting tardive dyskinesia.

Anticholinergic drugs may interact with amantadine (Symmetrel) to cause confusion and hallucination, so the two should be used cautiously together. They may also decrease the effectiveness of cimetidine (Tagamet) used to heal ulcers. There have been reported instances of occasional patients with schizophrenia getting a mild "high" from anticholinergics; I had one patient who was known in every emergency room in the city of Washington for his ability to mimic the symptoms of an acute dystonic reaction in his nightly quests for an injection of benztropine (Cogentin).

Lithium.   Lithium is the most useful drug to be introduced to psychiatry since the antipsychotics were discovered in the early 1950s. In fact, lithium was originally discovered even earlier—by Dr. John Cade in Australia in 1948—but for a variety of reasons it was not introduced to the United States until the 1970s. It rapidly became a mainstay of treatment and prevention for manic-depressive psychosis, and in recent years has been found effective in many patients with schizophrenia as well.

Like the antipsychotics, precisely how lithium works is as yet unknown; its effectiveness may be related to its ability to control the transport of substances across the cell membrane. What is clear is that, when used in conjunction with an antipsychotic, lithium is effective in decreasing symptoms such as hallucinations, delusional thinking, and thought disorders in perhaps one-third of patients with schizophrenia and that it often works when antipsychotics by themselves have failed. Patients with schizophrenia should not be categorized as "treatment unresponsive" until they have been given a trial on lithium with an antipsychotic.

Lithium is available as tablets or liquid. Previously it was thought that lithium must be given in divided doses two or three times a day but recent studies have suggested that it can be given once daily or even every other day. Before starting lithium, the patient should have a blood test for kidney and thyroid function (usually a TSH and creatinine), and women should certainly have a pregnancy test; lithium may harm the fetus and should not be given in pregnancy except in very unusual circumstances. Women on lithium should also bottle-feed rather than breast-feed their babies.

Lithium differs from the antipsychotic drugs in being potentially much more dangerous if taken in overdose. For this reason blood must be drawn for lithium level testing initially every few days, then in decreasing frequency as the person becomes stabilized on the drug. Blood tests should also be done approximately every six to twelve months to check thyroid and kidney function. The therapeutic blood level of lithium is 0.6–1.2 meq (milliequivalents) per liter, although a few patients can be maintained successfully in the 0.4–0.6 meq range and a few require a 1.2–1.6 meq range to be effective. To get a therapeutic blood level may require 2 or 3 tablets a day in one patient, 6 or 8 tablets in another. Older patients need lower doses.

Side effects of lithium in a normal dose range may include thirst, frequent urination, a tremor of the fingers or hands, diarrhea, fluid retention (edema) of the hands or lower legs, weight gain, altered hair texture, acne, or the worsening of psoriasis if the person has it. In my experience the two most troublesome side effects are tremor and frequent urination, especially at night. If the person is clearly responding to the lithium, then the tremor can often be treated using beta blocker drugs (e.g., propranolol) and the frequent urination with amiloride or other diuretics; the use of diuretics with lithium, however, may be risky in some cases and should be done only by physicians who are very familiar with these drugs.

If the lithium level goes too high, it can be a serious, even life-threatening, situation. Symptoms of toxicity include vomiting, diarrhea, weakness, confusion, stupor, staggering, incoordination, slurred speech, dizziness, blurred vision, convulsions, and coma. Lithium should *never* be given to a patient with any of these symptoms without first checking with a doctor. Even if the person has only vomiting or

diarrhea from a suspected gastrointestinal upset, stop the lithium until
the person is better. Lithium levels also tend to rise in very hot weather
when the person is sweating heavily, and fluid intake should be increased.

Lithium interacts unfavorably with many other drugs. There has
even been controversy regarding the advisability of using lithium with
antipsychotic drugs, such as is useful in schizophrenia, because of rare
reports of serious toxicity between lithium and haloperidol. The general
consensus is that using lithium in combination with antipsychotic drugs
is safe as long as a physician is involved in following the patient. Many
other lithium interactions bear watching, such as the following:

Lithium may interact with	Causing
acetazolamide	decreased lithium effect
amiloride	increased lithium toxicity
aminophylline	decreased lithium effect
carbamazepine	increased carbamazepine toxicity
furosemide	increased lithium toxicity
ibuprofen	increased lithium toxicity
indomethacin	increased lithium toxicity
mazindol	increased lithium toxicity
methyldopa	increased lithium toxicity
naproxen	increased lithium toxicity
phenylbutazone	increased lithium toxicity
phenytoin	increased lithium toxicity
piroxicam	increased lithium toxicity
sodium bicarbonate	decreased lithium effect
spectinomycin	increased lithium toxicity
spironolactone	increased lithium toxicity
sulindac	increased lithium toxicity
tetracycline	increased lithium toxicity
theophylline	decreased lithium effect
thiazide diuretics (e.g. hydrodiuril)	increased lithium toxicity
ticarcillin	increased blood sodium
triamterene	increased lithium toxicity
verapamil	increased lithium toxicity
zomepirac	increased lithium toxicity

Carbamazepine. Since 1980, carbamazepine (Tegretol) has been
used as a backup drug for selected cases of manic-depressive psychosis.
Widely used for epilepsy and effective for psychiatric disorders, this

drug is another piece of evidence suggesting that some patients with psychosis, like patients with epilepsy, have underlying neuroelectrical disturbances.

Carbamazepine figures in the treatment of schizophrenia as a substitute for lithium in patients who are responsive to lithium but, because of side effects, cannot long be maintained on that drug. Carbamazepine has also been claimed to be useful in schizophrenia with excited or violent patients. In most such cases carbamazepine has been used in conjunction with antipsychotic medication and not alone.

Like lithium, the drug carbamazepine with its wide range of side effects must be monitored carefully. Drowsiness, double vision, dizziness, unsteadiness, nausea, and vomiting may occur when the drug is first used. More serious side effects include severe depletion of white blood cells (leukopenia, which should be monitored initially by blood counts), aplastic anemia, hepatitis, and cardiac toxicity. Carbamazepine should not be taken by pregnant women or nursing mothers. Blood levels of carbamazepine can be monitored by most laboratories and are useful. In addition to the listed side effects, carbamazepine may also interact adversely with several other drugs.

Carbamazepine may interact with	Causing
anticoagulants	decreased anticoagulant effectiveness
cimetidine	increased toxicity of both drugs
contraceptives, oral	decreased contraception
doxycycline	decreased doxycycline effect
erythromycins	increased carbamazepine toxicity
isoniazid (INH)	increased toxicity of both drugs
lithium	increased carbamazepine toxicity
phenytoin	decreased effect of both drugs
primidone	decreased primidone effect
propoxyphene	increased carbamazepine toxicity
theophylline	decreased theophylline effect
troleandomycin	increased carbamazepine toxicity
valproic acid	decreased valproic acid effect
verapamil	increased carbamazepine toxicity

Antidepressants. These drugs have been in use for many years for depression. Only recently, however, it was realized how many patients with schizophrenia are also depressed, either due to the effects of the schizophrenia itself, the reaction of the patient to the illness, or the side effects of antipsychotics. The increasingly visible, high suicide rate among persons with schizophrenia also focuses attention on the prevalence of depression in this condition.

Therefore, for valid reasons antidepressants are being used increasingly widely for selected patients with schizophrenia in whom depression is evident. The well-established tricyclic antidepressants are usually selected, although newer antidepressants or monoamine oxidase (MAO) inhibitors can also be used. Tricyclic antidepressants take approximately two to four weeks to be effective.

The early side effects of tricyclic antidepressants may include dry mouth, constipation, blurred vision, and drowsiness. Occasionally they may worsen the psychiatric symptoms or cause heart problems. Interactions of tricyclic antidepressants may also occur with other drugs, as listed here:

Tricyclic antidepressants may interact with	Causing
baclofen	loss of muscle power
barbiturates	decreased antidepressant effect
bethanidine	decreased bethanidine effect
cimetidine	increased antidepressant effect
clonidine	decreased clonidine effect
coumarin anticoagulants	increased bleeding
debrisoquine	decreased debrisoquine effect
disulfiram (Antabuse)	psychiatric symptoms
epinephrine	decreased blood pressure
guanadrel	decreased guanadrel effect
guanethidine	decreased guanethidine effect
levodopa	decreased levodopa effect
quinidine	cardiac changes
phenothiazine antipsychotics	increased antidepressant toxicity
phenytoin	increased phenytoin toxicity
propoxyphene	increased toxicity of doxepin antidepressant

NEW AND EXPERIMENTAL DRUGS

Considering the magnitude and severity of schizophrenia, there have been remarkably few new drugs introduced to treat it in recent years. One major reason for this is the paucity of research attention and funds which schizophrenia has received (see chapter 6). Applications to test or market a new drug in the United States must be approved by the Food and Drug Administration (FDA), an arm of the Department of Health and Human Services, in Washington. This organization has been accused of unnecessarily delaying the availability of new drugs. In fact the FDA has, I believe, a desirable record of caution in light of past tragedies such as thalidomide. And when a new drug which appears to be useful for treatment-resistant cases is still in the testing stages, it can be made available for selected cases by a special mechanism (see clozapine, below). Occasionally the drug companies are also blamed for the lack of drugs, but drug companies are profit-making organizations and will follow up any promising lead which appears to be translatable into sales; they know that schizophrenia has great potential for them. The blame for not having more new drugs to treat schizophrenia, then, should not be directed at the FDA or drug companies but rather at the failure of the nation's research establishment to support more research on this disease.

Clozapine.   Despite having one major drawback, clozapine is potentially the most exciting drug for schizophrenia to come along in several years. Chemically a first cousin of the dibenzoxapine family, it has been used to treat schizophrenia in Europe and China for many years. It is undergoing extensive testing by Sandoz, Incorporated, in East Hanover, New Jersey, and preliminary tests suggest its efficacy in some patients with schizophrenia who are resistant to treatment by all other drugs currently available. It is also alleged that clozapine causes no tardive dyskinesia, although this is not yet as firmly established. Its major drawback is that it may precipitate a lowering of the white blood cells (leukopenia or agranulocytosis), which, if not detected, can lead to death. By getting a blood count every week once clozapine is being administered, it may be possible to monitor this. It may be obtained by psychiatrists for treatment-resistant patients or patients with tardive dyskinesia through a "compassionate" investigational new drug mechanism by applying to Sandoz, Inc.

Sulpiride.   This drug, not yet available in the United States, has been used to treat schizophrenia in Europe for many years, especially in France. It is a benzamide, a chemical family completely different from other drugs currently available, and its efficacy appears to be similar to that of haloperidol but one study found that sulpiride had fewer side effects. Other benzamide family members being tested for use in schizophrenia are metoclopramide, remoxipride, and amisulpride.

Pimozide.   Also used in Europe for schizophrenia for many years, pimozide (Orap) in 1986 was approved in the United States for use in Tourette's syndrome. Practically, this means that the drug is available to any physician who wishes to use it. Pimozide is a member of the butyrophenone family; whether it will turn out to be more useful than haloperidol remains to be seen.

Propranolol.   As a member of the beta blocker family, propranolol (Inderal) is widely used in hypertension and thus is available to any physician. It has been tested for efficacy in schizophrenia but when used by itself the results were not impressive. When used in conjunction with an antipsychotic, however, it shows more promise; one study found it to be especially effective in controlling "impulsively aggressive behavior" in patients with schizophrenia. The person's pulse and blood pressure must be monitored.

Valproic Acid.   Valproic acid (Depakene) is an anticonvulsant widely used in the United States for epilepsy. It has also been used experimentally in manic-depressive psychosis as a substitute for lithium. Some researchers have claimed that it may also be helpful in schizoaffective disorders, taken in conjunction with an antipsychotic, but sufficient data on this are not yet available.

Clonazepam.   Like valproic acid, clonazepam (new trade name Klonopin, old trade name Clonopin) is an established anticonvulsant used for epilepsy. It has also been found to be a substitute for lithium in manic-depressive psychosis, and to be effective in some cases of panic disorder and agoraphobia. There are also reports of its usefulness in cases of schizoaffective disorder and further work on it is in progress. It belongs to the benzodiazepine family and causes sedation as a major side effect.

Diazepam, Lorazepam, Alprazolam, Estazolam.   These are all benzodiazepines whose main use as minor tranquilizers has been to treat anxiety. In the first edition of this book, I indicated that such drugs have no place in the treatment of schizophrenia. Since that time preliminary studies have become available suggesting that they may have a minor role. Diazepam (Valium) used by injection may reverse acute catatonia and lorazepam (Ativan) by injection may help calm very disturbed patients. Alprazolam and estazolam are still experimental drugs, but claims have been made for their efficacy in selected schizophrenic patients with high levels of anxiety or in patients whose auditory hallucinations have not responded to other drugs. The problem with these drugs, unlike the antipsychotics, is that they have the potential to be addicting; since schizophrenia is a disease which often requires medications for many years it seems unlikely that these drugs will ever be useful for more than the short term.

Clonidine. Widely used as a drug in hypertension, clonidine (Catapres) has also been used experimentally to treat manic-depressive psychosis. It is not yet clear whether it may also be useful to treat schizoaffective disorder.

Verapamil. A member of a new class of drugs called calcium-entry blockers which are being widely used in cardiac conditions, verapamil (Isoptin, Calan) is also being researched for possible effectiveness in manic-depressive psychosis and schizophrenia. There is insufficient data to assess its usefulness.

Reserpine. There is an irony in listing reserpine (Raudixin) on a list of new and experimental drugs since it is the oldest antipsychotic known. Because of its relative weakness as an antipsychotic and its propensity for causing depression, it was discarded and today is used in medicine only for hypertension. It should be kept in mind as a backup drug for schizophrenia, especially in patients with early symptoms of tardive dyskinesia; reserpine has never been known to cause this condition.

Long-Acting Drugs. Until the introduction of haloperidol decanoate (IM Haldol), the only long-acting injectable medication for schizophrenia in the United States was fluphenazine decanoate (IM Prolixin). This was fine for those patients who responded to fluphenazine but not fine for those who did not. Long-acting haloperidol is a major addition. There are also available in Europe other long-acting injectable medications in the phenothiazine family (perphenazine and pipotiazine), the thioxanthine family (flupenthixol and cis-clopenthixol), and the butyrophenone family (fluspirelene). There are also long-acting oral antipsychotic agents available in Europe, though not yet available here, such as the phenothiazine pipotiazine and the butrophenone penfluridol. The more such drugs are available to treating physicians, the easier it becomes to treat schizophrenia.

Other Drugs. Several other medications are being looked at for possible use in schizophrenia. These include perlapine, fluperlapine and trebenzomine, all related to clozapine; melperone, a butyrophenone available in Europe; ritanserin, an antagonist of serotonin; GR 38032 F, which blocks serotonin receptors and is being tested in Europe; rimcazole (formerly known as BW 234-U); and amantadine (Symmetrel) used in conjunction with an antipsychotic.

Drugs for "Negative" Symptoms. Perhaps the single most pressing need in the drug therapy of schizophrenia is to develop medications which treat the "negative" symptoms as well as the "positive" symptoms. Currently there is no such drug available; even worse, it is suspected that antipsychotic drugs may worsen "negative" symptoms in some individuals with this disease. Preliminary claims have been made that some newer and experimental drugs may be more useful in treating negative symptoms but these claims have not yet been substantiated; among the newer drugs tried have been pimozide, penfluridol, fluspirilene and sulpiride. Alprazolam, a benzodiazapine, and trazodone, a new antidepressant, have been claimed to improve negative symptoms in occasional cases. Other drugs being tried for negative symptoms include methylphenidate and levodopa.

TREATMENT PLAN FOR MEDICATION

Once a diagnosis of schizophrenia has been established by a complete diagnostic workup, what should an antipsychotic medication treatment plan look like? It will vary, of course, depending on the symptoms of the patients (e.g., more affective symptoms, early signs of tardive dyskinesia) and the familiarity of the physician with different medications. With full recognition of such variations, however, a proposed model is outlined in the chart on the facing page.

MEDICATION TREATMENT PLAN

Begin with 5 mg. fluphenazine, haloperidol, or thiothixene. Increase 5–10 mg. every 2–3 days until maximum improvement or side effects limit further increase. Maximum dose 60–100 mg. per day for fluphenazine and haloperidol; 100–180 mg. for thiothixene.

If dysphoric effect after first dose, stop drug and begin next alternative.

Plus

Anticholinergic drug to prevent side effects if under age 30; e.g., benztropine (Cogentin) 2 mg., procyclidine (Kemadrin) 5 mg. Continue for 3–4 weeks, then gradually reduce. If side effects appear, resume anticholinergic drug.

Patients who fail to respond after 2–3 weeks should be switched to one of other three original antipsychotic medications.

If patient improves, slowly reduce medication over several weeks.

If relapses, resume medication.

For first episode of schizophrenia, discontinue completely.

If fails on second, try the third antipsychotic medication.

Intermittent medication for selected patients.

For subsequent episodes, reduce to maintenance level.

For continued failures, review medication procedures to ensure that patient is actually swallowing the medication.

Select one of three strategies:

Look for therapeutic window; try minidoses and also megadoses of the antipsychotic that the patient responded to best.

Trial of lithium used in conjunction with the antipsychotic that the patient responded to best. Carbamazepine is alternative.

Trials of molindone and loxapine (separately).

If one strategy fails, try the other two.

Trials of: clozapine
antidepressants
pimozide
propranolol
clonazepam
valproic acid
reserpine
sulpiride (not available in U.S.)
others

The truly treatment-resistant patient (less than 10 percent of total).

INEFFECTIVE TREATMENTS

Psychoanalysis and Insight-Oriented Psychotherapy

Psychoanalysis is to schizophrenia as Laetrile is to cancer. Both have enjoyed surprising popularity considering the fact that they lack scientific basis, are completely ineffective, may make the patient worse if administered in toxic doses, and still attract patients who are willing to pay vast sums of money in desperation for a cure. Freud himself recognized that schizophrenic patients "are inaccessible to the influence of psychoanalysis and cannot be cured by our endeavors," but that observation has not stopped his followers from trying.

It is important to distinguish psychoanalysis and insight-oriented psychotherapy from what is popularly known as supportive psychotherapy. Psychoanalysis and insight-oriented psychotherapy begin with the premise that the person's problems are caused by toxic early childhood experiences; the focus of therapy, therefore, becomes the exploration of those early childhood experiences. It is also referred to as uncovering, exploratory, intensive, or psychodynamic psychotherapy and its goal is a basic restructuring of the patient's personality through the exploration of unconscious conflicts with mother, father, and significant others in childhood. Supportive psychotherapy, on the other hand, is the teaching of living skills so that people can manage day-to-day activities despite their handicaps (in this case schizophrenia); its role in the treatment of schizophrenia will be discussed in chapter 9. Differentiating between insight-oriented psychotherapy and supportive psychotherapy can be reliably accomplished by the "Mother test": if on the first visit the psychotherapist asks the patient anything about Mother other than what she does for a living, then it is psychoanalysis and insight-oriented psychotherapy.

Several studies have now demonstrated that insight-oriented psychotherapy is of no value for schizophrenia. Probably the best-known of these studies was done by Philip R. A. May and his colleagues at Camarillo State Hospital, California. May randomly assigned 228 schizophrenic patients to five separate wards where they were treated by (1) psychotherapy alone, (2) psychotherapy plus drugs, (3) drugs alone, (4) milieu alone, and (5) electroconvulsive therapy. The patients who did best were those treated by drugs alone or psychotherapy plus drugs, and there were virtually no differences between the two groups;

the patients who did worst were those treated by psychotherapy alone or milieu alone. The inescapable conclusion is that psychotherapy added nothing to the treatment regimen in this study. These patients were followed up for from three to five years after the initial treatment and the results did not change: "Analysis of variance indicated an extremely significant effect from drug . . . , no significant effect from psychotherapy."

May's study was criticized by some for utilizing psychotherapy which was not "intensive" enough and for having it done by psycho-therapists who were relatively inexperienced. Another study was there-fore designed to treat schizophrenic patients with explicitly psy-choanalytically oriented psychotherapy (two hours a week for two years), using highly experienced psychotherapists. At the end of the study period the outcome was said to be that "psychotherapy alone (even with experienced psychotherapists) did little or nothing for chronic schizophrenic patients in two years." Such studies were sum-marized by Donald Klein, one of America's most respected psychia-trists: "There is no scientific basis for the affirmation of clinical benefit from the individual psychotherapy of schizophrenic patients."

There is some evidence that psychoanalysis and insight-oriented psychotherapy may not only be useless for treating schizophrenia, but may in fact be harmful. In the May study, for example, the "outcome for patients who received only psychotherapy was significantly worse than the outcome in the no-treatment control group." In other words, getting no treatment at all led to better outcomes than being treated with psychotherapy alone. This correlates with the individual experi-ence of many psychotherapists who have given up treating schizo-phrenic patients with insight-oriented psychotherapy, because many of their patients seemed to get worse. In following up Freud's original formulation about unconscious homosexual impulses being the cause of paranoid schizophrenia, one psychiatrist "checked the therapeutic suc-cesses of psychoanalysts and found to our surprise that it is common experience, frequently admitted and often implied, that not only are 'paranoid' patients not improved by homosexual interpretations, but even made worse."

Given what we now know about the brains of persons with schizo-phrenia, it should not be surprising to find that insight-oriented psycho-therapy makes them sicker. Such persons are being overwhelmed by external and internal stimuli and are trying to impose some order on the chaos. In the midst of this a psychotherapist asks them to probe their unconscious motivations, a difficult enough task even when one's brain is functioning perfectly. The inevitable consequence is to add insult to injury, unleashing a cacophony of repressed thoughts and wishes into the existing internal maelstrom. To do insight-oriented psychotherapy on persons with schizophrenia is analogous to directing a flood into a town already ravaged by a tornado. Or, to use another comparison from a recent review entitled "The Adverse Effects of Intensive Treament of Chronic Schizophrenia," insight-oriented psychotherapies are "analogous to pouring boiling oil into wounds because they ignore the chronic schizophrenic's particular vulnerability to over-stimulating relationships, intense negative affects, and pressures for rapid change."

It is remarkable how many people (including even some mental health professionals) still believe that insight-oriented psychotherapy is effective for treating schizophrenia. I still regularly meet wealthy families who have paid exorbitant sums—$100,000 to $200,000 a year—to have their schizophrenic son or daughter treated by psychoanalysis or insight-oriented psychotherapy in a private hospital. This is one of the last areas of American medicine where a Laetrile-type treatment—not only useless but probably harmful—may be legally purchased.

Recognition of the harmful role played by insight-oriented psychotherapy in patients with schizophrenia is not new. In a 1976 study of harmful effects of psychotherapy, Hadley and Strupp noted that "psychotic breaks resulting from psychotherapy were also frequently mentioned as a clear-cut negative effect . . . an occurrence would most typically be due to ego disintegration brought on by therapy." In 1978 the President's Commission on Mental Health observed that "there is some evidence that suggests that certain chronic schizophrenic patients respond adversely to psychological treatments." Shortly thereafter Dr. Gerald Klerman, at that time the highest-ranking government psychiatrist and a respected researcher, also acknowledged that "recent evidence suggests that high intensity psychotherapy may actually have negative effects in schizophrenia."

What, then, is the proper role for psychoanalysis and insight-oriented psychotherapy in the treatment of schizophrenia? It has none, and should be explicitly avoided. As summarized by Dr. T. C. Manschreck in a 1981 New England Journal of Medicine: "To offer traditional psychotherapy as the only treatment for schizophrenic disorder is generally regarded as inadequate and possibly negligent. Psychoanalysis and other insight-oriented psychotherapies have little demonstrated value in this illness." Given what is now known about schizophrenia, to treat it by utilizing these approaches is not only negligent, it is malpractice.

Group Therapy

Group psychotherapy, like individual psychotherapy, may run a broad range from insight-oriented groups to supportive meetings with an educational and/or social focus. Traditional group psychotherapy with its emphasis on interpersonal processes (e.g., "Sam, why did you ignore Sally just now when she was talking to you?") or intrapersonal processes ("Edna, can you explain to the group why your self-esteem is so low?") is of no value for patients with schizophrenia. Of nineteen studies done on group psychotherapy with such patients, "sixteen either failed to demonstrate an effect or were uninterpretable or irrelevant . . . two showed possible but very dubious effects" and "only one showed a minor clinical effect that was clearly not due to group therapy." Another reviewer of these studies concluded that "most controlled evaluations of group therapy with schizophrenics (especially long-term inpatients) showed meager, if any, therapeutic benefit from groups."

As with individual psychotherapy, there is some evidence that traditional group therapy with schizophrenic patients may even be detrimental. One study of aftercare centers for schizophrenics found that those centers which emphasized group psychotherapy had poorer results maintaining patients in the community compared with centers without this emphasis. Others have reported that group psychotherapy may precipitate the psychosis of persons who are becoming schizophrenic or bring about the relapse of those who previously had been sick. The finding of detrimental effects in traditional group therapy with schizophrenic patients is not surprising. Individuals with this disease are often being overwhelmed with sensory stimuli and thought which cannot be sorted out because of the brain dysfunction. What is needed in the early stages of a schizophrenic onset or relapse is a *decrease* in stimuli, yet group therapy offers exactly the opposite. As observed by Keith and Matthews summarizing research in this field: "Because group therapy is, in fact, a multiple stimulus situation frequently high in intensity, it may be counterproductive early in treatment."

Traditional group psychotherapy with an emphasis on interpersonal or intrapersonal processes must be distinguished from group meetings of patients with schizophrenia which have an educational or social focus. The latter group meetings may be very useful and will be discussed in chapter 9; they should not be referred to as "group therapy" so as to avoid confusion with traditional group therapy, which is not helpful and may even be harmful.

Shock Therapy, Diet, and Other Treatments

The use in schizophrenia of shock therapy, more formally called electroshock therapy (EST) or electroconvulsive therapy (ECT), is a controversial and unresolved issue in psychiatry. In the United States it is used very seldom, and most follow-up studies indicate that any benefits derived from it are transient. In Europe, in contrast, shock therapy is used frequently on patients with schizophrenia and follow-up studies are more positive. Its use has been vigorously opposed by ex-patient groups in the United States, and in states like California approval for its use must go through a special state-controlled board. In November, 1982, in a local referendum the city of Berkeley even voted to ban its use altogether, although this was later reversed by the courts. It is, therefore, not a realistic therapeutic alternative for most patients with schizophrenia.

No diet has been shown to be effective for schizophrenia, although many different diets utilizing vitamins have been advocated by proponents of orthomolecular theories (see chapter 6). Gluten-free diets have also been tried with contradictory results. Some families with schizophrenic members are convinced that the patient does better (or worse) when certain things are added to or deleted from his or her diet. My advice in such cases is to encourage the family to persist in the use of such a diet if it seems helpful and if the diet is nutritionally balanced and does not contain toxic amounts of any substance.

Other therapies are primarily of historical interest. Psychosurgery was utilized prior to the advent of antipsychotic drugs but no longer has a place in the treatment of schizophrenia. Similarly insulin shock therapy was commonly used during the two decades following World War II but is no longer thought to be of value. Newer therapies are tried from time to time, usually with great initial hopes and publicity; a recent example of this was hemodialysis, in which the blood of the schizophrenic patient is passed through a filter and returned to the body. Unfortunately, careful studies of this innovative attempt have failed to demonstrate that it has any effectiveness.

RECOMMENDED FURTHER READING

Baldessarini, R. J. *Chemotherapy in Psychiatry: Principles and Practice.* Cambridge, MA: Harvard University Press, 1985. This is the best standard textbook for professionals on the use of medications in psychiatry.

Biological Therapies in Psychiatry. Subscriptions from PSG, Inc., 545 Great Rd., Littleton, MA 01460. A monthly newsletter from the Department of Psychiatry of the Massachusetts General Hospital, it provides accurate and current assessments of medications for schizophrenic patients and is the easiest way to stay up-to-date in this rapidly changing area.

Davis, J. M. "Overview: Maintenance Therapy in Psychiatry. I. Schizophrenia." *American Journal of Psychiatry* 132 (1975): 1237–45. This is the best summary of studies showing the importance of continuing maintenance medications for schizophrenic persons, and an analysis of relapse rates when the medication is stopped.

New Directions in Drug Treatment for Schizophrenia. DHHS Publication no. ADM 84-1355. Rockville, MD: National Institute of Mental Health, 1984. This is a collection of articles originally published in the *Schizophrenia Bulletin* in 1983, concerning low-dose medication, intermittent medication, and related topics.

Scheifler-Roberts, P., and R. W. Mullaly. *Medication Maze.* Keene, NH: Intuition Press, 1985. Written in nontechnical terms, this is a useful guide for patients with schizophrenia and their families.

Wender, P. H., and D. F. Klein. *Mind, Mood and Medicine: A Guide to the New Biopsychiatry.* New York: Farrar, Straus & Giroux, 1981. An overview of schizophrenia and other mental illnesses, the book provides a particularly helpful perspective on recent advances in drug therapy. The biological causes of schizophrenia are assumed and discussed. The authors are two of the foremost researchers in psychiatry.

8

THE ORGANIZATION
OF OUTPATIENT PSYCHIATRIC
SERVICES FOR SCHIZOPHRENIA

With the knowledge that state hospitals required 100 years to achieve
their maximum size, the precipitous attempt to move large numbers
of their charges into settings that in fact did not exist, must be seen
as incompetent at best and criminal at worst.

John A. Talbott, "Deinstitutionalization:
Avoiding the Disasters of the Past"

Most persons with schizophrenia will require continuing outpatient
psychiatric services for many years. Like persons with diabetes or
hypertension, their medications will need to be increased, decreased, or
changed from time to time as the course of their disease fluctuates,
concurrent medical illnesses intervene, or side effects of the medication
mandate change. People with schizophrenia require a variety of services in addition to medication maintenance, as will be discussed in
chapter 9, but without adequate medication the other services usually
cannot be effectively used.

Up to the mid-1950s nobody worried about posthospital psychiatric services for people with schizophrenia, for a good reason—almost
no schizophrenic patients left the hospital. Once Aunt Elizabeth or
Uncle John went there, they simply stayed, sometimes for life. When
I began work at St. Elizabeths Hospital in 1977, I found many patients
who had spent most of their lives there; one elderly gentleman had been

there since 1909 and many had been there for over fifty years. The same thing could be found in any state hospital.

Following World War II, two changes took place, which were destined to transform psychiatric services. President Truman and influential members of Congress had been deeply impressed by the number of young men who were rejected for military service or discharged medically during the war because of serious psychiatric illnesses. Clearly these illnesses were much more common than anybody realized, and research on them was vital. Consequently, in 1946 Congress created the National Institute of Mental Health as part of the National Institutes of Health, with the intent of fostering research on serious mental illness. NIMH had no mandate to deliver services and only a very small amount of money for training psychiatric personnel; it was created primarily as a research institute for mental illness.

At the same time that NIMH was coming into existence, a series of exposés occurred, depicting the lives of inmates in state mental hospitals. Foremost among these were Albert Deutsch's *The Shame of the States,* published in 1948; Mike Gorman's Oklahoma newspaper series, followed by his book *Every Other Bed,* published in 1955; and the film *The Snake Pit,* released in 1949. Deutsch's work was particularly devastating, for it included both pictures and facts. After visiting hospitals in New York, Pennsylvania, Ohio, Michigan, and California he wrote:

> In some of the wards there were scenes that rivaled the horrors of the Nazi concentration camps—hundreds of naked mental patients herded into huge, barnlike, filth-infested wards, in all degrees of deterioration, untended and untreated, stripped of every vestige of human decency, many in stages of semi-starvation. The writer heard state hospital doctors frankly admit that the animals of near-by piggeries were better fed, housed and treated than many of the patients in their wards. . . .
>
> Actual physical brutality toward patients is not the rule and plays a small part in the real complaint against our state hospital system. The most serious defects arise from the deadly monotony of asylum life, the regimentation, the depersonalization and dehumanization of the patient, the herding of people with all kinds and degrees of mental sickness on the same wards, the lack of simple decencies, the complete lack of privacy in overcrowded institutions, the contempt for human dignity.

Deutsch received support from many mental health professionals, such as Dr. Kenneth E. Appel, who was professor of psychiatry at the University of Pennsylvania:

> Conditions in public mental hospitals are shocking, monstrous, and horrible. The majority of hospitals do not give treatment. They give custody—poor at that. Patients are herded like sheep. . . . Automobiles get better attention than most mental patients today. The grass surrounding the state hospitals receives more care and consideration than the patients inside.

There evolved a consensus, then, in the years following World War II, that something was seriously wrong in the care (or lack of care) for the seriously mentally ill. The average person had not been confronted with the issue before and felt something should be done. Congress, responding to this feeling and to a skilled lobbying effort by a handful of concerned individuals, established a Joint Commission on Mental Illness and Health in 1955 to study the problem and make recommendations for improvements.

In retrospect it is easy to discern the wrong turns taken in the ensuing years and to understand why outpatient psychiatric services for the seriously mentally ill are so inadequate today. Hindsight is always 20-20. Perhaps the most disturbing thing about the mistakes, however, is that they were not made maliciously, but by well-intentioned individuals. The road to hell *is* paved with good intentions.

THE FAILURE OF COMMUNITY
MENTAL HEALTH CENTERS

The Joint Commission on Mental Illness and Health met intermittently over the following five years and in 1961 issued its report, *Action for Mental Health*. The report focused on serious mental illness and the need for improvement of the state mental hospitals; as one solution it proposed a series of mental health centers in the community to treat the mentally ill closer to home. Such centers would be funded by federal tax dollars, a radical departure from almost two hundred years of exclusive state fiscal responsibility for the seriously mentally ill, and would function as the "main line of defense in reducing the need of many persons for prolonged or repeated hospitalizations."

Even before the report was officially issued, the Joint Commission's recommendations were appropriated by the Democratic Party. At its July, 1960, party convention in Los Angeles, the Democrats included in the platform a recommendation for "community mental health programs to help bring back thousands of our hospitalized mentally ill to full and useful lives in the community." John Kennedy was elected President that November, and sometime during the next two years he decided that mental illness and mental retardation should be priorities for his administration.

In his January, 1963, State of the Union message, Kennedy spoke of "the abandonment of the mentally ill and the mentally retarded to the grim mercies of custodial institutions" and the following month delivered his historic special message to Congress, entitled "Mental Illness and Mental Retardation." Kennedy proposed Community Mental Health Centers (CMHCs) as "a bold new approach" by which "when carried out, reliance on the cold mercy of custodial isolation will be supplanted by the open warmth of community concern and capability. . . . It has been demonstrated that two out of three schizophrenics—our largest category of mentally ill—can be treated and released within six months." No longer would it be necessary for the seriously mentally ill to undergo "a prolonged or permanent confinement in huge, unhappy mental hospitals. . . . If we launch a broad new mental health program now, it will be possible within a decade or two to reduce the number of patients now under custodial care by 50 percent or more." CMHCs, then, were set up for the seriously mentally ill as alternatives to the state hospitals. Kennedy made no mention of services for married couples who had difficulty communicating, young adults concerned about their relations with the opposite sex, or middle-aged individuals undergoing existential crises. President Kennedy was proposing a program for the suffering sick, not the worried well.

If there were any questions in anyone's mind regarding what the CMHCs were supposed to do, these should have been removed by the testimony of government officials on the proposed CMHCs in front of Congress. In March, 1963, a Department of Health, Education and Welfare (HEW) official testified that the proposed CMHCs would "move the care of the mentally ill into the community and out of these large mental institutions." HEW Secretary Anthony Celebrezze added:

> It is clear that huge custodial institutions are not suited for the treatment of mental illness. . . . Therefore, the national program for mental health

is centered on a wholly new emphasis and approach—care and treatment of most mentally ill persons in their home communities.

The CMHC bill was passed in 1963 and funds were approved by Congress. Authority was given to NIMH to write regulations for the CMHCs. NIMH, however, had no interest in the seriously mentally ill, and the regulations which emerged in May, 1964, reflected that lack of interest. They made no provision for these patients or their care by CMHCs whatsoever. As summarized by one study, the regulations prescribed "no plans, mechanisms, nor procedure to guide centers in determining their relationship to state hospitals; no methods to divert potential state hospital admissions to community mental health centers; and no procedures whereby patients released from state hospitals could be rehabilitated and assisted back into the community. Indeed, the regulations contain not a single reference to the goal of supplanting state hospitals!" The regulations simply defined the size of catchment areas and specified the *type* of services (e.g., inpatient, outpatient, partial hospitalization) without saying *who* was supposed to be served.

The consequences were predictable. Federal funds flowed directly to the CMHCs, bypassing state governments, so that states had scant leverage in determining how the funds were spent. The CMHCs had no more interest in the seriously mentally ill than NIMH had. Such patients were viewed as dull, uninteresting, and poor candidates for psychodynamic psychotherapy. Once the schizophrenic patients with their peculiar habits were deemed undesirable for the milieu of CMHC waiting rooms, they quickly got the message: they were not wanted.

From the beginning it was clear to anyone with eyes that the "bold new approach" primarily provided psychotherapy for individuals with interpersonal problems, and that patients with serious mental disorders were being ignored. In 1969 a NIMH study showed that one-third of all schizophrenic patients being released by state hospitals were being given no referral for aftercare, and a report of the American Psychiatric Association claimed "that some centers consciously discriminated against poor and chronically ill patients who came to them for help." In 1972, an internal NIMH report pointed out multiple abuses of CMHCs including the use of federal funds to build swimming pools in them and their use by private psychiatrists to hospitalize private patients.

The only people with improved lives appear to be the professionals who run the program. . . . If a Center is not doing what it said it would, NIMH is not really interested in knowing. This is the heart of the problem—the slow, sad steps which lead to a minuet of mutual deception.

In 1973, an article in the *American Journal of Psychiatry* was entitled "Care of the Chronically Mentally Ill: A National Disgrace." The same year a NIMH report, examining the relationship between state hospital discharges and CMHCs, concluded that "there is no large consistent relationship between the opening of centers [CMHCs] and changes in state hospital resident rates. This finding suggests a failure by individual centers to contribute to one of the major stated goals of the center program." The following year, under the direction of the Public Citizen Health Research Group, Franklin D. Chu and Sharland Trotter published *The Madness Establishment,* a scathing indictment of the CMHCs and NIMH. "The deficiencies of the program," it concluded, "are now too glaring to be brushed aside." Furthermore, NIMH data showed that between 1970 and 1975 the proportion of patients with schizophrenia being admitted to CMHCs *decreased* from 15 to 10 percent. In 1978, schizophrenic patients admitted to CMHCs were 12 percent, contrasting with 52 percent of admissions diagnosed with "transient situational disturbances," "social maladjustment," "other nonpsychotic," or "no mental disorder."

Incredibly, NIMH and the states paid virtually no attention to the accumulating data showing that the patients being emptied out of state hospitals were not being provided services by the CMHCs. Where mental health professionals and planners thought these people were going, or what might happen to them, is an abiding mystery.

NIMH continued to fund CMHCs with virtually no changes. To date, over 800 centers have been funded with cumulative federal grants of over $3 billion. Most CMHCs specialize in psychotherapy and counseling services for marital crises, family problems, stress management, better communications, and similar interpersonal problems. For example, a CMHC in Fort Wayne, Indiana, after receiving $12.7 million in federal funds between 1977 and 1981, changed its name from Community Mental Health Center to "The Park Center." The old name connoted services to the seriously mentally ill, while the new name, said the center newsletter, "would enable Park Center to better reach those persons who need counseling services for life adjustment problems such as marital, family, and personal problems." When CMHCs in Indiana were criticized in a 1986 national survey for failing to provide care for the seriously mentally ill, Indiana Governor Robert D. Orr *defended* the program by saying that *14 percent* of patients seen in Indiana's thirty CMHCs were seriously mentally ill.

Most public officials and CMHC directors have, of course, long since forgotten the original purpose of the centers, as clearly illustrated in an article published in 1986 by the director of a CMHC in Florida. The author bitterly assailed state pressure on his CMHC to accept the seriously mentally ill as patients, and concluded his article by saying: "Now is the time to go back to the John F. Kennedy administration philosophy of a *balanced* mental health system which has as its focus *psychotherapy*" (italics in original).

THE DEBACLE OF DEINSTITUTIONALIZATION

Given the failure of CMHCs to provide psychiatric aftercare for patients released from state mental hospitals, the process of deinstitutionalization was doomed to become a disaster. Between 1955 and the present, hundreds of thousands of seriously ill psychiatric patients have been discharged from state hospitals, often after a stay of many years, having no locus in the community for psychiatric aftercare. In 1955 there were 557,000 patients in public mental hospitals in the United States; now there are approximately 112,000. In the peak years of deinstitutionalization, between 1965 and 1980, 358,000 hospital beds were emptied and these patients released into the community to live. Some states deinstitutionalized patients more quickly than others; in California the number of patients was reduced from 37,000 to 3,000; in Massachusetts from 23,000 to 2,400. Despite massive transfers of patient responsibility from the state level to the community, however, there was no concomitant transfer of psychiatric staff or fiscal resources to cope with them in the community. In New York State, the state hospital population shrank from 93,000 patients in 1955 to 24,000 in 1981. Yet, despite this reduction, not a single state hospital was closed and the total of state hospital employees during this period *increased* from 23,800 to 37,000. In 1955 there were four patients for each employee; in 1981 for each patient there were 1.5 employees.

There were, to be certain, many discharged patients who did well in the community. This was especially true of the first patients released, who were the least disabled and most ready to live in the community.

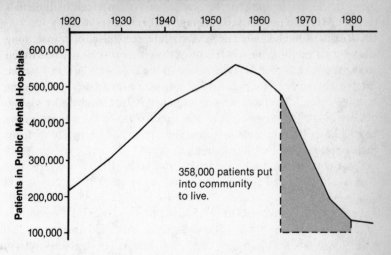

THE DEINSTITUTIONALIZATION OF AMERICA'S SERIOUSLY MENTALLY ILL

Patients in Public Mental Hospitals

358,000 patients put into community to live.

Approximately two-thirds of these early discharges went to live in their own or relatives' homes, indicating that they had a social support network. This was not true for later groups of discharged patients, only one-quarter of whom returned to family settings.

The failure of CMHCs represents the largest single cause of the debacle of deinstitutionalization, but other mistakes have compounded the problem. Antipsychotic drugs were oversold, for example; mental health professionals implied that a mere injection of Prolixin every two weeks was sufficient, when in fact seriously ill psychiatric patients require a wide array of support and rehabilitation services (see chapter 9). Furthermore, a romantic notion prevailed in the 1960s that mental hospitals themselves *cause* serious mental disease and that once the patients were released they would be much better because they were living in the community. It became radical chic to liberate the mental patients and return them to the community. Erving Goffman's sociological study *Asylums* promoted this view, as did Ken Kesey's fanciful *One Flew Over the Cuckoo's Nest.* Chief Broom, who runs away from the hospital at the end of the novel to avoid the malicious ministrations of Big Nurse, would in Kesey's imagination live happily ever after, spearing salmon in the Columbia River. In fact, like most such patients, Chief Broom, receiving neither medication nor aftercare, would diminish into a mentally ill, homeless person with frostbitten toes, hallucinating in the streets of downtown Portland.

Mistakes in funding services for the seriously mentally ill further compounded the problem. Prior to 1963, fiscal responsibility for psychiatric patients had always been a state responsibility. That year, however, at the time the CMHC program was starting, the mentally ill were made eligible for the federal Aid to the Disabled (ATD) program for the first time. The ATD program, which had been rising at an average rate of 9 percent a year prior to 1963, increased at a rate of almost 18 percent a year in the 10 years following the change, going from $3.8 million in 1963 to $16 million in 1973. At that time it was incorporated into the Supplemental Security Income (SSI) program and the costs of SSI continued rising rapidly. By 1984 it was estimated that total federal SSI payments to disabled persons with serious mental illnesses had reached over one *billion* dollars ($1,037,859,000) and the federal payments to disabled persons with serious mental illness in the companion SSDI program (Social Security Disability Insurance) had also passed one *billion* dollars ($1,279,510,000). Together they totaled $2.3 billion.

While federal SSI and SSDI programs were accepting fiscal responsibility for the discharged seriously mentally ill, other federal programs were also enacted. Medicaid, begun in 1965, paid some of the medical bills for patients in the community, while others were covered by Medicare, begun in 1966. Also in 1966, the federal food stamps program was enacted and the discharged seriously mentally ill, because they had no income, were eligible.

The net effect was to set up a giant, tragic shell game between state and federal governments. As long as the patients were hospitalized in state mental hospitals they were the fiscal responsibility of the state, but once placed in the community they became eligible for SSI, Medicaid, and food stamps. It did not take state legislatures long to realize this and pressure built rapidly to empty the state hospitals. Where the patients went in the community was less important, the mandate was to get them out. Some states (e.g., New York) directly rewarded state hospital superintendents for their success in emptying their hospitals.

As states began to shift their fiscal responsibility for the seriously mentally ill from themselves to the federal government, they told state taxpayers that money was being saved. What they really meant was that *state* money was being saved. In fact taxpayers were still footing the bill through their federal taxes (e.g., increased SSI and SSDI costs), but the states did not publicize that point.

Other serious mistakes exacerbating the debacle of deinstitutionalization over the past two decades have been the mistakes of well-meaning lawyers. The problems began in 1963 with the publication of Thomas Szasz' *Law, Liberty and Psychiatry,* in which he advocated the abolition of all involuntary psychiatric hospitalizations. Lawyers became interested in the civil rights of mental patients, and in 1971 brought suit against the State of Alabama, demanding minimum levels of care in the psychiatric hospitals *(Wyatt* v. *Stickney).* The following year the Mental Health Law Project, dedicated to legally improving psychiatric patients' rights, was begun. In 1975, another landmark case was brought against state hospital psychiatrists for failure to treat *(Donaldson* v. *O'Connor)* and subsequent cases have mandated release of patients from state hospitals and placement in "the least restrictive setting" in the community (e.g., *Dixon* v. *Weinberger* in the District of Columbia). The effect of both the minimum-level-of-care suits and the least-restrictive-setting suits has been to markedly increase the exodus of patients from state mental hospitals, often providing states with a legal rationalization for doing what they wanted to do anyway to reduce state costs. Clearly for both individual patients and state systems the involvement of lawyers has often been a well-meaning disaster.

The last, but certainly not the least, mistake which contributed to the failed services for the seriously ill was the failure of NIMH or the states to do research on the effects of deinstitutionalization. In effect a massive shift in social policy took place, the emptying of state mental hospitals which had been performing a function for over one hundred years, with no pilot studies, no data base to suggest that it would work, and no ongoing research to ascertain whether it was working. There has probably not been such a major shift in public policy in the United States in recent decades which was initiated and carried out with such a paucity of research findings to support it. The policies behind deinstitutionalization were implemented on blind faith. In retrospect, the key word is blind.

In summary, then, deinstitutionailzation has been a debacle primarily because of the failure of CMHCs to accept responsibility for seriously ill patients as they left state hospitals. Other errors further compounded the situation. Making mistakes is not necessarily fatal, however, if we can learn from them, and such learning truly measures good public administration. Despite the many missteps of recent decades, the elements of good outpatient psychiatric services for the seriously mentally ill have become clear.

ELEMENTS OF GOOD PSYCHIATRIC SERVICES

In 1986 the Health Research Group, the health arm of Public Citizen, Inc., founded by consumer advocate Ralph Nader, issued a report rating state programs for the seriously mentally ill. According to the summary of the report: "The single most important finding in this survey is that there are local programs in some states, and a small number of state programs, providing high-quality services for the seriously mentally ill. They demonstrate conclusively that such programs are possible and that the seriously mentally ill and their families need not accept mediocre services as a fact of life." Wisconsin, Rhode Island, and Colorado were singled out as the most highly rated state programs.

From this survey and other reports there is emerging a consensus on the elements of good outpatient psychiatric services for the seriously mentally ill, as follows:

Targeting the Seriously Mentally Ill as First Priority. Psychiatric outpatient services are obviously a finite resource for an almost infinite series of demands which may be placed upon such services. Married couples having problems, poor or minority groups with no jobs and low self-esteem, elderly persons who are lonely, and children underachieving in school because of emotional problems are only a few of the groups which may view local psychiatric outpatient services as a primary solution to their problems. The needs of these groups are both worthy and compelling, yet if psychiatric resources are utilized for them in large numbers, soon no resources are left for the seriously mentally ill. This is precisely what has happened in many CMHCs in the United States. It is, in short, a choice between promoting "mental health" or treating mental illness.

The allocation of public psychiatric resources is ultimately an ethical question. Which group is most worthy? Which group needs the services more? Which group can utilize the services best? What is the benefit to society of providing psychiatric services to each group? Dr. J. R. Elpers, in a recent discussion of this question, argued that the seriously mentally ill have fewer alternative resources and are also sicker, and on these grounds require first priority. What has become abundantly clear in recent years is that state programs which have targeted the seriously mentally ill as having priority for psychiatric services (e.g., Wisconsin, Colorado, Oregon) have much better programs than states which have not done so.

Fiscal Policies in Which Funds Follow Patients. One of the most striking findings of the Health Research Group study involved the lack of any relationship between the amount of money being spent by states on public psychiatric services and the quality of services being provided for the seriously mentally ill. New York State, for example, spends three times as much per capita as states like Wisconsin or Colorado, yet has mediocre services for the seriously mentally ill compared with the leaders.

How do some states do a better job with less money? They do so by utilizing fiscal policies in which the funds follow the patient. For example, Wisconsin allocates funds to each county for psychiatric services. Each time a patient enters a state hospital, the county must pay the state per diem costs for the patient. When the patient is discharged from the hospital the county no longer has to pay the state. The effect of such fiscal policies, now being implemented in many other states, is to encourage local psychiatric services to take care of the seriously mentally ill and prevent rehospitalizations. Failure to do so costs the county money.

One question frequently arises: Is it more expensive to maintain seriously mentally ill individuals as inpatients or as outpatients? The answer, of course, depends in part on which seriously mentally ill individuals are being discussed, for some demand many more resources than others. It will depend, too, on the quality of inpatient care (high patient-to-staff ratio vs. warehousing) and the quality of outpatient care (good support and rehabilitation programs vs. dumping patients at the local bus station). To date, some studies show that it is more expensive to maintain seriously mentally ill individuals in the community, and other studies show that it is less expensive. My strong impression from the data is that the cost is probably about the same.

Continuity of Care. Although this principle is paid widespread lip service, it is in fact rarely achieved. Seriously mentally ill patients transfer from one ward to the next and, once they leave the hospital, are often assigned a new treatment team each time they change residences. Sadly typical of the situation in much of the United States is the continuity of treatment offered Sylvia Frumkin, the focus of Susan

Sheehan's *Is There No Place on Earth for Me?*, who over an 18-year period had 27 separate admissions to 8 different hospitals with a total of 45 changes in treatment settings.

It may well be that the key element in continuity of care is continuity of the caregiver. In other words, a single individual or team should be responsible for the psychiatric care of a person with serious mental illness, no matter where that person goes within a defined geographic area. A description of such an arrangement was provided by Dr. Mary Ann Test, one of the nation's acknowledged leaders on the organization of psychiatric services, who defined continuity of caregiver as taking "responsibility for seeing to it that a chronically mentally ill person's needs are met. . . . The team members do not necessarily meet all the client's needs themselves (they may involve other persons or agencies). However they never transfer this obligation to someone else. The buck stops with the team . . . the team remains responsible for the client no matter what his or her behavior is. This fixed point of responsibility means that the client always has a consistent resource." Elsewhere I have called such an arrangement "continuous treatment teams."

Continuity of caregivers is logical in theory, considering the needs of patients. People with serious mental illness, especially schizophrenia, often have great difficulties in establishing human relationships and to expect them to transfer their trust from one treatment team to another is exceedingly unrealistic. Continuity of caregivers also has many advantages from the point of view of mental health professionals, allowing them to get to know patients in depth, assessing their medication history and potentials for rehabilitation, and working with their family.

Organizational Elements.   Leadership of the county and state mental health service system is an important determinant of the quality of psychiatric services for the seriously mentally ill. In a few states the governor and/or state legislature have also taken a special interest in this problem which has been very helpful. Decentralization of responsibility for such services from the state capital to the county level appears to increase chances for producing good services. Psychiatric care systems in which the mental health professionals regularly leave their offices to see patients in community settings (e.g., halfway houses, shelters, workshops) are almost always better than those in which this rarely happens. Finally, those psychiatric outpatient systems in which the directors and administrators retain some day-to-day clinical responsibility, along with their executive responsibilities, invariably surpass those in which the leaders no longer see patients. This principle applies at all levels; many of the disastrous decisions made by NIMH over the years issued forth from pundits devoid of experience with or clinical responsibility for the seriously mentally ill.

Use of Outpatient Commitment.   Many people with serious mental illnesses remain functional and relatively well as long as they take medications, but relapse when their medications are stopped. The revolving doors of state mental hospitals are kept in perpetual motion by such patients as they come in, get well on medications, leave, stop taking medications, relapse, and start the cycle one more time. It is not unusual in such hospitals to find patients who have been admitted twenty or more times over several years. A few of the patients stop taking the medications because of side effects, but the majority stop because they simply do not recognize that they have an illness and need the medications. The brain, an organ used in thinking about ourselves and assessing our needs, is the same body part which is functionally impaired in the seriously mentally ill.

Outpatient commitment and conditional release are effective means of stopping the revolving door. They allow the patient to be released from the hospital *on the condition that* the person continue taking medication. Compliance with medication-taking can be assessed by utilizing injections (e.g., fluphenazine, trade name Prolixin, or haloperidol, trade name Haldol) or by checking blood levels (e.g., lithium). Outpatient commitment and conditional release are grossly underutilized. A recent study found that, although it is legally sanctioned in two-thirds of the states, most mental health professionals are not aware of outpatient commitment and less than 5 percent of all commitments are to outpatient status. North Carolina, Hawaii, and Georgia were the first states to pass outpatient commitment laws, allowing individuals to be committed as outpatients without having first been committed as inpatients.

Modification of Services for Rural Areas.   Outpatient psychiatric services for the seriously mentally ill need tailoring to suit specific varieties of subcultures and geography, especially in rural areas where patients may be very widespread. Psychiatric services planned for a million people in a state like Rhode Island simply demand modification when the same number of people extend over a big state like Montana.

The most successful rural outpatient psychiatric services in North

America are found not in the United States but in the Canadian province of Saskatchewan. Deinstitutionalization has been carried out there in an orderly fashion: in 1957 there were 3,400 psychiatric inpatients in the province, and by 1978 that number had been reduced to 291, less than 9 percent of the original. Unlike many states, however, Saskatchewan made certain that psychiatric outpatient care was available in the community before discharging the patients. Care was arranged with general practitioners and community nurses who were given special training and support; the few psychiatrists available in Saskatchewan were used as consultants. In rural areas more support must be given to the families of patients, since most of the patients return home to live. The families become, in essence, the primary caregivers, and their effectiveness increases as this fact is recognized by those administering the psychiatric services.

Manpower Development. Psychiatric services are only as good as the personnel who deliver them. Furthermore, since 80 percent of the costs of psychiatric services in most states fund personnel costs, one would have thought that great efforts would have been put into manpower development.

That is not the case, however. Most psychiatric manpower systems are encrusted with civil service bureaucracy and union regulations; innovations and attempts to improve psychiatric manpower have been remarkably rare. One innovative approach that did work was the program implemented by the State of Maryland to recruit better psychiatrists by giving them joint appointments in the University Department of Psychiatry. Personnel systems allowing for advancement on the basis of excellence in clinical work should also be encouraged; all too often the only way an outstanding mental health professional can gain promotion is by giving up clinical work and becoming a full-time administrator. The system, in essence, values pushing papers and writing memos over taking care of patients.

The elements of good psychiatric services, then, are known and reasonably well agreed-upon by mental health professionals and planners. Transforming these elements from mere plans to reality is the task few counties or states have yet shown an inclination to take on. In late 1986 the U.S. Congress passed a bill authorizing grants to states to help develop mental health plans for the chronically mentally ill, which would incorporate some of the elements of good psychiatric services (Public Law 99-660). It is unfortunate that federal funds cannot also be used to purchase sufficient willpower to implement the plans.

DANE COUNTY: A MODEL PROGRAM

Of all the counties in the United States, Dane County, Wisconsin, is widely acknowledged to have the best outpatient psychiatric services. Ironically, the county has achieved this status with a Community Mental Health Center that was one of the few never to receive any federal funds. Their keynote is comprehensiveness, including a full range of services available to meet the needs of approximately 1,100 seriously mentally ill adults in the county of 323,000 persons. The use of inpatient hospitalization has been reduced dramatically from 10,100 hospital days per year in 1977, to 2,600 in 1985. The seriously mentally ill are maintained in the community with medications and "assertive case management," which takes mental health professionals onto the streets where they actively seek out patients who have not come in for scheduled appointments. At the same time the housing and vocational needs of these persons are addressed through contracts between the Dane County Unified Services Board and the YMCA (which runs small housing units) and Goodwill Industries (which provides job training). The case management of approximately 10 percent of the seriously mentally ill is done by an experimental program funded by NIMH (Program of Assertive Community Treatment, or PACT) and the others by the CMHC.

One could speculate why a county in southern Wisconsin has moved so far in front of other counties in the United States in a program for the seriously mentally ill. Wisconsin's long history of decentralizing responsibility for services to counties forms one element, strengthened in 1974 when the counties were given full responsibility for both inpatient and outpatient funds for seriously mentally ill county residents. Thus a county could spend its money hospitalizing such individuals, or utilize the same money to provide services in the community, which is what Dane County did. The PACT program which began in 1972 has also been important by providing a nucleus of well-trained and committed mental health professionals. Such individuals attract similar others so that now the county has an outstanding group of mental health professionals dedicated to public service. Dane County was also the origin of one of the earliest National Alliance for the Mentally Ill (NAMI) family consumer groups in 1977, and they have acted as an impetus for the development of services. Finally, the general intellectual milieu of Dane County, which includes the city of Madison and the University of Wisconsin, is innovative and encouraging of experimental programs.

The Dane County program is still far from perfect. There are waiting lists for many services, some families complain that hospitalization is not used enough, and some seriously mentally ill persons still fall between the cracks. But it is cost-effective and significantly more comprehensive than any other program. There are a handful of other counties scattered around the United States which are rapidly improving their services for the seriously mentally ill, and Dane County's leadership is likely to be challenged in the near future; some of these counties are mentioned in the state summaries in appendix D. What such programs do is demonstrate that deinstitutionalization truly *can* work if outpatient psychiatric services are organized appropriately.

THE CONCEPT OF ASYLUM

When the deinstitutionalization of seriously ill psychiatric patients began in the early 1960s, most people assumed that some patients could be placed in the community but that many others would continue to need long-term hospitalization. By the early 1970s that assumption had been steadily eroded, and in some states (e.g., California, Massachusetts) there was serious talk of closing state hospitals altogether. Another decade later we have come back, full circle, to where we began, and most mental health professionals who work with seriously ill patients believe that there is, and will continue to be, a need for state hospitals for some patients.

The kinds of patients who will continue to need state hospitals are those whose symptoms are the most severe and/or whose behavior makes placement in the community very difficult. They include the 10 to 20 percent of seriously mentally ill who respond minimally or not at all to antipsychotic drugs, those with a propensity toward aggression or violence, those with inappropriate behaviors such as setting fires or disrobing in public, and those who are so helpless and/or dependent that they need the protection of the institution. It would be nice if there were no such patients, but there are and—until we learn the causes of brain diseases like schizophrenia—there will continue to be. Because of the push to close down hospitals and because of legal decisions mandating the placement of patients in the community as "the least restrictive setting," many patients are currently being returned to the community who should not be.

How big a group of patients is this? The answer will depend in large measure on the quality of outpatient psychiatric and rehabilitation services available. A county with excellent programs, such as Dane County, Wisconsin, may be able to successfully maintain in the community all except 10 percent of the seriously mentally ill, whereas in an area with few services less than half of all seriously ill patients may be better off in the community. The point is that in every system there comes a point where you have to ask hard questions. Is this patient really better off living in the community than remaining in the hospital? Is the quality of his/her life really going to be better? Is the community truly the "least restrictive setting" for this person? In our rush to return everybody to the community, we have avoided asking such questions in recent years, and yet many of them have ended up in nursing homes, boarding homes, and public shelters much worse than the hospital ward they left. In my eight years of placing patients in the Washington, D.C., community from St. Elizabeths Hospital, I would estimate that at least one-quarter of them were *worse* off, in terms of quality of life, than they had been in the hospital. And such patients often told me that they would gladly return to the hospital if they had the opportunity.

We need to acknowledge, then, the need for some long-term psychiatric beds for the severely disabled. It is reviving the concept of asylum in the benevolent sense that the term was originally used—as protection for those who cannot protect themselves. We do not expect everyone who gets paralytic polio to necessarily be able to walk again, and we do not place them in boarding homes in the community if they are clearly unable to look after themselves. We maintain long-term hospital beds for patients with other severe brain diseases, such as multiple sclerosis and Alzheimer's disease, who are unable to care for themselves. Why shouldn't we do the same for schizophrenia?

RECOMMENDED FURTHER READING

Bassuk, E. L., and S. Gerson. "Deinstitutionalization and Mental Health Services." *Scientific American* 238 (1978): 46–53. This is a complete review of the rise and fall of Community Mental Health Centers and the origins of deinstitutionalization. It puts contemporary changes into historical perspective and is not an optimistic article.

Chu, F. D., and S. Trotter. *The Madness Establishment.* New York: Grossmans, 1974. The Health Research Group investigation of CMHCs in the early 1970s shows their deficiencies from the earliest years of the program.

Lamb, H. R., and R. Peele. "The Need for Continuing Asylum and Sanctuary." *Hospital and Community Psychiatry* 35 (1984): 798–802. A clear and concise analysis describes the need for asylum for some patients.

Torrey, E. F. "Continuous Treatment Teams in the Care of the Chronic Mentally Ill." *Hospital and Community Psychiatry* 37 (1986): 1243–47. This addresses the issue of continuity of care, one of the most critical variables in successfully maintaining persons with schizophrenia in the community.

Torrey, E. F., and S. M. Wolfe. *Care of the Seriously Mentally Ill: A Rating of State Programs.* Washington: Health Research Group, 1986. The survey rates the quality of services for the seriously mentally ill for each state, and gives examples of some good programs. A new survey will be published in September, 1988.

Wasow, M. "The Need for Asylum for the Chronically Mentally Ill." *Schizophrenia Bulletin* 12 (1986): 162–67. An excellent argument for the continued availability of asylum care for some patients.

9

WHAT THE PATIENT NEEDS

Expecting the chronically ill patient to use the current mental health system is like expecting a paraplegic to use stairs.

J. Halpern et al., *The Illness of Deinstitutionalization*, 1978

Proper medication is the single most important ingredient in the treatment and rehabilitation of persons with schizophrenia. But beyond that, what else do they need? Is a visit to an outpatient psychiatric clinic every other Wednesday for an injection of long-acting fluphenazine or haloperidol the sum total of treating schizophrenia? Many public mental health systems, unfortunately, have operated as if this were indeed the case.

Persons with schizophrenia, of course, need much more than medication. Services provided for them while in the hospital must still be provided once they leave the hospital. Too often we take for granted the provision of needs without thinking through the problems released patients may have in obtaining them. This was expressed clearly by Dr. John Talbott, who wrote: "To expect patients with major ego deficits and residual dysfunctioning, without families and social networks, to suddenly be able to obtain for themselves the professional and custodial services they formerly took for granted in a total institution, seems the stuff of sheer fantasy."

Patients with schizophrenia, then, are more than mere receptacles into which medications may be poured or injected. They are human beings and, as such, they have the same needs and desires as all of us. If you want to know the needs of someone with schizophrenia other than medication, simply think of your own needs and you will have a reasonably precise answer.

FOOD AND HOUSING

The need for food and housing of persons with schizophrenia is so self-evident that even to list it seems fatuous. And yet the past decade has witnessed the discharge from hospitals of tens of thousands of patients with schizophrenia with *no provision* made for their basic needs. Such individuals end up living on the streets and in public shelters, in some cases even being encouraged to do so by the hospital personnel discharging them. For several years I have worked with women with schizophrenia living in shelters for the homeless in Washington, D.C., and on a regular basis I encounter women who have been discharged from hospitals with no plans for food or housing. Were it not for volunteer groups, especially religious groups, which run most of the shelters and soup kitchens, many of these discharged schizophrenics would have literally starved to death.

Where housing is available for persons with schizophrenia, it varies chiefly in how much supervision is provided. The different types of housing can be divided as follows:

Professional Supervision.   This type of housing has professionally trained persons who provide supervision for most or all of the 24-hour day. It includes crisis houses, halfway houses, quarter-way houses, and similar facilities.

Nonprofessional Supervision.   These facilities have a supervisor in residence, part or all of the time, but the supervisor has no training. These include foster homes, board-and-care homes, boarding houses, group homes, congregate care homes, and similar facilities which go by different names in different locales.

Intermittent Supervision.   These residences include apartments and group homes set up for persons with schizophrenia to live basically on their own. Usually a social worker or other mental health professional stops by periodically (e.g., once a week) to make certain that there are no major problems.

No Supervision.   Many persons with schizophrenia live on their own with no supervision. Some live quite comfortably in their own home or apartment, others at the YMCA or YWCA, and still others in rundown SROs (single-room-occupancy hotels).

Live with Family. The single largest number of schizophrenics in the United States live with their families. This will be discussed in chapter 10.

The quality of housing for persons with schizophrenia varies widely. On one end of the spectrum are small foster homes where each patient has a room, the food is adequate, and the foster home sponsors watch over and worry about their charges as if they were their own children. A larger version of this may be a renovated hotel where the manager hires staff which organizes social activities for the residents, checks to be sure they are taking their medicine, reminds them of dentist appointments, and helps them fill out applications for food stamps.

But at the other extreme are foster homes with sponsors who provide insufficent heat, blankets, and food, steal the patients' meager funds, use them as cheap labor, and sometimes even rape them or pimp for them. The larger versions of these homes are old hotels that provide no services other than a rundown room and perform similar kinds of exploitation.

Predictably the deinstitutionalization movement has spawned many foster homes, boarding houses, and hotels on both ends of the spectrum and at all points between. Media exposés of abuses have been relatively frequent. In one foster home that was closed in the nation's capital, according to a newspaper story, an unannounced inspection found dirty pans growing mold and covered with roaches, "hundreds of roaches living in the oven feeding on a bag of prunes," multiple electrical and fire hazards, termites throughout the house, swollen cans of home-canned fruit, and for sleeping, only "one folding bed with a thin uncovered mattress which was urine stained and odorous."

I have personally been in foster homes and boarding houses for released psychiatric patients which were as bad as the one described, and which were within eight blocks of the White House. Why we allow such housing to exist for individuals who often cannot defend their own interests is an important question. It is as if society is implicitly saying that people with psychiatric disorders are third-class citizens and do not deserve decent housing. Given the suffering most persons with schizophrenia undergo, it seems morally more reasonable to provide the best housing for these people, rather than the worst.

Supervision in many homes for released psychiatric patients often exists on paper only. In a group home in Baltimore, which was licensed as a "graduated independent living program" with 24-hour supervision, the staff failed to discover a young diabetic until three days after he had died in his room. And in New York City "the police found the decaying corpse of a former patient lying undisturbed in one home inhabited by six other residents."

Because the living facilities are so poor in many places, the mental health professionals in charge of discharging patients from state hospitals are frequently caught in an ethical dilemma. Is the patient really better off in the community than in the hospital? Are the living conditions and exposure to potential victimization really an improvement? I am always surprised to find how many released patients with schizophrenia express satisfaction with their living conditions in the community when I know how shoddy the living conditions are. In one study of patients living in board-and-care homes in Los Angeles, 40 percent claimed to be content or reasonably content. I suspect the contentment is in comparison to being back in the hospital or having to live in public shelters or on the streets.

What are the common denominators of good housing for schizophrenics living in the community? There are four characteristics which can be identified. First, the people living there are treated with dignity and warmth, not simply as sources of income. Second, the best housing appears to set a maximum of ten to twelve persons living in a single facility. Boarding homes or congregate care homes for 50, 100, or even more released patients almost invariably become mental hospital wards called by another name; this is transinstitutionalization rather than deinstitutionalization.

Third, good community housing for psychiatric patients exists in a coordinated continuum whereby a person can be moved to a residence with more or less supervision depending on the needs of the person. Because schizophrenia is a disease of remissions and relapses, it is unrealistic to expect a patient to remain in the same kind of facility indefinitely. Many of the clubhouse models (see pages 265–72), such as Thresholds in Chicago, furnish a continuum of housing, and a few public systems such as in Ogden, Utah, have pioneered in this direction.

Finally, community housing for patients with schizophrenia is most useful where it is integrated with other activities of the patients.

An excellent example of this principle is the Fairweather Lodges, in which patients live together and contract for jobs as a group. Such facilities have been deemed to be very successful where they have been tried.

A practical problem that frequently arises with community housing for psychiatric patients is the issue of zoning and community resistance to such housing. Everybody applauds the placement of patients in the community, it is said, as long as the placement is not in their neighborhood. In some towns and cities in the United States, local fights over this issue have been very bitter. There have now been forty studies done on the effect of residential group homes for the mentally ill and mentally retarded on the surrounding neighborhood. A review of these studies found that "the presence of group homes in all the areas studied has *not* lowered property values or increased turnover, *not* increased crime, *not* changed the character of the neighborhood." Persons with schizophrenia in fact make very good neighbors. This assumes, of course, that they are being followed for their illness and supervised for medication by responsible mental health professionals.

INCOME

Some persons with schizophrenia who are able to work part-time or full-time can be self-supporting. The majority, however, must rely on their families or two government programs, Supplemental Security Income (SSI) and Social Security Disability Insurance (SSDI), for the money to pay for their food and housing.

SSI, a program to provide income for needy aged, blind, and disabled persons, is administered by the Social Security Administration. It defines disability as "an inability to engage in any substantial gainful activity by reason of any medically determined physical or mental impairment which . . . has lasted, or can be expected to last, for a continuous period of not less than twelve months." SSDI is a similar operation, except that to be eligible the person must have worked prior to becoming ill and accumulated sufficient credit under Social Security. Benefits from both programs vary; SSDI functions according to how long the person had worked before becoming ill, while SSI varies from state to state depending upon how much that state supplements the federal SSI payment. Although the precise number of persons with schizophrenia receiving SSI and SSDI is unknown, the range probably falls between 400,000 and 500,000; this would be between 33 and 42 percent of all persons with active schizophrenia in the United States and would include most of those residing in foster homes, board-and-care homes, and similar group facilities. The total federal expenditure for the SSI and SSDI programs for individuals with serious mental illnesses in 1984 was $2.3 *billion,* not including state supplements.

During the early 1980s considerable public attention focused on the SSI and SSDI programs when officials in the Reagan administration decided to tighten the criteria for eligibility for such payments. In 1981 and 1982 it was estimated that almost one-half million disabled persons were dropped from the program, including many persons with schizophrenia. Court challenges to these changes followed, and in 1986 the U.S. Supreme Court ruled in favor of the disabled and the majority of those who had been cut off the SSI and SSDI programs were reinstated.

Applications to establish disability and receive SSI funds should be made at the local Social Security office. The person's assets and other income are taken into consideration in computing eligibility. If he or she has assets worth more than $1,500 he may not be eligible; in computing assets a home and basic household goods do not count toward the $1,500. Income from a job of over $65 a month will also reduce the amount of the SSI payment. Thus a person with schizophrenia who is trying to go back to work must compute work income carefully to be certain that this income offsets the loss of SSI benefits. SSDI is more liberal in allowing individuals to work part-time before benefits are reduced.

The application for SSI is evaluated by a team consisting of a disability examiner and a physician; they may request additional medical information or even request an examination of the applicant in selected cases. In evaluating the application they pay special attention to evidence of a restriction of daily activities and interests, deterioration in personal habits, marked impairment in relating to other people, and the inability to concentrate and carry out instructions necessary to hold a job. Assessing eligibility for SSI is necessarily a subjective task, and studies have reported disagreement among SSI reviewers as much as 50 percent of the time.

If the applicant is denied SSI, he/she has the right to appeal. This must be done within sixty days of the denial, and additional evidence of disability can be included at that time. The initial reconsideration of the appeal occurs in the local Social Security office and results in approval only 15 percent of the time. However, the applicant may appeal again, and this time the hearing is before an administrative law judge of the Bureau of Hearings and Appeals of the U.S. Department of Health and Human Services. At this level 58 percent of appeals were approved in 1980. Further appeals are possible to a Department of Health and Human Services appeals council and then to a U.S. district court. It is clear that persistence in pressing a legitimate claim for SSI benefits will result in success most of the time.

Schizophrenics usually require assistance with SSI applications and, when necessary, with the appeals processes. Social workers who are doing these on a regular basis are often very helpful, especially in ensuring that the correct clinical information is included so that the person's degree of disability can be assessed fairly. Persons applying for SSI for psychiatric disability for the first time would be wise to utilize the services of a knowledgeable social worker. Application forms and appeals processes are confusing even for persons whose brains are working perfectly; to a schizophrenic they must appear completely Kafkaesque.

SSI payments, but not SSDI payments, are reduced by one-third when the disabled recipient lives with his/her family. In theory this takes account of the room and board the person receives, but in fact it penalizes schizophrenics for living at home. Many families of schizophrenic persons resent this discriminatory living aspect of the SSI program and claim that they have expenses for the person just as surely as a boarding house operator does. SSI payments are also stopped if a person is hospitalized for more than thirty days. A portion of the SSI monthly payment is intended for the disabled person to use as spending money for clothes, transportation, laundry, and entertainment. The amount of spending money varies by state and currently averages $30 to 40 per month.

It is important for persons with schizophrenia to establish eligibility for SSI benefits if they can. Even if they have other income, thereby reducing the monthly SSI check to a very small amount, it is still worthwhile. The reason is that eligibility for SSI may also establish eligibility for several other assistance programs which can be worth much more than the SSI benefits by themselves. Such programs include Medicaid, vocational rehabilitation services, food stamps, and some housing and rental assistance programs of the Department of Housing and Urban Development. In some states eligibility for SSI automatically confers eligibility for the other programs, while in other states a separate application must be submitted.

Individuals with schizophrenia who do not receive support from their families or from the SSI and SSDI programs must rely on other income. Many of them, especially those living in public shelters, utilize public assistance or welfare checks. Schizophrenics who were in the military at the time they first became ill often qualify for disability payments from the Veterans Administration; these are often very generous and may total over $1,000 a month when all benefits are included.

Food stamps are another supplementary source of support for persons with schizophrenia and are underutilized. To be eligible a person must have an income below the poverty level; this level includes many or most persons with schizophrenia. When the food stamp program first started, persons who were eligible were required to contribute some money of their own to get the food stamps (e.g., for $20 a person could purchase food stamps worth $50). This requirement was dropped in 1977 so that food stamps are now free to those who are eligible. The amount of food stamps a person can receive varies by state and with income. It also varies with the cost of food and so has been rising as food prices have been rising. Food stamps can be obtained through local welfare or social services offices.

EMPLOYMENT

In their interest in working, people with schizophrenia extend over the same broad range as persons without schizophrenia. At one end of the spectrum are individuals who will do anything to work and will often continue working even when not being paid; individuals at the other end will do anything to avoid work. The only difference in work attitudes between persons with and without schizophrenia is that those with the disease often have problems working closely with other people, thereby making work more difficult for them.

A large number of persons with schizophrenia have residual disabilities, such as thinking disorders and auditory hallucinations, which are sufficiently severe that full-time employment is impossible. Some of these people can do part-time jobs, however. Estimates of the number of persons with schizophrenia capable of full-time work range as low as 6 percent; from my own experience I would estimate that approximately 20 percent of schizophrenics can work full-time and probably

another 20 percent can work part-time *if* proper medication maintenance and rehabilitation programs are available. Past employment is the
best single predictor of future employment for a person with schizophrenia; a person who becomes sick after having a job is more likely to find
work than a person who becomes sick without ever having worked.

Work provides several potential benefits for schizophrenics, not
the least of which is additional income. Improved self-esteem is equally
important, for to hold a job is evidence that one is like other people.
England's Douglas Bennett, one of the few mental health professionals
who has fought for vocational opportunities for persons with schizophrenia, says that a job magically transforms a patient into a person.
Schizophrenics will often work very hard to control their psychiatric
symptoms in work situations because work is so important to them. It
has been observed, for example, that "in the morning at the day center,
the same person is fulfilling the role of patient and acts like a patient,
exhibiting symptoms and bizarre behavior never seen in the workshop
the same afternoon." Work also provides schizophrenics with a daily
structure, a reason to get out of bed in the morning, an identity, and
an extended social network.

It is ironic that the civil rights efforts which led to the release of
so many patients from psychiatric hospitals also led to sharply decreased availability of jobs for them. In the past many of these patients
had worked on the hospital farms, on the grounds, and on housekeep-
ing and kitchen details. Undoubtedly there was some abuse of this
captive work force, and civil rights lawyers went to court with cases of
"peonage." The result was a pendulum which swung too far in efforts
to correct the situation; hospitals became reluctant to employ patients
at all because they could not afford to pay them the minimum wage and
other employee benefits. The consequence is thousands of patients in
hospitals and in the community who are capable of, and enjoy, working
for brief periods but who are not capable of full-time employment. The
jobs of the past which were often tailored to their needs are gone.

The largest impediment to vocational opportunities for persons
with schizophrenia is stigma. Employers, like most people in our society, do not understand what schizophrenia is and so react negatively
when asked if they would consider employing persons with this disease.
"I can't have any psychos working in my place" is a common visceral
reaction. Another major impediment is that government rehabilitation
programs and sheltered workshops have traditionally shunned the
mentally handicapped in favor of the physically handicapped. Voca-

tional rehabilitation in the United States is still stuck in the polio era, and if you don't have a visible physical disability you need not apply. Some other countries do a much better job of providing job opportunities for schizophrenics. Sweden, England, and the Netherlands all have a greater availability of sheltered workshops for long-term partial employment of psychiatric patients. In the Soviet Union employment of schizophrenics in sheltered workshops is the rule and not the exception; such workshops work closely with psychiatric hospitals.

Scattered around the United States are occasional programs that demonstrate what can be done when vocational opportunities are opened to persons with schizophrenia. Goodwill Industries has been very active in this regard; other jobs programs have been started by clubhouses such as Fountain House in New York (see page 265), Alliance for the Mentally Ill support groups, local chapters of the Mental Health Association, and by interested individuals. In Georgia a worm farm (the worms were sold to fishermen) employed schizophrenic patients, while in Wisconsin patients were trained to help refinish antique furniture.

In Duluth, Minnesota, Dr. Gregory Bambenek, a psychiatrist at the Community Mental Health Center and an inveterate fisherman, discovered a liquid lure to attract fish which he sold under the name of "Dr. Juice"; he contracted with Goodwill Industries to employ up to fifty mentally ill patients to work in his bottling plant.

Another jobs program for persons with serious mental illnesses was begun by the Alliance for the Mentally Ill of Rock Island and Mercer Counties in Illinois. The original jobs were as home helpers and contract jobs. In 1984, the group opened the Mes Amis Deli and Ice Cream Parlor and added job training for food preparation, waiter/waitress, and cashier. In 1985, the jobs program provided employment to 76 individuals and paid out over $30,000 in wages. Initial funding for the program came from the City of Rock Island. Current funding is approximately half from project income, and half from the Illinois State Department of Mental Health and Developmental Disability and the Rock Island County Mental Health Board.

Perhaps the single most impressive vocational program for persons with schizophrenia I have seen is a restaurant in Hayward, California, called the "Eden Express." Opened in 1980 by Ms. Barbara Lawson, a dynamic restaurant owner with a mentally disabled daughter, the "Eden Express" trains persons with mental disabilities to do restaurant jobs including food preparation, catering, aide to cook, busing, waiting on tables, hostessing, cashiering, dishwashing, and janitorial. Between 1980 and 1985 a total of 315 persons completed the 15-week training program, which was 80 percent of those who enrolled. Approximately 25 trainees are enrolled at any given time, and several job counselors make up the training staff. The staff also teaches trainees how to interview for jobs at the completion of their training, and 94 percent of the graduates have obtained jobs.

The trainees bear a variety of mental disabilities. Sixty percent have been diagnosed with schizophrenia, 25 percent have learning disabilities, and 15 percent are mentally retarded. Their acceptance by employers has been very good. As the manager of a Burger King who had hired eight of the graduates said: "They are more reliable than other employees." The "Eden Express" is largely self-supporting, serving over 4,000 customers each month. Salaries for the job counselors are derived primarily from training funds from the California State Departments of Rehabilitation and Education. The program has been cited for its excellence in the Congressional Record and by the National Restaurant Association, and the latter helped sponsor two-week training seminars in 1986 to train others to open similar restaurants for training the disabled.

FRIENDSHIP, LOVE, AND SEX

Friendship is needed by persons with schizophrenia, just as it is by everyone. For the schizophrenic, however, there are often barriers to friendship. One such barrier encompasses the symptoms and brain dysfunction from the disease.

One young man I provided care for recovered from most of his symptoms and was living at home. He attempted to return to his social group of peers, going to taverns and drinking with them as he had done prior to his illness. He found this very difficult, however, complaining that "I can't make out their words, I don't know what to say. It's just not like it used to be." Another patient complained that in social situations "I get lost in the spaces between words in sentences. I can't concentrate, or I get off into thinking about something else." In view of such difficulties it is not surprising that many schizophrenics often respond inappropriately in social situations and eventually withdraw. Studies of schizophrenic patients living in the community report that 25 percent are described as very isolated, 50 percent as moderately isolated, and only 25 percent as leading active social lives. Almost half have no recreational activity whatsoever, other than watching television.

Another major barrier to friendship for someone with schizophrenia is the stigma attached to this disease. We have become accustomed to tales of the past, such as the schizophrenic woman who is hidden in the attic so her family will not be disgraced. What is important to realize is that stigma in the present is almost as pervasive as it was in the past. In 1986 in Ireland I was introduced to a woman whose mother and father had recently died. Shortly after their deaths, she was shocked to receive a call from the county psychiatric hospital asking if she would be willing to take her brother, diagnosed with schizophrenia, home for the weekend. Her shock came from the fact that she did not know that she had a brother; he had become sick when she was a very young girl and his existence had never been mentioned by her parents.

It would be nice if such stories were apocryphal but they are not. Ask anybody with this disease and they will tell you what the stigma is like. One older man, who returned to the hospital because the stigma encountered was so pervasive, expressed it well:

> I just can't make it out there. I know who I am and they know who I am—most of the people out there won't come near me or they spit me in the eye. I'm just like a leper in their eyes. They treat most of us like that. They're prejudiced, you know. They are either afraid or hate us. I've seen it a thousand times. I don't feel good on the outside. I don't belong. They know it and I know it.

Dr. Kenneth Terkelson, one of the leading American spokesmen for the seriously mentally ill, encourages families and mental health professionals to become sensitive to what patients experience as the humiliation of having schizophrenia.

Because of this stigma many people with schizophrenia rely on their family and other patients for friendship. Social networks formed through clubhouses or through patient self-help groups (see page 265) are especially useful. Another excellent program is the Compeer Program begun in Rochester, New York, which has spread rapidly across the country since 1981. Volunteers are matched with psychiatric patients (many of whom have schizophrenia) living in the community. The two get together once a week to shop, go to a movie, go to dinner, play checkers, or share some common interest. As of 1986 there were over 3,000 ongoing Compeer relationships. The volunteers include not only large numbers of retired persons but many younger persons as well who want to be a friend.

Another aspect of friendship for a person with schizophrenia is the nonhuman variety. Pets often make excellent companions, just as they do for some persons without schizophrenia. Dogs are especially good, for they love indiscriminately, are not at all bothered by a person's thought disorders or auditory hallucinations, and are usually understanding when things are not going well. Providing pets for persons with schizophrenia can often bring them much pleasure; this has been discovered by families as well as by some mental hospitals that have allowed the patients to keep pets.

Sigmund Freud said that the essence of being human is to love and to work. It is therefore not surprising to find that many persons with schizophrenia, just like the rest of us, are frequently interested in extending friendship to love and sex. A prevalent stereotype among psychiatrists and psychologists holds that most persons with schizophrenia lose interest in sex. In fact this is true for only a small group—probably 20 percent—and it is unclear how many in this group had much interest in sex even before developing schizophrenia. It is also true that some patients are affected by antipsychotic medications so that they have decreased libido or, among males, impotence; such side effects appear to affect males more than females in the few studies done to date.

The fact remains, however, that many people with schizophrenia desire an active sex life and pursue it to the best of their ability. In a study done on a long-stay ward of a Tennessee state hospital, 78 percent of schizophrenic women ranging in age from 20 to 58 expressed an interest in having an active sex life, and 65 percent had had intercourse during the previous three months while in the hospital. Most nursing staff who have worked in hospitals with schizophrenic patients are aware of this, and there is an unspoken agreement among staff to neither notice nor discuss such activity. At St. Elizabeths Hospital in Washington, D.C., I had several patients, both male and female, who used sexual activity as their major form of recreation. In two instances (one male, one female) I was told by patients that they had intentionally misbehaved while living in foster homes so that they would be returned to the hospital where their social—and sexual—life was much more satisfactory.

It is also true, however, that achieving a satisfactory sexual relationship is even more difficult for persons with schizophrenia than for persons without this disease. Imagine how complex and difficult sex would seem if you had delusions that the person was trying to harm you, or you were hearing constant auditory hallucinations. Dr. M. B. Rosenbaum, in a sensitive article on the sexual problems of persons with schizophrenia, described one patient who "vividly described all the angels and devils in his bedroom telling him what and what not to do" while having intercourse. Dr. Rosenbaum concluded: "It is hard for most of us to 'get it together' sexually—how much harder for the schizophrenic with his or her many very real limitations!"

Increasingly as persons with schizophrenia have been deinstitutionalized from state hospitals to the community, and as they are forced by the stigma of their disease to spend time primarily with each other, long-term liaisons and marriages inevitably result. Some of these relationships are disasters, but others are stable and may be the best thing that has happened to the two people. Sharing a disease like schizophrenia and supporting each other through the crises of the disease can forge very strong bonds indeed.

Pregnancies are especially difficult problems to deal with in schizophrenia, especially the issues of competency and informed consent. It is easy to empathize with, for example, a 36-year-old schizophrenic woman who has just been released from the hospital after fifteen years and wants to have a baby before it is too late; it is also easy to empathize with the infant who is born into such a situation and who is totally dependent for care on its mother. The genetic facts on a baby born to two persons with schizophrenia are harsh—an estimated 46 percent of these children will eventually develop schizophrenia (see chapter 11). It is also true that most people with schizophrenia have enough difficulties looking after their own needs without the burden of a dependent infant.

I frankly discourage people with ongoing schizophrenia from parenthood and make available or direct them to contraceptives. Oral contraceptives are able to be used by women who can take responsibility. Condoms can be utilized by some men, and have become increasingly acceptable because of the fears generated by AIDS. IUDs are often satisfactory, but are becoming less widely available because of medical complications with them. For women who are unable to take contraceptive precautions, I have occasionally used injections of medroxyprogesterone (Depo-Provera), which provides contraception for three months; it has not yet been approved by the Food and Drug Administration in the United States because of remaining questions about cancer risks, but I believe risks to the offspring in some cases outweigh the risks of cancer. Depo-Provera is used as a contraceptive in many other countries and is legally available to physicians in the United States for other uses. An alternative long-acting contraceptive which can be implanted beneath the skin in the woman's upper arm is currently being tested for release in this country; it appears to be very promising and potentially useful for women with schizophrenia.

Once a baby has been conceived, the couple and their families are often caught between a rock and a hard place. Abortion and adoption should both be considered; responsible decisions frequently involve consultation with the psychiatrist, family physician, lawyer, religious adviser, and social worker. Often from such consultations a consensus will emerge on the best course of action, and this sharing of decision-making will alleviate the burden on both the patient and the patient's family.

COUNSELING AND SUPPORTIVE "PSYCHOTHERAPY"

Counseling and supportive "psychotherapy" can be helpful for individuals with schizophrenia, especially if the person providing these services remains constant for long periods of time. I put the term "psychotherapy" in quotations to differentiate it clearly from insight-oriented psychotherapy, discussed in chapter 7, which for schizophrenia sufferers is a discredited and even harmful mode of treatment.

Supportive "psychotherapy," on the other hand, may provide a patient with friendship, encouragement, practical advice such as access to community resources or how to develop a more active social life, vocational counseling, suggestions for minimizing friction with family members, and, above all, hope that the person's life may be improved. Discussions focus on the here-and-now, not the past, and on problems of living encountered by the patient as he or she tries to meet the exigencies of life, despite a handicapping brain disease. The opening approach I take with my own patients is something like the following: "Look, I'm sorry you have this lousy brain disease, which is not your fault, but let's see what you can do to live better with it." It is exactly the same approach which one might take for a patient with multiple sclerosis, polio, chronic kidney disease, severe diabetes, or any other long-term disease.

The person who provides counseling or supportive "psychotherapy" can be the physician who also oversees medication, or it may be any other mental health professional who enjoys meeting regularly with schizophrenic patients. The frequency and periodicity of such meetings are highly variable. Dr. Werner M. Mendel, one of the few American psychiatrists who has followed individual schizophrenic patients for over twenty-five years, tells the story of one of his patients whom he treated for schizophrenia many years ago. The man, who still has residual symptoms but is able to function as an engineer abroad, flies to Los Angeles approximately once a year just to meet briefly with Dr. Mendel and get his chlorpromazine prescription refilled. The man only rarely has to take the chlorpromazine, but he carries it around in his pocket continuously and is reassured by the rattle of the pills. It takes about a year for the pills to turn to powder; the rattling stops, and so the man returns to Los Angeles for another refill. Mendel cites this as an appropriate and supportive long-term relationship, the pills being the daily reminder that Dr. Mendel will be there to help if the schizophrenia recurs.

There is scientific evidence that such a supportive relationship, when it is used *in addition to drug therapy,* is helpful in reducing the rehospitalization rate for schizophrenia. In one study patients were followed for one year after release from the hospital and offered one of four modes of follow-up: (1) placebo alone (a placebo is an inert or dummy medication with no physiological action), (2) placebo plus supportive "psychotherapy," (3) drugs alone and (4) drugs plus supportive "psychotherapy." At the end of the year the rehospitalization rates were:

Treatment	Percentage of Patients Hospitalized
Placebo alone	72
Placebo plus "psychotherapy"	63
Drugs alone	33
Drugs plus "psychotherapy"	26

The "psychotherapy" used in this study included social services and vocational counseling provided by someone who was predictably available to the patients. The results suggest again that drugs are the single most important element in preventing rehospitalization but that a supportive relationship provides a measure of additional improvement.

A supportive and educational relationship for a person with schizophrenia may be carried out in groups as well as individually. Such groups should be distinguished, however, from traditional group therapy, discussed in chapter 7, in which the focus of the group is on intrapersonal and interpersonal relationships. Effective support groups for persons with schizophrenia have a practical and educational focus.

As summarized by one reviewer of group psychotherapy studies, "It is tempting to conclude that the most effective types of psychosocial treatments for schizophrenia are those that provide the most comprehensive, corrective, and sustaining social support systems." Helpful groups may span a range from an in-hospital formal class on the nature of schizophrenia, such as has been tried at one Veterans Administration hospital, to predominantly social and affiliative clubhouse atmospheres, such as those described on pages 265–72.

INSIGHT INTO RELAPSES

Individuals with schizophrenia who almost invariably manage most effectively with this disease are those who know when they are relapsing. As mentioned in chapter 7, the signs and symptoms of relapse tend to be constant for any one person, so the changes that heralded the relapse last time are likely to be the same ones that will signal relapse next time.

Changes in the person's sleep pattern are especially common signs of relapse; the person may be up much of the night and sleep much of the day. Some people with schizophrenia habitually have such a sleep pattern and in them it does not necessarily indicate an impending relapse. As in all signs and symptoms of relapse, it is *change* in the usual pattern which should be looked for.

Other common developments in schizophrenic individuals who may be relapsing are changes in activity levels (e.g., becoming tense, nervous, pacing, restless), changes in appetite (e.g., becomes less interested in eating), changes in sexual activity (e.g., becomes preoccupied with masturbation), changes in social activity (e.g., withdraws and refuses to see friends), changes in the intensity of sounds (e.g., needs to play the record player much softer or much louder), changes in the expression of feelings (e.g., hostility or episodes of euphoria increase), changes in bodily sensations (e.g., pains or aches), and changes in personal care (e.g., stops bathing or changing clothes).

Some individuals become aware that they are relapsing when they can no longer concentrate as well, as when listening to the radio, watching television, or reading. One man with schizophrenia informed me that his "litmus test for how I'm doing is if I try to read the sports page and if it doesn't make sense then it is time to call the doctor." Other individuals become preoccupied with one or two ideas, e.g., religious ideas, sexual ideas, or ideas that people are watching them, and spend much of the day thinking about these ideas.

What a person with schizophrenia needs to do is to develop his/her own "relapse list," the signs and symptoms which are indicative of impending relapse for that person. A person's family, counselor, or supportive "psychotherapist" can often be very helpful in working with the person to develop such a list. The list should then be posted on the person's mirror so that it is always available.

When signs and symptoms of a relapse appear, what should be done? Consultation with the counselor, supportive "psychotherapist," or psychiatrist should be a top priority. Often a small adjustment in the person's medication will take care of the problem. It should be remembered that schizophrenia takes an up-and-down course unrelated to anything going on in the person's life; it is the natural fluctuations of the disease itself and in that sense is similar to multiple sclerosis, which also has natural fluctuations.

The person should also develop strategies that may decrease the chances of relapse when the signs and symptoms begin. Some people do this successfully by reducing their work hours, spending more time alone so as to reduce social stress, getting more rest, exercising, etc. Any one of these may be helpful. Whatever the individuals' coping strategies are should be added to the "relapse list" to remind them what they should be doing. Individuals with "relapse lists" and coping strategies may thereby decrease the time they are disabled or hospitalized substantially.

MEDICAL CARE AND SAFETY

Two services, medical care and safety, are automatically provided to patients with schizophrenia while in hospitals but cease once they leave. The magnitude of medical problems can be measured by specific studies, such as one in which schizophrenics living in the community were found to have the following problems: 7 percent had heart disease, 7 percent hypertension, 6 percent respiratory disease, 4 percent diabetes, and 11 percent obesity or malnutrition. Such medical problems, when untreated, are one cause of the increased mortality among persons with schizophrenia (see chapter 5).

The main sources of medical care for schizophrenics living in the community are arrangements made by their family, Medicaid, and free clinics. Medicaid is available to those who have been approved for SSI or SSDI, but benefits vary widely from state to state and many private physicians will not accept Medicaid patients. For individuals age 65 and over, Medicare can be used to pay for medical care once the annual deductible has been paid by the patient.

Failure to consider the safety of discharged patients has been a very serious omission of deinstitutionalization. Patients are placed in community facilities as if they were as capable of defending themselves and calling the police as are any other citizens. Because of the residual symptoms of their schizophrenia, however, self-defense is often a myth and incidents of robbery, rape, and serious bodily harm are routine among released patients. In one survey of psychiatric patients living in board-and-care homes, one-third reported being robbed and/or assaulted during the preceding year; furthermore, patients with schizophrenia were most likely to have been victims of violent crimes. Such assaults occur with greater frequency because of the placement of many boarding houses, halfway houses, and foster homes in those areas of the inner city with the highest crime rate. When schizophrenic patients do call the police or attempt to bring charges, they may be confronted by their inability to explain to the police what happened, skepticism on the part of the police, and the reality that if the case should go to court the patient would be a very poor witness. Most released schizophrenic patients learn these facts of life soon after leaving the hospital and are forced to accept assaults as a part of life if they wish to remain in the community. Many cite this as a major reason for wishing to return to the hospital, the "asylum," where they feel safer.

COMMUNITY SUPPORT PROGRAMS

By the mid-1970s it was clear to everyone who even occasionally ventured downtown that considerable numbers of released mental patients were not getting the services they needed to survive. Even the National Institute of Mental Health, which bore large responsibility for the problem because of its failure to ensure that Community Mental Health Centers served the seriously mentally ill, perceived the seriousness of the situation and in response began the Community Support Program (CSP). I was personally skeptical of the CSP initially, because to expect NIMH to respond to the problem seemed like sailing a second time with the captain of the *Titanic*. My skepticism was ill-founded, for CSP has turned out to be an excellent program for devising and coordinating services needed by schizophrenics living in the community.

CSP began in 1977 with federal grants to twenty states to promote the development and coordination of the services discussed above: housing, income, employment, social life, counseling, medical care, and safety. The federal money was intended to promote the kinds of activities that states and counties should have been running themselves but were not. By the mid-1980s the CSP program had spread to all fifty states and, although still modest by federal standards (approximately $15 million per year), it was having an important impact in many communities. Most CSP programs utilize a case manager to coordinate services for a patient, and it is this person's task to ensure that the needs are met. Case managers "provide the glue that binds otherwise fragmented services into arrangements that respond to the unique and changing needs of patients."

How do CSP programs work at the local level? Take the Community Support System in Oneida County, New York, as an example. This is a good CSP program, which I am familiar with because it is utilized by my sister. At the center of the system is a group of case managers who provide social services, coordination, and counseling. Two clubhouses (Spring House in Utica and Rainbow House in Rome) provide social and recreational day programs and are linked to a cooperative apartment program to provide housing. Vocational assessment, training, and a sheltered workshop are available within walking distance at the Mohawk Valley Workshop, Inc. Public transportation is arranged at reduced rates and legal services are provided through the Legal Aid Society. Psychiatric medications and medical care are available at a clinic in Utica, which is run as an outpatient clinic of the state hospital serving the area, so the patient's past psychiatric records are available to the clinic personnel. Such CSP programs are not perfect, but certainly constitute a vast improvement over the nonprograms that existed for released psychiatric patients in most communities prior to CSP.

PATIENT SELF-HELP GROUPS

A significant step forward for persons with schizophrenia began in the mid-1980s with the formation of patient self-help groups. There had been forerunners of such groups throughout the 1970s, but the earlier groups, known by such names as the Network Against Psychiatric Assault and the Mental Patients' Liberation Front, were based upon Szaszian or Laingian philosophy and committed to the premise that mental illness does not exist and that nobody should ever be hospitalized or treated involuntarily.

The newer groups, on the other hand, accept the reality of mental disorders like schizophrenia but wish to change the consequences of having such disorders. The groups are known locally by different names such as On Our Own, but in 1985 they came together nationally to form the National Mental Health Consumer's Association (see appendix D for a state contact). In several communities these groups have opened houses that can be used as meeting and recreational facilities. They also operate information exchanges and lobby for such improvements as better low-cost housing. Above all, such groups are committed to the fight against stigma, and members of such groups appear increasingly often on television and radio to educate the public about schizophrenia and other serious mental disorders.

Patient self-help groups have much in common with clubhouses (see below) and in fact such groups exist within many of the clubhouses. They also share many goals with family support groups, such as AMI, the Alliance for the Mentally Ill (see chapter 10). If patient self-help groups and family support groups forge a coalition and work with mental health professionals and politicians committed to improving services for the seriously mentally ill, then there will be real hope for the future.

THE CLUBHOUSE MODEL

The clubhouse model has achieved wider acclaim than any other approach for meeting the needs of persons with schizophrenia living in the community. Fountain House in New York City was the original clubhouse and began in 1948; few others followed until the late 1970s, when the idea began spreading. By 1986, 180 clubhouses in 38 states were patterned after Fountain House.

The clubhouse model is justifiably popular because it meets patients' (they are always referred to as "members") needs in an integrated and humane manner. Clubhouses are first and foremost precisely that—a house where members can gather, socialize, feel comfortable, and be with friends. Since all members have had some kind of serious mental disorder, no stigma enters there; the clubhouse is a stigma-free island set in a community awash with stigma.

Most clubhouses are also allied with housing for their members. Typically the clubhouse sponsors a series of apartments in which three or four members live together. Some clubhouses also include halfway houses for more intense supervision. Employment programs are likewise incorporated into almost all clubhouses, frequently with two members sharing a single full-time position so that each is working half-time. Counseling is available from clubhouse staff, and more formal classes are often offered. During a 1985 visit to Thresholds in Chicago, one of the oldest and most highly regarded clubhouses, I saw a class on the mechanism of action of antipsychotic drugs, being given for individuals taking these drugs, while downstairs in a nursery young mothers with schizophrenia were being taught how to care for their children.

Clubhouses have also been shown to be cost-effective, because they decrease the rehospitalization rate of members. In studies done at Thresholds in Chicago and its allied program, The Bridge, the rehospitalization rate after nine months among members was 14 percent, compared with a rate of 44 percent for a control group that utilized existing community resources. For people with schizophrenia, who regularly go through the revolving door of community-hospital-community-hospital, it was found that the savings in treatment costs averaged $5,700 per member per year: "These findings imply that an outreach program like The Bridge can literally pay for itself while producing tangible benefits for the members it serves." One wonders how much better off persons with schizophrenia would be in the United States if the $3 billion in federal funds that were used to set up Community Mental Health Centers had been used instead to set up clubhouses.

The following is a brief description of Fellowship House, a clubhouse in Miami, Florida, which I visited in 1980:

> Mark was describing how he used to think he was Tarzan. He would stand in the middle of the street, take off his clothes,

and stop the traffic right in the middle of Miami. Having spent two years in the Marines before developing schizophrenia and becoming Tarzan, he acquired some karate and other skills that stood him in good stead as Tarzan, until he was sent off to the state hospital in a straitjacket.

He recalled his days as Tarzan with a touch of humor. All that was in the past, he said. He was standing in the open courtyard of Fellowship House, where he had been coming daily for three months. "This time I'm going to make it here," he said. He had tried once before but had "gotten crazy" again. "Stopped taking my medicine and bang I was right back in the hospital." Now he was on 30 milligrams of Haldol a day and swore he was going to continue it. He liked Fellowship House very much and hoped that he would eventually get a job as a mechanic. He claimed to be a good one and clearly took much pride in his skills.

Mark is one of over three hundred former mental patients being served by Fellowship House. Almost all have been diagnosed schizophrenic and almost all are veterans of numerous psychiatric wards and state hospitals. They come by bus, Metrorail, and van to the refurbished warehouse in South Miami that serves as the clubhouse and main focus of the program. Next door, in what used to be the Eagle Family Discount Store, are the administrative offices. The buildings are just a few yards off the Dixie Highway in a semi-industrial area. A mall with office towers and hotel is under construction across the highway.

Jason is another regular. Having spent over twenty years in the state hospital and long since having been abandoned by his family, he comes to Fellowship House because he is wanted there. It has become his family. Staff members and other House members greet Jason affectionately. He really is wanted; there is no mistaking it or putting it on. Jason knows it, too, negotiates a loan to cover his lunch, and quietly mingles with the other members. It has been a long, long time since Jason had a place to go where he was really wanted.

When asked what he likes about coming to Fellowship House, Jason says the activities. And activities there are. On any given day there is the appearance of a community recreation center with pool, Ping-Pong, piano, television, and volleyball and basketball in the courtyard. Then there are regular monthly trips, and special nights, such as a talent show, a Hispanic festival, black culture night, and a four-day camping trip. The day before I visited they had had a rummage sale of donated items to raise money. The members, of course, do most of the work getting ready for these events. Jason also likes it because he will soon have a regular job at the House cataloging and caring for the teaching materials and videotapes being developed. It is not a paying job, but it recognizes Jason's talents and his worth, which is more than anyone else had done for him in over twenty years.

Many other members like Fellowship House because it helps arrange for a place for them to live. There are a variety of options spread out around Miami. The most closely supervised of these is currently located in the upstairs of the clubhouse, pending the finding of a community site. Staff are always present and help integrate these twenty members into the vocational and social programs downstairs. This facility provides housing and living skills development to people coming directly out of the state hospital. It is the newest residential program, established as part of the state's deinstitutionalization efforts. The extended nature of the program recognizes that for some, it may take more than a few months of closely supervised living to progress to a more independent residential setting. There are no time limits on this residential opportunity, although in just the first year 25 percent of the residents moved on to other Fellowship House options.

The Fellowship Manor, a transitional house offering 24-hour supervision for fifteen residents, is located about a half hour away from the main building. This program is designed for people who will need up to six months to gain (or regain) enough independent living skills to move to a less supervised residence. A member may also move back to Fellowship Manor on a temporary basis if he/she is getting sick or needs more individual supervision.

There are two kinds of apartments under the aegis of Fellowship House. Ten supervised apartments, each housing four persons, are in a nearby suburban apartment complex, where Fellowship House rents a staff apartment as well for on-site supervision. Two staff people assist residents with cooking, cleaning, marketing, bus travel, and interpersonal relationships. Twelve satellite apartments, each with four members, are clustered around town and have only on-call supervision. Rent money for the apartments comes from the members' SSI and welfare checks or from job earnings. Altogether, 40 percent of the Fellowship House members live in housing maintained by the organization. The

WHAT THE PATIENT NEEDS

remainder live with their families, in boarding houses, or alone.

Fellowship House works closely with the nearest state hospital to assure a smooth transition from hospital to clubhouse. Staff from the Membership Department (what Fellowship House calls its Intake Department) sit on a district committee meeting weekly to review all patients awaiting discharge from the hospital. Those for whom membership at Fellowship House is recommended go through the membership process at the hospital and are brought to Fellowship House for several visits before discharge to acquaint them with the programs and ease the transition. Membership remains voluntary.

Another important facet of the Fellowship House program is its vocational rehabilitation program. For those members who are capable of working, there is a program of graduated responsibilities with guidance and supervision. This process begins in the main center, where members are assigned regular responsibilities in the day-to-day running of Fellowship House. Members participate in one of eight work areas: food service (cooking and serving the daily lunch), plant care, maintenance, clerical, data collection, video (creating a daily news show), industrial (woodworking), and computers.

When members progress to the point of being ready for regular employment, there is a transitional employment program for approximately forty people. Staff seek entry-level positions throughout Miami, then train and work along with the member until the member feels comfortable on the job; the staff work at no additional expense to the employer. Members work half-time, so full-time jobs are filled by two people. Fellowship House guarantees job performance and reliability by training two persons for every position; thus, if one is sick, the other can fill in. Transitional employment opportunities, for which the members receive regular wages, include microfilming at Ryder System, Inc., varied tasks at Don Carter's Bowling Center, and food service jobs at the University of Miami. Members may hold the transitional job for three to twelve months, at which time they turn it over to (and help train) a new member. It is possible for members to have several different transitional employment jobs if they need to broaden their experience and increase their employability.

At times, members do so well on a transitional job that the employer expands the job responsibilities beyond entry-level skills. Staff continue to work with the member by providing ongoing and regular support. Supported work positions are not transitional but are the members' own jobs. Supported work is also developed for individual members who have skills that do not lend themselves to the transitional employment system as a way to aid them in obtaining employment without competitive pressures.

> Marie, a Cuban refugee, developed schizophrenia at age 17; she is now 23 and about to begin transitional employment in a cafeteria. She had worked on the data-processing work detail for six months, then switched to the food service unit. She is excited about the possibility of getting a real job; her shyness and residual schizophrenic symptoms would have made it impossible for her to have done so on her own. Yet when talking to her there seems little doubt that she will make an excellent employee, for her motivation is exceptionally high.

All of these programs were put into operation over a period of fourteen years. Fellowship House began in 1973, when a parent of an individual with schizophrenia volunteered to help organize a halfway house. The local Miami chapter of the Mental Health Association and a helpful local psychiatrist, Dr. James Sussex, provided early support. A social worker from Detroit, Marshall Rubin, was hired, and Fellowship House was under way. Mr. Rubin has provided skilled leadership during its growth, and it now has eighty staff members. As in most of these programs, the staff is a mix of social workers, college graduates, and people generally committed to human services. The atmosphere is similar to that found on a Vista or Peace Corps project, where staff know that they are performing a useful function and are proud of it.

Funding for Fellowship House has come from a variety of sources. Initially, $35,000 in seed money was obtained from the U.S. Department of Health and Human Services, and this was later supplemented by county, state, and other federal funds. Long-term funding of such programs is problematical, with neither the local, state, nor federal government prepared to commit itself.

A unique and exciting aspect of Fellowship House is the mutual support relationships it has developed with a variety of corporations and civic groups. The South Miami City Commission asked to have its meetings videotaped for cable television, and Fellowship House staff and members volunteered the time; after half a year, the Commission voted to pay for the video services, providing supported employment to two members. The relationship with South Miami Kiwanis is another good example. Individual Kiwanis members have assisted the agency with professional help, such as giving legal advice in obtaining apartments or donating architectural services for design of the administrative offices. A Kiwanis physician offered his services without charge for a few hours a week, and this has now grown into a panel of twenty physicians and dentists, whom Fellowship House members can consult. Mr. Rubin is a member of Kiwanis, and Kiwanis members are on the governing board of Fellowship House; other staff and Fellowship House members have also become Kiwanians. When a new Fellowship House facility needed painting, members of Kiwanis helped out, and when the Kiwanis has its annual pass-the-can fund-raising drive, Fellowship House members help out, proudly collecting one-third or more of the total each year. Several transitional employment positions have been developed in businesses owned by Kiwanians, and in turn Kiwanis bulk mailings have been shifted from a commercial firm to Fellowship House work areas. In the support and opportunities it is providing for members of Fellowship House, Kiwanis has demonstrated what community service really means; this model could profitably be adopted elsewhere. The Kiwanis relationship has expanded to involve members and staff with the Merchants Association, Rotary, Lions, Civitan, Jaycees, and the Chamber of Commerce. In 1987, for the third year, the month of May (Mental Health Month) was "Buying South Miami Is Good Fellowship" month with the Mayor (as Campaign Chairman), local businesses (contributing to a 2-for-1 coupon book fund-raiser), and civic clubs all participating in a fund-raising and community awareness campaign for Fellowship House. The kickoff event was a Fellowship House Night Baseball Game at the University of Miami (College World Series Champions of 1983 and 1985), with 3,500 free tickets for friends of Fellowship House and a $1,500 cash scramble, which is contributed by a local bank, to the lucky number holder.

Another unusual feature of Fellowship House involves training programs. Under a state contract, Fellowship House trained twelve other Florida communities in how to set up and run similar programs. Training has been given to professionals in twenty-five other states as well. A professionally produced series of video training tapes were made and have been distributed nationally. Currently, a federal grant is enabling Fellowship House to create and demonstrate a graduate-level curriculum to train future mental health administrators from social work, nursing, and health administration by teaching both psychosocial rehabilitation principles and those of management and marketing. Training efforts for staff, students, and concerned citizens are aimed at developing better community programs nationwide for long-term mentally ill adults.

Finally, it should be stressed that the recurring theme of the program, made explicit by Marshall Rubin, is the message which the members receive daily: "We need you." Fellowship House depends on its members to operate, just as the members depend on Fellowship House for their social needs and often their housing and vocational needs as well. On the day I visited, one member announced excitedly that she had been coming to Fellowship House for exactly one year on that day. Everyone sang "Happy Birthday" to her.

RECOMMENDED FURTHER READING

Beiser, M., J. H. Shore, R. Peters, et al. "Does Community Care of the Mentally Ill Make a Difference? A Tale of Two Cities." *American Journal of Psychiatry* 142 (1985): 1047–52. A comparison of the services for discharged mental patients in Vancouver, B.C. (good services), and Portland, OR. (poor services), with the advantage of good services clearly shown.

Bond, G. R. "An Economic Analysis of Psychosocial Rehabilitation." *Hospital and Community Psychiatry* 35 (1984): 356–62. This paper details the economic savings by preventing rehospitalizations in providing good community services for patients with serious mental illnesses. A good paper to distribute to cost-conscious public officials.

Carling, P. J., F. L. Randolph, and P. Ridgway. *Providing Housing and Supports for People with Psychiatric Disabilities.* Boston: Center for Psychiatric Rehabilitation, 1986. This is a useful compendium of ideas for developing housing for mentally disabled persons.

Stroul, B. A. *Models of Community Support Services: Approaches to Helping Persons with Long-term Mental Illness.* Rockville, MD: National Institute of Mental Health, 1986. This describes different types of CSP programs and illustrates approaches to providing services for the seriously mentally ill.

Talbott, J. A., ed. *The Chronic Mentally Ill: Treatment, Programs, Systems.* New York: Human Sciences Press, 1981. This is a collection of descriptions of "model" programs for the chronic mentally ill. It is the best book of its kind, but discouraging in that many of the "models" are, as models, not much. This is an accurate reflection of the state of the art.

There Goes the Neighborhood. White Plains, NY: Community Residences Information Services Program (CRISP), 1986. This summarizes studies showing that community residences for the mentally disabled do not depreciate property values or the neighborhood.

Uhlhorn, B. *Creating a Caring Community: Developing Housing for Persons with Mental Illness.* Arlington, VA: National Alliance for the Mentally Ill, 1987. An excellent "how-to" manual on setting up decent housing for the mentally ill.

IO

WHAT THE FAMILY NEEDS

Lunacy, like the rain, falls upon the evil and the good; and although it must forever remain a fearful misfortune, yet there may be no more sin or shame in it than there is in an ague fit or a fever.

Inmate of the Glasgow Royal Asylum, 1860

Schizophrenia is a devastating illness not only for the person afflicted but for the person's family as well. There is probably no disease, including cancer, which causes more anguish. After interviewing eighty families in which one member was afflicted with schizophrenia, Clare Creer and John Wing concluded, "Of all types of handicapping conditions in adults, chronic schizophrenia probably gives rise to the most difficulties at home."

The family atmosphere is often like the interval waiting for a time bomb to explode. The patient is faced with "seemingly endless questions and doubts. Needing motives for almost every action, comment, or even hobbies. Having to curb one's natural emotions, fearing they may be misconstrued as symptoms . . ." As described by one patient, "One lives closeted with the appalling picture of oneself out of control, while relations and some friends in their kindness try to pretend the thing never happened." On the other side the family lives with the constant fear that the symptoms will recur. "Because it's happened before you always fear it will happen again, so you are constantly trying to avoid saying the wrong thing. You're like a taut string, not knowing what will set him off next."

In such an atmosphere trivial problems become magnified and substantial problems become overwhelming. Family members blame the patient, one another, and themselves. Family schedules, social life, and finances are frequently put in total disarray. The needs of other family members are neglected. And at the beginning of each day the same recurring question presents itself to both the patient and the family: Is this the day the symptoms will recur or get worse? This element of unpredictability represents the most difficult aspect of schizophrenia and the source of the greatest tension.

Several studies have been done on family problems caused by persons with schizophrenia. The problems which recur most frequently are the person's failure to care for his/her personal needs (e.g., to take a bath); inability to handle money; social withdrawal; strange personal habits (wandering around talking to himself in the middle of the night); suicide threats; interference with the family's work, school, and social schedule; and fears for the safety of both the ill person and the family members. Clearly there is no shortage of serious problems. If families are to survive schizophrenia they have to develop coping strategies as well as practical solutions to the many problems which arise.

THE RIGHT ATTITUDE

Developing the right attitude is the single most important thing a family can do to survive schizophrenia. The right attitude evolves naturally once the family resolves the twin monsters of schizophrenia—blame and shame. These lie just beneath the surface of many families, impeding the family from moving forward, souring relations between family members, and threatening to explode in a frenzy of finger-pointing, accusations, and recriminations. Blame and shame are the Scylla and Charybdis of schizophrenia.

As should be clear from chapter 6, feelings of blame and shame are completely irrational. There is no evidence whatsoever that schizophrenia is caused by how people have been treated either as children or as adults; it is a biological disease of the brain, unrelated to interpersonal events of childhood or adulthood. But many families believe otherwise, and their feelings have often been based on what a mental health professional has said (or at least implied) to them. An excellent description of this process is recounted by Louise Wilson in *This Stranger, My Son:*

> Mother: "And so it is we who have made Tony what he is?"
> Psychiatrist: "Let me put it this way. Every child born, every mind, is a tabula rasa, an empty slate. What is written on it"—a stubby finger shot out, pointed at me—"you wrote there."

The consequences are predictable, with the mother lying awake at night remembering all the things she did that might have caused the schizophrenia.

> We had moved too often during his early years. . . . My tension during the prenatal period when his father was overseas . . . His father's preoccupation with his profession . . . No strong companionship and father image . . . A first child, and too many other children coming along too rapidly . . . Our expectations were too high . . . He had been robbed of his rightful babyhood, had grown up too fast . . . Inconsistent handling . . . Too permissive . . . Too much discipline . . . Oedipal fixation . . .

There is, of course, not a mother, father, brother, or sister in the world who has not done things he or she regrets in past relationships with other family members. We are, after all, rather imperfect human beings, and it is not surprising that at times we all speak or act impulsively out of jealousy, anger, narcissism, or fatigue. But fortunately we have resilient psyches, capable of absorbing random blows without crumbling or being permanently damaged. People do not cause schizophrenia; they merely blame each other for doing so.

Moreover, not only do the well family members blame each other for causing the schizophrenia in the family, but the person with schizophrenia may also do so. James Wechsler's son, in *In a Darkness,* once turned to him and angrily exclaimed, "You know, Dad, I wasn't *born* this way." And in *This Stranger, My Son,* Louise Wilson recounts the following conversation with her son:

> "I read a book the other day," Tony said. "It was in the drugstore. I stood there and read it all the way through."
> We waited, alarmed by the severity of his expression.
> "It told what good parents ought to be. It said that people get . . . the way I am . . . because their parents weren't qualified to be parents."
> "Oh Tony," I began, but Jack's signal silenced me.
> "I'm a miserable wreck, because both of you are, too. You're queers and you never should have had a child."
> "In what way are we queer?" Jack asked quietly.

"You never played ball with me. All you ever wanted to do was tramp around looking at birds or read. Or work in the damned hospital."

"Well, maybe it would have been more fun for you if I'd been an athlete. I can see that. But I really don't see why that should make me such a terrible father."

"Read the book!" Tony exclaimed.

"Tony, there are a lot of things written in books, a lot of opinions that are inaccurate, distorted, or just plain wrong. Besides, I'm sure the book—"

"Listen, even the doctor that I've got here agrees! He says nobody's born with problems like mine!"

The blaming of one another for the illness magnifies the tragedy of schizophrenia manyfold. By itself it is a chronic disease of the brain and a personal and family disaster of usually manageable proportions. But when family members add blame to its burden, the disease spreads its roots beneath the whole family structure and becomes a calamity of boundless dimensions. The pain that blame causes in such circumstances must be seen to be believed. One woman wrote to me:

> My mother died twelve years ago, tormented by my sister's illness. After reading every book and article published on the subject, she decided that she was to blame. My father, who is in his seventies, brought my sister home from the state hospital for five years following my mother's death, in memory of my mother, trying to prove that she wasn't sick. My sister was so sick he finally had to return her to the hospital.

Few members of the mental health profession have focused on the amount of harm that has been done by the idea that parents and families cause schizophrenia. Psychiatrists especially, as members of the medical profession, see themselves as unlikely to cause harm. We now know that this is not so, and it is likely that in the twentieth century psychiatrists as a group have done more harm than good to persons with schizophrenia. The harm has not been done maliciously; indeed I know of few psychiatrists who could be characterized as mean-spirited. Rather the harm has been done inadvertently because of prevailing psychodynamic and family interaction theories of the disease (see chapter 6). But it is harm nonetheless. William S. Appleton is one of the few professionals who have written about this, and he has analyzed the undesirable consequences that follow when professionals blame the families for causing the disease:

Badly treated families retaliate in ways that are detrimental to the patient. They become less willing to tolerate the problems he causes, are less agreeable to changing their behavior toward him, do not give much information when interviewed, and pay few visits to the hospital.

Occasionally, families are reluctant to give up the blame and guilt they feel. This may occur, for example, in a family where there are still young children; if the parents believe themselves to be responsible for the schizophrenia in their older child, then by changing their behavior they can theoretically prevent it in the younger children. If, on the other hand, they believe that schizophrenia is a random biological happening, as all the evidence suggests, then they are helpless to prevent it. Guilt in such families provides an illusion of control. Another type of family sometimes encountered that resists giving up guilt is one in which guilt is the family's way of life. Usually one or more members of such families are in psychoanalysis and the family seems to thrive on guilt, wallowing in it and blaming each other as their principal pastime. In such families, as one mother explained to me, "guilt is the gift which keeps on giving." I encourage individuals with schizophrenia who come from such families to minimize time spent within the family setting because it is detrimental to progress and to getting on with life despite a handicap.

The obverse of blame is shame. Inevitably, if families believe that they have somehow caused the schizophrenia, they will try and hide the family member affected, deny the illness to their neighbors, and otherwise dissociate themselves from the victim in a multiplicity of ways. Persons with schizophrenia sense this and feel more isolated than ever. It is not unusual for the patient then to react angrily toward the family, retaliating by making less effort to control bizarre behavior, and perhaps disrobing in front of elderly Aunt Agatha. Such behavior generates more shame in the family, producing more isolation and anger in the patient, and the downward spiral of shame and anger continues.

Education may resolve the problem of blame and shame. When family members come to understand that they did not cause the disease, the blame and shame felt by them are usually markedly reduced and the living situation for the schizophrenic member improved. The question of who is responsible for the disease should be asked of all family members, and the schizophrenic person should participate in the discussion if possible. Once this is opened up, the beliefs and fears that will sometimes emerge in the ensuing discussion are extraordinary. And once the issue of blame and shame is resolved and put to rest, schizophrenia becomes much easier to live with. One parent expressed it this way:

> Once you have unloaded your guilt, laid upon you by well-meaning professionals, the next step is easier. If you have done nothing wrong and have been doing the best you can, then you have nothing to be ashamed of. You can *come out of the closet.* The relief experienced by this act gives you strength to go on, and support starts coming out of the woodwork.

Once blame and shame have been put aside the right attitude naturally evolves. The right attitude has four elements and can be called a SAFE attitude: Sense of humor, Acceptance of the illness, Family balance, and Expectations which are realistic.

Sense of Humor. At first glance, a sense of humor seems antithetical to schizophrenia. How can the most tragic disease known to mankind elicit humor of any kind? And yet it is precisely because schizophrenia is such a tragic disease that a sense of humor is mandatory. Without humor the family burns out and loses its resiliency to handle the inevitable ups and downs inherent in the disease. The families I have seen that were most successful in coping with schizophrenia were those who had retained a sense of humor and an appreciation of the absurd.

What do I mean by a sense of humor? I certainly do not mean laughing *at* a person with this disease. Rather it is laughing *with* them. For example, one family in which the schizophrenic son relapsed each autumn and required rehospitalization had a standing family joke with the son that he always carved his pumpkins in the hospital. And when I sent my sister with schizophrenia a new suit as a gift she replied that "the suit looks ghastly on me and I gave it away." It is the kind of ingenuous reply which is often found in schizophrenia, a reply stripped of the social graces to which we have become accustomed, a reply which we would all like to make on occasion but usually do not. Being able to laugh with a person with schizophrenia on such occasions is good therapy for everyone; becoming indignant is not.

Perhaps the best example of the benign sense of humor so necessary in schizophrenia was told by researcher H. B. M. Murphy, while surveying a small Canadian village for schizophrenia:

One of our other informants learnt first of another case in a fashion which still less suggests shame or embarrassment. To use his own words, it happened that my wife had been making a social visit to them and she noticed a blanket over the parlour sofa as if some stuff had been covered up there. After a time, while they were having tea, it moved. She must have seemed a little startled, for they said: "Oh, that's just Hector. He always hides himself like that." Then they went on with tea!

Acceptance of the Illness. For both the patient and the family, this is the second important ingredient in the right attitude. Acceptance does not mean giving up, but rather an acknowledgment that the disease is real, that it is not likely to just go away, and that it will impose some limitations on the person's abilities. It is acceptance of things *as they are,* not things as you wish them to be.

Many individuals with schizophrenia and their families never learn to accept the disease. They go on, year after year, denying it and pretending it does not exist. When acceptance can be achieved it becomes easier for everyone. One mother wrote about her sick daughter's reaction when the daughter fully realized her diagnosis and that she had been the 1 in 100 to get the disease: "Well, I guess if it's percentage-wise it might as well be me. I have such a terrific family to hold my hand, and since I've been tagged someone else has escaped." Such an extraordinary attitude is an ideal to be striven for but rarely achieved, because such insight and kindness are so unusual.

More common, unfortunately, is anger in both the patient and the family. The anger may be directed at God for creating a world in which schizophrenia exists, at fate for dealing a bad hand, at the patient for becoming sick, or at each other for causing the illness. It varies from being a mild resentment bubbling to the surface when social activities must be curtailed because of the schizophrenic, to a more virulent bitterness flowing beneath the surface of their daily activities like a caustic acid. Occasionally the anger does not achieve overt expression but rather turns inward; it is then seen as depression.

Whenever I encounter such families I wish I could send them to a Buddhist monastery for a month. There they might learn the Oriental acceptance of life as it is, an invaluable attitude in surviving this disease. Such acceptance puts schizophrenia into perspective as one of life's great tragedies but stops it from becoming a festering sore eating away at life's very core. As one mother told me, "You can't stop the bird of sorrow from flying over your head, but you can stop it from making a mess in your hair."

Family Balance.   An important aspect of the right attitude in surviving schizophrenia is an ability to weigh the needs of the ill family member against those of others in the family. Families that selflessly sacrifice everything for the person with schizophrenia are usually doing so because they feel irrationally guilty about possibly having caused the disease. To provide care for a seriously disabled schizophrenic living at home may be a job requiring 168 hours per week; furthermore, it is unpaid and offers few thanks. Who is to care for the caregiver, who more often than not is the mother? How are we to weigh the needs of other children? Or the needs of the parent or parents to get away periodically? It is important to weigh these conflicting needs calmly and rationally, recognizing that the person with schizophrenia does not always come first. It may be necessary, for example, to occasionally rehospitalize a person with schizophrenia for the needs of the family and not the needs of the patient; perceptive mental health professionals recognize such dilemmas and support the family in such decisions.

Expectations Which Are Realistic.   Modifying assumptions about a person's future is difficult to accomplish but important to attempt, for it often follows directly from acceptance of the disease. It is especially difficult if the person with schizophrenia had been unusually promising prior to becoming ill. Such families tend to hang on to the hope, year after year, that the schizophrenic will someday become normal again and resume his or her career. Grossly unrealistic plans are made, money is saved for college or a big wedding, and family members fool each other with the shared myth of "when he gets well again."

The problem with the myth is that the ill person knows it is a myth, and it puts him/her in a no-win situation. There is nothing the person can do to please the family except to get well, and that is beyond his or her control. Several observers have noted this problem and have urged families to lower their expectations for the person. If this is done, the families themselves become happier. Creer and Wing noted in their interviews with such families:

> Several relatives mentioned that giving up hope had paradoxically been the
> turning point for them in coming to terms with their unhappiness. "Once
> you give up hope," one mother said, "you start to perk up." "Once you

realise he'll never be cured you start to relax." These relatives had lowered their expectations and aspirations for the patient, and had found that doing this had been the first step in cutting the problem down to manageable size.

Another parent said, "You've got to reach bedrock, to become depressed enough, before you are forced to accept the reality and the enormity of the problem. Having done that, you don't allow your hopes to become too high and thus leave yourself open to disappointment when they are not fulfilled."

This does not mean that families should have no expectations at all of the person with schizophrenia. H. Richard Lamb, one of the few psychiatrists who have worked assiduously on the rehabilitation of schizophrenic patients, has said, "Recognizing that a person has limited capabilities should not mean that we expect nothing of him." Expectations must be realistic, however, and consonant with the capabilities of the schizophrenic. Just as the family of a polio victim should not expect the person's legs to return to complete normality, so too the family of a schizophrenic should not expect the person's brain to return to complete normality. Psychiatrist John Wing wrote:

> A neutral (not overemotional) expectation to perform up to *attainable* standards is the ideal. This rule, if difficult for the specialist to adopt, is a thousand times more difficult for relatives. Nevertheless, we should be humbled to recognize that a large portion of relatives, by trial and error, do come to adopt it, without any help from professionals.

The effect of lowering one's expectations is often to be able to enjoy and share things with the schizophrenic individual for the first time in many years. Thus if someone who was an accomplished flutist prior to becoming ill takes up the flute again to play simple pieces, both the person and the family can enjoy that accomplishment. It no longer is going to be seen, implicitly or explicitly, in the light of when-you-are-well-you'll-be-able-to-give-concerts-again-dear. Similarly, if the person is able to ride a bus for the first time alone or go to the store by himself or ride a bicycle, these accomplishments can also be celebrated for what they are—often magnificent accomplishments for a person whose brain is not functioning properly. The person with schizophrenia and the family need to be able to find joy in such accomplishments just as a polio victim finds joy in relearning to walk. Oliver Sacks, in his book *The Man Who Mistook His Wife for a Hat,* expresses this attitude well

in his story about brain-damaged and deformed Rebecca who could still
see beauty in life:

> Superficially she *was* a mass of handicaps and incapacities . . . but at some
> deeper level there was no sense of handicap or incapacity, but a feeling of
> calm and completeness, of being fully alive, of being a soul, deep and high,
> and equal to all others. . . . We paid far too much attention to the defects
> of our patients, as Rebecca was the first to tell me, and far too little to what
> was intact or preserved.

ANSWERS TO COMMON PROBLEMS

Families with a schizophrenic member face an incredible array of
problems requiring solutions. Books and advice from other families
may be helpful in offering suggestions, but in the end each patient with
schizophrenia and each family are unique. In thinking through such
problems it is important to keep in mind the underlying personality of
the patient; it then becomes possible to separate what portion of the
problems arises from the personality and what portion from the schizophrenia superimposed on that personality. Schizophrenia randomly
selects personality types, and families should remember that persons
who were lazy, manipulative, or narcissistic before they got sick are
likely to remain so as schizophrenics. This problem is very similar to
that faced by families of physically handicapped, diabetic, or otherwise
chronically disabled patients who may utilize their condition to manipulate their families and environment.

Should the Person Live at Home?   The most important decision
to be made by most persons with schizophrenia and their families is
where the person should live. This was not always an issue. Thirty years
ago brother John and Aunt Kate were sent off to the state hospital when
they became schizophrenic, never to be seen again. The question of
where they should live never came up—it was simply assumed that they
would remain at the hospital. That has all changed, and now brother
John and Aunt Kate will probably be on their way home from the
hospital within a few weeks. The question of where they will live is a
very real one.

As a general rule, I believe that most persons with schizophrenia do better living somewhere other than at home. I have come to this conclusion after working with many schizophrenic persons and their families for several years; but it is a fact often learned painfully, and at great emotional cost, by families. The reasons for living elsewhere are complex. They include the facts that most people who are not schizophrenic do better living away from the family home once they are grown and that persons with schizophrenia often function at a higher level living away from home. Most persons with schizophrenia I have known do better, and are happier, in a halfway house or similar setting.

This does not mean that *no* persons with schizophrenia should live at home. A minority can, and it may work out well. This is true for females more often than it is for males. Nor does it mean that the schizophrenic family member who is living elsewhere should not come home to visit overnight or for weekends; this arrangement is often mutually satisfactory. Such persons may also live at home temporarily while they are waiting, for example, for an opening in a halfway house.

If the person lives at home, two things are essential—solitude and structure. A person with schizophrenia needs his or her own room, a quiet place that can be used for withdrawing. Families solve this problem in a variety of ways, including putting a small house trailer in the backyard. Structure is also helpful for most persons with schizophrenia, and they function better with regular meal hours, chores, and a predictable daily and weekly routine. One mother said:

> I found structure was very important during the more difficult days. Things were done similarly each day and at designated times, and every day of the week had its individual character which was kept as consistent as possible. This seemed to give him a sense of order, that life was predictable, and also established a sense of time.

In *Autobiography of a Schizophrenic Girl* the patient also comments on the importance of routine in counteracting hallucinations and other abnormal sensory stimuli:

> What saved me that day was activity. It was the hour to go to chapel for prayer, and like the other children I had to get in line. To move, to change the scene, to do something definite and customary, helped a great deal.

At the same time that routines are established, realize that the person with schizophrenia may deviate from them for no apparent reason. This is especially true of sleeping and eating routines. One father complained about his son, "My wife will cook a meal, and then

he doesn't want it. Then two hours later he suddenly decides he does."
An admirable solution to this kind of problem was outlined by this
mother:

> The second practical suggestion concerns the schizophrenic's need for a
> sudden intake of food. At least in the case of our son, available wholesome
> snacks are very important. I've learned to keep yogurt, cheese, cold meat,
> etc., in the refrigerator; fruit on the table; and quick canned meals on the
> shelves. All this has seemed more important than a regular schedule of
> meals, although three good meals a day helps, too. The strict time doesn't
> matter. If Jim fixes himself a can of stew at four in the afternoon, I simply
> leave his dinner ready for him to heat up when he's ready.

Occasionally it is necessary for the family to insist that a person
with schizophrenia move out of the house. This may occur for some of
the same reasons it occurs for nonschizophrenics (e.g., dependency,
laziness, abuse of alcohol or drugs) or it may occur for reasons having
more to do with the illness (e.g., gross disruption of family, aggression,
threatening behavior). When it is necessary it should be carried through
with consistency and conviction.

*How Should Family Members Behave Toward Someone with Schiz-
ophrenia?*   In general, the people who get along best with schizophrenics are those who treat them most naturally as people. This can
be verified by watching the nursing staff in any psychiatric hospital. The
staff who are most respected by both professionals and patients treat
the patients with dignity and as human beings, albeit with a brain
disease. The staff who are least respected treat the patients in a conde-
scending manner, frequently reminding them of their inferior status.
Often this is because the staff person does not understand schizophrenia
or is afraid of it. The simple answer, then, to the question, How should
I behave toward a schizophrenic? is, Kindly.

Beyond this, however, there are certain aspects of schizophrenia
as a disease which do modify to some degree one's behavior toward a
person who has it. These modifications arise directly and predictably
out of the nature of the brain damage and the symptoms of the disease
as described in chapter 2. Persons with schizophrenia have great difficulty in processing sensory input of all kinds, especially two or more
simultaneous sensory stimuli. If this is kept in mind, then determining
how to behave toward a schizophrenic becomes much easier.

Make communications, for example, brief, concise, and unambiguous. As explained by one family member: "Look at the person. Talk in short, concise, adult statements . . . be clear and practical . . . give one set of directions at a time with no options."

Another mother described how she communicates with her adult son with schizophrenia:

> My son seemed to have difficulty dealing with all the stimuli around him. He responded slowly and said that he had difficulty with "everything coming at me." At those times it was important for me to speak in simple, slow sentences. Requests were made for one thing at a time. Keeping down complexity was very important. Strong emotion increased his difficulty in processing what I was saying. However much in a hurry I felt, there was no way to hurry him. Patience was absolutely necessary.
>
> I learned finally the futility of arguments. When S. was in more acute stages, it was easy to get into impossible rounds of arguments. Often he could not be reasoned with, but I didn't know how to back off. I learned to choose carefully what had to be done, plan ahead how I would handle the situation, and not respond to all the objections. For example, I might say in a clear, firm, simple statement, "You must be ready to leave at 8:00 o'clock." Then I stood expectantly, even handing him his coat, and opening the door.
>
> Sometimes leaving requests by way of memo or over the telephone seemed to work better than face to face—I am not sure why—sometimes he seemed to be overstimulated by my presence.

Ask the schizophrenic person one question at a time. "Did you have a nice time, dear? Who went with you?" may seem like a straightforward two-part question for a normal person, but for a person with schizophrenia it may be overwhelming.

It is also counterproductive to try to argue schizophrenics out of their delusional beliefs. Attempts to do so often result in misunderstanding and anger, as described by John Wing:

> Patients tended to develop sudden irrational fears. They might, for instance, become fearful of a particular room in the house. Maybe they would tell the family the reason for their fear. "There's a poisonous gas leaking into that room" or "There are snakes under the bed in that room." At first relatives are baffled by this. Some admitted they had grown frustrated with a patient's absolute refusal to abandon some idea, despite all their attempts to reason with him, and had lost their temper. But they found this only resulted in the patient becoming very upset,

and in any case the idea continued to be held with as much conviction as ever.

Rather than arguing with the patient, simply make a statement of disagreement; this can be done without challenging or provoking him or her. Thus a reasonable response to "There are snakes under the bed in that room" is "I know you believe there are snakes there, but I don't see any and I doubt that there are," rather than a peremptory "There are *no* snakes in that room." The patient has some reason for believing that there are snakes there—perhaps he/she heard them or even saw them. It is often useful for the family member to acknowledge the validity of the patient's sensory experiences without accepting the person's interpretation of the experiences. Such a statement might be "I know you have some reason to believe there are snakes there, but I think that the reason has to do with the fact that your brain is playing tricks on you because of your illness."

Family members and friends of schizophrenic patients are often tempted to deal with the patient's delusional beliefs in a sarcastic or humorous manner. The statement about snakes, for example, might be responded to as follows: "Oh yes, I saw them there too. And did you see the rattlesnakes in the kitchen as well?" Such statements are never useful and are often very confusing for the patient. It also reinforces their delusional belief and makes it more difficult for them to separate their personal experiences from reality. One patient, who believed he had a rat in his throat and asked the doctors to look at it, was told sardonically by the doctors that the rat was too far down to see. When the patient recovered he recalled that "I would have been grateful if they had stated quite plainly that they did not believe that there was a rat in my throat." This is good advice.

Another useful way to handle the delusional thinking of schizophrenic patients is to encourage them to express such thinking only in private. Talking about snakes being under the bed is not harmful within the context of family and friends, but if said in a crowded elevator or announced to the saleslady in a store, it can be embarrassing for everyone concerned. Discuss this frankly and straightforwardly with the patient and it will often be appreciated. As Creer and Wing point out: "A more realistic aim is to try to limit the effect of such ideas upon the patient's public behavior. Many patients were well able to understand this and to limit odd behavior, such as talking to themselves, and the expression of odd ideas, to private occasions."

An impediment to communicating with schizophrenic persons is their frequent inability to participate in normal back-and-forth conversation. "One patient returned home each evening from the day center, ate in complete silence the meal her aunt provided, and then went straight to her room. . . . Her aunt, who was lonely and elderly, would have been very glad for a chat in the evenings. She was puzzled by the patient's almost total lack of communication." Such patients often are aware of conversations around them but are unable to participate. "One young man generally sat in silence, or muttering to himself, while his parents were conversing about family matters. Later, however, they learned that he had quite often spoken to a nurse at the hospital about such topics of conversation at home and had clearly been taking in what was said despite all appearances to the contrary." Many such schizophrenic patients like to have other people around them but do not like to interact with them directly. "One lady said she had been surprised to hear from a friend that her nephew suffering from the disease liked to come and visit her. 'I would never have guessed it because when he comes he just sits in a chair and says absolutely nothing.' "

An analogous problem families have in their efforts to relate to persons with schizophrenia is their impaired ability to express emotions. Frequently the patient will relate to even close family members in what appears to be a cold and distant way. This emotional aloofness is quite normal for many persons with this disease and should be respected. Difficult though this coldness may be, do not take it personally. The schizophrenic patient may find it easier to express emotion or verbal affection toward a family pet, and it is often a good idea to provide the person with a cat or dog for this purpose.

A common problem is how the family should behave toward a schizophrenic member when he/she is withdrawn. It is important to recognize the need of many persons with this disease to withdraw. One mother wrote me that while chatting with her ill daughter as they were doing the dishes, the daughter turned and said: "Leave me alone now, Mom, so I can enjoy my own world." Sometimes the withdrawal can be pronounced. I once had a patient who remained in her room at home for weeks at a time, coming out only during the night to eat.

It can be puzzling to know what to do in these cases of social withdrawal. Should you insist that the person emerge from the bedroom and interact socially, or should you leave him or her alone? The answer is, as a general rule, to leave the person alone. If the withdrawal seems excessive or too persistent, it is possible it may herald the recurrence of more severe symptoms and will require evaluation by the patient's psychiatrist. But in most cases the withdrawal is being used as a means for coping with the internal chaos in the patient's brain and is an appropriate response. Family members should remind themselves not to take such withdrawal as a personal rejection but should keep themselves available. As described usefully by the mother of a schizophrenic: "When our son was acutely ill we managed best by not being too intrusive, by not trying too hard to draw him out of his world and into ours, but by always being available at the times when he needed our support and tried to communicate."

In social situations it is important not to expect too much from persons with schizophrenia. Remember that they may be having problems assimilating sensory input or understanding what is being said. Minimize the number and scale of social events in the house in order to relieve pressure on the schizophrenic. Patients can often handle one visitor at a time, but groups are usually overwhelming to them. Similarly, taking the schizophrenic to group gatherings or parties outside the home is often a difficult and confusing experience for the person.

Experiment to find leisure time activities which are enjoyable. Those with a single (or dominant) sensory input are usually most successful. Thus a person with schizophrenia will often enjoy cartoons or a travelogue on TV but will not be able to understand a show with a plot. A boxing match may be preferable to a baseball game. Visual spectacles, such as a circus or ice show, are often very enjoyable, while a play is usually a total failure. Individuals are, of course, different in this regard, and it is necessary to explore different possibilities. The fact that people enjoyed something before they became ill does not mean that they necessarily will enjoy it after they become ill.

A common trap that families with a schizophrenic member frequently fall into is to blame *all* the person's undesirable or unwanted behavior on the disease. It should be called "the disease trap." Every little shortcoming, including the person's failure to pick up dirty socks or replace the cap on the tube of toothpaste, is blamed on schizophrenia. Families need to remind themselves that human beings come with peccadilloes built in and that there are few around who have achieved perfection. Resist the temptation to blame everything on schizophrenia and ask how many mistakes *you* made in the last week. Along the same line, allow individuals with schizophrenia to have a bad day now and then, just as we allow those of us without schizophrenia to have a bad day. We all need such days since our neurochemical and neurophysiological machinery does not work perfectly all the time; extending the privilege of a bad day to individuals with schizophrenia is both common sense and common courtesy.

Above all, cultivate the art of being unflappable. Radiate quiet confidence that you can handle any idea, however strange, that your schizophrenic relative may come up with. If the person's auditory hallucinations are worse that morning simply comment on it matter-of-factly, just as if you noticed that a person's arthritis is worse: "I'm sorry to see that the voices are bothering you more today." One parent said, "The most remarkable lesson I have learned about managing a schizophrenic person at home is to try to stay as calm as possible. The upsets and delusions have not been caused by me, and being calm keeps my son that way also. I might be heaving inside but my behavior on the outside is controlled."

How Much Responsibility?   One of the most challenging problems for families with a schizophrenic member is to assess how much responsibility the person is able to take and how much control he or she has over his or her own behavior. Most patients have some control and can take some responsibility, but these vary from patient to patient and may even fluctuate over time in a single patient. The dilemma for the family was expressed nicely by Dr. John Wing:

> Part of the peculiar difficulty in managing schizophrenia is that it lies somewhere between conditions like blindness which, though severely handicapping, do not interfere with an individual's capacity to make independent judgments about his own future, and conditions like severe mental retardation, in which it is clear that the individual will never be able to make such independent judgments. There is frequently a fluctuating degree of insight and of severity.

When the patient disrobes in front of Aunt Agatha, is it because his voices told him to, or because he is angry at his family for a real or imagined slight? Some persons with schizophrenia become highly skilled at utilizing their symptoms to manipulate those around them and get what they want. Patients who are placed where they do not want to live, for example, know exactly what to do behaviorally to ensure that they will be returned to the hospital or wherever they were living previously. And I have had many patients improve and tell me explicitly, "Doc, I'm a little better but I'm not well enough to go to work."

Management of a schizophrenic's medication is exceedingly important. Since continuation of the medication is often essential for remaining out of the hospital (see chapter 7), I encourage families to be very conservative in giving responsibility for taking medication to their relative. Many mental health professionals and families have defined "self-medication" as a highly desirable goal, a milestone to be achieved by schizophrenic persons on the road toward greater autonomy. I realize that I am in a minority on this issue, but I do not include self-medication as an important target. There are some patients who can handle it, but they are relatively infrequent. I have been much more impressed by the tragic relapses of those who were doing well but then decided by themselves that they did not need the medicine any more.

Traveling alone, staying out late, and the ill person's personal safety raise similar kinds of problems. As a general rule persons should be given as much autonomy and independence as they can handle, and this should be done in a graduated series of steps. For example, a schizophrenic person who believes he or she should be able to travel alone to a concert and stay out late should be given the opportunity to demonstrate readiness by successfully going to the store regularly, traveling alone to the halfway house during the day, avoiding street drugs, and not getting into trouble in public because of bizarre behavior. I have known families who discreetly followed their schizophrenic family member on initial forays into the community to ensure that no harm befell the patient. When the patient asks for more autonomy, the family should set up a series of conditions which must be met before the autonomy can be granted; for example, a patient who asks to travel home alone from the halfway house might be told that this can be tried once the patient has demonstrated familiarity with the bus route and has successfully gone for two weeks without forgetting to lock the door of the house.

Chores are another means by which persons with schizophrenia may demonstrate their readiness for more independence. Sweeping, cleaning, doing the dishes, taking out the garbage, feeding the dog, and weeding are all examples of chores which may be appropriate to assign to the schizophrenic family member. Families are sometimes reluctant to assign such chores, fearing that any stress will cause a recurrence of the patient's symptoms. Patients who are lazy may encourage such fears, pleading illness whenever there is work to be done. One mother described the resentment which is an inevitable consequence of this situation: "It's so annoying when you've got lots of housework to do, and there he is, a fine healthy-looking young man, and he just *sits* there doing absolutely nothing." Doing chores will not cause a patient to become sicker, and such chores are used extensively in halfway house settings and clubhouse programs, such as those described in chapter 9. They are an ideal way for patients to assume more independence and they increase the person's self-esteem at the same time. I have seen some extremely psychotic patients doing chores quite nicely and feeling better for having done so.

The management of the patient's money may cause the most diffi-culty of all. Many patients know that a portion of their SSI check is earmarked for their personal needs, and they believe they should have the right to spend it however they please. They should be reminded, however, that the personal portion of the check is intended to cover necessities, such as clothes, as well as cigarettes and sodas.

Occasionally persons with schizophrenia can take total responsi-bility for their money and can manage it with minimal difficulties. I know one severely affected paranoid schizophrenic, for example, who is very delusional much of the time but is able to take monthly trips to the bank and manage her funds. Predictably, she will not tell the doctors or nurses how much money she has. More common, however, is the schizophrenic who cannot manage money at all; some patients, for example, will repeatedly give away any money they have to the first person who asks for it. For such persons it may be useful to link autonomy in money management to other behavior indicating indepen-dence. For example, if patients have difficulty with personal hygiene and grooming, it may be appropriate to agree to give them more money to spend as they wish every week that they successfully take a shower without being told. The successful performance of chores is another way that schizophrenic patients can demonstrate that they are ready for greater financial responsibility.

Issues of independence and money management may also cause problems for families because of the family's inability to understand that their schizophrenic member is getting better. When one has lived with a severely psychotic individual who may have even needed help in dressing himself, it is often difficult to recognize a few weeks later that the person is now able to travel by bus alone and manage a weekly allowance. Families have often been both scared and scarred, and their ability to respond and adapt sometimes becomes constricted.

Some parents are reluctant to give autonomy to their schizo-phrenic children because they themselves need to continue their parental role. This is, of course, true for some parents of nonschizophrenics as well, and it often leads to retarded maturity in the young adult. It is another reason why living away from home is preferable for most released schizophrenic patients.

Finally, the responsibility issue arises around the question of how much control the person has over his or her symptoms. As discussed previously, the majority of schizophrenics have some control most of the time although this may fluctuate. Many of them can and do control their responses to auditory hallucinations on public buses and may learn not to talk about their sexual delusions to Aunt Agatha. A few patients have told me that they can even "command" their hallucinations to stop for brief periods. Others have learned to control some symptoms by diversionary activity, such as listening to music (earphones are sometimes effective in decreasing auditory hallucinations), watching television, playing pool, or withdrawing into their room.

How should families and patients resolve the responsibility and independence issue? It should be done in the same way families should resolve it for nonschizophrenic family members—by an open discussion of what is expected, what is fair, and what the person has to do to achieve more independence. It is often useful to include the patient's psychiatrist, counselor, social worker, or case manager in such discussions.

Violence and Aggression. These qualities are found in many families without schizophrenia, prominently in those with alcoholics. They present especially difficult problems, however, in families in which one member has schizophrenia. Violence and aggression lurk as specters on the periphery of consciousness, never completely out of view, quietly repeating "what if," "what if," "what if . . .?" In fact, schizophrenic patients as a group are remarkably nonviolent, but statistical assertions are of no value in predicting behavior for an individual patient.

Patients with schizophrenia may be involved in three types of aggressive behavior: destruction of property, aggression against oneself, or aggression against others. Regarding the first, there appears to be a consensus that patients with schizophrenia living in the community have a higher arrest rate for crimes against property than the general population.

Given the release of large numbers of them from state institutions and their poor psychiatric follow-up (see chapter 8), this increased arrest rate should not be surprising. As their schizophrenic symptoms recur, such persons do things or behave in ways which bring them to the attention of the police, who frequently arrest them in order to return them to the hospital. One man smashed a store window because he saw a dinosaur jumping out at him. Another was arrested for repeatedly following two men who he believed were CIA agents and had kidnapped his imaginary benefactress. A woman was arrested for repeatedly eating in restaurants and then refusing to pay; she said she was the reincarnation of Jesus Christ and was therefore not required to pay. Patients I have known have been arrested for throwing stones at cars, attacking a telephone booth with an ax, and walking nude on public streets.

Aggression against oneself can take the form either of suicide (discussed in chapter 5) or self-mutilation. The latter, although rare, is dramatic and often highly publicized. Almost always individuals who mutilate themselves have schizophrenia and are acutely psychotic at the time. One of my patients tried twice to cut off his penis with a piece of glass when he was very ill. Voices had told him to do it to atone for his sins. Another patient went to Sears, purchased a chain saw, then calmly took it to the women's room and cut off her leg; she too had been told to do it by voices. Other patients with schizophrenia have been known to take out their own eye or set themselves afire. Such patients usually give warnings of their impending behavior and do not commit such acts when they are properly medicated. Self-mutilation, then, is preventable in most instances with good psychiatric care and follow-up.

Aggression against others by persons with schizophrenia has become a subject of much public concern and controversy. In New Jersey a man who felt his neighbors were persecuting and belittling him made a list of his persecutors, then systematically killed thirteen people in twenty minutes. In Pennsylvania a woman, hospitalized psychiatrically fifteen times in ten years, opened fire in a crowded shopping mall, killing three people. In New York a woman with schizophrenia stabbed a stranger in the restroom of Pennsylvania Station, another pushed a stranger in front of a subway, and a man whose voices commanded him to kill was released by a hospital and thereupon stabbed to death two strangers on a Staten Island ferry. Reports of attacks by schizophrenic persons upon family members, sometimes fatal, circulate quietly within family support networks.

Are such episodes more common than in the past or just more highly publicized? There is no consensus on this. What is known is that aggression by persons with schizophrenia against others is more likely to occur in those who have paranoid delusions ("I'll get them before they get me") and in those who have command hallucinations (voices which order the person to do things). And it is known that most such attacks occur in patients who are undermedicated or unmedicated and/or who are concurrently using alcohol or street drugs, such as PCP. One study of violent behavior among schizophrenic patients in the hospital, for example, found a direct relationship between lower antipsychotic blood levels and more episodes of violence. In another study 94 percent of schizophrenic patients arrested for any crime were receiving no psychiatric care at the time.

What this implies is that the majority of arrests and attacks are preventable if our system of psychiatric care and aftercare was working as it should. If, on the other hand, we persist in deinstitutionalizing large numbers of patients with schizophrenia into the community without providing follow-up and aftercare—including ensuring medication compliance in patients prone to aggression and violence—then we must not be surprised if the number of such violent episodes increases.

What should families do when faced with a schizophrenic relative who may be violent or assaultive? First, it should be stressed that such problems almost always have forewarnings through threats and other signs of impending trouble; placid, withdrawn schizophrenic patients do not suddenly metamorphose into violent, homicidal individuals. Those with paranoid schizophrenia are the group which merits most concern, and if patients with this diagnosis start talking about "I'll get them before they get me," then an immediate reevaluation by a psychiatrist is mandatory.

When faced with threats of violence, the family of a schizophrenic patient should not ignore them but rather should discuss them openly. Is the patient simply seeking attention and/or trying to intimidate the family? Are the threats based upon rational manipulation, or do they arise in irrational, usually delusional, thought processes? Does the patient have a past history of violence, which is the single best predictor of future violence? Has the patient ingested street drugs or been drinking heavily? The family should usually consult with the patient's psychiatrist, who may help them assess the seriousness of the threat. If such threats are being heard for the first time, reevaluation of the patient by the psychiatrist is probably indicated. In all instances the family should convey to the patient that violence of any kind will not be tolerated, and the penalty for acting out the threats may well be expulsion from home. Families with such problems often learn to "schizophrenia-proof" their homes as well, including locking up sharp objects and weapons, removing the inner locks from the schizophrenic person's bedroom and bathroom, and ensuring that sufficient help is nearby if the person appears to be disturbed. The mother of one assaultive patient has a college student stay in the house as a companion when her son is at home; it gives her protection which she feels she needs and it gives her son somebody to spend time with who is closer to him in age. And families are learning increasingly to require their family member to take medication as a condition of living at or even visiting home.

The problem of violence and aggression by individuals with schizophrenia also is linked with problems of responsibility. Legally they comprise the problems leading to the insanity defense, to be discussed in chapter 11. In the eyes of the law, individuals with schizophrenia are either wholly responsible or wholly irresponsible for their behavior; actually, as discussed above, individuals with schizophrenia are capable of degrees of responsibility which may fluctuate over time. This is certainly true for aggressive acts as well. I had one patient, for example, who killed her husband because she grew tired of his physical abuse and philandering; she was modestly psychotic at the time but she knew exactly what she was doing and acted as many nonschizophrenic women have acted in similar circumstances.

A family within which the schizophrenic patient has been assaultive or violent is particularly poignant and lives in a special circle of Hell. Its members are often afraid of the patient, yet at the same time feel sorry for him/her and recognize that the behavior was a product of abnormal brain function. The ambivalence inevitably felt by the family members is formidable; fear and love, avoidance and attraction rest uneasily side by side. Afterward, no matter how well the patient gets, no matter how much time elapses, the memory of the past assault or violence never fully recedes.

Caffeine, Nicotine, Alcohol, and Street Drugs.   Excessive coffee drinking is frequently found among persons with schizophrenia and is often of concern to families. One speculation is that patients use coffee to offset the sedative effects of their medication. In some psychiatric hospitals, coffee, both in liquid form and as jars of instant coffee, is used as a form of currency. There have been indications that excessive amounts of coffee may make the symptoms of schizophrenia worse; it was also reported in the early 1980s that coffee and tea drinking might impair the absorption of antipsychotic drugs but subsequently this was shown probably not to be the case.

What should be the attitude of families toward coffee drinking in individuals with schizophrenia? It is known that excessive coffee drinking for anybody is bad, producing jitteriness and nervousness, what is known as caffeinism. The amount of coffee needed to produce this varies with the individual, the strength of the coffee (drip coffee is usually stronger than instant coffee), the size of the cup, the number of colas and other caffeine-containing substances also consumed, and the time period over which it is consumed. It is also known that many people with schizophrenia have few real pleasures in life, and we should not remove these pleasures without good reason. As a general rule, therefore, I suggest limiting coffee drinking in persons with schizophrenia to a maximum of five regular-size cups per 24-hour period, and to serving no coffee at the time medications are taken, for half an hour thereafter, or in the evening.

Smoking among persons with schizophrenia is almost universal. One study found that 88 percent of schizophrenic outpatients smoked regularly, a higher percentage than for any other psychiatric diagnosis and almost three times the rate for nonpsychiatric controls. In my own experience among inpatients with schizophrenia, I have been impressed by the strength of nicotine addiction among many of them; cigarettes are a frequent cause of fights and women in psychiatric hospitals occasionally turn to prostitution in order to acquire them.

The reason persons with schizophrenia smoke so heavily is unknown. It has been speculated that it is a product of boredom or the culture of the wards and clinics where everybody else smokes. It is also possible that nicotine offsets sedation or other unpleasant side effects of antipsychotic drugs, or that the biochemistry of the schizophrenic disease process somehow makes the person more nicotine-addicted. Finally, it is quite possible that smoking makes the symptoms of schizophrenia less bothersome for the person, for it is known that nicotine decreases the level of arousal; if this is true then the person with schizophrenia who smokes is simply self-medicating. It is unknown why lung cancer does not appear to be especially prevalent among persons with schizophrenia, despite their heavy use of nicotine.

What should be the attitude of families toward smoking in family members with schizophrenia? They should certainly demand good smoking habits (e.g., no smoking in bed), for lighted cigarettes are potentially dangerous to everyone in the home. Further, it is important to consider the pleasure patients get from smoking and not to take away one of the few pleasures they have. Given the strength of nicotine addiction, stopping smoking in a schizophrenic is not the battle a family is likely to win, and the first rule in life (masochists and martyrs excepted) is to fight no battles that are lost before you begin fighting. Cigarettes can also be used in a positive way in schizophrenia to encourage patients to take their medication; this used to be called bribery but is now called positive reinforcement. It works.

Alcohol consumption by persons with schizophrenia is often a worrisome problem for families. Many clinicians urge persons with schizophrenia not to drink alcohol at all, saying that the alcohol will make their symptoms worse and/or interact adversely with their anti-psychotic medicine. It has been my experience that the majority of persons with schizophrenia living in the community take a drink now and then and discover that the dire warnings of adverse effects do not materialize. Most patients can, in fact, have a social drink, and they appreciate doing so because it makes them feel more like "normal" people.

Like all life's pleasures, however, alcohol is best used in moderation and this may be as difficult for some schizophrenic persons to do as it is for some nonschizophrenic persons. This is especially true if the person gets symptom relief from the alcohol (e.g., a decrease in auditory hallucinations), and such patients frequently become addicted to alcohol. Whether alcohol addiction is more common among those with schizophrenia than it is among the general population is an issue yet to be settled. Both schizophrenia and alcoholism are common conditions, and so statistically one might expect some people to be afflicted by both. It is also undetermined whether alcoholism occurs more often in families of persons with schizophrenia, and vice versa.

What should be the attitude of families toward alcohol use in individuals with schizophrenia? If the person does not abuse alcohol and wishes to have an occasional social drink, then that may be reasonable. I have found it useful to set specific, well-defined *maximum* amounts of alcohol which may safely be consumed; for example, in any 24-hour period I tell patients not to exceed two cans of beer, two small glasses of wine, or one ounce of alcohol. For persons with a low tolerance to alcohol, even this may be too much. For some others with schizophrenia, alcohol should be prohibited, including anyone with a history of aggressive or violent behavior, anyone in whom the alcohol increases paranoid symptoms, anyone who abuses alcohol or is addicted to it.

The treatment of concurrent alcoholism and schizophrenia is a problem. Disulfiram (Antabuse) can be used but the patient must be capable of understanding that drinking alcohol while on disulfiram may produce a severe, even fatal, reaction. Disulfiram should also not be given to any patient taking the antipsychotic perphenazine (Trilafon), because it will decrease the antipsychotic effect of the medication, and should be given with medical supervision to patients taking tricyclic antidepressants. Alcoholics Anonymous is also effective for some schizophrenia sufferers with alcoholism, if the person's symptoms are under control with medication. The problems with Alcoholics Anonymous are that some chapters actively exclude members who have schizophrenia (they do not want the public to confuse alcoholism with "craziness") and the anti-all-drugs stance of Alcoholics Anonymous often leads to advising schizophrenic patients to throw away *all* drugs, *including* their antipsychotic medication.

Street drug use by persons with schizophrenia can be summed up in one word. NO. For many patients, even marijuana may set off psychotic symptoms in an unpredictable way, and it may take days to recover from them fully. One young man I treated remained virtually symptom-free on medication except when he smoked marijuana; he then become floridly psychotic for several days. Not every person with schizophrenia reacts so dramatically, of course, but there is no way to predict which will do so. Stronger drugs, especially PCP and amphetamines ("speed"), are like poison for anyone with schizophrenia. Families should discourage their use in every way possible, and should not allow a family member with schizophrenia in the home if street drug use is suspected. This rule is absolutely mandatory if the person has a history of assaultive or violent behavior; many of the homicides committed by those afflicted with schizophrenia appear to occur following use of street drugs. Draconian measures to discourage street drug use are perfectly legitimate, including requiring the person with schizophrenia to periodically submit to urine testing for street drug use as a condition of living at home, receiving support from the family, or remaining out of the hospital.

Religious Concerns.   Like all human beings, persons with schizophrenia have a need to relate to a god or philosophical worldview which

WHAT THE FAMILY NEEDS

allows them to place themselves and their lives within a larger context. For persons with schizophrenia this can be particularly problematical for many reasons. For one thing, the onset of the disease often occurs during the same period of life when religious and philosophical beliefs are in great flux, thus making resolution extremely difficult. Another complicating factor is that many persons with this disease undergo intense heightened awareness, or "peak experiences" (as described in chapter 2), during the early stages of their illness and conclude that they have been specially chosen by God. When auditory hallucinations are experienced, these usually reinforce such a belief. Still another impediment to resolutions of religious concerns is the schizophrenic person's inability to think metaphorically and in symbols, which most formalized religious belief systems require.

It is therefore not surprising that religious concerns continue to be important for many persons with this disease throughout the course of their illness. Most psychiatric hospitals provide chaplains to assist the patients; schizophrenia victims living in the community frequently utilize ministers, priests, and rabbis in their neighborhoods. I have been impressed by the quality of the spiritual ministrations shown by many of these people and their patience in answering the schizophrenic persons' questions.

Occasionally schizophrenic persons resolve their religious concerns by joining a religious cult of one kind or another. The variety of available cults is wide and includes the Unification Church ("Moonies"), Hare Krishna, Divine Light Mission, Jesus People, Scientology, and many smaller groups. A study reported that 6 percent of members from the Unification Church and 9 percent of members from the Divine Light Mission had been previously hospitalized for psychiatric problems. However, psychiatrists who have studied such groups believe that most of these previously hospitalized members were severely neurotic rather than schizophrenic. The groups themselves tend to exclude seriously disturbed individuals as too disruptive to the closely cooperative living and working conditions demanded by the groups.

For schizophrenic patients who are accepted into these cults there may be some advantages. A highly structured belief system and life style are inherent in such groups, as is also a sense of belongingness and community. These in turn lead to increased self-esteem in the member. Some cults also value unusual religious experiences, and in such settings a person with schizophrenia may feel more comfortable with his/her "peak experiences" or auditory hallucinations.

The cults also pose additional potential dangers, however. Many such groups emphasize the desirability of not taking any drugs; schizophrenics who are doing nicely on maintenance fluphenazine or haloperidol may be encouraged to stop the drug, with resultant relapse. The groups may also encourage the schizophrenic person to deny the reality of his or her illness, casting problems such as delusional thinking and auditory hallucinations into the mold of spiritual shortcomings rather than acknowledging that they are products of a brain disease. Some groups may also encourage paranoid thinking in schizophrenic persons who are already inclined in that direction, as there is often a siege mentality in the cults, a "we-they" feeling that the world is out to persecute them as a group. Finally, a few religious cults may exploit the money or property of schizophrenic members, as they sometimes do of nonschizophrenic members as well.

Sexual Issues.   As mentioned in chapter 9, some persons with schizophrenia have little interest in sexual relationships and therefore pose no problems in this area for their families. Many others, however, do have an interest. Among the biggest problems for their families are contraception (discussed in chapter 9) and genetic counseling (discussed in chapter 11). But the problems do not stop there.

Delusional thinking about sexual issues may be troublesome, especially if the person lacks social discretion and expresses the thoughts publicly. I once had a patient who delighted in announcing to each stranger who came on the ward that she had been pregnant for five years and might deliver at any time. Allegations of familial incest on a crowded elevator can also be a show stopper. Patients inclined to make such remarks must be educated and strongly encouraged to learn discretion, and such discretion should be one requirement for living in the community. If persons with schizophrenia cannot appreciate the necessity for verbal discretion in such socially sensitive areas, then their judgment is probably so impaired that they are incompetent to care for themselves in other social areas as well.

It should not be surprising that many persons with schizophrenia exhibit both anxiety and confusion about sexual issues. Many persons who do not have schizophrenia also exhibit anxiety and confusion. In addition, schizophrenia begins in most patients precisely at the time that sexual identity and sexual concerns are being resolved by young adults. Persons who develop schizophrenia are unable to complete the process of resolution, so these problems continue to occupy their thinking for many years. Delusional ideas that the person is homosexual, or is really of the opposite sex, are examples of ideas very common among persons with schizophrenia.

Families in which the person with schizophrenia is interested in sexual activities must first confront their own embarrassment about that interest. As mentioned in chapter 9, the mentally ill are consigned in our imaginations to the realm of nonlibido inhabited by the elderly and by persons with chronic physical illnesses, just as if physical pleasure, sharing, and intimacy are desired only by the young and the healthy, which is, of course, nonsense. Coming to grips with the reality of physical desire and accepting it as legitimate will often relieve some of the sexual concerns of the family.

The next problem is how to assess whether the patient is a consenting adult or is being taken advantage of in the sexual situation. This usually applies to women, although occasionally schizophrenic men will be taken advantage of by homosexuals. Questions which the family should ask itself include: Is she able to say no to men in nonsexual situations? Is her judgment reasonably good in other areas of her day-to-day functioning? Is she discreet, which suggests good judgment, in her sexual encounters? Is she trying to avoid men or is she seeking them out? Is she agreeing to sex primarily to obtain specific payment, most often cigarettes or food?

Consultation with the patient's psychiatrist and/or nursing staff at the halfway house or the psychiatric ward where the patient is known will often clarify the consent issue for the family. The family of one woman, for example, became upset when they found that she was having intercourse regularly at the halfway house and she told her parents she was being taken advantage of. Discussion with halfway house staff established that the woman was seeking out the sexual encounters, and her claim of being taken advantage of was designed to assuage the disapproval of her parents. If a woman really is being taken advantage of, however, increased supervision and restrictions in her activity may be indicated. Women who consent to intercourse merely to acquire cigarettes or food need a plan formulated by the families and psychiatric staff to provide these items reliably, so the schizophrenic person will be less tempted to prostitute herself.

SUPPORTIVE SIBLINGS

Supportive siblings can be a major asset in helping families to survive schizophrenia. It is not easy being a brother or sister to a person with this disease, however. If there is a belief within the family that psychosocial events caused the disease, then the brother or sister may share the family guilt. Which of us has not done things to our own siblings which we did not later regret? When looking for "causes" of the person's schizophrenia, all of these past misdeeds and memories may be dredged up, accompanied by the barnacles of guilt encrusted on them. Another source of guilt, often not conscious, is the survivors' syndrome, in which persons who survive a disaster feel guilty for not having perished with the others; well siblings may similarly feel guilty that they have escaped the disease and are able to lead normal lives.

Embarrassment is another common and understandable feeling among brothers and sisters of schizophrenics, especially prominent during the teen years when peer pressure and social concerns are at their peak. Imagine a sixteen-year-old, for example, walking with a schizophrenic sibling through a park when the person with schizophrenia suddenly "jumped on one of the statues and yelled, 'I'm the king of the castle and you're all the dirty rascals.' " And the sister of one of my patients never asks anyone to visit when the patient is home because he unpredictably takes off his clothes. The embarrassment felt by the brother or sister is also likely to be greater if the parents, too, are embarrassed.

Siblings almost invariably feel anxiety as well, especially if they are younger than the affected person and still in an age range where the possibility of sickness is plausible. Comments such as "I often wonder if they think I'm likely to be as mad as my brother" or "We all do stupid things when we're with friends, but I can't help feeling that every odd action or word that I say is taken as evidence that I could develop into a schizophrenic" are not uncommon. The specter of the disease, of becoming insane, lurks in the minds of these young people throughout their formative years.

Jealousy is sometimes a problem. This may become exacerbated if large amounts of the family's financial resources, such as the money set aside for college for the well children, must be commandeered in order to pay for treatment of the schizophrenic child.

Louise Wilson expresses this dilemma from the mother's point of view in *This Stranger, My Son,* when told that her son's care will cost $50,000 a year.

> Surely you will do anything for your child. But you have to live along the way. You have to take care of your other children who are not sick. They are entitled to their share, too. How much ought you to spend on the sick one? How ought you to apportion what you have? . . . Some will say: "Everything for the sick one because the healthy can take care of themselves." Others will say: "The well have a future, therefore give to them; don't sacrifice them for the sake of the hopelessly ill."

Siblings may also be angry at the special attention or privileges given to the brother or sister with schizophrenia, as in the following example:

> One thing that really bothered me was Mom's overprotectiveness, especially when Peter came home from the hospital. She would let Peter have anything and say anything. She told us specifically not to get him upset. "Just act like yourselves," she said. Fine and good. But every time I'd be reading or watching TV she'd say, "Why don't you go and talk to Peter or play ball or do something with him? You're his sister." I got really angry. If he wanted to, he'd ask me. I tried to tell her but it would go in one ear and out the other. She'd make all his favorite meals, and he'd never have to wash dishes or do a single chore around the house.
>
> Sometimes I don't think Peter wants to help himself. He seems to let everyone else do the worrying for him—what he's going to do, where he's headed. He's just content to sit back and live at home here and have not a care in the world. I suppose that's what rubs me the wrong way about Peter. He's got so much to offer but he does nothing with it.

Despite these problems, the siblings of schizophrenics can be extremely helpful. As parents age and die, the responsibility for care or support of the schizophrenic family member may devolve onto them. And because they may be involved in the long-term care, siblings should be included in family discussions of financial arrangements for the ill person.

An excellent resource for siblings of schizophrenics is the Sibling Network, an organization set up under the National Alliance for the Mentally Ill (see page 304). Julie Johnson, who has a brother with schizophrenia and who began the Sibling Network, advocates eight steps for siblings to consider in coming to terms with the disease:

1. Acknowledge that the sick sibling has an influence on our lives.
2. Identify our feelings about the sick sibling.
3. Realize that we cannot control the other person's behavior.
4. Realize that we can change our past attitudes and our stereotypical thinking.
5. Recognize that schizophrenia is a disease of the brain for which nobody is to blame.
6. Forgive ourselves for mistakes we might have made toward our sibling.
7. Recognize our own needs, as well as those of the sibling.
8. Set specific goals to help improve the situation.

FAMILY SUPPORT GROUPS

To survive schizophrenia, the single most important step which should be taken by families with a schizophrenic family member is to join a family support group. Such groups existed sporadically around the United States in the 1970s but have mushroomed in the 1980s. Most are affiliated with the National Alliance for the Mentally Ill (NAMI), which formed in 1979 and now has over 800 chapters; appendix D lists addresses for the national NAMI office, as well as state NAMI offices which can provide information on the nearest group. In a few states, family support groups have been formed by the local Mental Health Association, and occasional groups still exist that were formed in the past under the American Schizophrenia Association, committed to the principles of megavitamin treatment and orthomolecular psychiatry (see nutritional theories, chapter 6).

Family support groups vary in character and purpose. Almost all of them include mutual support and education. Either in large group meetings or in smaller groups (such as "sharing nights"), the families exchange information about psychiatrists, financial resources for patients, commitment laws, places for schizophrenic patients to live, and problems they are encountering with their schizophrenic relatives. One study of such groups found that it was this sharing of common experiences and problems, not merely practical information, which was their most useful function. Most family support groups supplement this private information exchange with a monthly newsletter, and some have undertaken public education. Many NAMI groups have undertaken advocacy, such as lobbying for better treatment of patients in state psychiatric hospitals, changing state commitment laws to make it easier to hospitalize patients who need treatment, getting more low-cost housing, or improving vocational programs. Some family support groups have even begun their own housing projects (e.g., halfway houses) or jobs programs. At the national level NAMI has become effective as an advocate for more research expenditures for schizophrenia as well as a force to combat stigma by public education. Many of these activities are discussed in more detail in chapter 14.

Support groups for families with schizophrenic members have begun in several other countries. In Britain the National Schizophrenia Fellowship began in 1970 and has been very active. There is now a Schizophrenia Association of Ireland, while Australia and New Zealand each have Schizophrenia Fellowships and Canada has a Canadian Friends of Schizophrenics. Similar organizations operate in Austria, Chile, France, Israel, Japan, the Netherlands, Sweden, South Africa, and West Germany.

GOOD MEDICAL INSURANCE

Medical insurance with good coverage for psychiatric disorders is exceedingly useful in enabling families to survive. Unfortunately, however, such insurance is not widespread. While between 85 and 90 percent of Americans are covered by some form of medical insurance, only 6 percent of these policies provide benefits for psychiatric disorders which are comparable to benefits provided for medical disorders. Most policies limit inpatient psychiatric coverage to a specified amount per year and/or a total amount for a lifetime. Outpatient psychiatric coverage is usually confined to a maximum number of visits or total cost per year. Many medical insurance policies require the person insured to meet a larger deductible or pay higher co-payments for psychiatric disorders. Day treatment programs are usually covered but psychosocial rehabilitation programs (e.g., clubhouses) usually are not.

The reasons for discrimination against psychiatric disorders in medical insurance policies are many. Insurance policies do not differentiate serious psychiatric disorders like schizophrenia from problems of living; thus an individual with unlimited coverage could seek psychoanalytic psychotherapy five times a week for years. If many people utilized their insurance coverage in this manner the insurance company would soon be bankrupt. Coverage of serious psychiatric disorders like schizophrenia can also be very expensive because the majority of such patients require ongoing care for many years.

Medical insurance that covers schizophrenia is most useful in the early stages of the disease when the initial diagnostic workup and trials of various antipsychotic medication should be taking place. Costs of hospitalization alone, even without laboratory tests or physician's fees, may be $600 per day or more. Families who have limited lifetime total benefits on their policy are best advised to use those benefits in these early stages.

For individuals not covered by insurance, it may be possible to use Medicaid (for the indigent) or Medicare (for the elderly and disabled) to cover the costs of brief inpatient hospital care. Medicaid coverage varies from state to state, including the number of days of psychiatric hospitalization that Medicaid will cover. In some states Medicaid will pay for hospitalization on the psychiatric ward of a general hospital but not in a psychiatric hospital. Medicaid may also pay for care in nursing homes classified in either the "intermediate" or the "skilled" care category, allowing some elderly schizophrenic patients to be cared for in these facilities if they prefer. Medicaid does not cover halfway house costs, an omission which many people would like changed. Medicaid covers outpatient psychiatric visits in some states, but the amount reimbursed to the psychiatrist varies widely from state to state.

Medicare also covers inpatient psychiatric costs for those who qualify but is limited to a maximum of 190 days for an entire lifetime. Therefore, for someone with schizophrenia who qualifies for Medicare, it may be most sensible to use the lifetime coverage early in the course of the disease. Medicare covers some outpatient psychiatric costs, but under a deductible and maximum allowable annual ceiling. In contrast to short-term psychiatric hospitalization coverage, there is virtually no insurance program to cover the cost of long-term care. Monthly fees for long-term care in private hospitals can be $12,000 or even higher and are thus affordable by only the very wealthy. Ironically, many of the most expensive private psychiatric hospitals are psychoanalytically oriented, anachronisms of the past, and therefore offer mediocre care for schizophrenia. It is a sad but common experience to learn of a wealthy family paying $150,000 per year for the care of a schizophrenic family member, and to find that the care the patient is receiving is psychiatrically worse than on most of the wards of the local state hospital. Psychiatry is one area of medicine where paying more money does not necessarily buy you better care.

GUARDIANSHIP AND PLANS FOR THE FUTURE

One of the most troubling problems for families with a schizophrenic family member is what will happen after the family members who are providing the care die. Typically it is a mother and father who provide much of the care needed by a schizophrenic son or daughter, although in other cases the same problem may arise for an aging or sick person who is providing care for a schizophrenic sibling. In the old days such care was transferred to the extended family or the state hospital. Now, however, the extended family has disappeared and the state hospital will simply discharge the person with schizophrenia to live in the community. The specter of their family member ending up living in public shelters and on the streets haunts many families.

Guardianship is one mechanism used by families to ensure care for the family member and safeguard his or her assets after the death of the well family members. The guardian may be either a relative or friend of the patient or, if none is available or appropriate, another person selected by the judge. The appointment of a guardian occurs most frequently when the patient owns large amounts of money or property or is likely to inherit some. Guardianship is a legal relationship authorizing one person to make decisions for another and is based upon the same *parens patriae* tenet of English law which permits involuntary hospitalization. When the guardian has jurisdiction only over the property of the patient, it is frequently referred to as a conservatorship. When both property and personal decisions are involved it is called a guardianship.

Guardianship (and conservatorship) laws are remarkably outmoded in most states. In many instances no distinction is made between personal and property decisions, and a guardian automatically is granted decision-making permission for both. Personal decisions affected by a guardianship may include where the patient may reside, the right to travel freely, and the right to consent to medical or psychiatric treatment; property decisions may include the right to sign checks or withdraw money from a bank account. Most guardianship laws are all-or-nothing affairs and fail to take into account the ability of schizophrenic patients to manage some areas of their lives but not others. The laws are often extremely vague: the law in California, until recently changed, said that a guardian could be appointed for any "incompetent person . . . whether insane or not . . ., who is likely to be deceived or imposed upon by artful and designing persons." This could include most of us! The actual appointment of a guardian is usually done without legal due process and without the patient present; nor is there periodic review to determine whether the guardianship is still necessary.

Another mechanism used by some families to plan for the future are nonprofit organizations founded by groups of families. These organizations will accept responsibility for the schizophrenic family member after the death of the well family members. For many years such organizations have been utilized by families with mentally retarded members; recently groups under the National Alliance for the Mentally Ill have been setting them up on a local level. For example, in Virginia and Maryland there is the Planned Life Assistance Network (PLAN), with family members serving on the organization's board of directors. A person who joins pays a membership fee and annual dues, then develops a plan of care for the family member with schizophrenia to be activated after the death of other family members. At that time the professional staff and volunteers of PLAN will assume the responsibilities previously provided by the family, including visiting the person regularly, maintaining contact with the schizophrenic person's doctor or case manager, paying the person's bills, acting as payee for SSI payments, and assuming other fiscal or supervisory functions as needed.

SOME EXPRESSED EMOTIONS
ABOUT EXPRESSED EMOTION

Expressed emotion has achieved great prominence in the schizophrenia research literature in recent years; because of this prominence, families need to have some understanding of what it is about. Expressed emotion originated in England in the 1960s, when it was observed that some patients with schizophrenia relapsed when they returned home to live with their families. Out of this observation came a series of studies attempting to identify the family characteristics which were likely to produce relapse. These characteristics included being overly critical, hostile, overinvolved and overidentified with the ill family member, intrusive, and highly expressive of emotions. The mother in a high expressed-emotion (high EE) family says things like: "John, you look like a dirty slob. Why can't you ever change your clothes? It's very embarrassing to me." By contrast, the mother in a low EE family handles the same situation by saying things like: "John, you would probably feel much better if you put on some clean clothes."

The corollary which follows from high EE research is that families exhibiting such characteristics can be educated to be less critical, less involved, etc., and that when this occurs the family member with schizophrenia is less likely to relapse. As described by one of the major researchers in this field, the relapse rate can be lowered "by teaching the patients and their families better methods of coping with stressful events and by changing the attitudes of key family members in the direction of greater support, less destructive criticism, and less emotional overinvolvement."

At first glance, research on expressed emotion seems reasonable enough. On closer inspection, however, this research elicits from me personally some thoughts and emotions which can be summarized as follows:

Surprise: Given what is known about the difficulties schizophrenics have in sorting sensory stimuli and messages (see chapter 2), it would be surprising to find that they were not affected by overtly expressed criticisms, hostility, or overinvolvement by family members. The main thesis of EE research appears to be, in short, self-evident. It is therefore surprising to find so much attention and research resources devoted to demonstrating the obvious. In 1985 alone, for example, NIMH awarded grants totaling $687,000 for EE research, and during the year four new books deriving from this work were published with such titles as *Expressed Emotion in Families, Working with Families of the Mentally Ill, The Family and Schizophrenia,* and *Family Management of Schizophrenia.*

Skepticism: Given the manpower and hours devoted to working with high EE families, teaching them to become more tolerant, etc., it is difficult to imagine that the findings of these studies will ever be of more than academic interest. Compliance with medication-taking remains by far the single most important factor determining relapse rates; if half the energy currently being devoted to educating families about high EE was devoted instead to ensuring compliance with medications, the relapse rate of schizophrenics would decrease much more dramatically than anything demonstrated by EE. There remain many methodological problems with EE research which elicit skepticism of its importance; included are the well-known Hawthorn effect (things will change just because they are being closely studied) and the apparent confusion between cause and effect in many of the research projects (e.g., did the family's high expressed emotion cause the relapse or did the characteristics of the patient elicit the expressed emotion?).

Suspicion: Although most of the EE researchers seem genuinely convinced that families do not *cause* schizophrenia in their family member, that is not true of all of them. Dr. Michael J. Goldstein of the University of California, Los Angeles, one of the more prominent researchers in the EE field, has carried out research on disturbed adolescent boys which he claims "provides evidence that family attributes measured during adolescence are associated with the *subsequent* presence of schizophrenia or schizophrenia-related disorders in the offspring once they entered young adulthood." In other words, the family causes schizophrenia. In *The New York Times,* Goldstein was quoted as claiming that "the parents of these kids engaged in character assassinations." Such assertions make families of schizophrenics justifiably suspicious of EE research. Is EE research merely the offspring of Gregory Bateson's double-bind?

What, then, is the role of EE in schizophrenia? People with schizophrenia do best in situations where people are calm and communicate clearly and directly. The attributes of the right attitude discussed above (sense of humor, acceptance of the illness, family balance, and expectations which are realistic) are the antithesis of high expressed emotions; insofar as families are striving to achieve these, they should not worry about expressed emotion.

What about counseling or family "therapy" to help the family learn to live with the disease? If families wish to seek help from a mental health professional, that may be useful in some instances. Be very careful, however, that the mental health professional has an educational approach and will help you learn ways to manage the family situation, not a psychoanalytic approach that will merely produce guilt and blame. Families with schizophrenic family members need to be educated, not "treated," and to do everything they can to learn how to live with a difficult situation. This is precisely the same for families with members affected by multiple sclerosis, polio, severe diabetes, renal disease, or any other long-term disabling disease.

HOW MENTAL HEALTH PROFESSIONALS
CAN HELP FAMILIES

Families faced with schizophrenia in a family member can be helped immeasurably by mental health professionals. In the past such help was usually not forthcoming, and in fact mental health professionals, armed with textbooks describing schizophrenogenic mothers and double-binds, often made the burden much heavier. Increasingly in recent years, however, a growing group of professionals have emerged who can help families to survive the catastrophe of schizophrenia.

How can mental health professionals be most helpful to families? The following are some suggestions:

1. Provide information to families about the disease (e.g., referral to written materials) and tell them about the local family support group.

2. Utilize families as one point of a therapeutic triangle with the patients and yourself as the other two points. Information about the patient's condition needs to flow in all directions. Families are in fact the primary care providers for large numbers of schizophrenics and can give important information regarding premorbid personality characteristics, symptoms, response to medication, and signs of relapse. Professionals must not hide behind the facade of confidentiality or "therapeutic alliance," but rather must share information regarding the patient's condition, exactly as if the patient had multiple sclerosis or Alzheimer's disease.

3. Be cognizant of the multiple needs of patients with schizophrenia, such as housing, vocational training, and social needs, and be supportive of the families' efforts to identify community resources to fill such needs. After the dopamine dysfunction has been corrected as best it can be, there are still human beings who need help in reconstructing their shattered lives.

RECOMMENDED FURTHER READING

Appleton, W. S. "Mistreatment of Patients' Families by Psychiatrists." *American Journal of Psychiatry* 131 (1974): 655–57. This unique account by a psychiatrist tells how psychiatrists cause damage by blaming family members for causing schizophrenia.

Bernheim, K. F., and A. F. Lehman. *Working with Families of the Mentally Ill.* New York: W. W. Norton, 1985. Practical suggestions for families.

Bernheim, K. F., R. R. J. Lewine, and C. T. Beale. *The Caring Family: Living with Chronic Mental Illness.* New York: Random House, 1982. The strengths of the book are its discussion of the emotions faced by families with chronic mental illness and practical suggestions on how to cope and respond. Its weaknesses are its paucity of factual data and its attempt to group all chronic mental conditions (alcoholism, severe anxiety, schizophrenia) into a single entity.

Busick, B. S., and M. Gorman. *Ill Not Insane.* Boulder, CO: New Idea Press, 1986. One of the recent books about schizophrenia written by the families, this one stresses the medical aspects of the disease.

Creer, C., and J. Wing. *Schizophrenia at Home.* London: Institute of Psychiatry, 1974 (National Schizophrenia Fellowship, 78/79 Victoria Road, Surbiton, Surrey, England KT6–4NS). A summary of interviews with eighty families with a schizophrenic member, it also describes major problems encountered.

Dearth, N. S., B. J. Labenski, M. E. Mott, et al. *Families Helping Families.* New York: W. W. Norton, 1986. Another recent book written by families affected by schizophrenia, this one has helpful portions but is enamored of orthomolecular treatment.

Hatfield, A. *Coping with Mental Illness in the Family: A Family Guide.* Washington, D.C.: National Alliance for the Mentally Ill, 1984. Course outline and material for six two-hour educational seminars for families. The purpose of the course "is to help families develop the knowledge and skills which will enable them to cope with severely mentally ill persons."

Hatfield, A. B., ed. *Families of the Mentally Ill: Meeting the Challenge.* San Francisco: Jossey-Bass, 1987. Ten chapters providing an overview of the family support movement and the family's response when a member is diagnosed with a serious mental illness.

Hinckley, J., and J. A. Hinckley. *Breaking Points.* Grand Rapids, MI: Chosen Books, 1985. This is the Hinckleys' account of discovering their son's schizophrenia after he had attempted to assassinate the President.

Johnson, J. *The Silent Witness.* New York: Doubleday, 1988. Written by a woman whose brother has schizophrenia, this is a very helpful book for brothers and sisters.

Kantor, J. S. *Coping Strategies for Relatives of the Mentally Ill.* Bethesda, MD: Threshold AMI, 1982. A summary of steps which families can take to survive this disease.

Park, C. C., and L. N. Shapiro. *You Are Not Alone.* Boston: Little, Brown, 1976. Although now somewhat dated, this is an encyclopedia of useful information for families of the mentally ill. The book does not focus on schizophrenia exclusively but is an invaluable reference and is well written for a lay audience.

Riley, J. *Crazy Quilt*. New York: William Morrow, 1984. This is an excellent fictional account of a thirteen-year-old whose mother has schizophrenia. It is written for children.

Rollin, Henry, ed. *Coping with Schizophrenia*. National Schizophrenia Fellowship. London: Burnett Books, 1980. This book brings together several previously published pamphlets by the National Schizophrenia Fellowship with some new material. The chapters "Schizophrenia from Within" and "Schizophrenia at Home" are especially good and will be very useful to families of patients with this disease. The ten-year history and exciting work done by the National Schizophrenia Fellowship in England is summarized in the last chapter and offers many ideas which could be utilized in the United States.

Russell, L. M. *Alternatives: A Family Guide to Legal and Financial Planning for the Disabled*. Evanston, IL: First Publications, 1983. This is a very useful summary of wills, trusts, guardianship, etc.

Seeman, M. V., S. K. Littmann, J. F. Thornton, et al. *Living and Working with Schizophrenia*. Toronto, Canada: Toronto University Press, 1982. This is an excellent synopsis of problems written for families and includes personal accounts of the disease.

Seywert, F. "Some Critical Thoughts on Expressed Emotion." *Psychopathology* 17 (1984): 233–42. This is a concise summary of many of the methodological problems with expressed emotions research.

Terkelson, K. G. "Schizophrenia and the Family." *Family Process* 22 (1983): 191–200. This piece might be subtitled "Confessions of an Ex-Family Therapist," for it details the damage mental health professionals can cause. Strongly recommended.

Vine, P. *Families in Pain: Children, Siblings, Spouses, and Parents of the Mentally Ill Speak Out*. New York: Pantheon, 1982. This book provides useful case histories which clearly describe the effects of schizophrenia (and other serious mental illnesses) on the patients' families. Its limitations are its loose, rambling style and its paucity of factual material.

Walsh, M. *Schizophrenia: Straight Talk for Family and Friends*. New York: William Morrow, 1985. This is the best book written for families by a mother. She demonstrates the right attitude for surviving schizophrenia better than anyone else has done.

Wasow, M. *Coping with Schizophrenia: A Survival Manual for Parents, Relatives and Friends*. Palo Alto: Science and Behavior Books, 1982. The opening chapter is a moving account of the illness of the author's son. After that the book becomes disorganized; for example, medications are in chapter 4 but treatment in chapter 8. Despite this, the book is worth buying for its common sense and compassion.

II

LEGAL AND ETHICAL DILEMMAS
IN SCHIZOPHRENIA

When I tell them that I suffer from schizophrenia I often get blank
looks and sometimes a wary one. I have often felt that the mad cannot
explain and the sane cannot comprehend.

Schizophrenic patient, quoted in Henry R. Rollin,
Coping with Schizophrenia

Providing care for someone with a chronic illness is a difficult task.
Diseases such as polio, multiple sclerosis, kidney failure, and slowly
progressive cancer can drain a family physically, emotionally, and
sometimes also financially. When the chronic illness affects the person's brain, however, then the task becomes herculean. It has no-win
qualities, so that whatever the relative or friend does, there is always
the lingering feeling that it wasn't enough or it wasn't right. Like
Sisyphus condemned forever to roll a huge stone uphill, only to have
it roll down again, the unremitting process of caring for someone
with schizophrenia will tax the inner resources of even the strongest
person.

One major reason for this is the many legal and ethical dilemmas
raised by this disease. Relatives and friends of people with schizophrenia are caught frequently in damned-if-you-do and damned-if-you-
don't situations. They want to be helpful and do the right thing for the
patient, but often when they try they are confronted by these dilemmas.
This chapter will not solve the dilemmas, but it will at least articulate
them forthrightly, and thus allow them to be thought through as rationally as possible.

INVOLUNTARY HOSPITALIZATION

The most common of the legal and ethical dilemmas posed by people with schizophrenia is if and when to hospitalize them against their will. Consider the following case:

A young woman is observed to be living in a train station for several days. She asks passers-by for money but otherwise does not bother them. She is often seen talking to herself or to imaginary people. A newspaper reporter talks with her and discovers that she is a college graduate who has been recently released from a psychiatric hospital. The woman's conversation does not make sense. A policeman takes her to the local psychiatric hospital but the psychiatrists there refuse to admit her because they say she has done nothing to suggest that she is a danger to herself or others. She also indicates unwillingness to go back into the hospital voluntarily. She returns to the train station. A few days later she is found raped and murdered nearby.

This woman represents all the dilemmas of involuntary hospitalization. On one side are those who would argue against hospitalizing her against her wishes. Opponents of involuntary hospitalization include psychiatrists such as Dr. Thomas Szasz, civil liberties lawyers such as Bruce Ennis of the American Civil Liberties Union, and many ex-patient groups. Szasz has been working for the abolition of involuntary psychiatric hospitalization for over two decades, and in 1970 helped found the American Association for the Abolition of Involuntary Mental Hospitalization (AAAIMH). His many books, especially *Law, Liberty and Psychiatry* and *Psychiatric Slavery,* articulately expound the case against involuntarily hospitalizing persons with strange behavior or strange beliefs. Ennis, the forerunner of an increasing group of civil liberties lawyers concerned with mental illness, in 1972 published *Prisoners of Psychiatry,* in which he said, "The goal should be nothing less than the abolition of involuntary hospitalization." And ex-patient groups publish periodicals, such as the *Madness Network News,* which offers "all the fits that's news to print" and vividly describes the many injustices perpetrated on incarcerated mental patients.

The arguments used by these people against involuntary hospitalization include the deprivation of civil liberties and the violation of various constitutional rights guaranteed us as individuals. They cite thinkers such as John Stuart Mill and Thomas Jefferson, and argue that the state has no right to protect people from themselves. We allow people to smoke, drink, climb mountains, race automobiles and do many other things which clearly are dangerous to themselves. Doesn't one have the right to do what one wishes with one's own body provided no one else is harmed? Furthermore, dangerousness is a vague and relative concept, and what one person finds dangerous the next person may call pleasurable. And to confine people because they *might* do something to hurt themselves or hurt others is just preventive detention; if we can confine people for what they *might* do, then we must confine all criminals forever because we know that when they are released their dangerousness is much greater than the dangerousness of mental patients. Opponents of involuntary psychiatric hospitalization also point to the lifelong stigma which accrues to psychiatric hospitalization and to the accompanying loss of the right to vote, the right to make a contract, and the right to drive an automobile, which may accompany such hospitalization in some states.

Another argument against involuntary hospitalization is its potential for abuse. If the state has the right to hospitalize people against their will, then it may create arbitrary criteria for such hospitalization and thereby use it to remove dissenters and political opponents. This has in fact happened in the Soviet Union and other East European bloc countries and is well described by Sidney Bloch and Peter Reddaway in *Psychiatric Terror: How Soviet Psychiatry Is Used to Suppress Dissent.* Such hospitalizations are doubly effective as political tools because they not only incarcerate dissenters with indeterminate sentences but tinge them with the brush of insanity, thereby discrediting them.

The strongest arguments put forth against involuntary psychiatric hospitalization, however, are the horror stories of individual cases. There is no doubt that there has been much abuse of involuntary commitment, so there is much ammunition which can be used in the battle. People have indeed been locked up for thirty, fifty, even seventy years for strange behavior. Combine with this the fact that conditions in public psychiatric hospitals where they are locked up are so often grim, and you have the ingredients necessary for lurid testimonials of beatings, forced labor, and other inhumane conditions.

What about the young woman at the train station? Opponents of involuntary psychiatric hospitalization would argue that it was correct to let her remain free. Her behavior, they would say, may have been strange but then behavior is a relative concept. As long as she was not harming anyone she should have been left free. They, too, would mourn her death but would say that the price you must pay for liberty is the possibility that a few people may be killed.

Supporters of involuntary psychiatric hospitalization include most psychiatrists, many other mental health workers, the policemen and social workers who face these crises on a daily basis, and large segments of the general public. The major argument for hospitalizing people against their will is that they are unable to care for themselves because of their illness or because they are dangerous to themselves or to others. The idea of *parens patriae* (see chapter 7) says that the state has an obligation to protect people who cannot protect themselves and that mentally ill individuals have a right to be both protected and treated so that they will get well. Temporarily confining them and restricting their liberties is a small price to pay for this protection and treatment.

Another reason used to hospitalize patients against their will is the protection of others. A few psychiatric patients are genuinely dangerous. The problem arises when you try to quantify dangerousness. How dangerous do they have to be? What must they have done? Is a threat enough? I once had a young man under my care who had threatened the life of one of the nation's leaders. In addition to the threat, a rifle with a telescopic sight and dozens of rounds of ammunition were found in his car. Do we require actual dangerous acts to justify incarceration, or is circumstantial evidence sufficient? These are real dilemmas faced daily in the admissions departments of the nation's psychiatric hospitals.

The key to resolving the dilemma of involuntary hospitalization is the nature of schizophrenia. If it is nothing other than a euphemism for unusual behavior, then it is hard to justify involuntary hospitalization. If schizophrenia is really one or more brain diseases, however, then the justification becomes much easier. When the brain is diseased, it does not function properly and one could not reasonably expect a person with a diseased brain to be able to make accurate judgments. When you say to persons with schizophrenia, "Look, I think you are getting sick again and you need to go back to the hospital," and they answer that they are not sick and refuse to return, then the refusal does not necessarily have to be taken as an absolute. The brain which is causing the sickness is the same brain deciding on the need for treatment. In one study of chronic schizophrenic patients, for example, it was found that only 13 percent of them understood that they were mentally ill. Even though we know that the entire brain is not sick in such persons, we have no way of knowing which of its parts are ailing and which are functioning normally; to say that the person's refusal of hospitalization is coming from the healthy parts is absurd. Thus the concept of a diseased brain provides sufficient rationale for invoking the *parens patriae* role of the state and hospitalizing persons against their will when necessary. Using such reasoning, the young woman in the vignette at the beginning of this chapter could be hospitalized against her will, at least until it was ascertained whether she could be improved with medications. To let such people alone, perhaps to die because they cannot take care of themselves, is to let them "die with their rights on."

Now that we are on the threshold of delineating the biological underpinnings of schizophrenia, the dilemma of involuntary hospitalization may become easier. Even Szasz has said that he would permit involuntary hospitalization *if* there was something wrong with the body which could be measured objectively. As an example of what he means, he gives the measurement of abnormal chemicals in the body in a person withdrawing from alcohol addiction. Schizophrenia is now developing such measurements (see chapter 6), and it will be interesting to watch the development of scientific criteria for involuntary hospitalization.

If people with schizophrenia really have a brain disease, then the medical model also provides justification for involuntary hospitalization to protect other people. We do not argue against the regulation that persons with smallpox and tuberculosis can be confined involuntarily to protect others. So can persons with epileptic attacks or brain tumors that cause them to strike out at other people.

The 1970s saw state laws for involuntary hospitalization become increasingly narrow in defining who could be hospitalized. In many states a person had to demonstrate overt dangerousness to self or others before he or she could be confined. By the mid-1980s there was an increasing consensus among mental health professionals and large segments of the public that the criteria for commitment had become too narrow. Increasing hordes of homeless mentally ill individuals crowded the sidewalks and public shelters of cities, poignantly described by one observer: "Patients wander our streets, lost in time, as if in a medieval city. We are protecting their civil liberties much more adequately than we are protecting their minds and their lives." Dr. Alan Stone, a noted scholar on legal aspects of psychiatry, added: "The liberty of psychotic persons to sleep in the streets of America is hardly a cherished freedom, but a cruel and immoral consequence of failed libertarian reform."

Individual horror stories abounded of clearly psychotic persons who could not be involuntarily hospitalized because of the stringent interpretation of "dangerousness to self or others" by law enforcement and judicial officials. In 1984 in the District of Columbia, I personally examined a homeless woman who was blatantly hallucinating and carrying an axe around town; the police refused to take her to a hospital for possible commitment because they said she had not yet *done* anything to demonstrate dangerousness. In Wisconsin "a man barricaded himself in his house and sat with a rifle in his lap muttering 'Kill, kill, kill.' A judge ruled that the man was not demonstrably violent enough to qualify for involuntary commitment." At another commitment hearing in Wisconsin, a man with schizophrenia, mute and refusing to eat food or bathe, was noted to be eating feces while being held in jail. He was released because such behavior did not qualify as dangerous. The dialogue at the commitment hearing included the following:

> Public defender: "Doctor, would the eating of fecal material on one occasion by an individual pose a serious risk of harm to that person?"
>
> Doctor: "It is certainly not edible material. . . . It contains elements that are considered harmful or unnecessary."
>
> Public defender: "But, Doctor, you cannot state whether the consumption of such material on one occasion would invariably harm a person?"
>
> Doctor: "Certainly not on one occasion."
>
> The public defender then moved to dismiss the action on the grounds that the patient was in no imminent danger of physical injury or dying.

The case was dismissed.

It is such absurd and inhumane legal decisions as these that have spurred a growing movement toward broadening grounds for commitment. The State of Washington was one of the first to move in this direction in 1979, and since then several others have begun to follow. In North Carolina, for example, "impairments to judgment" was added as a legal ground for commitment. In 1983 the American Psychiatric

Association proposed a model commitment statute which would allow commitment of psychiatrically ill persons whose behavior indicates "significant deterioration" of their psychiatric state and who clearly are in need of treatment. I believe it is a good model for state laws because it permits the treatment of a relapsing schizophrenic patient *before* the person has had to demonstrate dangerousness, with its frequent tragic consequences.

Arguments about involuntary hospitalization have become increasingly heated, as psychiatrists in favor of broadening commitment laws confront lawyers opposed to the change. Dr. Alan Stone has claimed that the lawyers' stand "demonstrates their great concern for abstract rights, but it also demonstrates their lack of concern for the prevention of human suffering or public protection." Dr. Loren Roth, another psychiatrist prominent in urging the broadening of commitment laws, observed: "A large number of patients have been kidnapped by a small number of lawyers in order to make a philosophical point on their own behalf." The lawyers in turn accuse the psychiatrists of arrogance and of overreaching professional knowledge by claiming to be able to predict dangerousness when all studies show that they cannot. As summarized in 1985 by one observer: "The two warring camps are at each other's throats."

There is one additional dilemma which has recently made itself known, as involuntary commitment laws begin to be reliberalized. Committing a person to a hospital is no guarantee of treatment; the two *should* go hand in hand but do not always do so. Thus in the State of Washington, when the law was changed in 1979, many more individuals were admitted to the two state hospitals. The hospitals were not prepared to treat them, however, leading to serious overcrowding. This in turn led to the need to open additional hospital beds and the transfer of some mental health resources from the community back to the hospitals. As resources in the community decrease, the availability of community care further deteriorates, leading to the need to rehospitalize more patients and a vicious cycle is under way. The way to avoid such a cycle is through active, aggressive treatment programs in the hospital. With good inpatient treatment programs the length of rehospitalization for most individuals with schizophrenia should not exceed two or three weeks, and many can be stabilized and returned to the community in a matter of days *if* there is good coordination and follow-up between inpatient and outpatient.

THE INSANITY DEFENSE

The responsibility of schizophrenic persons for criminal acts becomes a problem for their families if they break the law. Most persons with schizophrenia are not dangerous and do not commit major crimes. Minor violations of the law are not uncommon, however, when the person becomes confused or psychotic. Often such persons are judged not competent to stand trial. In the past, incompetency to stand trial was used as grounds for long-term commitment to a psychiatric hospital, but in recent years there has been a tendency for courts to either bring the person to trial or drop the charges.

If the person is brought to trial, the lawyer may plead him/her not guilty by reason of insanity. This is the insanity defense. It dates back to the thirteenth century, when it was known as the "wild beast test" (insofar as persons are like wild beasts they cannot be held accountable). In England in the nineteenth century it was modified in the M'Naghten case to the "right or wrong test" (insofar as persons do not know right from wrong they cannot be held accountable). In the United States in recent years this has been replaced in many states by the "product test" (insofar as their acts were a product of mental disease persons cannot be held accountable) or by various modifications and compromises between the "right or wrong test" and the "product test." Most of these incorporate a volitional element, stating that the person acted on an "irrestible impulse."

Among the arguments urging the insanity defense for persons accused of crimes is the fact that it protects them from being simply convicted and punished as if they had been fully responsible. Thus, a schizophrenic who steals a car with the key in it because he thought it was his car or because voices told him to do so is not treated in the same way as a car thief who steals it to sell to others.

Arguments against use of the insanity defense are impressive, and many people have suggested that it be abolished. Deciding whether a person's behavior is a "product" of his or her mental illness is an exceedingly difficult and subjective task. As one observer has noted, "Almost all crimes, by definition, involve transgressions of societal norms that could be called insane." And in terms of an "irresistible impulse" it has been noted that "the line between an irresistible impulse and an impulse not resisted is probably no sharper than that between twilight and dusk." Such judgments are made even more difficult by the fact that they are retrospective. Who can really know what was in a person's mind when a criminal act was being committed months before he or she comes to trial?

The biggest problem with the insanity defense is that, because it is so imprecise, it has been abused. The well-publicized trials of Sirhan Sirhan, in which psychiatrists tried to convince the jury that Sirhan had hypnotized himself with mirrors before he shot Robert Kennedy, or of Patty Hearst, who was said to have been brainwashed prior to holding up a bank, strongly discredited the insanity defense. Even more damaging was the trial of Dan White, accused of killing San Francisco mayor George Moscone and supervisor Harvey Milk. One of White's defense psychiatrists proposed a "Twinkie defense" to excuse White's actions, claiming that his habit of eating junk food had caused changes in his brain that diminished control over his behavior.

Unhappiness with the insanity defense was translated into action in 1982, when John Hinckley was acquitted by reason of insanity after attempting to assassinate President Reagan. A torrent of criticism followed with calls for reform or abolition of the insanity defense. Three states (Idaho, Montana, and Utah) abolished it altogether and a majority of the other states passed legislation restricting its use. At least twelve states have instituted a modification of the insanity plea that permits a defendant to be found guilty but mentally ill.

Many proposals to change the insanity defense have included a two-part trial in which the issues of guilt for the crime and extenuating circumstances (including insanity) would be separated. In the first part the only question addressed would be whether or not the accused actually committed the crime. If the person was found guilty, *then* psychiatrists and other witnesses would be allowed to testify on the person's mental state and other extenuating circumstances; this testimony would be used to help decide where the person should be sent (prison or psychiatric hospital) and for how long.

If the second part of the trial specifically addressed the question of responsibility, such a system would be a definite improvement over the current legal quagmire engendered by the insanity defense. The insanity defense as currently practiced includes an assumption that persons are either responsible or not responsible for their actions. Sane persons are considered to be responsible, insane persons to be not responsible; it is an all-or-nothing determination. Such simplistic thinking, however, contradicts the experience of everyone who has ever lived with or taken care of persons with schizophrenia. As discussed in chapter 10, schizophrenics are almost never wholly responsible or wholly irresponsible; further, their level of responsibility may fluctuate over time. Included in the second part of the trial, therefore, should be a determination by a jury of the level of responsibility that they believe the person had at the time of the crime. For example, a schizophrenic who kills another man because he believed he was an alien creature from another planet may be judged to have a very low level of responsibility, whereas a schizophrenic who kills her philandering husband out of anger may be judged to have a high level of responsibility. No longer would a defendant like John Hinckley be said to be totally responsible or totally not responsible.

THE RIGHT TO TREATMENT

For the 1970s, the emerging issue in law and psychiatry was the right to treatment. It came to the forefront in 1971, when Judge Frank Johnson in Alabama issued a court order in the case of *Wyatt* v. *Stickney*. This order dealt with the deplorable conditions in Alabama's mental hospitals and mandated that the conditions must be improved so that treatment of the patients could take place. As Judge Johnson phrased it: "To deprive any citizen of his or her liberty upon the altruistic theory that the confinement is for humane and therapeutic reasons and then fail to provide adequate treatment violates the very fundamentals of due process." He then went on to recommend specific staff-to-patient ratios and minimal conditions which were to be implemented. It was the first time the courts had entered mental hospitals and legally mandated that things must be improved.

The next major thrust in this direction came when the United States Supreme Court in 1975 ruled in favor of Kenneth Donaldson in the case of *Donaldson* v. *O'Connor*. Donaldson had been a patient in a Florida state hospital for many years and sued the hospital superintendent, Dr. O'Connor, for failing to treat him and failing to discharge him since he was not being treated. Lower courts had found in favor of Donaldson and had awarded him monetary damages. The Supreme Court ruled that a psychiatric patient who is not dangerous to himself or others, who can survive safely outside the hospital, and who is not getting treatment must be released from the hospital. It reversed the award for monetary damages and did not rule specifically on the right to treatment *per se*.

Also in 1975, a judge in Washington, D.C., ruled in favor of psychiatric patients in the case of *Dixon* v. *Weinberger*. This suit had been raised in behalf of patients at St. Elizabeths Hospital, a federal psychiatric facility serving the District of Columbia, in the name of Dixon (a patient) against Weinberger (then Secretary of the Department of Health, Education and Welfare, which had jurisdiction over the hospital). It stated that patients not only have a right to treatment but have a right to treatment in the least restrictive setting. This meant that patients who don't require full-time hospital care must be moved to alternative facilities, such as foster homes, halfway houses, and nursing homes. The right to treatment had been carried an additional step.

Right-to-treatment suits continued to appear sporadically. In 1981 the U.S. Department of Justice and the State of Texas agreed to a review panel to monitor care in the Texas state hospitals; the panel has made specific recommendations regarding the use of medications and staff-to-patient ratios which should be achieved by the hospitals. In 1982 the U.S. Supreme Court ruled on the rights of a mentally retarded man, Nicholas Romeo, in a Pennsylvania state institution. It ruled that the patient had a right to safety, to a reasonable amount of physical freedom, and to training to improve his level of function. Although the ruling was specifically aimed at institutions for the mentally retarded, it is generally assumed that it will be invoked in court actions for the mentally ill as well.

What relevance do these legal suits have for schizophrenic patients and their families? Most important, they illustrate how the courts may be used to promote better treatment in state hospitals and better community facilities for chronic mental patients. It is not yet clear whether they will be successful, however. The courts can mandate minimum staff ratios, as they did in Alabama, but the courts cannot magically produce nurses and psychiatrists to work in the hospitals and improve the ratios. The courts can mandate alternative community facilities, as they did in Washington, D.C., but the courts cannot build the foster homes or halfway houses if the local government refuses to do so. Most disturbing, the suit for monetary damage by Donaldson against the state hospital superintendent in Florida might have the reverse effect and frighten away psychiatrists from working in the state hospital system. It may also be argued that one of the effects of these legal proceedings has been to increase the speed of deinstitutionalization, with the states dumping unprepared ex-patients onto unprepared communities, such as has happened in Texas, in order to comply with mandated staff-to-patient ratios.

Right-to-treatment suits are an exciting and potentially valuable tool which may force improvement in the facilities available for treating schizophrenic patients over time. In the short run, however, the suits may have some undesirable effects, and this should be monitored closely. Organized groups of patients' families can be invaluable in assisting the legal groups to initiate and then follow up the suits. It is a legal area in flux and one which will almost certainly evolve further.

THE RIGHT TO REFUSE TREATMENT

If the right to treatment was the emerging forensic psychiatric issue of the 1970s, then the right to refuse treatment is the issue of the 1980s. The issue was joined in 1979 in the U.S. District Court in Boston, when Federal Judge Joseph L. Tauro, in the case of *Rogers* v. *Okin,* ruled that psychiatric patients in state mental hospitals could no longer be required to take medicine except in emergency situations "when there is a substantial likelihood of extreme violence, personal injury, or attempted suicide." Since then similar rulings have been made in courts in Oklahoma, Colorado, and New York, all mandating stringent safeguards and court reviews before psychiatric patients may be medicated involuntarily except in emergencies. The Rogers suit, often used as an example by courts in other states, went from the Massachusetts district court to the appellate court to the U.S. Supreme Court, then back to appellate court, and in November, 1983, a final ruling was handed down by the Massachusetts Supreme Judicial Court.

The Rogers case decision states that psychiatric patients have the right to refuse antipsychotic medications unless they are found incompetent by a judge following a formal hearing. Emergency medication is allowed for a brief period "to prevent the immediate, substantial, and irreversible deterioration of a serious mental illness." The court decision explicitly stated that "the patient has the right to be wrong on the choice of treatment."

Proponents of patients' rights have hailed the Rogers case and similar rulings in other states as landmark decisions. They argue that forcing medication on patients violates constitutional rights, such as the right to privacy, freedom from harm, freedom of speech and thought; and it may also represent cruel and unusual punishment. Forcing medication on patients, insofar as medication sedates them or impairs their thinking, may also impair their ability to defend themselves at legal hearings and may influence the judge or jury by making them appear to be unable to think clearly. The potential for abuse of forced medication is enormous, and in the Soviet Union many political dissidents have described having been involuntarily given antipsychotic and sedative drugs which made clear thinking very difficult.

Proponents of the right to refuse treatment have used medication side effects as their strongest argument. They cite those studies showing that antipsychotic medications cause frequent and irreversible tardive dyskinesia (see chapter 7) and other unpleasant or undesirable side effects. In response to the argument that schizophrenic patients cannot make rational judgments on these matters, they claim that "mental illness often strikes only limited areas of functioning, leaving others areas unimpaired, and consequently many mentally ill persons retain the capacity to function in a competent manner." Furthermore, they counter that even if such persons were thinking completely normally, they would decline to take such drugs because of the threat of these side effects.

Opponents of these decisions claim that they will lead only to "the right to rot," as patients needing medication languish without necessary treatment. They argue that the loss of civil rights, such as privacy, can be balanced by the right to be free of disease. Such freedoms are meaningless if the person is sick. As articulated by one observer, psychiatric patients "will suffer if a liberty they cannot enjoy is made superior to a health that must sometimes be forced on them." It can also be argued that giving schizophrenic patients medication improves their thinking and their ability to defend themselves at hearings. The dangers and frequency of tardive dyskinesia and other side effects of these drugs vary widely in different studies, and for every report showing the drugs to be dangerous, another report can be brought forth showing that they are relatively safe drugs.

Other arguments supporting the right of psychiatrists to administer medications involuntarily to schizophrenic patients focus on benefits to society as a whole. With medications dangerous persons with this disease may be rendered nondangerous. And the drugs usually allow patients to leave the hospital and return to the community much sooner; this not only is better for the patient (by avoiding institutionalization) but also saves society the cost of long-term hospitalization of individuals too sick to be released untreated. Advocates of this position are collecting horror stories about the effects of Judge Tauro's decision and related cases, such as the patient in Massachusetts who could not be medicated for seven months while the court was securing a guardian, or the patient in New Jersey whose refusal to take medication cost an additional $35,350 for extra time in the hospital and legal fees.

Finally, it can be argued that because people with schizophrenia have diseases of the brain, they cannot give informed consent and cannot make an informed judgment on their own need for medication. Supporting this position is a study of chronic schizophrenic patients, showing that only 27 percent of them understood that they needed medication.

Underlying much of the debate over this issue is, many suspect, long-standing acrimony between the legal and the psychiatric professions. And since most judges are graduates of the former, the decisions to date have bent significantly toward the lawyers. This would be harmless enough if we were dealing only with a urinating contest among adolescent boys, but in fact many patients have been and are being hurt by legal decisions that ostensibly protect their rights but in reality do so at the expense of their health. As succinctly summarized by a prominent New York State legislator: "The state must begin now to reorder its priorities for the mentally ill; instead of first guaranteeing a client's right to refuse treatment, we must first guarantee his right to receive it."

Families of schizophrenic patients are increasingly likely to be drawn into the arguments as courts move into this area. Psychiatrists will ask families more and more frequently for permission to give their relative antipsychotic medication against his or her wishes. This may put the relatives in an awkward position, but court mandates may make it necessary.

I myself come down strongly on the side of giving schizophrenic patients medication against their will if they need it. Checks and balances should certainly be built into the system to protect the patient in the same way that involuntary hospitalization should be periodically reviewed. But the fact is that persons with schizophrenia are really sick, and to withhold medication usually hurts rather than helps them. I would urge those who advocate an elaborate court proceeding before involuntary medication can be given to spend a day on an acute psychiatric admission ward for schizophrenics where the patients have not been medicated; it will be an unforgettable experience. Finally, I would recommend that the process of involuntary commitment to a psychiatric hospital should automatically include the right to administer medications involuntarily if needed. To commit a patient to a hospital but say simultaneously that drugs cannot be given involuntarily, as some courts have done, is illogical and unworkable.

INFORMED CONSENT

The issue of informed consent comes up repeatedly in the care of persons with schizophrenia. Is their admission to the hospital truly voluntary or is it subtly coerced? Can they understand details of possible side effects of the medication, especially tardive dyskinesia? Is their agreement to participate in a research protocol based on a real understanding of what they have agreed to?

Studies on informed consent in severely ill psychiatric patients suggest that they understand much less than we have assumed. In one study "most patients stated they had understood the informed consent information" but "objective assessment of their understanding did not confirm this." It was also evident that patients' decisions on whether or not to consent to the taking of medications had very little to do with any information they had been given.

The issue of informed consent is especially pertinent to tardive dyskinesia. Suits for damages against psychiatrists prescribing antipsychotic drugs have been brought by several patients who subsequently developed tardive dyskinesia, and questions inevitably arise about what the patient was told and what he or she understood. A useful discussion of this issue, with practical suggestions for informed consent regarding tardive dyskinesia, can be found in *Understanding and Treating Tardive Dyskinesia* by Dilip V. Jeste and Richard J. Wyatt.

OUTPATIENT COMMITMENT

Outpatient commitment is exactly what it sounds like—the commitment of an individual to an outpatient program. It differs legally from a conditional release (the release of a patient from a hospital on condition that the patient follows through on treatment) in that the conditional release is a continuation of the original inpatient commitment, whereas an outpatient commitment is a separate legal proceeding. In effect, however, either one may be used to help ensure that the patient continues to take medication.

Although outpatient commitments are legally permissible in approximately two-thirds of states, they have been little used. The main reason is that for outpatient commitment the treating psychiatrist must initiate a legal proceeding, then go to court and testify. It is far easier simply to discharge the patient, which is what usually happens.

Since 1983 outpatient commitments have become the subject of lively discussion among professionals and families concerned about the seriously mentally ill. That year North Carolina became the first state to pass legislation allowing the commitment of an individual to outpatient status directly, without first having gone through an inpatient commitment. Since 1983 Hawaii and Georgia have passed similar laws and several other states have such legislation under consideration. In order for outpatient commitment to work, however, there must be an effective system of outpatient care; the commitment process itself is no guarantee of treatment.

Given the expanding use of outpatient commitment and its apparent effectiveness in keeping patients on their medication while living in the community, it is likely that civil rights lawyers will raise such cases in court increasingly often. The legal justification for outpatient commitment is likely to be questioned. Must the person have demonstrated dangerousness in the past? How many times must the person have failed to take medication on his/her own before the state has the right to mandate it? And what about the specter of a therapeutic state, the brave new world of psychiatry, in which legions of individuals living in the community are forced by the state to take medication they do not want and who can be picked up by the police if they stop taking it? Despite such objections, I believe that outpatient commitment will become—and should become—widely used because it is the most effective and humane option available for large numbers of individuals with schizophrenia who lack insight to realize they need treatment.

FAILURE TO TREAT AND NEGLIGENT RELEASE

If the right to treatment was the legal issue of the seventies for schizophrenia, and the right to refuse treatment is the legal issue of the eighties, then failure to treat and negligent release will likely prove the issues of the nineties. Both have been raised sporadically to date, but litigation will doubtless increase as families of schizophrenic patients become more sophisticated about their rights. For example, New York State in 1984 was successfully sued by a woman who had been attacked and stabbed by a schizophrenic outpatient. It was alleged that the patient was not being properly treated by the psychiatrist in charge of the case. A similar but unsuccessful suit was brought against the Colorado psychiatrist who treated John Hinckley prior to his attack on President Reagan.

Negligent-release suits have been brought to courts in situations where a patient was released from a psychiatric hospital while still dangerous and then harmed somebody. One of the early, successful negligent-release suits was litigated in Washington, D.C., where a patient had been released from a hospital and then killed a young woman in a private girls' school. A variant in negligent release was utilized by a psychologist at the Philadelphia State Hospital in 1983, who charged hospital officials with releasing one hundred seriously mentally ill patients into the community without considering their inability to care for themselves.

CONFIDENTIALITY

The need for confidentiality of communications between persons with schizophrenia and mental health professionals, including the confidentiality of their records, periodically raises ethical problems for both professionals and the families of patients. Persons with schizophrenia who are involuntarily committed to hospitals are often committed on the basis of what they have voluntarily told psychiatrists; they have, in one sense, incriminated themselves. More serious is the situation when a person with schizophrenia (or any other mental disorder) confides to a mental health professional a wish or plan to harm another person. In the past such communications were considered to be confidential and legally exempted from disclosure under physician-patient confidentiality. In 1976, however, courts in California ruled that mental health professionals have a duty to warn the potential victim in such situations. This ruling, generally referred to as the Tarasoff decision, has been extended to many other states. Vermont recently extended it to cover potential damage to property (e.g., burning down a barn), as well as potential harm to persons.

The biggest problem of confidentiality for patients' families is the reluctance of mental health professionals to share information about the family member's illness because of the fear of breaking confidentiality. State laws vary in this regard but such confidentiality has been invoked to an absurd degree by professionals in many states. The following, for example, is an account of a mother's attempts to get information about her son during the six months he was committed to a psychiatric hospital in Boston:

> I was never told how he was doing. I was in complete darkness about his prognosis, whether positive or negative. Each time I questioned the social worker assigned to his case, which was almost daily, the answer would be, "Danny would not give us permission today to tell you how he was doing."
>
> This was the reply I received for the first month or so. Then one day, moved by pity because of the state of anxiety I was in, she replied to my inquiry, "Danny would not give us permission today to tell you how he was doing but the patients on the ward are doing well today."
>
> I grasped at her coded message with much relief. But after hearing that same coded message and only that for the remainder of his commitment, it became quite evident to me that the system was as ill as my son and needed much help.

This is a travesty of confidentiality. More often than not, such reluctance to share information under the guise of confidentiality simply reflects the disinterest of the mental health professionals in having anything to do with the families. It may also represent the lingering psychoanalytic orientation of the professionals with an implicit message: "You the family caused this disease, so now as punishment you have no right to know what is going on."

What can the family do? Become knowledgeable about the state laws regarding confidentiality. Get the laws changed if they appear to be too restrictive. On individual cases complain to the professional's supervisors and act in concert with other organizational consumers as outlined in chapter 14. Do not accept any less information than you would expect to be forthcoming from professionals if your family member had another brain disease, such as multiple sclerosis or Alzheimer's disease.

RESEARCH ON PERSONS WITH SCHIZOPHRENIA

Mental patients confined to institutions have occasionally been used to test new procedures and experimental drugs. This practice came into sharp public focus in the early 1970s, when it was disclosed that mentally retarded patients in New York's Willowbrook Hospital had been experimentally infected with hepatitis virus. Since then public awareness of the issue has increased, and the 1978 *Report of the President's Commission on Mental Health* contains a concise and enlightening summary of the problem.

There are three kinds of experimentation or research which are theoretically possible. The first is the use of procedures or drugs which have little or no direct relationship to the illness for which the person is confined. Experimentally infecting retarded patients with hepatitis is an example of this. Hepatitis is a disease which is widespread in society and, while it occurs among retarded institutionalized patients more frequently than in the general population, it cannot be said to be a major threat to the health or life of such patients. Most important, hepatitis is not the reason these patients are hospitalized; retardation is the reason. Thus there is no justification for experimenting on retarded patients with the hepatitis virus or with any other procedure which is not directly related to their underlying condition. As stated by the President's Commission: "Experimentation which is neither directly beneficial to individual subjects nor related to subjects' mental condition and which poses any degree of risk to such subjects should not be permitted with institutionalized mentally handicapped individuals."

The second kind of experimentation is the use of procedures or drugs which may be directly beneficial to the person with schizophrenia. This possibility arises frequently with chronic schizophrenic patients on whom all the generally accepted modes of therapy have been tried to no avail. A conscientious psychiatrist will not be satisfied at this point but may want to go on and try newer and more experimental approaches. If this is done in a reputable hospital, it should be encouraged by the patient's family, for the alternatives are usually continued psychosis and indefinite hospitalization. Reputable hospitals ensure that all experimental procedures have passed a research review board and that experimental drugs are used only under protocols approved by the Food and Drug Administration. The protection of the patient's rights under such procedures is adequate, usually ensuring that there has been a careful consideration given to the benefits weighed against the risks to the patient, and that the risks have been explained to the patient and/or family. Even if the patient objects, it may be legitimate to try the experimental drug if the patient is not competent to decide and if the family gives consent.

The third kind of experimentation is directly related to finding the cause or treatment of schizophrenia, but realistically is unlikely to benefit that particular patient. For example, I perform lumbar punctures on many schizophrenic patients under my care in an attempt to find the causes of the disease. Such a procedure is virtually harmless and causes little more discomfort than drawing blood. For a 20- or 25-year-old patient I can honestly say that the procedure might be of direct benefit if it helps find the causes of schizophrenia. But for a 50-year-old patient, direct benefit is much less likely. Is it justifiable to use experimental procedures or unproven drugs on that patient?

Such a question raises the general problem previously alluded to, of informed consent in psychiatric patients. Patients who are legally competent can give informed consent in such instances and pose no problem. Patients who are legally incompetent, however, raise further issues, for it is illogical to call a patient incompetent in some matters (e.g., understanding the need for medication) yet competent in others (understanding the risks in an experimental procedure). If the experimental procedure includes substantial risk, therefore, it is desirable to obtain consent from the patient's family. Furthermore, schizophrenic patients who are sickest are precisely the ones we should be studying to learn what causes the disease, and those who are sickest are frequently the best candidates for experimental drugs because they may not have responded to traditional antipsychotics. Families of schizophrenics are apt to be increasingly asked to give consent for the incompetent family member, and they should weigh all aspects of the question in giving their decision.

In general, the current situation regarding experimentation and research approaches a reasonable balance between protecting the rights of patients and allowing worthwhile experimentation and research to go forward. The trend, however, is toward increasing restrictions on psychiatric research, so that it will become virtually impossible to do this in the future. Real and well-publicized research abuses in the past, the vociferous defense of patients' rights by civil liberties lawyers, and the continuing rhetoric by Szasz, Laing, et al., that "mental illness is not really a disease," are all acting to swing the pendulum past the point of adequate protection toward an end which specifies overprotection. It is certainly possible to protect schizophrenic patients' rights so zealously that research on causes of the disease and on new treatments will be effectively terminated, and in some psychiatric hospitals research has already become a dirty word. It is urgent that this be guarded against, and families of schizophrenic patients can help in this regard. There is little enough research going on as it is; if it is made more difficult to perform, then current studies will further diminish. What we will then have is a generation of well-protected schizophrenic patients and the guarantee of more generations of similar patients to follow.

RESEARCH ON ANIMALS

The 1980s have witnessed the increasing militancy of animal rights activists in attempts to stop all medical experiments using animals. It is morally wrong, they claim, to utilize animals for research purposes, no matter how lofty the research goal. Extreme members of such antivivisection groups have broken into laboratories to "liberate" research animals, while others have dressed in monkey costumes and picketed government buildings in Washington.

It would be very nice if animals were not needed for research on schizophrenia and other diseases, but in fact they are. For schizophrenia research they are absolutely essential to learn the causes of the brain dysfunction, to develop new drugs for treatment by understanding how the drugs work on the brain, and for testing new drugs for side effects. Cell cultures, computer simulations, and human volunteers can be used for some research, but not for most; without the use of animals, schizophrenia research would come to a virtual standstill.

Animals used for research should of course be treated as humanely as possible, and the provisions of the Federal Animal Welfare Act should be strictly enforced. Animal research was essential for advances in tuberculosis, polio, and smallpox. In schizophrenia there would have been no development of antipsychotic drugs or lithium without animal research. We should be grateful to animals for these contributions, and should all look forward to the day when diseases are understood well enough that research on animals will no longer be necessary.

GENETIC COUNSELING

Since more and more people with schizophrenia are living in the community and socializing, it seems inevitable that increasing numbers of them will decide to have children. In such circumstances genetic work-ups should be undertaken. Counseling is also indicated when brothers and sisters of a person with schizophrenia ask about their own chances of getting the disease, or the chances of their children getting the disease.

A number of studies on the genetics of schizophrenia have been summarized by Dr. Irving Gottesman, a well-known schizophrenia researcher, who has calculated the risk of developing schizophrenia. Dr. Gottesman's calculations follow. It should be added that not all geneticists agree with the precise risk, and some others estimate the risks as modestly lower.

- Brother or sister of person with schizophrenia: *10 percent* if neither parent has schizophrenia. If either the mother or father also has the disease, the chances of the brother or sister becoming ill increase to 17 percent. Remember, however, that schizophrenia usually begins between the ages of 17 and 25; if the brother or sister reaches age 30 with no signs of the disease, then chances are very small that he or she will subsequently develop it.

- Child of person with schizophrenia: *13 percent.* If *both* parents have schizophrenia the chances of the child's eventually developing schizophrenia climb to *46 percent.* Thus my advice to any person with schizophrenia who insists on having a baby is to *please* conceive the baby with somebody who does not also have the disease.

■ Niece or nephew of person with schizophrenia: *3 percent.* The chances of getting schizophrenia if there is no family history at all is 1 percent, so this is only a little higher. Brothers and sisters of schizophrenics often worry about their own children but excessive worry is not warranted.

■ Grandchild of person with schizophrenia: *4 percent.* This question arises frequently from the unaffected son or daughter of a parent with schizophrenia.

In the end everyone must make his/her own decision whether to have children or not. It is rare to find any family pedigree without its share of undesirable diseases and personality characteristics thought to have genetic components; schizophrenia is simply one among them. Creating life is, and always has been, a genetic lottery. Knowing the odds in the game will not make the decision for you but will allow you to choose more intelligently.

RECOMMENDED FURTHER READING

Chodoff, P. "Involuntary Hospitalization of the Mentally Ill as a Moral Issue." *American Journal of Psychiatry* 141 (1984): 384–89. A lucid discussion of the philosophical issues of involuntary commitment by a widely respected psychiatrist.

Gottesman, I. I. *Schizophrenia and Genetic Risks.* Arlington, VA: National Alliance for the Mentally Ill, 1984. A good discussion of the intricacies of genetic predisposition and assessment of risk.

Hospital and Community Psychiatry 36 (1985): 966–89. This issue contains several articles discussing the model commitment law proposed by the American Psychiatric Association.

Mental Disability Law Reporter. Subscriptions from American Bar Association, 1800 M St., N.W. Washington, D.C., 20036. This bimonthly journal is published by the Commission on the Mentally Disabled of the American Bar Association. It contains a good analysis of rapidly changing mental health laws.

12

THE HISTORY AND DISTRIBUTION
OF SCHIZOPHRENIA

I doubt if ever the history of the world, or the experience of past ages,
could show a larger amount of insanity than that of the present day.

John Hawkes, "On the Increase of Insanity," 1857

The history and geographical distribution of diseases often offer clues
to their cause. From syphilis to atherosclerosis and multiple sclerosis,
historical and epidemiological studies have proven exceedingly useful
in enlarging our understanding.

The history of schizophrenia has been ignored by most scholars
but in fact is a most curious one. A perusal of what little history is
available raises two major questions: (1) Was schizophrenia a rare
disease prior to about 1800? (2) Between 1800 and 1900 did it increase
rapidly and become the relatively common disease it is today? Although neither question can be definitely answered at this time, it is
important to raise them in order to stimulate thinking about the disease.

MENTAL DISEASE IN ANCIENT TIMES

Virtually all textbooks of psychiatry and psychology suggest that schizophrenia has always existed in numbers not very different from the
rates today. As evidence for this the books often cite Emil Kraepelin,
the German physician who first proposed dementia praecox as a name

337

to cover the multiple syndromes we now know as schizophrenia. In 1919 Kraepelin wrote: "Only so much may be said, that the disease is probably extremely old, as indeed the descriptions of the old physicians often unmistakably point to the clinical pictures familiar to us."

Nobody would argue with the fact that there have been people with severe mental disorders since earliest recorded history. Even the cavemen, with their fondness for hitting each other over the head with clubs, inevitably caused some permanent brain damage. This would have produced retarded and demented individuals who would look identical to their counterparts today. It is also important to recall that modern obstetrics is of recent origin and that in centuries past many more individuals must have been brain damaged by difficult births. This would have produced proportionately more retarded individuals, even allowing for the most severely retarded, who probably would not have survived. To trauma and difficult births must be added other known insults to the brain which existed then and which can produce mental disease—strokes, tumors, malaria, syphilis, poisonings, vitamin deficiencies, hypothyroidism, temporal lobe epilepsy, viral infections—and a sizable group of mental patients would have been inevitable.

Thus it is not surprising to find occasional references to severely psychiatrically disturbed individuals in ancient texts, including the Old and New Testaments, early Sanskrit writings, and early Greek writings. The most interesting claim of an early case of schizophrenia is undoubtedly that concerning Jesus. In the early years of the twentieth century four books were published in German purporting to prove that Jesus had paranoid schizophrenia. In 1905 *Jesus Christ from the Standpoint of Psychiatry* and *Jesus: A Comparative Study of Psychopathology* appeared. These were followed in 1911 by *The Insanity of Jesus* and in 1912 by *Conclusions of a Psychiatrist*. All focused on the auditory hallucinations and delusions of grandeur of Jesus and cited various biblical texts in support of this claim. They were shown to be on very weak ground both clinically and historically, however, by Dr. Albert Schweitzer, who in 1948 published *The Psychiatric Study of Jesus* and demonstrated convincingly that there are really no solid grounds for suspecting that Jesus had schizophrenia. Rather, what the authors were doing was trying to discredit Jesus by tarring him with the brush of a psychiatric diagnosis, a practice which has been used more recently in the Soviet Union in an attempt to discredit political dissidents.

The strongest case for the existence of schizophrenia in ancient times has been made by Dilip V. Jeste and his colleagues, who state definitively that "schizophrenia has existed throughout history . . . there is definite evidence in support of the view that schizophrenia is an ancient illness." As evidence they cite Babylonian texts dating to 3000 B.C., claiming that "the existence of schizophrenia and especially paranoid schizophrenia . . . is unmistakable." In more detail they examine second-century A.D. texts of Celsus, who described a type of madness which was "the longest of all so that it does not injure life itself, and which is accustomed to be a disease of a strong body . . . some are deceived by false images" and "some are disordered in their judgment." Jeste et al. as well as C. V. Haldipur have also argued that schizophrenia was found in early Sanskrit writings.

While such passages undoubtedly describe mentally ill individuals, I personally am not impressed by them as clear descriptions of schizophrenia. They fail to emphasize the onset in young adulthood in previously healthy individuals, nor do they specify the auditory hallucinations which are the hallmark of the disease as we know it. Furthermore, if schizophrenia existed in ancient times in the same proportion now found, then approximately 3 or 4 of every 1,000 persons would have been afflicted at any one time.

Jeste et al. cite several possible reasons why schizophrenia may have existed in ancient times yet failed to be adequately described. Ancient physicians focused on specific signs and symptoms of disease, rather than on collections of these (called syndromes); since schizophrenia has no single sign or symptom which is unique to the disease, it might have been missed. Further, Jeste et al. claim that there was much less interest in chronic incurable diseases; that schizophrenia might have been considered to lie in the domain of religion rather than medicine; that the terminology for describing psychiatric symptoms at that time was very imprecise; and that families probably kept such patients at home rather than seeking help from physicians. Another possibility cited by Jeste et al., intriguing but unprovable, is that the clinical picture of schizophrenia was somewhat different two thousand years ago than it is now. It is known that diseases can change over time, as has been described, for example, for syphilis.

Ultimately the question is not answerable. The arguments offered by Jeste et al. are all plausible and could theoretically explain schizophrenia's sparse presence in ancient texts. On the other hand, we are left with a disease which in the middle years of the twentieth century occupied half of all hospital beds in the United States. The rarity of such a disease in ancient medical history seems curious indeed.

It was during the Middle Ages that insane patients were first gathered together. Initially they were herded onto ships and sailed from port to port (the "ships of fools"), but later they were placed in asylums or hospitals. One of the first such hospitals was opened at Geel, Belgium, in the thirteenth century; shortly thereafter others were begun in Spain and England. The earliest hospital in England, Bethlem Hospital, gave rise to the term "bedlam," meaning noisy confusion.

With the collection of the mentally ill in one place the opportunity for good clinical descriptions of diseases multiplied tremendously. Over the next three centuries some excellent accounts of other mental diseases were published, such as those by Bartholomaeus Angelicus and Johann Weyer, but almost none of schizophrenia. Probably the best case to be made was for a most eminent patient—King Henry VI of England, who lived from 1421 to 1471. At age thirty-one he had a psychotic breakdown with a sudden onset and remained ill for the next year and a half. His symptoms included "fright, loss of a sense of reality, poor judgment, stupor, and mutism." He recovered, relapsed twice again in the next two years, and according to some appears to have deteriorated into a chronic psychotic state. He was deposed, imprisoned, and eventually executed.

An especially interesting publication during these years was *Of Ghosts,* published in 1570, in which Johann Kaspar Lavater described delusions and hallucinations in great detail. It may well have been available to William Shakespeare, a young playwright in London who selected King Henry VI as the subject of his first play and was clearly intrigued by psychotic disorders. Hamlet is made to feign lunacy, Lear develops a senile psychosis (he was over 80 years of age at the time), and Ophelia becomes insane when she discovers that her father was killed by the man she loves.

English psychiatrist Nigel Bark claims that Shakespeare was describing schizophrenia in the person of Poor Mad Tom in *King Lear*. He cites passages suggesting that Tom's condition had begun in early adulthood, was chronic, and that he had delusions, hallucinations, bizarre behavior, social withdrawal, and a thought disorder (e.g., "Still through the hawthorn blows the cold wind; says suum, mun, hey no nonny. Dolphin my boy, my boy; sessa! let him trot by"). Bark allows for the possibility that Poor Tom was feigning madness in order to elicit sympathy as a beggar, but concluded "that Shakespeare did know schizophrenia, and that it did exist in the sixteenth century."

Whether or not Shakespeare was describing schizophrenia, observers such as Karl Jaspers have noted the rarity of symptoms corresponding with this disease throughout the Middle Ages and Renaissance. Psychiatrist Edward Hare is especially impressed by the absence of descriptions of auditory hallucinations without accompanying visual hallucinations, although these are very commonly found in present-day patients with schizophrenia. Kroll and Bachrach have addressed this question by comparing the hallucinations seen in present-day schizophrenic patients in Minnesota with descriptions of hallucinations (both visual and auditory) found in literary accounts of medieval religious visions. They concluded that auditory hallucinations did appear in the earlier years but that they were understood within a religious rather than a medical context: "Medieval people whose major forms of thought and behavior disturbances were expressed in a religious mode were not considered psychotic . . . When similar forms of religious behavior are manifested in present-day Minnesota, the people are considered psychotic."

ENTER SCHIZOPHRENIA

Whether or not schizophrenia was described prior to the seventeenth century will remain a subject for conjecture. From the seventeenth century onwards, however, all agree that it was present, even if sporadically. Perhaps honors for being history's first clearly described schizophrenic patient should go to George Trosse, an English minister who had a breakdown in 1656 and subsequently published an autobiographical account of his experience. Trosse's illness occurred at age 25 and included both delusional thinking and auditory hallucinations. Some of his behavior sounds catatonic: "For several days I would neither open my eyes nor my lips." He was hospitalized for several months in an asylum and then recovered. This may be the first actual description in literature of what we now call schizophrenia.

There were other accounts in the seventeenth century of mental illness which may have been schizophrenia. Felix Platter, Professor of Medicine at the University of Basel, described patients with delusions of being transformed into animals and other patients with bizarre somatic delusions. He also described mutism and catatonic postures. Thomas Willis, one of the most eminent physicians of his time, published a treatise in 1672 that distinguished the thought processes of "stupidity" or mental retardation from those of "foolishness." The latter were said to occur in "deteriorating illnesses" which may have been schizophrenia. "Foolish" people were said to "apprehend simple things well enough . . . and retain them firm in their memory, but by reason of a defect of judgment, they compose or divide their notions evilly, and very badly infer one thing from another. Moreover by their folly and acting sinistrously and ridiculously, they move laughter in the by-standers." One medical historian claims that this is the original description of loose associations and nominates Willis as the first to describe schizophrenia in psychiatric literature.

In the eighteenth century there are also a few scattered references to conditions which might have been schizophrenia, but they are remarkably few considering the magnitude of the disease as we know it. Dr. Samuel Johnson, who was a keen observer of the century's philosophy and politics, had a special interest in madness and believed that insanity was increasing in frequency. The increase, he believed, was due to a *decrease* in smoking, which was apparently becoming less fashionable. Smoking was thought to tranquilize the mind and as it decreased, Johnson reasoned, madness would increase. In his *Rasselas* in 1759 Johnson wrote: "Of the uncertainties of our present state, the most dreadful and alarming is the uncertain continuance of reason." The idea of increasing insanity was to become very important one hundred years later.

Up until 1800 descriptions of possible cases of schizophrenia are sporadic. Suddenly, however, it appeared. Simultaneously (and apparently independently) John Haslam in England and Philippe Pinel in France both described cases which were certainly schizophrenia. These were followed by a veritable outpouring of descriptions continuing throughout the nineteenth century and also by evidence that schizophrenia was increasing in frequency. It was a dramatic entrance for a disease. Haslam's publication in 1809 was an enlarged second edition of his 1798 book, *Observations on Insanity.* It is a remarkable book, with descriptions of delusions, hallucinations, disorders of thinking, and even autopsy accounts of abnormalities in the brains of some of the patients. His descriptions of patients leave no doubt that he was describing what we now call schizophrenia. At the time Haslam and Pinel were describing schizophrenia for the first time, they and many others expressed concern that insanity was becoming much more common. This was not wholly a new idea, as the quote by Samuel Johnson above illustrates, but from 1800 onward it became a subject of lively debate and speculation in both medical and philosophical circles.

In the preface to his 1809 book Haslam sounded a note which was to be heard increasingly often as the century progressed: "The alarming increase of insanity, as might naturally be expected, has incited many persons to an investigation of this disease." In the previous year the English House of Commons had passed a County Asylums Act establishing mental hospitals in many counties.

By 1829 Sir Andrew Halliday noted statistics "which not only show that insanity, in all its forms, prevails to a most alarming extent in England, but that the numbers of the afflicted have become more than tripled during the last twenty years." This was confirmed by J. C. Prichard, who said, "The apparent increase is everywhere so striking that it leaves in the mind a strong suspicion that cases of insanity are far more numerous than formerly."

As the century wore on, the increase in insanity was noted throughout the British Isles. By 1857 John Hawkes in England wrote, "I doubt if ever the history of the world, or the experience of past ages, could show a larger amount of insanity than that of the present day." Similar observations were made in Scotland, and in Ireland the apparent increase in insanity had produced a rapid building of asylums and much debate.

On the Continent similar pronouncements were being made. Pinel himself believed that the increased number of insane was in some way a product of the French Revolution. By 1856 Renaudin had published extensive data showing the increase in insanity in France. He noted that the increase had been most marked in younger age groups, which would be compatible with a diagnosis of schizophrenia: "Formerly insanity of early age was a very rare exception; now, on the contrary, we observe a marked precocity . . . it happens in all ranks of society and seems to be on the increase." He also noted the increased insanity was three times more common in urban areas compared with rural areas, an observation which was subsequently confirmed (see chapter 13). Other European countries which explicitly noted the increase in insanity during this period were Denmark, Greece, Germany, and Russia.

In the United States there was apparently less interest shown in the increase in insanity. It was noted, to be sure, by leaders such as Dorothea Dix and Isaac Ray, but it did not seem to evoke the alarm it did in Europe. Perhaps the main reason for this was that large numbers of immigrants were arriving in America during those years, and it was widely assumed that the increase in insanity, and many other diseases, was simply due to them. There were also major shifts of population within the United States as it pushed westward, which could make it more difficult to perceive changes in any given area.

What figures exist, however, certainly point to a rapid increase in insanity in this country during the nineteenth century. The first American mental hospital opened in Williamsburg, Virginia, in 1773, but no more opened until 1816. Then suddenly there was an explosion of them, with eight more opened between 1816 and 1828 and another fourteen opened by 1846. Census figures suggest that between 1840 and 1880 there was a threefold increase in the number of the insane. The number of those hospitalized rose from 2,561 in 1840 to 38,047 in 1880, and by 1904 this number had skyrocketed to 150,151. The 1871 *Report of the United States Commissioner of Education* included the following observations:

> The successive reports, upon whatever source or means of information procured, all tend to show an increasing number of the insane. In the United States, Great Britain, Ireland and other civilised nations, so far as known there has been a great increase of provision for the insane within forty years and a very rapid increase within twenty years. Hospitals have been built seemingly sufficient to accommodate all the lunatics within their respective States, counties, or districts. These have been filled, and then crowded and pressed to admit still more. They have been successively enlarged, and then other institutions created, and filled and crowded as the earlier houses were.

There is, of course, no way to be certain that the increase in insanity noted in Europe and in the United States was specifically due to schizophrenia. Theoretically it could have been due to manic-depressive psychosis or to other brain diseases. The great bulk of the evidence is against this, however. Not only do we have observations by people, such as Renaudin, who noted that the increase was occurring in the younger age groups, but examination of the old hospital charts of these patients suggests that schizophrenia was the correct diagnosis. I have studied such charts in two of the oldest mental hospitals in the United States and found that the clinical data supported a diagnosis of schizophrenia in most cases.

The major argument against the rapid increase in schizophrenia has been a sociological one. David J. Rothman in *The Discovery of the Asylum* claims that rapidly changing social customs in the United States led to the building of large institutions such as asylums, and that patients with schizophrenia who had been living at home were then placed in the asylums. A variant of sociological theory was put forth by Cooper and Sartorius, who indicted industrialization and breakdown of the family as the primary causes of schizophrenia's rise: "It is suggested that the social and family structures found historically in pre-industrial societies . . . exert a comparatively benign effect upon patients with schizophrenia, and that these effects are lost during and after industrialization." It was not that schizophrenia increased, then, but rather that those who had the disease did not fare so well in the industrialized society.

Other explanations for the apparent increase have also been put forward. Schizophrenic patients were thought to live longer when put into asylums and thus their numbers increased. Legal changes, such as the "Four Shillings Act" of 1874, in which the English government gave local authorities four shillings for each person maintained in local asylums, provided an incentive to hospitalize patients. Increasingly mild cases of psychiatric disorders were hospitalized, some argue. The tolerance of the community for bizarre behavior decreased as the industrial revolution progressed, claim others. And the diagnostic criteria for schizophrenia changed dramatically during those years producing an illusory effect of an increase. As summarized by Dr. Assen Jablensky: "If the evidence for the apparent rarity of schizophrenic disorders until the beginning of this century is placed in the context of the dramatic changes in psychiatric theory and nosology that occurred between the middle and the end of the 19th century, it becomes highly plausible that schizophrenia was not identified earlier because clinicians were seeing reality from a different angle."

All of these arguments are plausible and probably explain some of the apparent increase in schizophrenia observed during the nineteenth century. And yet, at least for me personally, they are not very satisfying. Essentially they argue that schizophrenia occurred at about the same prevalence in 1800 that it occurs today, but that the patients were, so to speak, in the closet. The dramatic rise in schizophrenia observed in the nineteenth century, under these theories, was simply emptying the closets, labeling these patients with disease for the first time, and building asylums to house them.

Like the question of whether schizophrenia existed in ancient times, the question of whether there was a nineteenth-century increase is not definitively answerable without further studies. It comes down in the final analysis to the problem of the chicken and the egg: Did schizophrenia increase rapidly, causing asylums to be built, or were asylums built in response to social-industrial changes and then filled with schizophrenics who had been waiting in closets? Further analysis of nineteenth-century psychiatric hospital records might provide resolution to the question and to the curious history of this disease.

GEOGRAPHICAL VARIATIONS IN THE UNITED STATES

Just as there have been differences of opinion about the history of schizophrenia, so there are lively arguments about the geographical distribution of the disease. These arguments are difficult to resolve because of methodological problems in interpreting prevalence data and in comparing one study with another. It should be pointed out, however, that all major diseases in which both genetic and nongenetic factors are thought to play a role show significant differences in geographic distribution. Heart disease varies approximately sixfold, rheumatoid arthritis tenfold, insulin-dependent diabetes thirtyfold, multiple sclerosis fiftyfold, and some cancers show even greater differences. Schizophrenia would be a unique disease if its prevalence were approximately the same everywhere in the world. The surprising finding, then, would be not that such differences exist, but rather that they did not.

As far back as 1840, it was recognized that the northeastern states in the United States had a higher rate of insanity than the midwestern or the southern states. Early figures were, of course, very unreliable, but it is noteworthy that this same pattern of distribution has been cited repeatedly up to the present. In 1903, for example, a well-known American psychiatrist surveyed the distribution of schizophrenia by states. He found that the greatest concentration was in the northeast and "if from this center of greatest prevalence of insanity we draw a line in any direction—west, south, or southwest—we see that no matter which way we go we find a steady decrease until we strike the Pacific Slope."

More recent data on schizophrenia admission rates to American mental hospitals support these earlier studies. The states with the greatest population density and with most people living in cities have approximately twice as high a schizophrenia rate as states with low population density and most people living in rural areas. Thus in 1960, for example, the rate of first admissions for schizophrenia per 100,000 population was 32 in Massachusetts and 16 in Maine, 22 in Illinois and 11 in Arkansas. When the figures for the different decades of the twentieth century are examined, there is an impression that the differences are becoming less over time; the difference between highest and lowest states in 1840 was fourfold, in 1903 it was threefold, and it now appears to be twofold.

There are, of course, many explanations for these differences. One which is certainly true is that people who develop schizophrenia tend to migrate away from their hometowns and go to cities to live. San Francisco and New York are well known as having collected more than their share of strange people, and the same thing is true of most major American cities. Therefore, in terms of the examples cited above, schizophrenic patients in Maine are more likely to migrate to Boston to live, thus inflating the Massachusetts rate, and schizophrenic patients in Arkansas are more likely to migrate to Chicago and thus inflate the Illinois rate.

Another commonly cited explanation for these differences is that it is easier for persons with schizophrenia to live in rural areas; thus they do not get taken to the hospital and counted in the statistics. It is said, for example, that a schizophrenic family member on a farm can remain there for longer than a schizophrenic family member in the city and that this produces the differences in the statistics. Though this may have been true one hundred years ago when rural America was truly isolated, it is much less clearly true today. People living in small towns and on farms are now constantly in touch with each other by telephone and automobile, and it is doubtful whether a schizophrenic family member can really be assimilated any more easily on the farm than in suburban or urban areas. Farm work is increasingly mechanized, and the farmer's wife is now quite likely to have a job in a small nearby factory or business.

Even with explanations, such as the migration of schizophrenic persons from rural to urban areas, and the possibility that schizophrenics can be more easily assimilated in rural areas, important differences in the distribution of schizophrenia still remain. There is clearly a disproportionate number of schizophrenics who come from the cities, and especially from those portions of cities where the poor live. This was noted over a twenty-year period in a well-known study of New Haven, Connecticut, and has been shown to be true in many other studies. One of the foremost researchers in this field reported: "The evidence that there is an unusually high rate of schizophrenia in the lowest socioeconomic strata of urban communities seems to me to be nothing less than overwhelming." Furthermore, the association of schizophrenia with lower socioeconomic class status appears to be strongest for the largest cities and to be less clearly evident in smaller cities.

Since large numbers of blacks live in the poorer sections of large cities, it is not surprising to find that blacks as a whole have a higher rate of schizophrenia than whites. Five separate studies have confirmed this in highly urbanized states such as New York, Maryland, and Ohio. The higher rate of schizophrenia among blacks holds up even when corrections are made for the age distribution of the population; thus in a very careful study in Rochester, New York, blacks still had a schizophrenia rate one and one-half times that of whites.

When blacks who live in rural areas are compared with whites who live in rural areas, however, the results are different. This was done in Texas and in Louisiana and no differences were found. This argues strongly against race as being the cause of the difference. Rather it suggests that it is because blacks live in the inner city, and not because they are black, that they have a higher schizophrenia rate. Others have claimed that blacks appear to have a higher rate of schizophrenia because most psychiatrists are white and unconsciously (or consciously) racist; such psychiatrists would more readily label a black patient than a white patient as schizophrenic. This may well be so and is impossible to measure. Even if it were so, however, it would explain only a small portion of the differences and we are left with the fact that poor people in inner cities, whatever their race, have a disproportionately high schizophrenia rate.

IS SCHIZOPHRENIA INCREASING
IN THE UNITED STATES?

As detailed in the preceding chapter, there are suggestions that the prevalence of schizophrenia increased rapidly in the nineteenth century. Between 1910 and 1950 there are studies indicating that the prevalence rate of schizophrenia among Americans was approximately unchanged.

The most recent prevalence studies of schizophrenia in the United States raise the question—and it is only a question—whether schizophrenia might not be again increasing in prevalence. In Baltimore, for example, a study in 1936 found a schizophrenia prevalence rate of 3.6 per 1,000. A multisite NIMH study in 1984 found approximately twice that number and a 1967 study was intermediate between them. In New Haven in 1958 Hollingshead and Redlich reported a schizophrenia prevalence rate of 3.6 per 1,000, but a 1984 NIMH study found twice as much. A pre–World War II study of rural Tennessee reported a schizophrenia prevalence rate of 2.0 per 1,000, while a 1984 NIMH study of rural North Carolina reported twice that rate. And in Rochester a case register of all cases in psychiatric treatment reported a schizophrenia prevalence rate of 4.1 per 1,000 in 1970 and 5.1 in 1975.

Comparisons of the older studies with the more recent studies are fraught with methodological problems, especially relating to differences in diagnosis and case finding. In the past the diagnosis of schizophrenia in the United States was applied more broadly than it is today, and precisely this fact makes the findings listed above so interesting. Given the narrower diagnostic criteria used in recent studies, one would have expected that the schizophrenia prevalence rate in New Haven or Baltimore, for example, should have gone *down* compared to the older studies. Instead it went up, despite narrower diagnostic criteria. Arguing on the other side, case finding methods using door-to-door surveys were better in the more recent studies, which would account for at least part of the higher rates. The net impression, however, is to raise the possibility of a real increase in schizophrenia prevalence rates in recent years. The question certainly merits further study.

Is there any evidence that the prevalence rate of schizophrenia has changed in recent years in other countries? The answer is yes, and the pertinent studies have recently been reviewed. Briefly, they suggest that changes may occur in either direction or the rate may remain relatively constant. In northern Sweden and in Finland there appears to have been an increase in schizophrenia. On the other hand, in southern Sweden, Scotland, Ireland, and in Buckinghamshire County, England, there are studies suggesting that schizophrenia has become less common. Finally, in Norway and Germany the available evidence indicates that there has been no significant change in the schizophrenia prevalence rate since approximately 1930. Thus there is no reason to assume that schizophrenia in the United States will necessarily remain constant over time. Indeed, if it did it would be an unusual disease, for other chronic diseases (e.g., heart disease, cancers) often change in prevalence over time. Such changes, if they can be understood, may offer important clues to the causes of the diseases.

WORLDWIDE PREVALENCE RATES

Schizophrenia prevalence rates reported in studies since World War II vary from less than 1 per 1,000 to 17 per 1,000. The range is at least tenfold although most studies, including those in the United States, fall into the 2 to 5 per 1,000 range.

At the lower end of the range are studies of the Amish and the Hutterites in the United States and studies done in Ghana and Taiwan. The methodology in these studies appears to have been sound; the Taiwanese study, in fact, was praised as having the best case-finding methodology of any study up to that time. The low prevalence rates cannot simply be dismissed, therefore, by the assumption that the researchers missed most cases of the disease. Furthermore, in the Taiwanese study 10 cases of schizophrenia were found among 11,442 aborigines; 2 of these had lasted less than 3 months and another 4 had recovered in less than 2 years. Schizophrenia, especially the chronic variety, appears to have been genuinely rare among this group of people.

Other areas have reported very low prevalence rates of schizophrenia, although the methodologies in the studies were often inadequate. Several studies in Africa reported low rates, corroborating impressions of physicians on that continent in the nineteenth and early twentieth century. An especially interesting study was done in Ghana where over a twenty-seven year period the prevalence of schizophrenia appeared to rise dramatically. Low schizophrenia prevalence rates have also been found in Papua New Guinea and several islands in the South Pacific.

In response to all such studies of schizophrenia in developing countries, it is common to reply that all the schizophrenic individuals were probably killed off by fights, famine, or neglect. This is simply not true. No doubt a few have so died, especially if they were violent or attacked other people. Most schizophrenic patients in virtually all these cultures are relatively harmless, however, and are treated humanely. They are given food by the extended family and often allowed to forage in the village gardens. If they become too much of a nuisance, they may be chained to a log or confined in huts, but they are not usually allowed to starve to death. Another myth which needs to be dispelled is that schizophrenic individuals in other cultures are given special roles, such as shamans or medicine men. This idea is, in a word, nonsense, and I have discussed it in detail elsewhere. There is no evidence at all that persons with schizophrenia in other cultures are used systematically in these special roles. Undoubtedly there is the occasional schizophrenic who becomes a shaman by chance, but then in our own culture there is also an occasional schizophrenic who becomes a psychiatrist.

There is also evidence from other countries that the prevalence of schizophrenia may vary from region to region. Yugoslavia is the best-researched example of this. The Istrian peninsula in Croatia had been rumored for many years to have a disproportionate number of individuals with psychosis, so it was subjected to extensive study. It was found that both schizophrenia and manic-depressive psychosis were higher in the study area, compared to other parts of Croatia; the schizophrenia prevalence rate (for people ages 20 to 64) was 7.4 per 1,000 in villages and 7.3 per 1,000 in an urban area in the Istrian peninsula, compared with 2.9 per 1,000 (villages) and 4.2 per 1,000 (urban) elsewhere in Croatia.

The affected area lies on the Adriatic just south of Trieste and is popular with tourists. It is an area of mixed genetic stock (Croats, Italians, Austrians, Hungarians, and Rumanians), very little inbreeding, and one which has had shifting political fortunes over the years as empires rose and fell. By Yugoslav standards it is comparatively prosperous. In 1978 I traveled through the high schizophrenia prevalence area of Yugoslavia. It is an attractive region, with villages clinging to hillsides overlooking the sea and old men in dark suits timelessly tilling the fields as their ancestors did. Wandering the back streets where small houses are surrounded by ancient brick walls, I wondered what made these villages different. Why should they have twice as much schizophrenia as their counterparts one hundred miles across the hills? If such villages will yield their secret, we will have gone a long way toward understanding and, hopefully, preventing this disease.

India is another country that has provided intriguing findings on the prevalence of schizophrenia. In a series of studies in villages in West Bengal, Nandi and his Indian colleagues found the prevalence rate for schizophrenia to vary from 2.2 to 5.6 per 1,000. The highest schizophrenia rates were found among Indians of the highest castes. This is the ninth group of researchers over the past 50 years to find that schizophrenia occurs more commonly in India among individuals of higher castes. This observation contrasts with claims in the United States and eastern Europe that schizophrenia occurs more commonly in lower socioeconomic groups. At least a partial explanation for the latter is "downward drift" of individuals prone to schizophrenia; it is difficult to imagine how "upward drift" could account for the Indian findings, however.

On the high prevalence end of the spectrum are Böök's two studies of northern Sweden done twenty-five years apart, Väisänen et al.'s study of communities in both northern and southern Finland, and the study by my Irish colleagues and myself of an area in western Ireland. It should be noted that both Böök and I selected areas for study which were reputed to have a high prevalence rate for psychosis, but this was not true for the Finnish study. Väisänen et al.'s comparatively high schizophrenia prevalence rates were confirmed by a restudy of the same communities five years later, in which the number of persons found with psychoses was 50 percent higher than the original study; unfortunately, the authors did not provide a diagnostic breakdown of the psychoses.

There are other suggestions that schizophrenia prevalence rates in northern Scandinavia are high. Bremer reported a rate of 5.3 per 1,000 for a northern Norwegian village; the village was restudied thirty years later and the number of persons with "functional psychosis" (no diagnostic breakdown given) had increased. Fugelli surveyed two northern Norwegian islands and found 10 cases of schizophrenia among 1,726 residents (5.8 per 1,000); in addition he diagnosed another 15 cases of "organic and senile psychosis" and 17 cases of "other psychosis," yielding a prevalence of all psychoses of 24.3 per 1,000. Anderson studied another area of northern Norway and found a prevalence rate for all psychoses (no diagnostic breakdown given) of 24 per 1,000 for the Norwegian inhabitants and 54 per 1,000 for the Lapps. The idea that Scandinavian countries have a high rate of schizophrenia compared with southern Europe is not a new one; it was noted by W. Charles Hood in 1862, when he published his *Statistics of Insanity.*

WESTERN IRELAND

The other area of the world known for its high rate of schizophrenia is Ireland, and especially western Ireland. The story goes back over one hundred years, and many nineteenth-century observers were impressed by the number of insane in Ireland. In 1808 Sir Andrew Halliday noted that in Ireland "insanity is a disease of as frequent occurrence among the lower classes of the people as in any other country in Europe."

Others made similar observations. In 1845 the disastrous famine began in Ireland, resulting in mass emigration to America and elsewhere. By 1864 it was noted that "it is remarkable that during the last ten years no perceptible diminution has taken place in the number of the insane, notwithstanding the decrease of population in that period." By the turn of the century it was claimed that "the insane have all but doubled, and the cry is, Still they come!"

Contemporary studies of the high Irish schizophrenia rates were begun in 1963 by Walsh, O'Hare, and their colleagues. They found that the number of schizophrenic patients resident in Irish mental hospitals was higher than anywhere else in the world. The rate was almost three times higher than in neighboring England and Wales. The rates were highest for westernmost counties, for example, Roscommon, Galway, and Mayo. Not only was the schizophrenia rate high but the rates for manic-depressive psychosis and alcoholism were also high.

The question next arose whether the schizophrenia rate in Ireland was high only because more patients were hospitalized there. To answer the question, a community survey was begun in three counties in 1973 and a case register set up to count all persons with schizophrenia (and other mental disorders) both in the hospitals and living in the community. The schizophrenia prevalence rate for the three counties in 1973 was 5.6 per 1,000; County Roscommon, the westernmost county of the three studied, had a rate of 7.1 per 1,000. In 1982 the same three counties were again studied by the case register and the schizophrenia prevalence rate had decreased to 4.9 per 1,000; in County Roscommon it had decreased to 5.9 per 1,000. Thus there is some evidence that schizophrenia is decreasing in western Ireland.

I have visited western Ireland several times and lived there for six months in 1982 in order to do research on schizophrenia in this fascinating area. The winding sloughs and rocky hills are inhospitable to crops, and the people poorer than in most other parts of Ireland. They live quietly in an area of bleak beauty. During my stay my Irish colleagues and I carried out a schizophrenia prevalence survey of an area of County Roscommon reputed to have a high prevalence. When I asked one psychiatrist who was knowledgeable about the area how much schizophrenia existed there he replied: "Well, let me put it this way. If you put a fence around the whole area you could call it a mental hospital."

The area studied contained 2,848 persons; of these 48 were diagnosed with active psychosis at the time of the study, and 8 others with a history of psychosis had fully recovered and were not taking any medications. Two additional individuals were suspected of having schizophrenia but could not be included because they were living very secluded lives and refused all requests to be interviewed. Of those diagnosed with active psychosis, 21 were diagnosed with schizophrenia (*DSM-III* criteria), 11 with schizoaffective disorder, 6 with manic-depressive psychosis, 4 had atypical psychosis, and 6 had psychosis with preexisting mental retardation or medical conditions. The schizophrenia prevalence rate for this area was found to be 12.6 per 1,000, thus more than twice as high as the 5.9 per 1,000 rate found for the county as a whole. Similar to the case register data, it was observed in this study that the highest schizophrenia prevalence rates were found in older age groups, suggesting a decreased rate in more recent years.

There seems little doubt that schizophrenia in Ireland, as in Scandinavia, is a major problem. Dr. Dermot Walsh of the Irish Medico-Social Research Board has estimated that in the western counties 4 percent of the people will be affected with this disease during their lifetime.

Many of the Irish in these areas are themselves aware of their unusual number of "mad people." In the high prevalence areas almost everyone has a relative or friend who has been "over at the county hospital," great old stone asylums dating to the middle of the nineteenth century. Many confided to me that the cause of the problem was "close marriages," and this is a common local belief. The problem with this theory is that there is no evidence that there are any more marriages between close relatives in western Ireland than in any other rural area in the world, and the Catholic Church strongly discourages such marriages. Neither are the Irish an unusually inbred population, as multiple invasions of Celts, Spaniards, Scots, and English in centuries past ensured a broad genetic mix. Since schizophrenia sometimes runs in families, however, it is possible that the tendency to have large families in Ireland is contributing to the higher prevalence of schizophrenia if the families which are genetically predisposed to the disease are also having disproportionately large families.

Emigration is the other commonly heard explanation for the high Irish schizophrenia rates. When the nineteenth-century famine came, the story goes, all the healthy young people left to go to America and the weak ones stayed behind. They in turn begat weak offspring, and the high schizophrenia rate is one consequence.

There are several problems with this explanation, too. First, the high Irish schizophrenia rate was clearly noted before the mass emigration began. More important, an equally high rate of schizophrenia was noted among those who left Ireland as among those who stayed behind. As early as 1850 a high rate of insanity was reported among Irish immigrants in Massachusetts. By 1913 in the same state it was said that "in the Irish we find a higher ratio of insanity than in any other people." In New York State in 1920 it was observed that "the Irish-born had then the highest age-standardized rates for schizophrenia in either sex among the eleven immigrant groups differentiated." Subsequent studies of immigrants in the 1930s and 1940s showed a continuing high rate for the Irish, but one which decreased over time. The children of the Irish immigrants had a lower schizophrenia rate than their parents. Clearly it is not possible to explain the high schizophrenia rate in Ireland by saying that the healthiest people went to America and only the weak remained behind.

There are three other aspects of schizophrenia in Ireland which are noteworthy. It has been found that, as in so many other countries, schizophrenia in Ireland occurs much more frequently among lower socioeconomic groups. (This may be why it is more prevalent in Ireland's western counties, which are generally poorer.) The Irish "far larger increase of alleged insanity among the poorer than the wealthy classes" was noted as far back as 1894. Second, several people have remarked that schizophrenia appears to have a later onset in Ireland; this is seen in the larger numbers of people in older age groups being admitted to hospitals for the first time. Finally, the high schizophrenia rate in Ireland is not shared by her neighbor, Northern Ireland, which was found to have a lower rate in 1911 and has continued to have a low rate up to the present. Given the history of constant turmoil and strife in Northern Ireland over the years, this would argue against stress being an important causative factor of the disease. On the other hand, Northern Ireland has always been wealthier than the rest of Ireland, and this socioeconomic difference may be a factor in the lower rate there.

In summary, the geographical distribution of schizophrenia presents intriguing research leads, which need to be pursued. Ongoing case registers should be set up in areas thought to have very high or very low prevalence. Groups such as the Hutterites and northern Swedes need to be reexamined in detail, with genetic, biochemical, nutritional, virological, and psychosocial information collected. The higher castes in India merit study. The suggestions of an urban-rural gradient or a north-south gradient must be examined. Migrants from suspected high prevalence or low prevalence areas need follow-up to see whether their prevalence rate changes in their new home, similar to the work done in multiple sclerosis. Differences in age and acuteness of onset, and in outcome in different regions require documentation. And data on the seasonality of schizophrenic births should be collected in many more countries to ascertain its possible relationship with the geographical distribution of the disease. All of this research and much more has to be pursued. Our failure to do so reveals that we are not really serious about researching the causes of this disease, despite the fact that the geographical distribution of schizophrenia provides us with many clues to follow.

RECOMMENDED FURTHER READING

Eaton, W. W. "Epidemiology of Schizophrenia." *Epidemiologic Reviews* 7 (1985): 105–26. Also his book *The Sociology of Mental Disorders.* New York: Praeger, 1980. Dr. Eaton covers many of the epidemiological methodological issues clearly and concisely.

Hare, E. "Was Insanity on the Increase?" *British Journal of Psychiatry* 142 (1983): 439–55. Dr. Hare makes the case for a nineteenth-century increase in schizophrenia in his usual erudite and lucid style.

Jablensky, A., and N. Sartorius. "Culture and Schizophrenia." *Psychological Medicine* 5 (1975): 113–24. These two respected researchers argue that many of the differences in schizophrenia prevalence are artifacts of methodology.

Jeste, D. V., R. del Carmen, J. B. Lohr, and R. J. Wyatt. "Did Schizophrenia Exist Before the Eighteenth Century?" *Comprehensive Psychiatry* 26 (1985): 493–503. This is the strongest case that has been made for the existence of schizophrenia in ancient medical texts.

Kroll, J., and B. Bachrach. "Visions and Psychopathology in the Middle Ages." *Journal of Nervous and Mental Disease* 170 (1982): 41–49. A fascinating analysis of visual hallucinations as found in medieval writings.

Torrey, E. F. *Schizophrenia and Civilization.* New York: Jason Aronson, 1980. An extended and earlier version of this chapter.

———. "Prevalence Studies of Schizophrenia." *British Journal of Psychiatry* 150 (1987): 598–608.

White, W. A. "The Geographical Distribution of Insanity in the United States." *Journal of Nervous and Mental Disease* 30 (1903): 257–79. A forgotten but classic paper by one of the best-known psychiatrists of his era.

13

MOTHERS MARCH FOR MADNESS: HOW THE SYSTEM CAN BE CHANGED

> We have traveled a long road upward from the ideal of repression to the ideal of prevention, from manacles to mental hygiene. But the contemplation of past triumphs leaves no room for a complacent attitude toward present conditions. We are too often inclined to ignore a present evil by recalling still greater evils of the past. Progress is achieved not by the philosophy of "things have been worse," but by the philosophy founded on the premise that "conditions could be made better."
>
> Albert Deutsch, *The Mentally Ill in America*, 1937

The history of schizophrenia in twentieth-century America is a history of unprecedented neglect. Here is a disease which affects one out of every one hundred individuals, which is bringing chaos and tragedy to over one million families on any given day, which costs state and federal governments billions of dollars each year. Yet what do we offer the sufferers of this disease? Frequently, mediocre psychiatric care in state hospitals. Eviction from the hospital to live in vermin-infested boarding houses and fear-infested back alleys. Minimal psychiatric and medical follow-up. Virtually no sheltered workshops or opportunities for partial employment. Inadequate research budgets to pursue the causes of the disease. And psychiatrists who are at best indifferent to the disease and at worst blame the families for having caused it. In terms of services for schizophrenia it has been said that patients with this disease "are not falling between the cracks—they are lost in the ravines."

In addition to services ranging from mediocre to nonexistent, people with schizophrenia and their families have to live with an extraordinary amount of stigma. Schizophrenia is the modern-day equivalent of leprosy, and in the general population the level of ignorance about schizophrenia is appalling. A recent survey among college freshmen found that almost two-thirds mistakenly believed that "multiple personalities" are a common symptom of schizophrenia, whereas less than half were aware that hallucinations are a common symptom. One poll found that 55 percent of the public does not believe that mental illness exists, and only 1 percent realizes that mental illness is a major health problem. On television persons with schizophrenia are portrayed as aggressive, dangerous, and homicidal; in one study 73 percent of psychiatric patients on television were characterized as violent and 23 percent were homicidal maniacs. There is no other disease in the western world which confers such social ostracism on the people afflicted and on their families.

There are signs, fortunately, that life for persons with schizophrenia may improve in the future. The turning point came in the early 1980s, when three separate trends converged and produced stirrings of change. First, the evidence that schizophrenia is a brain disease had accumulated rapidly in the 1970s and become more widely known; no longer could the disease be blamed on rejecting mothers or social conditions. Second, hundreds of thousands of patients dumped from state hospitals without adequate aftercare in that period had accumulated in the inner cities so that it was no longer possible to take a walk without noticing them. As long as there had been only a few hallucinating schizophrenics on the sidewalks and in the parks nobody noticed, but once their concentration passed a certain visibility threshold then everyone noticed. In sociological terms it became known as the Saks-Gucci principle (i.e., when it is no longer possible to walk from Saks to Gucci without passing at least three obviously mentally ill individuals, it is defined as a crisis), and the visibility threshold was exceeded in 1982.

Third, and most important, the families of persons with schizophrenia began coming out of the closets and organizing. Most of the family groups became affiliated as chapters of the National Alliance for the Mentally Ill (NAMI), and a rapidly growing advocacy movement was under way. By the mid-1980s NAMI groups had learned how to bring pressure on state and federal agencies. Some state mental health departments, which had for years conceptualized the seriously ill simply as bodies to be extruded from the state hospitals, began to reallocate resources to these patients. And the National Institute of Mental Health (NIMH), under the leadership of Dr. Shervert Frazier from 1984 to 1986, began to talk of major new initiatives for research on schizophrenia. To be sure, most of the new service being offered to persons with schizophrenia was lip service but the increasing visibility of the disease was encouraging, as major newspapers and television networks devoted more space and time to the disease.

THE POLITICS OF NEGLECT

Why, one might ask, was it necessary for families to organize in the 1980s before public attention was turned to schizophrenia? Why had not the American Psychiatric Association, the National Institute of Mental Health, or the National Mental Health Association provided leadership on this disease?

The American Psychiatric Association (APA) was an especially good candidate for such leadership. It had been begun in the 1840s as an association of superintendents of state hospitals and, until World War II, its major area of interest was the seriously mentally ill. With the ascendance of psychoanalysis in the United States and the 1930s influx of psychoanalysts from prewar Europe, however, the prestige and dominant interest of American psychiatry shifted sharply to private psychotherapy for the worried well. Patients with serious mental disorders were no longer viewed as interesting or desirable, and in fact the more prestigious a psychiatrist you were considered to be, the less chance that any of your patients would have schizophrenia.

Lack of APA interest in the seriously mentally ill was clearly demonstrated in the 1970s when Dr. John Spiegel, then president of the organization, toured the country to discuss with groups of psychiatrists the ten most important problems facing American psychiatry. The last problem on the list was that of the chronic mental patient. Dr. Spiegel noted that "although audiences tended to respond to the other points vigorously, on this issue, except for a rare complaint that something ought to be done about it by the leaders of psychiatry, there was a numbing silence." A study at that time showed that only 11 percent of patients seen by psychiatrists in private practice were diagnosed with schizophrenia, despite the fact that schizophrenia was by far the most serious problem facing America's psychiatrists.

By the mid-1980s the APA had evolved into being merely a union to protect the vested interests of the nation's private psychiatrists. The energy and resources of the organization were devoted to lobbying for insurance coverage to pay psychotherapy fees for the worried well and to keeping psychologists and psychiatric social workers from taking away private patients. An occasional leader, such as Dr. John Talbott, exhorted psychiatrists to take an interest in the seriously mentally ill, and occasional spasms of institutional guilt goaded the APA to hold conferences or convene task forces to "study" the problem. Most of the time, however, the APA continues to act simply as a union for the nation's privately practicing psychiatrists. As such it is no more likely to provide leadership for patients with serious mental disorders than is the Brotherhood of Teamsters or the AFL-CIO.

What about other mental health professionals—psychologists, psychiatric social workers, and psychiatric nurses? If American psychiatrists will not take the lead in championing the cause of the seriously mentally ill, why cannot these other professionals do so? In fact, they could if they wished. Unfortunately, however, virtually all of them look to psychiatry for their standards and try to emulate the psychiatric profession. Status within all these mental health disciplines accrues to the private practice model; taking care of schizophrenic or otherwise seriously disturbed patients is indicative of second-class professional status. There are individual psychologists, psychiatric social workers, and psychiatric nurses who defy the laws of social gravity and devote their careers to the seriously ill, just as there are psychiatrists who do so. They stand out as the exceptions, however, always considered somewhat aberrant by their peers. And when the official organizations of these professions take public stands apart from psychiatry, it is usually on issues of pay and insurance compensation, not on issues like quality of care for schizophrenic patients.

The National Institute of Mental Health (NIMH), created in the late 1940s as a research institute for serious mental illnesses, seemed a logical candidate to provide leadership on the seriously mentally ill. As was mentioned in chapter 8, however, NIMH was not interested in these patients. Instead it strove to become an institute of human behavior with tentacles extending to all problems of society, from poverty and racism to campus unrest, urban blight, child-rearing practices, and divorce. Its name, the National Institute of Mental Health rather than the National Institute of Mental Illness, was used to condone an interest in virtually every social problem in America *except* the problem of the seriously mentally ill.

If NIMH was not interested in the seriously mentally ill, then what did it spend all its money on? During the 1970s, at a time when each year tens of thousands of mental patients were being discharged from state hospitals and placed in inadequate community facilities, NIMH research funds were being spent on research projects such as the following:

1971	Training Student Leaders for Changes on Campus	$65,000
	Pupil Growth In and Out of School	33,000
1972	Methods to Promote Growth in Marital Relationships	126,000
	An Empirical Base for Planning Community Changes	162,000
1973	Problem-Solving Behavior of Family Groups	194,000
	Human Territoriality in Home and Neighborhood	21,000
1974	Study of Process of Adjustment of Families of Prisoners	169,000
	Earned Family Incomes and the Urban Crisis	210,000
1975	The Impact of Religious Belief on Voting Behavior	14,000
	Tenant Organization: Mobilization and Consequences	82,000
1976	Effect of Metropolitan Open Space on Community Life	72,000
	Factors in the Marriages of Older Couples	15,000
1977	Culture and Cooperation	53,000
	Oral History and World View	33,000
1978	Managing Grievance in the Urban Workplace	77,000
	Effects of Automation on the Lives of Longshoremen	34,000
1979	Pair-Bonding, Parental Care, and Reproduction	44,000
	Self-Regulation in Altruism	39,000
1980	Sex and Sexual Violence in Fiction	49,000
	Police Discretion in Relationship to Emergency Apprehension	75,000

Each of these research projects had of course some intrinsic merit and value; the problem was that together such research issues usurped NIMH's attention and resources. Whereas the problem of the seriously mentally ill should have been the primary focus of NIMH, it instead became a minor issue relegated to the back corridors and trotted out ceremonially for official occasions such as budget hearings. In such an atmosphere NIMH was about as likely to provide leadership for the seriously mentally ill as was the Smithsonian Institution. It was not until the late 1970s, with the advent of the Community Support Program (CSP), and especially in 1984 when Dr. Shervert Frazier became the Director, that NIMH began to pay attention to schizophrenia.

The National Mental Health Association (NMHA), an advocate group for the mentally ill, should theoretically have been another candidate to provide leadership for the seriously mentally ill. It had been, after all, founded in 1909 by Clifford Beers (who had himself been hospitalized with manic-depressive psychosis) with the express purpose of reforming care in state mental hospitals. By World War II, however, the Mental Health Association, like American psychiatry generally, had lost interest in the seriously mentally ill. It had instead supported the private practice, problems-of-living model of American psychiatry, acting as a handmaiden for psychiatrists and other mental health professionals and strongly supporting NIMH. On issues such as the coverage of individual psychotherapy under health insurance, the Mental Health Association became very active, mobilizing volunteers to visit and write their congressmen and otherwise lobbying for the rights of the worried well. Much of its rhetoric has focused on the need for good mental health, a concept as nebulous as it is all-inclusive. "Have you hugged your kid today?" Mental Health Association posters asked. Like motherhood and apple pie, it is difficult to be against hugging your kid, but if most of an organization's energy goes into hugging kids there is little energy left over to promote better services for the truly mentally ill.

At the local level in cities such as Pittsburgh, Philadelphia, and Honolulu, the Mental Health Association has worked hard on behalf of the seriously mentally ill. At the national level, however, it has continued to champion the ephemeral concept of "mental health" and shown little interest in the mentally ill. In 1977, in fact, the organization gave its annual research award to two researchers whose work was based on the thesis that families cause schizophrenia. In terms of the politics of mental illness, the National Mental Health Association is quietly slipping into oblivion, a relic of the past.

If the National Mental Health Association has been ineffectual, what about other mental health organizations whose offices dot the Washington landscape? The National Association of State Mental Health Program Directors, for example, is interested in the plight of schizophrenic patients since this group is composed of the state directors of mental health programs. By itself, however, it has limited power. It also suffers from political eunuchism insofar as the state governors can dictate deinstitutionalization needs to their state mental health directors; few such directors have risked their jobs by standing up to the governor or state legislators and saying that hospitalized patients would not be released until adequate community aftercare facilities were in place first. Other Washington mental health lobby groups, such as the National Council of Community Mental Health Centers, the National Association of Private Psychiatric Hospitals, and the Association of Mental Health Administrators, have functioned primarily to help secure a larger slice of the federal pie for their clients and have been irrelevant as far as the needs of schizophrenics are concerned.

THE POLITICS OF SCHIZOPHRENIA IN OTHER COUNTRIES

Neglect of the seriously mentally ill is not unique to the United States. Other countries are experiencing many of the same problems of deinstitutionalization, including England, France, Germany, Italy and Australia, and the homeless mentally ill roam the streets of Paris, Milan, and Sydney just as they do the streets of Philadelphia, Miami, and San Francisco. In general, however, the problems are not so severe in these other countries, because psychiatrists in other western countries did not become as enamored with psychotherapy nor did they abandon the seriously mentally ill to the degree that American psychiatry did. It is still respectable in Sweden or Germany, for example, for a psychiatrist with high professional standing to specialize in patients with serious mental illnesses.

A few unusual situations in other countries merit attention:

Japan.   There are reports that the rights of persons with schizophrenia in Japan are being seriously abused. There is great stigma within Japanese families in having a member with a serious mental illness, and pressure is put on psychiatrists to keep such patients in psychiatric hospitals. Eighty-seven percent of psychiatric hospital beds in Japan are private, mostly run by private companies. Over three-fourths of all psychiatric hospital admissions are involuntary and most psychiatric wards are locked. Allegations of abuse of the system had become so widespread that in 1986 an international commission visited Japan and confirmed the severity of the situation.

Soviet Union.   There have been allegations that psychiatry in the Soviet Union has occasionally been abused. Dissidents whose political views are contrary to those of the government have been arrested, labeled with schizophrenia, then forcibly medicated. The psychiatric label is used to rationalize indefinite involuntary hospitalization and also effectively to discredit the political views of the dissident. That this abuse of psychiatry has taken place, and that it has involved the collusion of some well-known Soviet psychiatrists, there is no doubt. Because of such abuse the Soviet Union was expelled from the World Psychiatric Association in 1977. A good review of Soviet manipulation of psychiatry and misuse of the label "schizophrenia" may be found in *Psychiatric Terror* by Sidney Bloch and Peter Reddaway.

Italy.   A law was passed in Italy in 1978 prohibiting new admissions to mental hospitals. Instead psychiatric patients, including those with schizophrenia, were mandated to be treated at outpatient facilities and, when necessary, in small psychiatric units in general hospitals. The "Italian experiment," as it is widely known, has been watched with great interest by other countries.

Assessments of how well it has worked vary widely, from calling it a glorious new era to an unmitigated disaster. In fact the results appear to be mixed and predictable. In some areas, such as Trieste and Verona, the experiment has worked nicely because outpatient facilities and alternative living arrangements have been made. Most people with schizophrenia appear to be better off in these areas. In other cities, where admission to mental hospitals was denied but no alternative community facilities were created, most patients with schizophrenia appear to be worse off. In southern Italy many jurisdictions have ignored the law altogether and gone ahead with business as usual in the large psychiatric hospitals.

West Germany and the Netherlands.   In these countries left-wing political organizations have agitated against psychiatry. Serious mental illnesses like schizophrenia, they argue, are products of inequitable social and economic conditions and are not brain diseases. Active distrust and occasional demonstrations against biological psychiatry have been the result, with a consequent slowing of research on schizophrenia. Because of the political climate against research in the Netherlands and threats against his family, one of that country's best psychiatric researchers moved to the United States.

England.   Deinstitutionalization and the closing of psychiatric hospitals is a very controversial topic in England, with dialogue between groups becoming increasingly politicized. In addition, animal rights activists have demonstrated against research establishments and threatened researchers. Reportedly, it is now more difficult to do schizophrenia research on animals in England than on humans.

"I'M NOT GOING TO TAKE IT ANYMORE"

In recent years it has become clear that organized efforts by persons with schizophrenia and their families can change the system and improve services. The gains to date have been modest, to be sure, but they have conclusively demonstrated that change can occur. That is the important lesson to be learned—that the decades of neglect for persons with this disease can be brought to an end. Nothing inherent in the disease schizophrenia mandates that it be neglected; nothing inherent in having schizophrenia assigns stigma and fourth-class citizenship.

It is feasible to change the public perception of schizophrenia and to decrease the stigma associated with the disease. For other conditions the National Association for Retarded Citizens and the Epilepsy Foundation have demonstrated that progress can be made, and the Alzheimer's Disease and Related Disorders Association is presently making some. Advocacy groups have successfully organized fights for diseases far rarer than schizophrenia. Take muscular dystrophy, for example, with its Jerry Lewis telethons and massive media blitz each September. In viewing such a drive next Labor Day, remember that for every patient with muscular dystrophy there are sixty patients with schizophrenia.

How can services for people with schizophrenia and research on this disease be improved? The answer: organized action by family support groups, like that taking place under local Alliance for the Mentally Ill (AMI) groups. Some of the activities such groups should consider include the following:

- Increase membership in your local family support group. Leave brochures for your group with all local mental health professionals. Give brochures to drug salesmen who visit physicians. Leave leaflets on the windows of cars parked in the visitors lot of the state hospital. Put notices on community bulletin boards, in church bulletins, company and local newspapers. One AMI group persuaded a grocery chain to print their name and telephone number on milk cartons. Another persuaded the telephone company to include information on their group with telephone bills.

- Develop a speakers bureau and offer to talk to community service organizations (e.g., Kiwanis, Lions, Rotary), school assemblies, and local companies. Mr. and Ms. Ron Norris in Wilmington, Delaware, persuaded the Du Pont Corporation to fund the making of a film that can be used for such presentations.

- Organize a chapter of the National Sibling Network for brothers and sisters of the seriously mentally ill. Support groups for wives and husbands of the seriously mentally ill are also beginning to form in some areas.

- Form an alliance with patient groups in your area to work on common interests. Patient groups are increasingly moving away from the rhetoric of Szasz ("schizophrenia does not exist") and Laing ("schizophrenia is a sane response to an insane world") and becoming effective in working for better services.

- Set up a formal course on schizophrenia and manic-depressive psychosis taught by a professional for family members or anyone who is interested. The National Schizophrenia Fellowship of Northern Ireland has a regular six-week course taught by a public health nurse and the Schizophrenia Fellowship of New Zealand has developed a correspondence course for families in rural areas.

- Volunteer to become a liaison between your family support group and the local public shelters. Visit the shelters and get to know the people running them. A large number of persons living in the shelters have schizophrenia and manic-depressive psychosis, and many of them have been listed as missing persons by their families. NAMI has established a network to link such persons with their families.

- Establish coalitions between family support groups and the 344,000 churches and synagogues in the United States. Offer to preach a guest sermon during Mental Illness Awareness Week. The clergy are natural allies for families with schizophrenic members. In some areas education of the clergy must accompany these efforts, for some clergy still teach that mental illness is a sign of sin. Religious groups are the main providers of care for the homeless mentally ill, since these groups operate most public shelters; they are therefore aware of the vast numbers of untreated schizophrenics.

- Volunteer to become a liaison between your family support group and the local jails. Get to know the law enforcement officials. Many persons with schizophrenia and manic-depressive psychosis are in jails. Explore with local mental health officials how psychiatric care for such individuals can be improved. Offer to give a lecture about schizophrenia to police trainees. Link your efforts to similar efforts in other family support groups under HELP-MI, a task force of the Alliance for the Mentally Ill.

- Volunteer to become a liaison between your family support group and local nursing homes. Visit the nursing homes and get to know the administrators. Explore with them and with local mental health officials how psychiatric care can be improved for the many persons with serious mental illnesses who are confined to nursing homes. Ask the administrator to make a presentation to your support group. Encourage the establishment of in-service education about serious mental illnesses to the nursing home staffs.

- Publish a resource book describing local mental health resources for persons with schizophrenia and manic-depressive psychosis. Several AMI groups that have done this can be used as models (e.g., Washington AMI, Colorado AMI, Missouri AMI).

- Become an expert on low-cost housing. Visit existing units being used by persons with schizophrenia living in your community, take pictures, and show them to the county council, etc. Visit model housing projects such as in Weber County, Utah, and Yolo County, California, and make people in your community aware of what can be done.

- Encourage the setting up of halfway houses by working against restrictive zoning ordinances and changing federal regulations (through the Department of Housing and Urban Development, etc.).

- If there is a great lack of halfway houses in your community, work with the local mental health agencies to set one up yourself. The Main Line Mental Health Group outside Philadelphia successfully did this, renovating a mansion adjacent to Haverford

State Hospital into what is almost certainly the most elegant and comfortable halfway house in the United States.

■ Become an expert on vocational training for the seriously mentally ill. Visit model programs such as the Eden Express restaurant in Haywood, California (see chapter 9). Meet with state vocational training officials and explore possibilities. Go to the state legislature if necessary.

■ Visit the nearest state-sheltered workshop. Ask the director why more persons with schizophrenia are not included. If, as in most such workshops, schizophrenics are few and far between, organize a letter and telephone blitz of the state legislature to get the policy changed. Look at model workshops, such as Boley Inc. in St. Petersburg, Florida.

■ Organize part-time jobs with local business and industry to be filled by persons with schizophrenia and manic-depressive psychosis.

■ Organize a local clubhouse for the seriously mentally ill, using the Fountain House model in New York City (see chapter 9). Encourage the state to fund such programs as Florida has done.

■ Become an expert on SSI and SSDI regulations. Do a brief survey to ascertain how many people with schizophrenia and/or manic-depressive psychosis are eligible for but are not in fact receiving their benefits. Meet with the local officials in charge of these programs. Ask families to bring to your attention instances where persons with these diseases have been rejected or cut off from benefits.

■ Lobby for the amending of Medicaid and Medicare so that they do not discriminate against persons with schizophrenia, and so that they cover persons living in halfway houses. A step in this direction took place in 1986, when Congress liberalized Medicaid coverage for the chronically mentally ill.

■ Work to get representatives of family support groups on all city, county, and state mental health boards and advisory commissions, as well as the boards of directors of CMHCs.

■ Become politically aware. Identify the legislators in your county and state who support the concerns of the mentally ill. Let these legislators know that you back them because of their stand. Organize political support for them in elections.

■ Become expert on the county and state mental health budget. Where is the money going? Who is getting services? Who is *not*?

Attend the key subcommittee meetings. Offer to testify as a family support group.

- Meet regularly with the director of the local CMHC. Push to raise the seriously mentally ill to top priority for clinic services.

- Lobby the state legislature to mandate the seriously mentally ill as prime candidates for expenditure of state mental health dollars. Accomplishing this in some states (e.g., Colorado and Oregon) has proved very helpful.

- Arrange for introduction of legislation in your state to change the name of the state Department of Mental Health to the Department of Mental Illness. It will help people to focus on the real problems. The Massachusetts AMI has attempted to do this.

- Lobby for establishment of a bill of rights guaranteeing minimum standards of service for the seriously mentally ill. For a model of such a bill, write to Deputy Commissioner for Mental Health, Iowa Department of Human Services, Des Moines, IA 50319.

- Set up a system of respite care among a group of families, with families covering for each other so they can get away on vacations. Suggest to local mental health authorities that they support such services and provide some of the necessary manpower.

- Organize a plan for providing continuing care for the seriously mentally ill after the well family members have died (e.g., Planned Lifetime Assistance Network (PLAN), described in chapter 10).

- Work to update guardianship laws in your state. The Mental Health Law Project in Washington, D.C., and the American Bar Association have published model statutes that can be used as guidelines.

- Educate insurance companies about the necessity of covering schizophrenia and manic-depressive illness in exactly the same way multiple sclerosis is covered. They should be encouraged to differentiate these brain diseases from problems of living, for which insurance coverage is not practical since there is no logical cutoff to the need. Take an insurance executive to lunch, or have your AMI group make a formal presentation to the company staff so that they will better understand the disease.

- Educate mental health professionals in training by offering to make presentations to local nursing schools, schools of social work, university departments of psychology, schools of medicine, and psychiatric residency training programs.

- Initiate a dialogue between your family support group and the local psychiatric society. Ask them to make a presentation to your group and ask to make one to their group. Both sides will emerge with a better understanding of each other's problems and with ideas on how you can be helpful to each other. The Northeast Ohio Alliance for the Mentally Ill in Cleveland has done this very effectively.

- Identify local physicians and psychiatrists who provide good care for persons with schizophrenia and manic-depressive psychosis and put out consumers' guides (see *How to Compile a Consumer's Directory of Doctors and Their Fees,* Health Research Group, 2000 P Street, Washington, D.C. 20036).

- Educate lawyers and judges about schizophrenia. Request time to make a presentation to the monthly meeting of the local Bar Association and offer to teach a class at the law school.

- Publish a booklet outlining commitment laws and procedures in your state, including the major impediments to hospitalizing seriously mentally ill family members. A good example is "Court Assistance Program," published by the Mental Health Association in Forsyth County, N.C. (390 S. Stratford Rd., Winston-Salem, NC 27103).

- Combat the negligent release of patients by state hospital or other psychiatric inpatient units. If the patient scheduled to be released is known to be a danger to himself or others, send a letter such as the following by registered mail:

Dear ———,

   You have under your care John Doe. I am informed that you intend to release John Doe. You should not do so. I know John Doe to be a danger to himself and to others. You already have information which puts you on notice of this fact. If there is any doubt, I now put you on notice.

   If in spite of this information you release John Doe and he causes injury to himself or to others, you will be responsible because were on notice that your release of John Doe will be the substantial factor in causing either harm to him or to others or to both.

Better yet, have a lawyer send it.

- Sue mental health professionals who endanger patients by negligently reducing medication to levels known to be too low, or who release patients from the hospital when it is clear that the patients cannot care for themselves.

- If laws in your state have tilted too far toward the patient's right to refuse treatment, begin a campaign to restore muscle to the laws, so that patients who need treatment will be treated. Open a public dialogue with lawyers and judges. Make it a political issue. Form an alliance with mental health professionals working for the same goal.

- Advocate wider use of outpatient commitment laws, which permit patients to live in the community only so long as they continue to take medication (see chapter 11).

- Work with the State Commissioner of Mental Health to set up quarterly meetings between family groups and mental health professionals to discuss problems. In Maine such a program has proved to be very successful.

- Work with state mental health officials to devise innovative ways to recruit good mental health professionals into the state system, such as Maryland has done (see chapter 8). Let good mental health professionals know that the families appreciate them.

- Establish public awards at the local and state levels for outstanding employees of the mental health system. Civil service systems do not reward excellence so family support groups must. Create a coalition with other community groups (e.g., Kiwanis, Rotarians, Elks, etc.) to form annual awards presentation ceremonies.

- If necessary, bring legal suits against city and state governments, insisting that they provide psychiatric aftercare and shelter for released mental patients (in 1982 examples of such class-action suits were initiated in Denver by the Legal Aid Society and in New York City by the Coalition for the Homeless).

- Institute regular inspections of the state hospital by the family support group. For details on how to do this, write AMI of South Carolina, P.O. Box 2538, Columbia, SC 29202; MHA of Illinois, 217 E. Monroe Street, Springfield, IL 62701; or see *Hospital and Community Psychiatry* 36 (1985): 393–95.

- Meet with Joint Commission on Accreditation of Hospitals (JCAH) inspectors every three years, when they make their inspection of the state hospital. JCAH welcomes such input. To find out when an inspection is scheduled, contact JCAH, 875 N. Michigan Avenue, Chicago, IL 60611. Tell the inspectors what is right and what is wrong with the hospital.

- If the state hospital flagrantly disregards the rights of patients, ask for an investigation by the Civil Rights Division, U.S. Department of Justice, Washington, D.C. 20530.

- Another means of safeguarding the rights of hospitalized mentally ill persons is through the 1986 Protection and Advocacy Law, which mandates that each state must have a patient protection and advocacy agency. Become familiar with how it can be used. Educate other families.

- In larger states, do a ranking of state hospitals and/or CMHCs on the quality of care they provide for the seriously mentally ill. Publicize the rankings. For a guide see E. F. Torrey and S. M. Wolfe, *Care of the Seriously Mentally Ill: A Rating of State Programs* (Health Research Group, 2000 P Street, N.W., Washington, D.C. 20036).

- Lobby your Senators and Congressmen to put more pressure on the National Institute of Mental Health (NIMH) to shift research funds to schizophrenia and manic-depressive psychosis.

- Raise research funds for the National Alliance for Research on Schizophrenia and Depression (NARSAD), a fund originated by NAMI.

- Support efforts of research organizations to maintain brain banks in which brains of persons who had serious mental illnesses are collected after death. These are exceedingly useful for research.

- Become a stigma-spotter. Be alert for evidence of prejudice against the seriously mentally ill in the media. Ask patients with these diseases about discrimination they encounter in housing and jobs. Establish a coalition with such patients to combat the stigma by letters, calls, and public education.

- Establish contact with officials of local newspapers and radio and television stations. Encourage them to consider more coverage of the problems of the seriously mentally ill, e.g., an exposé of a rundown boarding house. Educate them about schizophrenia and manic-depressive illness. Ask them to speak at a meeting of your family support group. Utilize the NAMI publication *Anti-Stigma: Improving Public Understanding of Mental Illness.*

- Organize a local advertising campaign to combat stigma. For example, the Ontario Friends of Schizophrenics and the New York State AMI funded a series of billboards and posters (e.g., on city buses), explaining what schizophrenia is and how widespread it is. An AMI group persuaded a local grocery chain to put on the grocery bags: "The brain is part of the body. It too can become ill. Schizophrenia and depressive disorder are *no fault* brain illnesses."

- Become the "lunatic fringe" of your local family support group. Threaten to lead marches of patients and families into county council meetings or state legislative meetings. Threaten to organize sit-ins at key offices or CMHCs unless specific needs of the seriously mentally ill are met. If necessary, carry out your threats. A "lunatic fringe" makes it easier for the mainstream majority in your organization to appear reasonable.

- If *none* of the above suits your aptitudes or abilities and you still want to help, there is one thing left. As advocated in the movie *Network*, when fed up with existing conditions you should lean out your window and yell loudly: "I'm mad as hell and I'm not going to take it anymore!" After doing this you will be forced to explain to your neighbors what is going on, and several more families will thereby become educated about schizophrenia.

These suggestions constitute a mere sampling of what can be done by families committed to changing the system. Since there are a minimum of 1.2 million persons with schizophrenia in the United States today, there are a minimum of 1.2 million families who can change the system. In fact, 1.2 million families can change *any* system; only reluctance and embarrassment prevent us from doing so.

The system will not change, however, until enough families become angry and get organized. Persons with schizophrenia will continue to be fourth-class citizens, leading twilight lives, often shunned, ignored, and neglected. They will continue to be, in the words of President Carter's Commission on Mental Health, "a minority within minorities. They are the most stigmatized of the mentally ill. They are politically and economically powerless and rarely speak for themselves. . . . They are the totally disenfranchised among us." The mad will become liberated only when those of us fortunate enough to have escaped the illness show how mad we really are.

RECOMMENDED FURTHER READING

Awakenings: Organizing a Support/Advocacy Group. Washington, D.C.: National Alliance for the Mentally Ill, 1982. The pamphlet outlines steps which can be used to form a support and advocacy group for families of schizophrenic patients.

Citizen Evaluation in Practice: A Casebook on Citizen Evaluation of Mental Health and Other Services. Rockville, MD: National Institute of Mental Health, 1984. DHHS publication no. ADM 84–1338. A compilation by fifty-one authors of examples of citizen attempts to monitor mental health service programs.

Hatfield, A. "Consumer Guide to Mental Health Services." Washington, D.C.: National Alliance for the Mentally Ill, 1985. Practical suggestions on how to work toward improving psychiatric services.

"Media Watch Kit." Washington, D.C.: National Alliance for the Mentally Ill, 1984. How to work with the media to decrease stigma against the seriously mentally ill.

Torrey, E. F., and S. M. Wolfe. *Care of the Seriously Mentally Ill: A Rating of State Programs.* Washington, D.C.: Health Research Group, 1986. This state-by-state rating of state programs can be used as a model for advocacy groups wishing to rank state hospitals or mental health programs within their own state. A new survey will be published in September, 1988.

APPENDIX
A

TEN BEST AND TEN WORST READINGS ON SCHIZOPHRENIA

The novitiate seeking knowledge of schizophrenia often samples the holdings of the local library in a random fashion. Depending purely on chance, a person may emerge from such archival encounters either modestly enlightened or thoroughly confused. The following lists are readings on schizophrenia that I consider especially helpful, as well as others I found distinctly unhelpful. There are undoubtedly many other candidates for these lists of merit and demerit; readers are invited to submit nominations. The order is entirely alphabetical.

TEN BEST

Andreasen, Nancy C. *The Broken Brain: The Biological Revolution in Psychiatry.* New York: Harper & Row, 1984. Of the many recent books and articles describing contemporary research on the brain, this is the best. Its especially clear description of the structure and function of the brain provides lay readers with everything they need to know to follow the current neuroscience revolution. It covers not only schizophrenia, but manic-depressive psychosis, Alzheimer's disease, and anxiety disorders as well.

Balzac, Honoré de. "Louis Lambert." A short story written in 1832 by the French novelist, included in collections of Balzac's work and also in *The Abnormal Personality Through Literature,* edited by A. A. Stone and S. S. Stone, Englewood Cliffs, NJ: Prentice-Hall, 1966. Although written more than 150 years ago, the story of Louis Lambert's breakdown into chronic catatonic schizophrenia has never been equaled for tragedy and for its poignant portrait of a brilliant mind taken over by disease. The dedication of Lambert's wife, and her insistence on seeing the dignified being of her lover beneath his chronic psychosis, is eloquent and touching even in translation.

Deutsch, Albert. *The Shame of the States.* New York: Harcourt, Brace and Company, 1948. Deutsch was a crusading New York journalist who undertook a twelve-state examination of public mental hospitals. His shocking descriptions of the conditions he found are matched in the photographs by a cameraman who accompanied him. The book stands as a monument to our past inhumanity to the seriously mentally ill, and a warning of what can happen to defenseless people who have no organized lobby to speak for them. "Could a truly civilized community permit humans to be reduced to such animal-like level?" Deutsch asked.

Diamond, Ronald. "Drugs and the Quality of Life: The Patient's Point of View." *Journal of Clinical Psychiatry* 46 (1985): 29–35. This sensitive and thought-provoking discussion explores the "invisible" side effects of medication experienced by some patients and the issue of noncompliance with medication. It encourages families and mental health professionals to consider all aspects of the quality of the patient's life, not just whether or not the person is hearing voices. It also reminds us to listen closely to persons with this disease, for they often have much to teach us. Dr. Diamond is on the staff of the Dane County, Wisconsin, treatment program, a model program for the seriously mentally ill.

Riley, Jocelyn. *Crazy Quilt.* New York: William Morrow, 1984. An unusual children's book, the fictional account of a thirteen-year-old girl whose mother has schizophrenia. It is a poignant reminder of the effects of this disease on other family members and the fact that children need education and support just as siblings and parents need them. We need many more such books so that children, too, may understand.

Sheehan, S. *Is There No Place on Earth for Me?* Boston: Houghton, Mifflin, 1982. Susan Sheehan's superb study originally appeared in *The New Yorker* magazine. It provides the best available description of the course of a chronic schizophrenic illness, the difficulties encountered by a person with the disease, the frustrations for the family, and the mediocre care available at the state hospital. It is searingly accurate and mandatory reading for anyone who wants to understand the tragedy of this disease. The patient described has the schizoaffective subtype.

Talbott, John A. "Deinstitutionalization: Avoiding the Disasters of the Past." *Hospital and Community Psychiatry* 30 (1979): 621–24. Dr. Talbott, a past president of the American Psychiatric Association, is one of the few members of the psychiatric establishment who has fought for better care for the seriously mentally ill. He is author and editor of several pertinent books and articles (e.g., *The Death of the Asylum, The Chronic Mentally Ill*), but in this short article he succinctly captures the disastrous aspects of deinstitutionalization, e.g., "The chronic mentally ill patient had his locus of living and care transferred from a single lousy institution to multiple wretched ones."

Vonnegut, Mark. "Why I Want to Bite R. D. Laing." *Harper's* 248 (1974): 90–92. A whimsical essay by a young man who believed Ronald Laing's quixotic theories about psychosis until he himself experienced a psychotic episode. Recovered, Vonnegut decides that the most rational response is to bite Laing, and he carefully plans the event. He is especially acerbic about Laing's calling schizophrenia a political label and his glossing over the suffering: "What shouldn't be lost in the fascination [of studying schizophrenia] is the fact that schizophrenia is sheer hell for millions of people."

Walsh, Maryellen. *Schizophrenia: Straight Talk for Families and Friends.* New York: William Morrow, 1985. This is the best account to date of schizophrenia from the point of view of the parent of a person afflicted. Articulate and angry, yet able to maintain a sense of humor, Ms. Walsh describes confrontations with the ignorance and the indignities faced by families. There is familiarity and comfort in sharing her ordeals, and hope in joining her fight to change the system.

Wasow, Mona. "The Need for Asylum for the Chronically Mentally Ill." *Schizophrenia Bulletin* 12 (1986): 162–67. Dr. Wasow, a Professor of Social Work, explores the issues engendered by placing marginal patients in the community. "Is being filthy, alone, totally without structure and without human contact better than being in humane, unlocked institutional housing of some kind?" she asks. She describes the plight of her own son with schizophrenia as an example of someone who is considered to be a "success statistic" in bureaucratic terms because he has been rehospitalized only once in twelve years, yet because of his living conditions "success" is the last adjective which is humanely appropriate.

TEN WORST

Barnes, Mary, and Joseph Berke. *Mary Barnes: Two Accounts of a Journey Through Madness.* New York: Ballantine Books, 1973. This is the book that made Ronald Laing's approach to schizophrenia widely known. Schizophrenia, it says, is a "career" which is "launched with the aid and encouragement of one's immediate family." The family member with schizophrenia is often "the least disturbed member of the entire group." Moreover, suffering from schizophrenia can be a growth experience— "psychosis may be a state of reality, cyclic in nature, by which the self renews itself." There is no end to such absurd drivel in this book.

Bateson, Gregory, Don D. Jackson, Jay Haley, and John Weakland. "Toward a Theory of Schizophrenia." *Behavioral Science* 1 (1956): 251–64 and reprinted in several books, including *Beyond the Double Bind,* edited by Milton M. Berger, New York: Brunner Mazel, 1978. This paper gave birth to the double-bind, the heads-I-win-tails-you-lose method of family com-

378   APPENDIX A

munication which the authors "hypothesize goes on steadily from infantile beginnings in the family situation of individuals who become schizophrenic." The authors admitted that "this hypothesis has not been statistically tested" and in fact it never was; nevertheless, it was adopted as fact by two generations of mental health professionals who proceeded to blame the family (especially the mother) for causing the disease. Schizophrenia, say the authors, is "a way of dealing with double-bind situations to overcome their inhibiting and controlling effect." What seems incredible in retrospect is that theoretically intelligent people could postulate the symptoms of schizophrenia as the product of such relatively innocuous family communications. The fact that psychiatrists, psychologists, and social workers bought it—untested—is a scathing indictment of their intelligence quotient.

Boyer, L. Bryce, and Peter L. Giovacchini. *Psychoanalytic Treatment of Schizophrenic, Borderline and Characterological Disorders.* New York: Jason Aronson, 1980. When this book was published, it was overtly ridiculed in a review in the *American Journal of Psychiatry* as "anomalous, atavistic." Representative of a small number of books that continue to be published, it advocates insight-oriented psychotherapy as the treatment of choice for schizophrenia. Another such book, by Bertram P. Karon and Gary R. Van den Bos, is titled *Psychotherapy of Schizophrenia: Treatment of Choice* (New York: Jason Aronson, 1981). Overwhelming evidence indicates that insight-oriented psychotherapy is not "the treatment of choice" for schizophrenia; since some patients subjected to it actually get worse it might be said to be the non-treatment of choice. But do not throw these books away; store them in your attic and in just a few years they will be collectors' items of historic interest, like old books on phrenology.

Breggin, Peter. *Psychiatric Drugs: Hazards to the Brain.* New York: Springer, 1983. Dr. Breggin in the past has published two works of fiction as well as scientific books; this should be catalogued with the former. A mixture of Szasz, Laing, and misinformation, the book defines psychosis "as utter irresponsibility for one's own thought processes and personal conduct. It is the ultimate expression of personal failure or abject psychological helplessness." After thus blaming the patient for getting sick, Dr. Breggin then cites the reasons antipsychotic medication should not be used. He describes the drugs used to treat schizophrenia as poisons, specifically as "neurotoxins that impair and eventually destroy cellular function." Predictably, he also inveighs against involuntary hospitalization. The book is little known, and deserves its obscurity.

Green, Hannah. *I Never Promised You a Rose Garden.* New York: Holt, Rinehart and Winston, 1964. If a prize were to be given to the book which has produced the most confusion about schizophrenia over the past twenty years, this book would win going away. The young woman with schizophrenia (in fact her symptoms are much more characteristic of hysteria) is helped to become well by psychoanalytic psychotherapy. Such therapy is about as likely to cure schizophrenia as it is likely to cure multiple sclerosis. The book belongs in the Kingdom of Ur with the young woman's fantasies.

Hill, David. *The Politics of Schizophrenia: Psychiatric Oppression in the United States.* Lanham, MD: University Press of America, 1984. This book was a dissertation for a Doctorate in Clinical Psychology. Perhaps the most remarkable thing about it is that Dr. Hill was given the degree. Patients with schizophrenia are presented as political prisoners being tortured by psychiatrists to maintain the capitalist system. The table of contents alone is all one needs to read: "The Invention of Schizophrenia," "Psychiatry and the C.I.A.," "Psychiatrists Are Still Killing People." There is a lot of Szasz here, but it is Szasz without wit or erudition. The book drags on for 589 pages, and anyone who can finish it wins an award for masochism.

Lidz, Theodore, and Stephen Fleck. "Schizophrenia, Human Integration and the Role of the Family." In *The Etiology of Schizophrenia,* edited by Don D. Jackson, New York: Basic Books, 1960. Almost any one of the multitude of papers authored by Dr. Lidz and his colleagues qualifies for this list. This particular paper, however, has a memorable opening line in which it is stated that "schizophrenic patients virtually always emerge from homes marked by serious parental strife or eccentricity." Lidz and his colleagues drew their conclusions from a study of the families of 16 patients with schizophrenia: "In each family at least one parent suffered from serious and crippling psychopathology, and in many both were markedly disturbed . . . at least 10 of the 16 families contained a parent who was an ambulatory schizophrenic or clearly paranoid." Lidz et al. argued strongly against the bias of other researchers who blamed the mother for causing schizophrenia; in their families "the father appeared to be seriously disturbed just as often as the mother." It appears that no controls were used, and the scientific aspects of their studies are worthy of "Peter Pan"; it is doubtful if ever in the history of psychiatric research so many papers have been published on so few patients in studies of such doubtful scientific merit.

Rubin, Theodore I. *Lisa and David.* New York: Macmillan, 1961. This book is included because it became a movie (*David and Lisa*) and thus influenced a generation of thinking about schizophrenia. Lisa, a thirteen-year-old girl with "hebephrenic schizophrenia," and David, a fifteen-year-old boy with "pseudoneurotic schizophrenia," are eloquently described in their daily activities in a residential treatment center in 1959 and 1960. Unfortunately, the author is a psychoanalyst whose only plan for treatment for the two is continued psychotherapy until they can "become involved in problems of . . . neurotic defenses, sexuality, and family relations." The two case histories cry out for antipsychotic drug therapy, which was available in 1959 and 1960, but is nowhere to be seen. One only hopes that in the intervening years the families of Lisa and David have taken them out of such an anachronistic treatment facility and found them more up-to-date treatment.

Szasz, Thomas. *Schizophrenia: The Sacred Symbol of Psychiatry.* New York: Basic Books, 1976. Dr. Szasz is a charming and intelligent man who has made major contributions to psychiatric theory and practice. Unfortunately, schizophrenia is not included among these contributions. Page for page, this book probably contains more specious reasoning than any other book on the subject. Schizophrenia is one of the "fake diseases," says Szasz, another of the myths of mental illness. The only myth is that Dr. Szasz knows anything whatsoever about schizophrenia.

Tietze, Trude. "A Study of Mothers of Schizophrenic Patients." *Psychiatry* 12 (1949): 55–65. Although Frieda Fromm-Reichmann used the term "schizophrenogenic mother" in a paper one year prior to Tietze's paper, this study was usually referenced to justify the concept. It is a classic of pseudoscience and should be read in all eighth-grade science courses as an example of what science is not. Tietze interviewed twenty-five mothers of schizophrenic patients and freely admits that "in order to arrive at valid conclusions it would be necessary to compare the twenty-five mothers of this series with a control group of mothers who have never produced a schizophrenic child." Alas, she says, she could not find any controls. Furthermore the twenty-five mothers were "hostile and resented the psychiatrist" [Dr. Tietze] for blaming them for causing their children's illness. Dr. Tietze is not discouraged by these minor methodological problems, and proceeds to draw conclusions which must qualify as true hallucinations. Should be read only on days when one wishes to froth at the mouth.

APPENDIX
B

RESOURCES ON SCHIZOPHRENIA

Here is a compilation of helpful resources for persons with schizophrenia and their families.

- *National Alliance for the Mentally Ill (NAMI)* family support groups. These now exist all over the United States. They can be located by using the state AMI office (listed in appendix D) or by contacting the NAMI office at 1901 N. Fort Myer Drive, Suite 500, Arlington, VA 22209 (703-524-7600). Included within NAMI are the Sibling Support Network for brothers and sisters of persons with schizophrenia (P.O. Box 300040, Minneapolis, MN 55403), groups for spouses, and other groups such as HELP-MI for families of schizophrenics who are in jail or prison. In some states there are also local Mental Health Association chapters which are useful for families.
- *National Mental Health Consumer's Association (NMHCA)* composed of local groups of patients who have (or have had) schizophrenia or other serious mental illnesses. These groups are relatively new but growing and are very useful. For the address of the nearest group contact NMHCA, 311 South Juniper St., Room 902, Philadelphia, PA 19107; these are also listed in appendix D.
- *Schizophrenia Research Branch,* National Institute of Mental Health (NIMH), 5600 Fishers Lane, Rockville, MD 20857. This is the government organization which develops schizophrenia research projects in the United States. Since NIMH was reorganized in 1986 the Schizophrenia Research Branch has been much more effective. It publishes the *Schizophrenia Bulletin* and in 1986 made available a useful booklet called "Schizophrenia: Questions and Answers" which is available without charge from NIMH, Room 15c-05, 5600 Fishers Lane, Rockville, MD 20857.
- *National Alliance for Research on Schizophrenia and Depression (NARSAD)* is an organization to raise money for research on schizophrenia, manic-depressive psychosis and depression. It is composed of NAMI, the National Mental Health Association, the Schizophrenia Research Founda-

tion, and the National Depressive and Manic Depressive Association. Contributions can be made through NAMI, 1901 N. Fort Myer Drive, Suite 500, Arlington, VA 22209.

- *American Mental Health Fund,* Box 17389, Washington, D.C. 20041. This organization, founded by Mr. and Mrs. Jack Hinckley, raises funds for public education on schizophrenia and other serious mental disorders and conducts a campaign to reduce stigma.

- *Videotapes:* Many videotapes about schizophrenia and manic-depressive psychosis are available on both VHS and Beta, and more are in the making. Most have been created by local family support groups (both AMI and MHA) and by professional filmmakers for public television to illustrate the symptoms and tragedy of the disease. The best, in my opinion, is "Madness," which was done as Part 4 of "The Brain" series first shown on public television in 1985; it is a superb introduction to the disease. Others which are very good are "Promise," originally shown on CBS in 1986 on the Hallmark Playhouse, "Strange Voices," shown on NBC in 1987, and "When the Music Stopped," created by the Du Pont Corporation in 1987. Many videotapes are kept by family support groups for loan. Another type of videotape is that made as a training instrument, such as the eight-part series "Approaches to Psychosocial Rehabilitation" showing how to organize a psychosocial clubhouse; it was made by Fellowship House in South Miami, Florida.

- *Journals:* Professional journals and newsletters are useful for keeping abreast of research developments and new approaches to the treatment of schizophrenia. The best of these for families with an affected family member are:

Hospital and Community Psychiatry, a monthly publication of the American Psychiatric Association (1400 K Street, N.W., Washington, D.C. 20005).

Schizophrenia Bulletin, put out four times a year by the Schizophrenia Research Branch of NIMH (5600 Fishers Lane, Rockville, MD 20852). In 1987 a particularly useful special issue was published on "Schizophrenia: The Experience of Patients and Families."

Newsletters of many local chapters of the Alliance for the Mentally Ill (AMI) as well as the *NAMI News* put out by the national AMI (1901 N. Fort Myer Drive, Suite 500, Arlington, VA 22209).

There are several other professional journals which publish articles about schizophrenia. These include:

American Journal of Psychiatry
Archives of General Psychiatry
British Journal of Psychiatry
Canadian Journal of Psychiatry
Comprehensive Psychiatry

Integrative Psychiatry
Journal of Clinical Psychiatry
Journal of Nervous and Mental Diseases
Journal of Psychiatric Research
Mental Disability Law Reporter
Psychiatry Research
Psychological Bulletin
Psychological Medicine
Psychosocial Rehabilitation Journal
Schizophrenia Research

- *New Directions for Mental Health*, a quarterly series of paperback books published by Jossey-Bass Publishers, 433 California Street, San Francisco, CA 94104. The series is edited by Dr. H. Richard Lamb and contains many useful volumes describing mental health services for persons with schizophrenia.
- *The Information Exchange (TIE)* publishes *Tie-Lines* (a quarterly bulletin) and other publications concerning young adult chronic patients, most of whom have schizophrenia. Write to TIE, P.O. Box 1945, New City, NY 10956.
- *Intuition Press* publishes *Getting Better*, a quarterly bulletin on schizophrenia, as well as other publications such as *The Medication Maze*. Write to Intuition Press, P.O. Box 404, Keene, NH 03431.
- *Community Residences Information Services Program (CRISP)* is an information clearinghouse for agencies which are establishing residences for mentally or developmentally impaired persons (e.g., a community residence for persons with schizophrenia). They put out many publications relative to this subject. Write to CRISP, 66 Fulton Street, White Plains, NY 10606.
- *Compeer* is a program which matches volunteers in the community with psychiatric patients also living in the community. The two meet weekly to shop, go to the movies, or share some common interests. Begun in 1981, it has expanded rapidly. Write to Compeer, 797 Elmwood Ave., Rochester, NY 14620.

APPENDIX
C

CENTERS FOR
SCHIZOPHRENIA RESEARCH

The following list identifies the leading centers for schizophrenia research; in such facilities three or more researchers are working on this disease. Those centers marked with an asterisk are the most outstanding. Individuals are also doing good research on schizophrenia in other places not named below. Centers specializing in research on psychiatric disorders other than schizophrenia are also not included here. It should be noted that there is no necessary correlation between centers that do good research on schizophrenia and centers that provide good clinical care for this disease.

UNITED STATES

Baltimore	Maryland Psychiatric Research Center
	Johns Hopkins University
Boston	*McLean Hospital
	Massachusetts Mental Health Center
	Brockton VA Medical Center
	Boston University
Chicago	Illinois State Psychiatric Institute
Cleveland	Case Western Reserve University
Columbus	Ohio State University
Iowa City	University of Iowa
Irvine	University of California at Irvine
Los Angeles	*UCLA
New Haven	*Yale University
New York	New York University
	New York State Psychiatric Institute
	Mount Sinai–Bronx VA Medical Center
	*Long Island Jewish–Hillside Medical Center
	State University of New York at Stony Brook
Palo Alto	Stanford University

Philadelphia	University of Pennsylvania	
	Eastern Pennsylvania Psychiatric Institute	
Pittsburgh	University of Pittsburgh	
Richmond	Medical College of Virginia	
St. Louis	Washington University	
San Diego	University of California at San Diego	
Washington	*NIMH and WAW Research Division, St. Elizabeths Hospital	

OTHER COUNTRIES

Australia	*Melbourne*	Mental Health Research Institute
	Sydney	University of New South Wales
Austria	*Vienna*	University of Vienna
Bulgaria	*Sofia*	Institute of Psychiatry
Canada	*Edmonton*	Alberta Hospital
	Toronto	Clarke Institute
China	*Shanghai*	Shanghai Medical University
Denmark	*Aarhus*	Risskov Hospital
	Copenhagen	Kommunehospitalet
Finland	*Oulu*	University of Oulu
Germany	*Bonn*	University Nervenklinik
	Konstanz	University of Konstanz
	Mannheim	Central Institute of Mental Health
	Munich	Max Planck Institute for Psychiatry
		University of Munich
	Würzburg	University of Würzburg
Great Britain	*Edinburgh*	Royal Edinburgh Hospital
	London	*Northwick Park CRC
		*Institute of Psychiatry
		Charing Cross Hospital
	Newcastle	Newcastle General Hospital
	Nottingham	University of Nottingham
Italy	*Milan*	Institute of Clinical Psychiatry
Sweden	*Goteborg*	University of Goteborg
	Lund/Malmo	University of Lund
	Stockholm	*Karolinska Hospital
Switzerland	*Bern*	University Hospital
	Geneva	WHO Division of Mental Health
	Zurich	University Hospitals
USSR	*Moscow*	Institute of Psychiatry

APPENDIX
D

INFORMATION ON
INDIVIDUAL STATES

The following is a brief synopsis of relevant information on the seriously mentally ill for each state. It includes the following:

AMI Family State Contacts. These are the state organizations of the Alliance for the Mentally Ill (AMI), the support and advocacy groups for families of individuals with schizophrenia, manic-depressive psychosis, and other serious mental illnesses. There are over 800 local AMI chapters in the United States. To learn more about your local group, write to the state contact listed below or to NAMI, 1901 N. Fort Myer Drive, Suite 500, Arlington, VA 22209.

NMHCA State Contacts. These are contacts for local affiliates of the National Mental Health Consumer's Association (NMHCA), the support and advocacy group of patients, ex-patients, clients, and consumers from state psychiatric systems. Formed in 1985, the group is growing rapidly. Interested individuals should contact the state affiliate listed below or NMHCA, 311 S. Juniper St., Rm. 902, Philadelphia, PA 19107.

State Public Psychiatric Systems. This is a brief description of the strengths and weaknesses of each state system as of 1987. It should be emphasized that the evaluations only refer to services for the seriously mentally ill, and states may rate quite differently in services for other groups (e.g., children or substance abusers). It should also be emphasized that such state systems change. For a 1988 update see *Care of the Seriously Mentally Ill: A Rating of State Programs,* 1988 edition, to be published in September, 1988 (Health Research Group, 2000 P Street, N.W., Washington, D.C. 20036).

Commitment Laws. This provides a brief synopsis of changes since 1983 in state laws for the involuntary commitment of mentally ill persons. It is an updating of the information on commitment in appendix A of the first edition of this book. Legislation for additional changes is pending in several states. For a general discussion of commitment laws see chapters 7 and 11.

ALABAMA

AMI Family Support Groups. Alabama AMI, 2061 Fire Pink Court, Birmingham, AL 35244.

NMHCA State Contacts. NMHCA, 311 S. Juniper St., #902, Philadelphia, PA 19107.

State Public Psychiatric System. In 1985 a U.S. District judge released Alabama's mental health system from 14 years of federal supervision, thereby ending the landmark *Wyatt* v. *Stickney* court case. Symbolically, it marked the transition of Alabama from disgrace to respectability. The Department of Mental Health and Mental Retardation has made impressive efforts, which are evident, for example, in Bryce and Searcy state hospitals. An increasingly strong AMI state group has helped. Resources remain thin in this state, however, with some areas (e.g., Birmingham) comparatively well-off while others (e.g., Huntsville) have very few.

Commitment Laws. No recent major changes.

ALASKA

AMI Family Support Groups. Alaska AMI, P.O. Box 2543, Fairbanks, AK 99707.

NMHCA State Contacts. Mental Health Consumers of Alaska, 406 G Street, Suite 2016, Anchorage, AK 99501.

State Public Psychiatric System. The delivery of good psychiatric services to a population spread out in a state this size is a herculean undertaking. Although overcrowded, the Alaska Psychiatric Institute in Anchorage is quite good as state hospitals go. Outpatient facilities, under twenty-seven locally controlled community mental health centers, are uneven and residential facilities for discharged patients seriously deficient with rare exceptions. Homeless mentally ill, abundant on the streets of Anchorage, are saved from the elements by the impressive dignity of the Brother Francis public shelter.

Commitment Laws. Outpatient commitment authorized as a less restrictive alternative for patients meeting the civil commitment criteria, if the alternative treatment program accepts the patient.

ARIZONA

AMI Family Support Groups. Arizona AMI, P.O. Box 60756, Phoenix, AZ 85032.

NMHCA State Contacts. Survivors On Our Own, 6545 N. 19th Ave., #C-40, Phoenix, AZ 85015.

State Public Psychiatric System. Arizona is distinguished by spending less per capita for its public psychiatric care system than any other state. The results are predictable, with virtually no outpatient or aftercare services and a 1985 state court order ordering Maricopa County (Phoenix) to provide services. In 1986 state legislation was enacted to improve the psychiatric care system and new leadership was brought into the Division of Behavioral Health; one hopes this is the start of long-overdue improvements.

Commitment Laws. The definition of "danger to others" was changed in 1985 to mean that the judgment of a person who has a mental disorder is so impaired that he is unable to understand his need for treatment and as a result of his mental disorder his continued behavior can reasonably be expected, on the basis of competent medical opinion, to result in serious physical harm. The term "gravely disabled" was added to the law, and it was defined as a condition evidenced by behavior in which a person, as a result of a mental disorder, is likely to come to serious physical harm or serious illness because he is unable to provide for his basic physical needs such as food, clothing, and shelter. Outpatient commitment was explicitly authorized in 1983 as a dispositional alternative for patients who meet the civil commitment criteria. Extensive provisions are included for administering the provision, indicating that it could be used in the future but to date has not been widely used.

ARKANSAS

AMI Family Support Groups. Arkansas AMI, Help and Hope Inc., Hendrix Hall 125, 4313 W. Markham, Little Rock, AR 72201.

NMHCA State Contacts. NMHCA, 311 S. Juniper St., #902, Philadelphia, PA 19107.

State Public Psychiatric System. The Arkansas State Hospital in Little Rock is among the better in the nation. Outpatient services vary in quality, with some community mental health centers accepting responsibility for the seriously mentally ill, while others do not. Psychosocial rehabilitation centers have been started (e.g., Pinnacle House in Little Rock) but need to be spread more widely. Overall, Arkansas ranks high compared with other states, and a strong state AMI group has helped.

Commitment Laws. Outpatient commitment was authorized in 1983 as a dispositional alternative for patients meeting the civil commitment criteria, if the person has been involuntarily committed within the past two years and the mental illness has been treated successfully with medication in the past. Legislation was also passed in 1987 to enable commitments to community placements without previous institutionalization, utilizing the same civil commitment standard, which includes a grave disability provision. The new law also mandates patient treatment plans; in the event of noncompliance, the patient can be brought in by police officers for another commitment hearing. The Arkansas law appears to be a good model for other states.

CALIFORNIA

AMI Family Support Groups. California AMI, 2306 J St., #203, Sacramento, CA 95816.

NMHCA State Contacts. NMHCA, 311 S. Juniper St., #902, Philadelphia, PA 19107.

State Public Psychiatric System. In the 1950s it was regarded as the best overall system in the United States, but California fell mightily under the governorships of Brown and Reagan. State hospitals were closed but community facilities and aftercare were not developed. There are sure to be good programs in such a huge and sprawling state, in which program responsibilities are decentralized to the fifty-eight counties; San Mateo, Marin, Napa, and Yolo counties have excellent programs, while others such as Monterey, San Francisco, and Los Angeles counties are disaster areas. Strong Alliance for the Mentally Ill and Mental Health Association groups pressure for improvements but they are slow in coming. The hordes of homeless mentally ill on the streets of Los Angeles bear mute testimony to a system which has failed.

Commitment Laws. The state considered but did not enact in 1986 legislation to broaden the current definition of "gravely disabled" to include deterioration without continued treatment and substantial likelihood that the person would not accept treatment voluntarily.

COLORADO

AMI Family Support Groups. Colorado AMI, 1100 Fillmore St., Denver, CO 80206.

NMHCA State Contacts. Denver Mental Health Consumers Support Group, 611 Marion, Denver, CO 80218.

State Public Psychiatric System. Colorado demonstrates the importance of strong consumer groups (Alliance for the Mentally Ill and Mental Health Association) combined with good leadership in the state Division of Mental Health; together they have made Colorado among the most highly rated states for the care of the seriously mentally ill. The state hospital in Pueblo, once an embarrassment, is now among the better state hospitals in the country. State law gives priority to the seriously mentally ill for mental health services, and the state mental health agency was the first to achieve designation as a federal housing authority. There are problems, to be sure, such as the mentally ill homeless on the streets of Denver, but compared with other states Colorado services rank high.

Commitment Laws. No recent major changes.

CONNECTICUT

AMI Family Support Groups. Connecticut AMI, 284 Battis Rd., Hamden, CT 06514.

NMHCA State Contacts. NMHCA, 311 S. Juniper St., #902, Philadelphia, PA 19107.

State Public Psychiatric System. Forty years ago Connecticut was regarded as one of the best state systems for the care of the seriously mentally ill for its time. It is not as good now, although still above average by national standards. Resources have been allocated disproportionately to the four regional state hospitals which are fully accredited. Aftercare and outpatient facilities, however, have been insufficiently developed, with community mental health centers not providing leadership for services for the seriously mentally ill.

Commitment Laws. No recent major changes.

DELAWARE

AMI Family Support Groups. AMI of Delaware, 3705 Concord Pike, Wilmington, DE 19803.

NMHCA State Contacts. NMHCA, 311 S. Juniper St., #902, Philadelphia, PA 19107.

State Public Psychiatric System. In 1948 the Delaware state mental health system was called one of the five best in the United States. Since that time it has been all downhill, so that by 1980 the state was relying heavily on unlicensed foreign medical graduates to staff the system. In the mid-1980s new leadership was brought into the Division of Alcohol, Drug Addiction and Mental Health and improvements began. How long the climb back to respectability will take depends in large measure on the strength of the AMI advocacy group and the will of the state's political leadership.

Commitment Laws. Outpatient commitment is now explicitly authorized as a dispositional alternative for patients meeting the civil commitment criteria.

DISTRICT OF COLUMBIA

AMI Family Support Groups. Threshold D.C. AMI, 422 8th St., S.E., Washington, D.C. 20003.

NMHCA State Contacts. Our Turn, 3169 Mt. Pleasant St., N.W., Washington, D.C. 20010.

District Public Psychiatric System. Those who believe that there is a correlation between money spent and quality of care for the seriously mentally ill need only visit the District of Columbia to have their thinking corrected. Outpatient and aftercare services are probably the worst in the nation despite huge budgets. St. Elizabeths Hospital is average in quality. There are rays of light, however, including the Green Door clubhouse and Anchor Club programs. Moreover, in October, 1987, the St. Elizabeths Hospital inpatient facility was finally merged with the District's outpatient program. The fact is that there is nowhere to go but up.

Commitment Laws. For patients meeting the civil commitment criteria, the court may order hospitalization or any alternative course of treatment in the best interests of the person or of the public. A published report on the use of outpatient commitment in the District of Columbia claimed that it decreased readmissions and length of hospital stays for patients.

FLORIDA

AMI Family Support Groups. Florida AMI, 400 S. Dixie Highway, Lake Worth, FL 33460.

NMHCA State Contacts. SHARE, 2609 Gorda Bella Ave., St. Augustine, FL 32086.

State Public Psychiatric System. The improvement in Florida's public psychiatric system in recent years is impressive. The state hospitals, once considered among the nation's worst, are now respectable. Outpatient services vary widely but local programs, such as Boley Inc. in St. Petersburg, are impressive. Florida is also the only state to systematically develop clubhouses to be used for psychosocial rehabilitation in all regions of the state, patterned after Fellowship House in South Miami.

Commitment Laws. No recent major changes.

GEORGIA

AMI Family Support Groups. Georgia AMI, 1362 W. Peachtree St., N.W., Atlanta, GA 30309.

NMHCA State Contacts. Alternative Atlanta, 1420 Southland Vista Ct., Apt. F, Atlanta, GA 30329.

State Public Psychiatric System. In 1948 an attendant at the Central State Hospital was quoted as saying that "a patient who could get well here could get well just as easy if he were lost out in the Okefenokee Swamp." Georgia's public psychiatric system has come a long way since that time but still has a way to go. Outpatient services, housing, vocational opportunities and rehabilitation for released patients are all deficient with the exception of a few mental health centers that are trying hard. The homeless mentally ill on Atlanta's streets bear testimony to the deficiencies of the system.

Commitment Laws. In 1985 the state enacted an explicit alternative disposition provision to allow courts to order outpatient treatment. In 1986, Georgia became the third state to enact a preventive commitment statute, enabling courts to order involuntary outpatient treatment directly from the community for patients who do not meet the commitment standard for inpatient treatment. An outpatient is defined as a person who is mentally ill and who will require outpatient treatment in order to avoid predictably and imminently becoming an inpatient; who, because of the person's mental status, mental history, or nature of his or her mental illness is unable to voluntarily seek or comply with outpatient treatment; and who is in need of involuntary treatment.

A wide variety of treatments are included in addition to medication, with the purpose of alleviating or treating the mental illness so as to maintain his functioning and prevent his becoming an inpatient. Physicians at CMHCs or state hospitals may initiate such treatment for persons who have never been hospitalized if they determine that the patient meets the stated definition, confirm that appropriate outpatient treatment is available, consider whether the person will comply with the proposed treatment, and prepare (with the outpatient facility) a treatment plan. The state already had an explicit authorization for outpatient treatment as a dispositional alternative for patients who meet the civil commitment criteria.

HAWAII

AMI Family Support Groups. Hawaii Families and Friends of Schizophrenics, Inc., P.O. Box 10532, Honolulu, HI 96816.

NMHCA State Contacts. Office of United Self-Help, 3627 Kilauea, Honolulu, HI 96816.

State Public Psychiatric System. Despite having abundant mental health professionals and a setting that should make it easy to attract good talent, the Hawaii state public psychiatric system is among the worst in the country. The state hospital has been allowed to deteriorate badly, while outpatient and community services have not been well developed. The few good pieces in the care system are fragmented, and continuity of care almost nonexistent. More optimistically, new leadership in 1987, renovations of the hospital which are under way, and active consumer advocacy groups (both the AMI Hawaii Families and Friends of Schizophrenics and the Mental Health Association) promise improvements in the near future.

Commitment Laws. In 1985 the state added the term "gravely disabled" as a criterion for involuntary hospitalization, defining it as a condition in which a person, as a result of mental disorder, is unable to provide for his or her own personal needs for food, clothing, or shelter, and is unable to make or communicate rational or responsible decisions concerning his or her personal welfare, and lacks the capacity to understand the need to do so.

In 1986, the legislature added another criterion—"obviously ill"— defined as a condition "in which a person's current behavior and previous history of mental illness, if known, indicate a serious mental or emotional illness, and the person is incapable of understanding the risks to health and safety involved in refusing treatment, the advantages of accepting treatment, and the alternatives to the particular treatment offered, after the advantages, risks, and alternatives have been explained to the person." Questions have been raised about the constitutionality of the "obviously ill" criteria. For outpatient commitment in 1984 Hawaii enacted the second preventive commitment law (after North Carolina), enabling people to be committed directly from the community. Its stated purpose was to enable the family court to order outpatient treatment for mentally ill individuals who need treatment but are incapable of deciding to voluntarily seek or comply with such treatment. The outpatient treatment may be ordered only if the person is in need of treatment to prevent a relapse or deterioration that would result in his becoming imminently dangerous to himself or others, if the current illness or disorder limits or negates his ability to make an informed decision to voluntarily seek treatment, *and* there is a reasonable prospect that outpatient treatment will be beneficial. Outpatient commitment has been little used to date.

IDAHO

AMI Family Support Groups. NAMI, 1901 N. Fort Myer Dr., Suite 500, Arlington, VA 22209.

NMHCA State Contacts. NMHCA, 311 S. Juniper St., #902, Philadelphia, PA 19107.

State Public Psychiatric System. Idaho is a large state with a small and widely dispersed population. Services for the seriously mentally ill are made even more difficult to deliver by the fact that the state has fewer psychiatrists and psychologists per capita than any state except Mississippi. The Department of Health and Welfare is attempting to improve the state hospitals at Blackfoot and Orofino but outpatient and rehabilitative services are sadly lacking. A strong AMI advocacy group is badly needed.

Commitment Laws. No recent major changes.

ILLINOIS

AMI Family Support Groups. AMI Illinois State Coalition, P.O. Box 863, Glenview, IL 60025.

NMHCA State Contacts. NMHCA, 311 S. Juniper St., #902, Philadelphia, PA 19107.

State Public Psychiatric System. "Neglected" is a succinct summary of the Illinois state mental hospitals and outpatient system, allowed to slowly deteriorate over the past 15 years. It is a low priority with recent governors and with a state legislature that refuses to provide funds for its adequate operation (Illinois is thirty-eighth in per capita expenditures for its mental health system despite being ninth in per capita income). Good programs exist, of course; Thresholds and The Bridge programs in Chicago are excellent, and counties such as McHenry offer good services but these stand in sharp contrast to the meager programs available for most of the seriously mentally ill in the state.

Commitment Laws. Outpatient commitment is now explicitly authorized as a dispositional alternative for patients who meet the civil commitment criteria, with extensive instructions regarding administration.

INDIANA

AMI Family Support Groups. Indiana AMI, Box 8186, Fort Wayne, IN 46808.

NMHCA State Contacts. Great Lakes Network Against Psychiatric Assault, P.O. Box 247, Huntington, IN 46750.

State Public Psychiatric System. Care for the seriously mentally ill in Indiana is of average quality despite good leadership in the Department of Mental Health. The major impediment to improving services has been the state's thirty CMHCs, which have shown little interest in the seriously mentally ill. Patients have regularly been discharged from the five state hospitals and then provided with very few community services.

Commitment Laws. Legislation was being actively considered in 1987 to expand the definition of gravely disabled and to authorize outpatient commitment.

IOWA

AMI Family Support Groups. Iowa AMI, 6521 Merle Hay Rd., Johnston, IA 50131.

NMHCA State Contacts. Darline M. Brown, MHA of Iowa, 3116 Ingersoll Ave., Des Moines, IA 50312.

State Public Psychiatric System. The Iowa state system for the care of the seriously mentally ill is among the more highly regarded in the United

States. It is completely decentralized, with program and fiscal responsibility vested at the county level. Its four state hospitals are above average and its program for the criminally insane highly rated. Iowa's biggest deficiency is a system of county homes in which the seriously mentally ill are often placed; many are less than therapeutic.

Commitment Laws. Outpatient commitment is now explicitly authorized as a dispositional alternative for patients who meet the civil commitment criteria.

KANSAS

AMI Family Support Groups. Kansas Families for Mental Health AMI, 4811 W. 77th Place, Prairie Village, KS 66208.

NMHCA State Contacts. LINC, 477 E. Loula, #4, Olathe, KS 66061.

State Public Psychiatric System. Kansas' three state hospitals are below average by national standards but its outpatient system is above average. A few of the community mental health centers, such as the one at High Plains, have been cited for excellence. The private Menninger Foundation in Topeka, mired in anachronistic psychoanalytic treatment programs, is influential and has slowed the state's program toward improving programs for the seriously mentally ill. Kansas also spends less on its mental health programs, compared to the state's per capita income, than most other states.

Commitment Laws. As part of sweeping changes to the civil commitment act in 1986, the legislature changed the definition of a mentally ill person from one who *is* dangerous to himself or others, to a new definition of one who is suffering from a severe mental disorder, lacks capacity to make an informed decision concerning treatment, and is *likely* to cause harm to self or others. The prospect of harm is further defined as likely in the foreseeable future to cause *substantial* physical injury or abuse to self or others or substantial damage to another's property; or who is substantially unable, except for reasons of indigency, to provide basic needs, thus causing a substantial deterioration of the person's ability to function.

The 1986 amendments also allow the court to enter an order for outpatient treatment (dispositional alternative) only if it finds that the patient is not likely to cause harm to self or others.

KENTUCKY

AMI Family Support Groups. Kentucky AMI, 145 Constitution Ave., Lexington, KY 40508.

NMHCA State Contacts. Just Friends, 33 E. 7th St., #200, Covington, KY 41011.

State Public Psychiatric System. Kentucky overall ranks above average in its state system for the seriously mentally ill, although it has problems. Its three regional state hospitals have been able to remain fully accredited despite chronic nursing shortages and past reliance on physicians not fully licensed. Community resources for patients discharged from the hospitals are limited but there are a series of clubhouses, such as Cardinal House in Richmond.

Commitment Laws. No recent major changes.

LOUISIANA

AMI Family Support Groups. Louisiana AMI, 1633 Letitia, Baton Rouge, LA 70808.

NMHCA State Contacts. Kendall Williams, 8060 Stroelitz St., New Orleans, LA 70125.

State Public Psychiatric System. With very few psychiatrists and psychologists per capita, and grossly inadequate community housing for discharged patients, Louisiana has more than its share of problems. Its four state hospitals are below average but improving, yet coordination of care with outpatient facilities is seriously deficient. There clearly are individuals in the Department of Health and Human Resources working to bring improvements, but the consumer groups such as AMI will have to bring more pressure to bear.

Commitment Laws. No recent major changes.

MAINE

AMI Family Support Groups. Maine State AMI, P.O. Box 5057, Augusta, ME 04330.

NMHCA State Contacts. LINC Social Club, 27 Weston St., Augusta, ME 04330.

State Public Psychiatric System. Throughout the early 1980s Maine improved steadily in its programs for the seriously mentally ill. An interested governor, excellent leadership in the Department of Mental Health and Mental Retardation, and an active AMI group were major reasons, while the state legislature was generous in providing program funds in this relatively poor state. Although old, the two state hospitals have been rehabilitated, while some rural programs in northern Maine are considered to be very good by national standards. Overall, Maine ranks high.

Commitment Laws. No recent major changes.

MARYLAND

AMI Family Support Groups. AMI of Maryland, Inc., 2500 N. Charles St., Baltimore, MD 21218.

NMHCA State Contacts. On Our Own, 213 Monroe St., Rockville, MD 20850.

State Public Psychiatric System. A decade ago the Maryland state hospitals were among the worst in the United States. They are substantially better now, partly due to an innovative program set up by the University of Maryland School of Medicine to recruit and retain competent psychiatrists to staff the hospitals. Outpatient services vary widely in quality, with good rehabilitation programs available in some locations (e.g., Way Station in Frederick, Omni House in Glen Burnie) but not elsewhere. A Consumer Coalition for Citizens with Longterm Mental Illnesses, comprising AMI groups, NMHCA groups, and others, makes an effective model for other states to follow.

Commitment Laws. The state has considered but not passed legislation to permit preventive outpatient commitment. A report to the governor on the subject in February, 1986, concluded that there was no need for statutory change. A pilot project on increased use of conditional release was initiated.

MASSACHUSETTS

AMI Family Support Groups. AMI of Massachusetts, Inc., 34½ Beacon St., Boston, MA 02108.

NMHCA State Contacts. Massachusetts Association of Social Clubs, P.O. Box 9216, Boston, MA 02114.

State Public Psychiatric System. A state that was once proud of its psychiatric services and state mental hospitals, Massachusetts slid downhill progressively during the 1970s and early 1980s. Its ignominy became public in 1985 when Worcester State Hospital became the first state mental hospital in the United States to be sued by the U.S. Department of Justice for "causing such residents to suffer grievous harm." This is even more embarrassing because Massachusetts has more psychiatrists and psychologists per capita than any other state. Things may improve, however, under Governor Dukakis, who in 1986 announced a major program to improve psychiatric services. There are isolated but solid programs on which to build, including good clubhouses (e.g., The Lighthouse in Springfield) and growing AMI family groups, who are demanding improvements.

Commitment Laws. No recent major changes.

MICHIGAN

AMI Family Support Groups. State AMI of Michigan, P.O. Box 51102, Livonia, MI 48151.

NMHCA State Contacts. Bernie Elbinger, 10574 Park Terrace, Detroit, MI 48204.

State Public Psychiatric System. Michigan's state hospital system was subject to a continuing series of scandals throughout the early 1980s. Outpatient and community services for the seriously mentally ill were not much better, except for occasional model programs under the Community Support Program. Despite a concerned governor and reasonably good leadership in the Department of Mental Health, the state has not yet taken major steps to turn the system around.

Commitment Laws. Outpatient commitment is now authorized as a dispositional alternative for patients who meet the civil commitment criteria, with extensive instructions for administration.

MINNESOTA

AMI Family Support Groups. Mental Health Advocates Coalition of Minnesota, Inc., 265 Fort Rd., St. Paul, MN 55102.

NMHCA State Contacts. Strive Inc., 328 E. Hennepin Ave., Minneapolis, MN 55414.

State Public Psychiatric System. Two decades ago Minnesota was nationally regarded as a leader in public psychiatric services. All that is but a distant memory in a state where services have deteriorated alarmingly. A 1986 report from the Governor's Mental Health Commission described the state system as "divided, inconsistent, uncoordinated, undirected, unaccountable, and without a unified direction"; it led directly to a series of public hearings throughout the state. Programs that focus on the seriously mentally ill (e.g., Range Community Mental Health Center) are sparse. There is now a consensus that the system must be improved, a necessary first step toward action. The homeless mentally ill living beneath the bridges of Minneapolis and St. Paul would certainly like to see the next steps taken.

Commitment Laws. Outpatient commitment was considered by the legislature in 1986, but did not pass.

MISSISSIPPI

AMI Family Support Groups. NAMI, 1901 N. Fort Myer Dr., Suite 500, Arlington, VA 22209.

NMHCA State Contacts. NMHCA, 311 S. Juniper St., #902, Philadelphia, PA 19107.

State Public Psychiatric System. Mississippi needs everything. It has fewer mental health professionals per population than any other state. Its per capita income is lower than any other state by almost a thousand dollars per person. The state hospitals in Meridian and Whitfield are seriously deficient. Outpatient and community services are not much better; community mental health centers which do exist often focus their efforts on psychotherapy for the worried well rather than providing services for the seriously mentally ill. A strong consumer advocacy movement would be the first step toward turning around this sorry state of affairs.

Commitment Laws. Outpatient commitment is now explicitly authorized as an alternative disposition, including various levels of treatment, or placement in the custody of a friend or relative.

MISSOURI

AMI Family Support Groups. Missouri Coalition of AMI, 10 Blackpool Lane, St. Louis, MO 63132.

NMHCA State Contacts. Project Share, 13339 Rosebank, St. Louis, MO 63122.

State Public Psychiatric System. Services vary widely for the seriously mentally ill in Missouri. For inpatients Western, Malcolm Bliss, and the Mid-Missouri Mental Health Center are reasonably good, Fulton and St. Louis State average in quality, while Farmington, St. Joseph, and Nevada are well below average. Outpatient facilities run a similarly wide range, with some community mental health centers having neglected their responsibility for patients with psychoses. Coordination between the hospitals and community mental health centers is also badly needed.

Commitment Laws. No recent major changes.

MONTANA

AMI Family Support Groups. MONAMI, P.O. Box 1021, Helena, MT 59624.

NMHCA State Contacts. Montana Mental Health CAP, Inc., 17 W. Meadow St., Billings, MT 59102.

State Public Psychiatric System. To deliver good psychiatric services to fewer than a million people spread over a state the size of Montana is virtually impossible. The state is divided into five mental health center regions, some of which are larger than small states. Throughout the 1970s Montana State Hospital was a traditional custodial facility and the state's community mental health centers ignored the seriously mentally ill. In 1981 the Department of Institutions established a new system of reimbursement to encourage the centers to care for these patients, and since then services have steadily improved. The newly built unit for the criminally insane at the state hospital should also improve things.

Commitment Laws. Legislation was under consideration in 1987 to expand the definition of mental illness to include more extensive grave disability criteria. Outpatient commitment is now authorized as a dispositional alternative for patients meeting the civil commitment criteria.

NEBRASKA

AMI Family Support Groups. AMI of Nebraska, 122 Westridge Ave., Bellevue, NE 68005.

NMHCA State Contacts. NMHCA, 311 S. Juniper St., #902, Philadelphia, PA 19107.

State Public Psychiatric System. Nebraska's system of care for the seriously mentally ill is above average compared to the rest of the country, yet not in the same class as neighboring Colorado. The three state hospitals (called regional centers) in Hastings, Lincoln, and Norfolk are reasonably good. Outpatient services bear the responsibility of six regional community health programs which do not always coordinate their care with that of the hospitals and have insufficient funds compared with the hospitals. There are six clubhouses; Cirrhus House in Scottsbluff and Liberty Center in Norfolk are especially good. An ongoing struggle between state and local mental health officials continues over the allocation of state funds.

Commitment Laws. Outpatient commitment is now authorized as a dispositional alternative for patients meeting the civil commitment criteria.

NEVADA

AMI Family Support Groups. Nevada AMI, P.O. Box 15445, Las Vegas, NV 89114.

NMHCA State Contacts. NMHCA, 311 S. Juniper St., #902, Philadelphia, PA 19107.

State Public Psychiatric System. Although the Division of Mental Hygiene and Mental Retardation has designated the chronically mentally ill as the top priority, the services in Nevada vary widely. In the south (Las Vegas and Clark County) a major effort has been made to provide community-based services including day treatment, housing, and case management. In the north (Reno and Washoe County), on the other hand, services continue to center on the aging state hospital with aftercare services poorly developed.

Commitment Laws. No recent major changes.

NEW HAMPSHIRE

AMI Family Support Group. NAMI in New Hampshire, P.O. Box 544, Peterborough, NH 03458.

NMHCA State Contacts. NMHCA, 311 S. Juniper St., #902, Philadelphia, PA 19107.

State Public Psychiatric System. New Hampshire has considerably improved services for the seriously mentally ill in recent years and rests among the more highly rated states. It has slowly phased out the antiquated state hospital, replacing it with a modern acute-care facility attached to the general hospital. An active AMI family support group has been a definite asset and has worked with state personnel and the Joint Commission on Accreditation of Hospitals (JCAH) to set up an innovative system for monitoring outpatient care. Clubhouses such as Friendship House in Dover have also helped.

Commitment Laws. Outpatient commitment has been authorized as a dispositional alternative for patients meeting the civil commitment criteria.

NEW JERSEY

AMI Family Support Groups. New Jersey AMI, 400 Route 1, #10, Monmouth Junction, NJ, 08852

NMHCA Support Groups. New Jersey Coalition of Mental Health Consumers, 906 Grand Ave., Asbury Park, NJ 07712.

State Public Psychiatric System. Following World War II, New Jersey was cited as having one of the nation's best mental health state systems. The state went steeply downhill in the 1960s and 1970s, especially the state hospitals, in which care deteriorated badly. In recent years good leadership in the Division of Mental Health and Hospitals has put New Jersey on the upswing. The Community Support System program is excellent although outpatient services under the twenty-one county boards are very uneven. Residential facilities for discharged patients are sadly lacking although a few clubhouses (e.g., The Club in Piscataway) provide good rehabilitative services for a small number of patients.

Commitment Laws. As of 1987 the state was considering significant reform legislation.

NEW MEXICO

AMI Family Support Groups. AMI–New Mexico, P.O. Box 9049, Santa Fe, NM 87504.

NMHCA State Contacts. NMHCA, 311 S. Juniper St., #902, Philadelphia, PA 19107.

State Public Psychiatric System. New Mexico's inpatient and outpatient system for individuals with serious mental illnesses is among the worst in the country. The state hospital in Las Vegas has been used as a jobs program by local legislators, while aftercare services and housing have been minimally developed. Signs of improvement appeared in the mid-1980s, when a capable superintendent took charge of the hospital and a five-year plan for developing community services was adopted. An active state AMI family support group has provided important advocacy; they will need all the help they can get to turn this state around, but a start has clearly been made.

Commitment Laws. Outpatient commitment is explicitly authorized as a dispositional alternative for patients who meet the civil commitment criteria.

NEW YORK

AMI Family Support Groups. AMI of New York State, 121 Wawanda Ave., Liberty, NY 12754.

NMHCA State Contacts. NMHCA, 311 S. Juniper St., #902, Philadelphia, PA 19107.

State Public Psychiatric System. It is difficult to generalize about a state psychiatric system as large as New York's but two facts stand out: it spends more per capita than any other state (except the District of Columbia) and achieves only average results. It is a system known for its bureaucracy and the strength of employees' unions, which have prevented resources from being shifted from the thirty-three state hospital units to community programs. Governor Cuomo has shown little interest and the system muddles on from year to year. In such a large system there are bright lights, to be certain: Rockland and Monroe counties; a system of clubhouses featuring the original Fountain House and twenty-one others (e.g., Bridges in Watertown, Four Seasons Club in Binghamton); and the Compeer program in Rochester. However, the homeless mentally ill on New York City's streets are the most accurate overall barometer of the system.

Commitment Laws. In 1986 the legislature considered but did not pass a bill to require a pilot involuntary outpatient treatment program. New York is the only state with a specific statutory prohibition on court-ordered involuntary outpatient commitment. It defines "in need of involuntary care and treatment" as having "a mental illness for which care and treatment in a hospital is essential." However, it does have conditional release.

NORTH CAROLINA

AMI Family Support Groups. North Carolina AMI, 4900 Water Edge Dr., Raleigh, NC 27606.

NMHCA State Contacts. NMHCA, 311 S. Juniper St., #902, Philadelphia, PA 19107.

State Public Psychiatric System. North Carolina has four reasonably good state hospitals at Morganton, Goldsboro, Raleigh, and Butner, and improving outpatient services. Clubhouses offering psychosocial rehabilitation for released patients have been developed (e.g., The Threshold in Durham), although housing and vocational training lag badly. The increasingly strong AMI support groups have provided an important impetus to improving the state system.

Commitment Laws. Inpatient commitment criteria were modified in 1985, when the legislature revised the definition of "dangerousness" to consider extreme destruction of property as dangerous to others and to allow previous episodes of dangerousness to self or others to be considered in determining predictability of future dangerousness. In 1983 North Carolina came to national attention when it became the first state to put into law a procedure for outpatient commitment directly from the community for patients who do not meet the criteria for involuntary inpatient commitment. The physician can recommend outpatient commitment if the patient is found to be mentally ill but capable of surviving safely with available supervision and treatment to prevent further disability or deterioration, which would result in dangerousness to self or others, and the patient's current mental status or the nature of the illness limits or negates his ability to make an informed decision to seek or comply with recommended treatment. A court hearing is required, but because of the lesser deprivation of liberty, counsel is provided only where the issues are complex or the patient is unable to speak for himself. The state's Mental Health Study Commission has analyzed experience under the new outpatient commitment system, finding that: (1) the program is underfunded and underutilized, (2) it is difficult to create supportive services in areas that are skeptical about preventive commitment, (3) use differs widely in different areas, and (4) commitments that continued beyond the first ninety days were likely to last indefinitely.

NORTH DAKOTA

AMI Family Support Groups. NAMI, 1901 N. Fort Myer Dr., Suite 500, Arlington, VA 22209.

NMHCA State Contacts. Therapeutic Community, 1808 Continental Dr., #304, Grand Forks, ND 58201.

State Public Psychiatric System. Except for a reasonably good state hospital at Jamestown, North Dakota has little to offer in services for the seriously mentally ill. Community mental health centers are not interested in these patients and coordination between inpatient and outpatient services is very poor. The state could surely use a strong advocacy group.

Commitment Laws. Outpatient commitment is authorized as a dispositional alternative for patients meeting the civil commitment criteria.

OHIO

AMI Family Support Groups. AMI of Ohio, 360 S. Third St., #102, Columbus, OH 43215.

NMHCA State Contacts. Clients for Better Care, 1038 Roseland Ave., Dayton, OH 45407.

State Public Psychiatric System. Ohio has publicly improved its state system in the 1980s more than any other state; much of this is attributable to a governor who demanded improvement and to excellent leadership in the Department of Mental Health. It had a long ways to come, for in the 1970s it was near the bottom nationally. As of 1987, the results are impressive, with the inpatient and outpatient systems being unified administratively, strong efforts to develop case management, and some areas (e.g., Toledo) rated very high. Strong AMI groups have provided advocacy for the seriously mentally ill.

Commitment Laws. No recent major change.

OKLAHOMA

AMI Family Support Groups. Oklahoma AMI, 10404 Sunrise Blvd., Oklahoma City, OK 73120.

NMHCA State Contacts. Share-N-Care Hope, Inc., 5621½ S. Youngs St., Oklahoma City, OK 73119.

State Public Psychiatric System. The three Oklahoma state psychiatric hospitals and aftercare system are average in quality compared with other states. It has traditionally relied on large numbers of unlicensed physicians, housing for released patients has been grossly inadequate, and the state legislature until recently has not been interested in the problems. Under good leadership in the Department of Mental Health the situation is slowly improving.

Commitment Laws. Outpatient commitment is now authorized as a dispositional alternative for patients meeting the civil commitment criteria, with extensive instructions for administration.

OREGON

AMI Family Support Groups. Oregon Alliance of Advocates for the Mentally Ill, 12955 N.W. Lordlaw, Portland, OR 97229.

NMHCA State Contacts. NMHCA, 311 S. Juniper St., #902, Philadelphia, PA 19107.

State Public Psychiatric System. Strong support in the Oregon legislature, good leadership in the state mental health agency, and a strong AMI advocacy group have made Oregon one of the more highly rated states in services for the seriously mentally ill. Particularly noteworthy is their system for funding, implemented in 1983, in which the sickest patients receive the highest priority for services. Mental health centers are free to provide services for the worried well, but the state insists that county or local funds, rather than state funds, be used to support such services. The state funds must be used for the sickest patients, a model which other states would do well to copy. Problems remain, of course, as can be seen by the mentally ill homeless on the streets of Portland.

Commitment Laws. In 1985 the legislature considered but did not pass legislation to broaden existing "unable to provide for basic needs" language. For outpatient commitment there is explicit authorization for placement of patients in the care of a legal guardian, relative, or friends, as a dispositional alternative for patients meeting the civil commitment criteria, if ability and financial resources for care can be shown. While no studies have been done for civilly committed patients, a report on the state's unique Psychiatric Security Board system for providing aftercare and supervision for insanity acquittees concluded that involuntary outpatient treatment was effective, where the treatment is actually available and close supervision was provided.

PENNSYLVANIA

AMI Family Support Groups. AMI of Pennsylvania, 1110 Cocklin St., Mechanicsburg, PA 17055.

NMHCA State Contacts. Peoples Oakland, 223 Coltart Ave., #3, Pittsburgh, PA 15213, *or* NMHCA, 311 S. Juniper St., #902, Philadelphia, PA 19107.

State Public Psychiatric System. A state with a history of sensational exposés of its state hospitals, Pennsylvania has improved its public psychiatric services significantly in the 1980s. The state hospitals have been upgraded except for forensic services, which still lag. An innovative system of funding, in which counties providing more care for the seriously mentally ill receive more funds, has helped outpatient and aftercare service development; Philadelphia is said to be especially progressive and clubhouses such as Peoples Oakland in Pittsburgh are good. There is still a long ways to go before the state will rank near the top, however. A state AMI advocacy group and strong Mental Health Association groups in Pittsburgh and Philadelphia help.

Commitment Laws. Legislation is under consideration to broaden commitment criteria. Outpatient commitment is authorized as a dispositional alternative for patients who meet the civil commitment criteria. The state has considered but not passed legislation to permit preventive commitment under broader criteria.

RHODE ISLAND

AMI Family Support Groups. NAMI, 1901 N. Fort Myer Dr., Suite 500, Arlington, VA 22209.

NMHCA State Contacts. Rhode Island Coalition of Consumer Self-Advocates, Cottage 404, MHRH, 600 New London Ave., Cranston, RI 02902.

State Public Psychiatric System. Care for the seriously mentally ill in Rhode Island has improved dramatically in the past thirty years. Perhaps more than in any other state, voters have approved bond issues (eleven of them in eighteen years) to create housing in the community for the mentally retarded and mentally ill. One major reason for success has been excellent leadership in the Department of Mental Health, Mental Retardation and Hospitals over the past decade. There are still problems, but compared with other states Rhode Island ranks very high.

Commitment Laws. A grave disability commitment category has been under consideration by the governor's council, but no legislation has been enacted. The state has also considered but not passed legislation to permit preventive commitment under broader criteria. An informal outpatient commitment program has been initiated in the courts through the efforts of a local psychiatrist; no explicit statutory procedures are available, but the definition of alternatives (which must be considered at every stage) includes "voluntary or court-ordered outpatient treatment," as well as specific community-based services, "or any other services that may be deemed appropriate."

SOUTH CAROLINA

AMI Family Support Groups. South Carolina AMI, P.O. Box 2538, Columbia, SC 29202.

NMHCA State Contacts. South Carolina SHARE, 1823 Gadsden St., Columbia, SC 29201.

State Public Psychiatric System. In the early 1980s South Carolina ranked near the bottom of the list of state psychiatric systems. South Carolina State Hospital was seriously deficient while outpatient and aftercare facilities varied from inadequate to abysmal. In 1986 new leadership in the Department of Mental Health and an increasingly strong AMI family consumer movement began to turn the situation around, and that has continued.

Bright lights in the system include services for seriously disturbed children (set up as a result of a court case) and three clubhouses (especially Gateway House in Greenville).

Commitment Laws. Outpatient commitment is authorized as a dispositional alternative for patients who meet the civil commitment criteria.

SOUTH DAKOTA

AMI Family Support Groups. NAMI, 1901 N. Fort Myer Dr., Suite 500, Arlington, VA 22209.

NMHCA State Contacts. NMHCA, 311 S. Juniper St., #902, Philadelphia, PA 19107.

State Public Psychiatric System. Although the state hospital at Yankton is of average quality by national standards, outpatient and aftercare services for the seriously mentally ill in South Dakota have been very slow to develop. Much of the problem arises from the fact that the responsibility for inpatients and outpatients is divided between two state agencies with a continuous power struggle and consequent administrative turmoil. A strong AMI advocacy group is badly needed.

Commitment Laws. Outpatient commitment is authorized as a dispositional alternative for patients meeting the civil commitment criteria.

TENNESSEE

AMI Family Support Groups. Tennessee AMI, 1900 N. Winston Rd., #502, Knoxville, TN 37919.

NMHCA State Contacts. CBI Counseling, 1000 Oak St., Chattanooga, TN 37403.

State Public Psychiatric System. The Tennessee Department of Mental Health and Mental Retardation is making steady progress toward achieving a respectable state system, strongly encouraged by AMI family support groups which are gaining strength. The state hospitals are still below average, and community mental health centers vary widely in their interest in seriously mentally ill patients. Continuity of care between the inpatient and outpatient sectors leaves much to be desired. The decades of neglect of the state mental health system are still clearly visible, but so are the evolving improvements.

Commitment Laws. Since 1981 the state has authorized outpatient commitment upon discharge from the hospital; the person can be rehospitalized for noncompliance. This differs from conditional release, where the authority to return the patient to the hospital comes from the original civil commitment order, and expires with the civil commitment period.

TEXAS

AMI Family Support Groups. Texas AMI, 902 Terrace Mountain Dr., Austin, TX 78746.

NMHCA State Contacts. Reclamation, Inc., 2502 Waterford, San Antonio, TX 78217.

State Public Psychiatric System. For over a decade Texas has been under federal court order to improve its state hospitals; progress has been slow but steady. The aftercare and outpatient system for the seriously mentally ill in the community has also been severely deficient. One problem is that Texas ranks forty-seventh in per capita spending on its public psychiatric system despite being eighteenth in per capita income. Another problem is a conservative state legislature that views state hospitals as local jobs programs and refuses to shift funds to community programs. There are good programs to be certain (e.g., Pyramid House in Houston) and active advocacy groups (both the Alliance for the Mentally Ill and the Mental Health Association). But the numbers of mentally ill homeless persons on the streets of Houston and Dallas are a measure of how far the state still has to go.

Commitment Laws. Outpatient commitment is authorized as a dispositional alternative for patients meeting the civil commitment criteria.

UTAH

AMI Family Support Groups. Utah AMI, P.O. Box 26561, Salt Lake City, UT 84126.

NMHCA State Contacts. Problems Anonymous Action Group, 1469 Darling, #303, Ogden, UT 84403.

State Public Psychiatric System. With a small, homogeneous and geographically concentrated population, Utah should be able to deliver good services for the seriously mentally ill. The state hospital in Provo is adequate, and some programs in Salt Lake County and the PAAG program in Ogden are especially impressive. Housing for released patients in most areas is a major problem, however, and the mental health system would be wise to take greater advantage of the extensive social services network of the Church of the Latter Day Saints (Mormons).

Commitment Laws. No recent major changes.

VERMONT

AMI Family Support Groups. AMI of Vermont, P.O. Box 1511, Burlington, VT 05402.

NMHCA State Contacts. Counterpoint, 38 Marble Ave., Burlington, VT 05401.

State Public Psychiatric System. Vermont is an unusual state in its care system for the seriously mentally ill—the state hospital is quite bad while the aftercare and outpatient system is quite good. This is especially noteworthy, considering that Vermont has a higher percentage of its population living in rural areas than any other state. The Community Support Program (CSP) is particularly good and clubhouses such as Evergreen House in Middlebury have been developed. The state legislature has also shown a willingness to spend money considering the fact that Vermont is a relatively poor state.

Commitment Laws. Outpatient commitment is authorized as a dispositional alternative for patients meeting the civil commitment criteria, with specific assessment of appropriateness and availability of the treatment. Vermont has a provision for preventive commitment on discharge from the hospital, allowing for rehospitalization for noncompliance. This differs from conditional release, where the authority to return the patient to the hospital comes from the original civil commitment order, and expires with the civil commitment period.

VIRGINIA

AMI Family Support Groups. Virginia AMI, P.O. Box 1903, Richmond, VA 23215.

NMHCA State Contacts. The Town House, 310 Randolph St., Farmville, VA 23901.

State Public Psychiatric System. Virginia keeps talking about improving its state system for psychiatric care but progress has been slow. Two small state hospitals are good but four large ones vary from mediocre to poor. Outpatient services are under the jurisdiction of forty local Community Service Boards and vary widely in quality. Despite occasional good programs (e.g., clubhouses such as Beach House in Virginia Beach and Lakeside House in Richmond), the state is below average overall.

Commitment Laws. Outpatient commitment is explicitly authorized as a dispositional alternative for patients who meet the civil commitment criteria.

WASHINGTON

AMI Family Support Groups. AMI of Washington State, P.O. Box 2174, Vancouver, WA 98684.

NMHCA State Contacts. NMHCA, 311 S. Juniper St., #902, Philadelphia, PA 19107.

State Public Psychiatric System. In 1979 Washington passed legislation making it easier to hospitalize seriously mentally ill persons in need of treatment. The two state hospitals were not up to the task, however, and became badly overcrowded. Outpatient services are above average but usually insufficiently coordinated with inpatient services; the homeless mentally ill on the streets of Seattle bear mute testimony to this. Strong AMI family support groups and a well-developed series of clubhouses (e.g., Chinook Center in Auburn) are among the state's more promising resources.

Commitment Laws. As one of the first states to rebroaden its commitment law, in 1979, Washington has also been one of the only states to study the effects of the change. The studies have reported that: (1) the new criteria started to be used even before the effective date of the statute, (2) involuntary commitment increased, including many patients who had no previous contact with state hospitals, (3) these patients stayed longer than others and became chronic users of state hospitals, (4) extreme overcrowding in the major state hospital occurred, leading to a lawsuit when the state sought to cap new admissions, and (5) voluntary patients were virtually excluded from state hospitals. Outpatient commitment is authorized as a dispositional alternative for patients who meet the civil commitment criteria.

WEST VIRGINIA

AMI Family Support Groups. AMI of West Virginia, 25 Clinton Hills, Triadelphia, WV 26059.

NMHCA State Contacts. NMHCA, 311 S. Juniper St., #902, Philadelphia, PA 19107.

State Public Psychiatric System. With a per capita income lower than any state except Mississippi and with few mental health professionals available, West Virginia has had an uphill battle to achieve respectability. That the state is trying is generally acknowledged, but success remains elusive. The three state hospitals have been under court order to improve since 1981. The backbone of outpatient services is fourteen community mental health centers, of which some (e.g., Eastern Panhandle) do a good job but others are woefully inadequate.

Commitment Laws. The state considered but did not pass a bill that would have broadened commitment criteria in 1986.

WISCONSIN

AMI Family Support Groups. AMI of Wisconsin, Inc., 1245 E. Washington Ave., #212, Madison, WI 53703.

NMHCA State Contacts. Lighthouse/Safehouse, P.O. Box 529, Madison, WI 53701.

State Public Psychiatric System. Dane County in Wisconsin has achieved a reputation as the best county program for the seriously mentally ill in the

United States (see chapter 8). The reputation of Dane County spills over to Wisconsin as a whole, although in fact some counties provide very good services, while others (e.g., Milwaukee) are only average in quality. The secrets of success in Wisconsin include decentralization of authority and decision-making from the state capital to the state's fifty-six Community Service Boards, fiscal policies in which the money follows the patients, good leadership, and a strong AMI group which has demanded that priority be given to services for the seriously mentally ill. It is not a perfect state system, but it is as good as any yet achieved in the United States.

Commitment Laws. Outpatient commitment is authorized as a dispositional alternative for patients who meet the civil commitment criteria, with emphasis on medication compliance. The state considered but did not pass a bill in 1986 to allow involuntary outpatient commitment under broader criteria than for hospitalization. A description of outpatient commitment in Dane County (Madison) and Milwaukee County found that 75 to 80 percent of all commitment hearings end in negotiated dispositions in which the patient typically agrees to accept outpatient treatment on a "voluntary" basis, and that almost all cooperate with their outpatient treatment and avoid hospitalization.

WYOMING

AMI Family Support Groups. Wyoming AMI, 1123 Beaumont Dr., Casper, WY 82601.

NMHCA State Contacts. NMHCA, 311 S. Juniper St., #902, Philadelphia, PA 19107.

State Public Psychiatric System. Providing adequate services for the seriously mentally ill thinly spread over a vast area is no easy undertaking. In Wyoming the task is made more difficult by the location of the state hospital in the distant southwestern corner of the state, far from all centers of population. Further compounding the problems is the organizational administration of the hospital under one state agency (with the prison), while outpatient psychiatric services are under an entirely different state agency. One would expect such a system to deliver mediocre services on the best of days and that is exactly what happens.

Commitment Laws. No recent major changes.

APPENDIX
E

SUPPORT AND ADVOCACY GROUPS
IN OTHER COUNTRIES

This is a list of support and advocacy groups for families of the seriously mentally ill who are active in other English-speaking countries. Such groups usually welcome visitors to their meetings, for the problems and issues faced in their attempts to improve services and research for serious mental illnesses are remarkably similar to those in the United States.

CANADA

Canadian Friends of
  Schizophrenics
95 Barber Greene Rd., #309
Don Mills, Ontario, Canada
  M3C-3E9

Local chapters exist in all
  Canadian provinces.

ENGLAND

National Schizophrenia Fellowship
78 Victoria Road
Surbiton, Surrey, England
  KT6-4NS

SCOTLAND

National Schizophrenia Fellowship
40 Shandwick Place
Edinburgh, Scotland EH2-4RT

IRELAND

Schizophrenia Association of
  Ireland
4 Fitzwilliam Place
Dublin 2, Ireland

NORTHERN IRELAND

National Schizophrenia Fellowship
Advice Centre, Bryson House
Bedford Street
Belfast, Northern Ireland

NOTES

EPIGRAPH

Van Gogh letter quoted by J. Rewald, *Post-Impressionism: From van Gogh to Gauguin* (New York: Museum of Modern Art, 1962), p. 321.

CHAPTER 1: OUT OF THE CLOSET

"Schizophrenia is": W. Hall, G. Andrews, and G. Goldstein, "The Costs of Schizophrenia," *Australian and New Zealand Journal of Psychiatry* 19 (1985) : 3–5. **"one of the most sinister":** L. Wilson, *This Stranger, My Son* (New York: Putnam, 1968), p. 174. **"the state of":** A. Deutsch, *The Mentally Ill in America* (New York: Columbia University Press, 1937), p. 165. **"kicking or":** "Executive Summary of Hearings on Institutionalized Mentally Disabled Persons," Senate Committee on Labor Subcommittee on the Handicapped, April 1–3, 1985. **"and there had":** Deutsch, pp. 166–67. **"two vicious":** "Ex-Patients Kept in Primitive Shed in Mississippi," *The New York Times*, October 21, 1982, p. A21. **In 1848:** *The Oneida Sachem*, Oneida, NY, January 16, 1858. **In 1986:** "City Inquiry in Ferry Slashing Criticizes Hospital for Release," *The New York Times*, July 12, 1986, p. A1. **"I'm sick":** *The New York Times*, editorial, October 25, 1985. **"passing on":** Deutsch, pp. 123–24. **"a poor":** Ibid. **"routinely reported":** R. Cohen, "Death by Freezing," *Washington Post*, December 6, 1985, p. A27. **"trying to give":** *The New York Times*, November 15, 1985, p. A1. **"rabbits forced":** "A Ferocious Crime Against the Helpless," *Cape Cod Times*, July 22, 1984. **A recent survey:** O. Wahl, "Public vs. Professional Conceptions of Schizophrenia," *Journal of Community Psychology* 15 (1987): 285–91. **John Bradley:** R. S. Kindleberger, "Rekindling Fear," *Boston Globe*, March 8, 1985. **Dennis Sweeney:** E. F. Torrey, "The Sweeney-Lowenstein Madness," *Psychology Today* (October, 1980): 1–5. **Lois Lang:** S. Raab, "Deak Murder Suspect Had Been Found Paranoid," *The New York*

Times, November 21, 1985. **Reagan's tax attorney:** S. Horak, "In Perfect American Family Tragedy Hits Twice in Two Years," *Washington Post,* March 27, 1983. **Phyllis Iannotta:** W. Herbert, "Lost Lives of the Homeless," *Washington Post,* October 19, 1985. **Director of NIMH, testifying:** Testimony of Dr. Shervert H. Frazier before Committee on Appropriations, U.S. Senate, November 20, 1986. **hospital beds:** C. Taube and S. Barrett, eds., "Mental Health, United States 1985," National Institute of Mental Health, DHHS publication number ADM 85-1378 (Rockville, MD: NIMH, 1983). **A 1977 study:** H. H. Goldman, J. Feder, and W. Scanlon, "Chronic Mental Patients in Nursing Homes: Reexamining Data From the National Nursing Home Survey," *Hospital and Community Psychiatry* 37 (1986): 269–72. **studies in Washington:** E. F. Torrey, E. Bargmann, and S. M. Wolfe, "Washington's Grate Society: Schizophrenics in the Shelters and on the Streets" (Washington, D.C.: Health Research Group, 1985). **Studies of prisoners:** H. R. Lamb and R. W. Grant, "The Mentally Ill in an Urban County Jail," *Archives of General Psychiatry* 39 (1982): 17–34. **"psychotic inmates":** E. V. Valdiserri, K. R. Carroll, and A. J. Hartl, "A Study of Offenses Committed by Psychotic Inmates in a County Jail," *Hospital and Community Psychiatry* 37 (1986): 163–66. **"voted friendliest":** "Man Who Blinded Self Is Moved from Prison," *Atlanta Constitution,* March 8, 1985. **$636,000:** A. E.

Moran, R. I. Freedman, and S. S. Sharfstein, "The Journey of Sylvia Frumkin: A Case Study for Policymakers," *Hospital and Community Psychiatry* 35 (1984): 887–93. **$4.5 billion:** "Funding Sources and Expenditures of State Mental Health Agencies: Revenue/Expenditure Study Results Fiscal Year 1983." Updated final report, National Association of State Mental Health Program Directors, August, 1985, table 2, p. 45. **$2.3 billion:** "Selected State and Federal Government Agency Mental Health Expenditures Incurred on Behalf of Mentally Ill Persons." Final report, National Association of State Mental Health Program Directors, June, 1985, pp. 132, 135. **$10 to $20 billion:** J. G. Gunderson and L. R. Mosher, "The Cost of Schizophrenia," *American Journal of Psychiatry* 132 (1975): 901. **$18 billion:** *ADAMHA News,* Rockville, MD, December 31, 1982. **$36 billion:** D. I. MacDonald in talk to the National Alliance for the Mentally Ill, Boston, July, 1986. **$48.2 billion:** R. J. Wyatt, "Science and Psychiatry," in J. T. Kaplan, B. J. Sadock, eds., *Comprehensive Textbook of Psychiatry,* 4th ed. (Baltimore: Williams & Wilkins, 1984), chapter 53, p. 2026. **In Australia:** G. Andrews, W. Hall, G. Goldstein, et al., "The Economic Costs of Schizophrenia," *Archives of General Psychiatry* 42 (1985): 537–43. **$180 billion:** Wyatt, p. 2027. **"It is expedient":** Deutsch, pp. 69–71. **"The insane":** Ibid., p. 137. **"miseries and":** Ibid., p. 177.

CHAPTER 2: THE INNER WORLD OF MADNESS: VIEW FROM THE INSIDE

"What then does": H. R. Rollin, *Coping with Schizophrenia* (London: Burnett Books, 1980), p. 162. **R. W. Emerson,** *Journals* (1836). **I Never Promised You a Rose Garden:** See C. North and R. Cadoret, "Diagnostic Discrepancy in Personal Accounts of Patients with 'Schizophrenia,'" *Archives of General Psychiatry* 38 (1981): 133–37. **"Perceptual dysfunction":** J. Cutting and F. Dunne, "Subjective Experience in Schizophrenia," *Schizophrenia Bulletin*, forthcoming. **"During the last":** A. McGhie and J. Chapman, "Disorders of Attention and Perception in Early Schizophrenia," *British Journal of Medical Psychology* 34 (1961): 103–16. **"Colours seem":** Ibid. **"Everything looked vibrant":** Cutting and Dunne. **"Lots of things":** Ibid. **"People looked deformed":** Ibid. **"I saw everything":** G. Burns, "An Account of My Madness," mimeo, 1983. **"These crises":** M. Sechehaye, *Autobiography of a Schizophrenic Girl* (New York: Grune & Stratton, 1951), p. 22. **"Everything seems":** McGhie and Chapman. **"Occasionally during":** Anonymous, "An Autobiography of a Schizophrenic Experience," *Journal of Abnormal and Social Psychology* 51 (1955): 677–89. **"I can probably":** M. Vonnegut, *The Eden Express* (New York: Praeger, 1975), p. 107. **"In these disturbing":** Sechehaye, p. 24. **"An outsider":** E. Leete, "Mental Illness: An Insider's View," presented at annual meeting of National Alliance of the Mentally Ill, New Orleans, 1985. **In one study:** Cutting and Dunne. **"Had someone asked":** Vonnegut, p. 107. **"Sometimes when people":** McGhie and Chapman. **"it was terrible":** M. Barnes and J. Berke, *Mary Barnes: Two Accounts of a Journey Through Madness* (New York: Ballantine, 1973), p. 44. **"decay in my":** Rollin, p. 150. **"a genital sexual":** Ibid. p. 150 **One psychiatrist:** See M. B. Bowers, *Retreat from Sanity: The Structure of Emerging Psychosis* (Baltimore: Penguin, 1974). **"My trouble is"** and **"My concentration is":** McGhie and Chapman. **"Childhood feelings":** Bowers, p. 152. **"All sorts of":** W. Mayer-Gross, E. Slater, and M. Roth, *Clinical Psychiatry* (Baltimore: Williams & Wilkins, 1969), p. 268. **"I was invited":** A. Boisen, *Out of the Depths* 1960. Quoted in B. Kaplan, ed., *The Inner World of Mental Illness* (New York: Harper & Row, 1964), p. 118. **"Fear made me":** Sechehaye, p. 26. **"Suddenly my whole":** M. Coate, *Beyond All Reason* (Philadelphia: J. B. Lippincott, 1965), p. 21. **"Before last week":** Bowers, p. 27. **"A few weeks":** Anonymous, "Schizophrenic Experience." **"as if a heavy":** B. J. Freedman, "The Subjective Experience of Perceptual and Cognitive Disturbances in Schizophrenia," *Archives of General Psychiatry* 30 (1974): 333–40. **"However hard":** Rollin, p. 150. **Decreased pain perception:** See W. E. Marchand et al., "Occurrence of Painless Acute Surgical Disorder in Psychotic Patients," *New England Journal of*

Medicine 260 (1959): 580–85; N. Geschwind, "Insensitivity to Pain in Psychotic Patients," *New England Journal of Medicine* 296 (1977): 1480; E. F. Torrey, "Headaches After Lumbar Puncture and Insensitivity to Pain in Psychiatric Patients," *New England Journal of Medicine* 301 (1979): 110; and G. D. Watson, P. C. Chandarana, and H. Merskey, "Relationship Between Pain and Schizophrenia," *British Journal of Psychiatry* 138 (1981): 33–36. **"At first it":** N. McDonald, "Living with Schizophrenia," *Canadian Medical Association Journal* 82 (1960): 218–21, 678–81. **"When people are":** McGhie and Chapman. **"I can concentrate":** Ibid. **"I used to get":** Cutting and Dunne. **"I have to":** J. Chapman, "The Early Symptoms of Schizophrenia," *British Journal of Psychiatry* 112 (1966): 225–51. **"Everything is in":** McGhie and Chapman. **"the teeth, then":** Sechehaye, foreword. **"This morning":** S. Sheehan, *Is There No Place on Earth for Me?* (Boston: Houghton Mifflin, 1982), p. 69. **"I can't concentrate":** McGhie and Chapman. **"I tried sitting":** B. O'Brien, *Operators and Things: The Inner Life of a Schizophrenic* (New York: Signet, 1976), pp. 97–98. **"During the visit":** Sechehaye, p. 28. **"If I do":** Chapman. **"My thoughts get":** McGhie and Chapman. **" 'Sun,' I intoned":** Peters (1949), quoted in C. Landis and F. A. Mettler, *Varieties of Psychopathological Experience* (New York: Holt, Rinehart & Winston, 1964), p. 160. **"I am not":** Nijinsky, quoted in Kaplan, p. 424. **"How**

could a": O'Brien, p. 100. **"I was extremely":** Sechehaye, pp. 66–67. **"I had no":** Peters, quoted in Landis and Mettler, p. 160. **"The worst thing":** Chapman. **"I am glad"** and **"I feel that":** Mayer-Gross, Slater, and Roth, pp. 281, 267. **"For instance, I":** G. Bateson, ed., *Perceval's Narrative: A Patient's Account of His Psychosis 1830–1832* (1838, 1840) (New York: Morrow, 1974), p. 269. **"I may be":** McGhie and Chapman. **"If I am":** Ibid. **"I would start":** Cutting and Dunne. **"Sometimes I commit":** Burns. **Chapman claims:** See Chapman. **"I am so":** Anonymous, "I Feel Like I Am Trapped Inside My Head, Banging Desperately Against Its Walls," *The New York Times,* March 18, 1986, C3. **"Why did she":** R. M. Rilke, *The Notebooks of Malte Laurids Brigge* (1910) (New York: Norton, 1949), p. 42. **"In the morning":** A. Chekhov, "Ward No. 6," quoted in A. A. Stone and S. S. Stone, eds., *The Abnormal Personality Through Literature* (Englewood Cliffs, NJ: Prentice-Hall, 1966), p. 5. **"I got up":** Bowers, pp. 186–87. **"Anxiety: like metal":** Poem by Robert L. Nelson, now deceased, and published with the permission of his mother. **"I should emphasize":** Sechehaye, p. 25. **"During the paranoid":** Anonymous, *"Schizophrenic Experience."* **"I felt that":** Ibid. **"I once believed":** R. Jameson, "Personal View," *British Medical Journal* 291 (1985): 541. **de Clerembault:** G. Remington and H. Book, "Case Report of de Clerembault Syndrome, Bipolar Affective Disorder and Response to Lithium," *American Jour-*

nal of Psychiatry 141 (1984): 1285–88. **"telepathic force"**: Rollin, p. 132. **"I like talking"**: Chapman. **"I was sitting"**: Ibid. **"One day we"**: Sechehaye, p. 20. **"This phenomenon can"**: J. Lang, "The Other Side of Hallucinations," *American Journal of Psychiatry* 94 (1938): 1090–97. **"No doubt I"**: Poe, "The Tell-Tale Heart." **"Thus for years"**: D. P. Schreber, *Memoirs of My Nervous Illness* (1903), translated and with introduction by I. Macalpine and R. A. Hunter (London: William Dawson & Sons, 1955), p. 172. **"The voices"**: *Perceval's Narrative*, quoted in Landis and Mettler, p. 122. **"There was music"**: Boisen, quoted in Kaplan, p. 119. **"For about almost"**: Schreber, p. 225. **born deaf**: E. M. R. Critchley, "Auditory Experiences of Deaf Schizophrenics," *Journal of the Royal Society of Medicine* 76 (1983): 542–44. **Julian Jaynes**: See *The Origin of Consciousness in the Breakdown of the Bicameral Mind* (Boston: Houghton Mifflin, 1976). **"At an early"**: Lang. **Silvano Arieti**: *Creativity: The Magic Synthesis* (New York: Harper Colophon, 1976), p. 251. **"On a few"**: Ibid. **"During the time"**: Bowers. p. 37. **"To the person"**: Lang. **"I was present"**: Sechehaye, pp. 80–81. **"Sometimes I did"**: Ibid., pp. 87–88. **"I saw myself"**: Coate, pp. 66–67. **"I get shaky"**: Chapman. **"This was equally"**: Sechehaye, p. 87. **"My breast gives"**: Schreber, p. 207. **"Now it was"**: Rilke, p. 59. **"During the first"**: J. Lang, "The Other Side of the Affective Aspects of Schizophrenia," *Psychiatry* 2 (1939): 195–

202. **"Later, considering them"**: Sechehaye, p. 35. **"I am lying"**: Rilke, pp. 60–61. **"I sat"**: M. Stakes, "First Person Account: Becoming Seaworthy," *Schizophrenia Bulletin* 11 (1985): 629. **"Half the time"**: McGhie and Chapman. **"one of the"**: Chapman. **"During my first"**: Anonymous, "Schizophrenic Experiences." **"Instead of wishing"**: E. Meyer and L. Covi, "The Experience of Depersonalization: A Written Report by a Patient," *Psychiatry* 23 (1960): 215–17. **"I wish I"**: J. A. Wechsler, *In a Darkness* (New York: Norton, 1972), p. 17. **One study found**: T. C. Manschreck et al., "Disturbed Voluntary Motor Activity in Schizophrenic Disorder," *Psychological Medicine* 12 (1982): 73–84; see also M. Jones and R. Hunter, "Abnormal Movements in Patients with Chronic Psychotic Illness," in G. E. Crane and R. Gardner, *Psychotropic Drugs and Dysfunctions of the Basal Ganglia,* Publication No. 1938 (Washington: U.S. Public Health Service, 1969). **In another study**: Cutting and Dunne. **"I became"**: Ibid. **eye blinking**: See J. R. Stevens, "Eye Blink and Schizophrenia: Psychosis or Tardive Dyskinesia," *American Journal of Psychiatry* 135 (1978): 223–26. **"[He] stood"**: H. de Balzac, "Louis Lambert" (1832), in A. A. Stone and S. S. Stone, eds., *The Abnormal Personality Through Literature* (Englewood Cliffs, NJ: Prentice-Hall, 1966), pp. 63–64. **"When I am"**: McGhie and Chapman. **"I don't like"**: Ibid. **"Everything is all"**: Chapman. **"I get stuck"**: McGhie and Chapman. **"My responses are"**:

Ibid. **"I am not"**: Ibid. **"As a matter"**: Sechehaye, pp. 40–41. **"As the work"**: Kindwall and Kinder (1940), quoted in Landis and Mettler, p. 530. **"The state of"**: Sechehaye, pp. 61–62. **"to help to"**: Chapman. **"There were two"**: *Perceval's Narrative,* quoted in Kaplan, p. 240. **Chapman believes**: Chapman. **"My feelings about"**: Anonymous, "Schizophrenic Experiences." **Schreber**: p. 146. **"an enchanted loom"**: Quoted by O. Sacks, *The Man Who Mistook His Wife for a Hat* (New York: Summit Books, 1985), p. 140. **John Hinckley**: "Hinckley Sr. Seeks Support in Fight Against Mental Illness," *Psychiatric News,* November 16, 1984. **"self-measuring ruler"**: Burns. **"Lost"**: Nelson. **cited by one woman**: A. Sobin and M. N. Ozer, "Mental Disorders in Acute Encephalitis," *Journal of Mt. Sinai Hospital* 33 (1966): 73–82. **"No doubt Louis"**: Balzac.

CHAPTER 3: THE DIAGNOSIS OF SCHIZOPHRENIA: VIEW FROM THE OUTSIDE

"Insanity is": Quoted in C. E. Goshen, *Documentary History of Psychiatry* (New York: Philosophical Library, 1967), p. 315. **Studies have shown**: C. S. Mellor, "First Rank Symptoms of Schizophrenia," *British Journal of Psychiatry* 117 (1970): 15–23. **patients with manic-depressive illness**: W. T. Carpenter, J. S. Strauss, and S. Muleh, "Are There Pathognomonic Symptoms in Schizophrenia?" *Archives of General Psychiatry* 28 (1973): 847–52. **DSM-III**: *Diagnostic and Statistical Manual of Mental Disorders* (Washington, D.C.: American Psychiatric Association, 1980). **Rosenhan study**: D. L. Rosenhan, "On Being Sane in Insane Places," *Science* 179 (1973): 250–58; see also R. L. Spitzer, "More on Pseudoscience in Science and the Case for Psychiatric Diagnosis," *Archives of General Psychiatry* 33 (1976): 459–70. **"If I were"**: S. S. Kety, "From Rationalization to Reason," *American Journal of Psychiatry* 131 (1974): 957–63. **Paranoid schizophrenia**: For a review see K. S. Kendler and K. L. Davis, "The Genetics and Biochemistry of Paranoid Schizophrenia and Other Paranoid Psychoses," *Schizophrenia Bulletin* 7 (1981): 689–709; there are other related articles in the same issue. **Soviet system of classification . . .**: See J. Holland and I. V. Shakhmatova-Pavlova, "Concept and Classification of Schizophrenia in the Soviet Union," *Schizophrenia Bulletin* 3 (1977): 277–87. **"positive" symptoms**: This subtyping is reviewed in an entire issue of *Schizophrenia Bulletin* (volume 11, no. 3, 1985) devoted to the subject; the articles by Drs. Crow and Andreasen are especially useful. **Researchers in Canada**: J. Varsamis and J. D. Adamson, "Somatic Symptoms in Schizophrenia," *Canadian Psychiatric Association Journal* 21 (1976): 1–6. **gender differences**: See M. V. Seeman, "Gender Differences in Schizophrenia," *Canadian Journal of Psychiatry* 27 (1982): 107–11; R. R. J. Lewine, "Sex Differences in Schizophrenia: Timing or Subtypes," *Psychological*

Bulletin 90 (1981): 432–44. **R. L. Taylor,** *Mind or Body: Distinguishing Psychological from Organic Disorders* (New York: McGraw-Hill, 1982). **CT scan:** D. R. Weinberger, "Brain Disease and Psychiatric Illness: When Should a Psychiatrist Order a CAT Scan?" *American Journal of Psychiatry* 141 (1984): 1521–27. **Lumbar puncture:** E. F. Torrey, "Functional Psychoses and Viral Encephalitis," *Integrative Psychiatry* 4 (1986): 224–36. **complains of headache:** E. F. Torrey, "Headaches in Schizophrenia," submitted for publication. **post-lumbar-puncture headaches:** E. F. Torrey, "Headaches After Lumbar Puncture and Insensitivity to Pain in Psychiatric Patients," *New England Journal of Medicine* 301 (1979): 110. **Most geneticists:** I. I. Gottesman and J. Shields, *Schizophrenia: The Epigenetic Puzzle* (Cambridge: Cambridge University Press, 1982). **recent follow-up:** J. G. Howells and W. R. Guirguis, "Childhood Schizophrenia 20 Years Later," *Archives of General Psychiatry* 41 (1984): 123–28. **L. Wilson:** *This Stranger, My Son* (New York: Putnam, 1968).

CHAPTER 4: WHAT SCHIZOPHRENIA IS NOT

"What consoles me": J. Rewald, *Post-Impressionism: From van Gogh to Gauguin* (New York: Museum of Modern Art, 1962), p. 320. **pair of identical twins:** J. T. Dalby, D. Morgan, and M. L. Lee, "Schizophrenia and Mania in Identical Twin Brothers," *Journal of Nervous and Mental*

Disease 174 (1986): 304–8. **triplets:** P. McGuffin, A. Reveley, and A. Holland, "Identical Triplets: Nonidentical Psychosis?" *British Journal of Psychiatry* 140 (1982): 1–6. **"are inflexible":** *Diagnostic and Statistical Manual of Mental Disorders* (Washington, D.C.: American Psychiatric Association, 1980). **Studies of families:** M. Baron, R. Gruen, J. D. Rainer, et al., "A Family Study of Schizophrenia and Normal Control Probands: Implications for the Spectrum Concept of Schizophrenia," *American Journal of Psychiatry* 142 (1985): 447–55; and K. S. Kendler, C. C. Masterson, R. Ungaro, et al., "A Family History Study of Schizophrenia-related Personality Disorders," *American Journal of Psychiatry* 141 (1984): 424–27. **low doses of antipsychotic drugs:** G. Serban and S. Siegel, "Response of Borderline and Schizotypal Patients to Small Doses of Thiothixene and Haloperidol," *American Journal of Psychiatry* 141 (1984): 1455–58; and S. C. Goldberg, S. C. Schulz, P. M. Schulz, et al., "Borderline and Schizotypal Personality Disorders Treated with Low-Dose Thiothixene vs. Placebo," *Archives of General Psychiatry* 43 (1986): 680–86. **Abuse of schizophrenia label in Soviet Union:** See W. Reich, "The Spectrum Concept of Schizophrenia," *Archives of General Psychiatry* 32 (1975): 489–98. **widely quoted study:** R. C. W. Hall, E. R. Gardner, S. K. Stickney, et al., "Physical Illness Manifesting as Psychiatric Disease," *Archives of General Psychiatry* 37 (1980): 989–95. **A larger study:** K. Davison, "Schizophrenia-like Psychoses Associated with Organic Cerebral Disorders: A Review," *Psychiatric Developments* 1 (1983): 1–34. **A postmortem study:** Davison. **Viral encephalitis:** E. F. Torrey, "Functional Psychoses and Viral Encephalitis," *Integrative Psychiatry* 4 (1986): 224–36. **One study:** Davison. **one recent report:** A. G. Awad, "Schizophrenia and Multiple Sclerosis," *Journal of Nervous and Mental Disease* 171 (1983): 323–24. **"a common":** Davison. **Psychosis following childbirth:** R. A. Munoz, "Postpartum Psychosis as a Discrete Entity," *Journal of Clinical Psychiatry* 46 (1985): 182–84. **Psychosis following trauma:** H. A. Nasrallah, R. C. Fowler, L. L. Judd, "Schizophrenia-like Illness Following Head Injury," *Psychosomatics* 22 (1981): 359–61. **Infantile autism:** The best recent book on this subject is M. Coleman and C. Gillberg, *The Biology of the Austistic Syndromes* (New York: Praeger Publishers, 1985). An older but still useful book is B. Rimland, *Infantile Autism* (New York: Appleton-Century-Crofts, 1974). **neuropathological changes in autism:** E. R. Ritvo, B. J. Freeman, A. B. Scheibel, et al., "Lower Purkinje Cell Count in the Cerebella of Four Autistic Subjects," *American Journal of Psychiatry* 143 (1986): 862–66. **one study:** E. F. Torrey, S. P. Hersh, and K. D. McCabe, "Early Childhood Psychosis and Bleeding During Pregnancy," *Journal of Autism and Childhood Schizophrenia* 5 (1975): 287–97. **one study has suggested:** J. L. Karlson, "Genetic Association of Giftedness and Creativity with Schizophrenia," *Hereditas* 66 (1970): 177. **creativity and schizophrenia:** See J. A. Keefe and P. A. Magaro, "Creativity and Schizophrenia: An Equivalence of Cognitive Processing," *Journal of Abnormal Psychology* 89 (1980): 390–98; and M. Dykes and A. McGhie, "A Comparative Study of Attentional Strategies of Schizophrenic and Highly Creative Normal Subjects," *British Journal of Psychiatry* 128 (1976): 50–56. **suspected manic-depressives:** J. Leo, "The Ups and Downs of Creativity," *Time* (October 8, 1974): 73–74. **alcoholics:** D. W. Goodwin, review of *The True Adventures of John Steinbeck, Writer: A Biography,* in *American Journal of Psychiatry* 143 (1986): 102–3. **"he could not sleep":** R. Ellmann, *James Joyce: New and Revised Edition* (New York: Oxford, 1982), p. 685. **A psychiatrist:** N. J. C. Andreasen, "James Joyce: A Portrait of the Artist as a Schizoid," *Journal of the American Medical Association* 224 (1973): 67–71. **"Joyce had":** Ellmann, p. 650. **"assailed by":** Rewald, p. 266. The other symptoms of his illness can be found on pp. 266–334. **"Oh, if I":** B. Schiff, "Triumph and Tragedy in the Land of 'Blue Tones and Gay Colors,' " *Smithsonian* (October, 1984), p. 89.

CHAPTER 5: PROGNOSIS AND POSSIBLE COURSES

"Such a disease": Quoted in V. Norris, *Mental Illness in London* (London: Oxford University Press, 1959), p. 15. **best summary:** J. H. Stephens,

"Long-term Prognosis and Follow-up in Schizophrenia," *Schizophrenia Bulletin* 4 (1978): 25–47. **"About three-fifths"**: L. Ciompi, "Catamnestic Long-term Study of the Course of Life and Aging of Schizophrenics," *Schizophrenia Bulletin* 6 (1980): 606–16. **"the current picture"**: C. M. Harding and J. S. Strauss, "The Course of Schizophrenia: An Evolving Concept" in M. Alpert, ed., *Controversies in Schizophrenia* (New York: Guilford Press, 1985), p. 347. **"The patient"**: W. Mayer-Gross, E. Slater, and M. Roth, *Clinical Psychiatry* (Baltimore: Williams & Wilkins, 1969), p. 275. **community survey in Baltimore**: M. Von Korff, G. Nestadt, A. Romanoski, et al., "Prevalence of Treated and Untreated *DSM-III* Schizophrenia," *Journal of Nervous and Mental Disease* 173 (1985): 577–81. **Miles**: C. P. Miles, "Conditions Predisposing to Suicide: A Review," *Journal of Nervous and Mental Disease* 164 (1977): 231–46. **The majority**: A. Roy, "Depression, Attempted Suicide, and Suicide in Patients with Chronic Schizophrenia," in A. Roy, ed., *The Psychiatric Clinics of North America* 9 (1986): 193–206. **Those at highest risk**: A. Breier and B. M. Astrachan, "Characterization of Schizophrenic Patients Who Commit Suicide," *American Journal of Psychiatry* 141 (1984): 206–9; R. E. Drake, C. Gates, P. G. Cotton, et al., "Suicide Among Schizophrenics," *Journal of Nervous and Mental Disease* 172 (1984): 613–17. **In 1981**: P. Allebeck and B. Wistedt, "Mortality in Schizophrenia," *Archives of General Psychiatry* 43 (1986): 650–53. **elevated pain threshold**: E. F. Torrey, "Headaches After Lumbar Puncture and Insensitivity to Pain in Psychiatric Patients," *New England Journal of Medicine* 301 (1979): 110. **percentage of patients**: N. Sartorius, A. Jablensky, and R. Shapiro, "Cross-Cultural Differences in the Short-term Prognosis of Schizophrenic Psychoses," *Schizophrenia Bulletin* 4 (1978): 102–13. **"the prognosis in the aboriginal"**: H. Rin and T. Y. Lin, "Mental Illness among Formosan Aborigines as Compared with the Chinese in Taiwan," *Journal of Mental Science* 108 (1962): 134–46. **And on Mauritius**: H. B. M. Murphy and A. C. Raman, "The Chronicity of Schizophrenia in Indigenous Tropical Peoples," *British Journal of Psychiatry* 118 (1971): 489–97. **data from the World Health Organization**: See N. Sartorius, A. Jablensky, and R. Shapiro; World Health Organization, *Schizophrenia: An International Follow-up Study* (New York: Wiley, 1979). **courses of schizophrenia**: M. Bleuler, "A 23-year Longitudinal Study of 208 Schizophrenics and Impressions in Regard to the Nature of Schizophrenia," in D. A. Rosenthal and S. S. Kety, eds., *The Transmission of Schizophrenia* (Oxford: Pergamon Press, 1968); E. H. Hare, "The Changing Content of Psychiatric Illness," *Journal of Psychosomatic Research* 19 (1974): 283–89; K. A. Achte, "The Course of Schizophrenic and Schizophreniform Psychoses," *Acta Psychiatrica et Neurologica Scandinavica* Supplementum 155 (1961).

CHAPTER 6: THE CAUSES OF SCHIZOPHRENIA

"Something has happened": L. Jefferson, *These Are My Sisters* (1948), quoted in Kaplan, p. 6. "the most robust": R. C. Shelton and D. R. Weinberger, "X-ray Computerized Tomography Studies in Schizophrenia: A Review and Synthesis," in H. A. Nasrallah and D. R. Weinberger, eds., *The Neurology of Schizophrenia* (Amsterdam: Elsevier, 1986). smaller brains: N. Andreasen, H. A. Nasrallah, V. Dunn, et al., "Structural Abnormalities in the Frontal System in Schizophrenia," *Archives of General Psychiatry* 43 (1986): 136–44. corpus callosum: H. A. Nasrallah, N. C. Andreasen, J. A. Coffman, et al., "A Controlled Magnetic Resonance Imaging Study of Corpus Callosum Thickness in Schizophrenia," *Biological Psychiatry* 21 (1986): 274–82. globus pallidus: T. S. Early, E. M. Reiman, M. E. Raichle, et al., "Left Globus Pallidus Abnormality in Never-Medicated Patients with Schizophrenia," *Proceedings of the National Academy of Sciences* 84 (1987): 561–63. since 1980: D. G. Kirch and D. R. Weinberger, "Anatomical Neuropathology in Schizophrenia: Post-mortem Findings," in Nasrallah and Weinberger. Stevens: J. R. Stevens, "Neuropathology of Schizophrenia," *Archives of General Psychiatry* 39 (1982): 1131–39. Bogerts: B. Bogerts, E. Meertz, and R. Schonfeldt-Bausch, "Basal Ganglia and Limbic System Pathology in Schizophrenia," *Archives of General Psychiatry* 42 (1985): 784–91. dopa-

mine receptors: J. E. Kleinman, "Postmortem Neurochemistry Studies in Schizophrenia," in Nasrallah and Weinberger. Wong: D. F. Wong, H. N. Wagner, L. E. Tune, et al., "Positron Emission Tomography Reveals Elevated D-2 Dopamine Receptors in Drug-Naive Schizophrenics," *Science* 234 (1986): 1558–63. "Although the": E. H. Rubin, "Imaging of Brain Activity and Behavioral Disorders," *Psychiatric Developments* 1 (1986): 65–76. Berman: K. F. Berman, R. F. Zec, and D. R. Weinberger, "Physiologic Dysfunction of Dorsolateral Prefrontal Cortex in Schizophrenia," *Archives of General Psychiatry* 43 (1986): 126–34. Gur: R. E. Gur, R. C. Gur, B. E. Skolnick, et al., "Brain Function in Psychiatric Disorders," *Archives of General Psychiatry* 42 (1985): 329–34. PET scans: L. E. DeLisi, "The Use of Positron Emission Tomography (PET) to Image Regional Brain Metabolism in Schizophrenia and Other Psychiatric Disorders: A Review," in Nasrallah and Weinberger. "a broad": J. A. Grebb, D. R. Weinberger, and J. M. Morihisa, "Electroencephalogram and Evoked Potentials Studies of Schizophrenia," in Nasrallah and Weinberger. BEAM: J. M. Morihisa, "Computerized Mapping of Electrophysiologic Data in Schizophrenia Research: Two Possible Organizing Strategies," in Nasrallah and Weinberger. grasp reflex: J. B. Lohr, "Transient Grasp Reflex in Schizophrenia," *Biological Psychiatry* 20 (1985): 172–75. gag reflex: T. J. Craig, M. A. Richardson, R. Pass, et al. "Impairment of

Gag Reflex in Schizophrenic Inpatients," *Comprehensive Psychiatry* 24 (1983): 514–20. **"The frequency":** L. J. Seidman, "Schizophrenia and Brain Dysfunction: An Integration of Recent Neurodiagnostic Findings," *Psychological Bulletin* 94 (1983): 195–238. **three additional:** T. C. Manschreck and D. Ames, "Neurologic Features and Psychopathology in Schizophrenic Disorders," *Biological Psychiatry* 19 (1984): 703–19; T. Kolakowska, A. O. Williams, K. Jambor, et al., "Schizophrenia with Good and Poor Outcome," *British Journal of Psychiatry* 146 (1985): 348–57; B. T. Woods, D. K. Kinney, and D. Yurgelun-Todd, "Neurologic Abnormalities in Schizophrenic Patients and Their Families," *Archives of General Psychiatry* 43 (1986): 657–63. **"clumsiness and":** T. C. Manschreck, "Motor Abnormalities in Schizophrenia," in Nasrallah and Weinberger. **23 separate:** D. L. Levy, P. S. Holzman, and L. R. Proctor, "Vestibular Dysfunction and Psychopathology," *Schizophrenia Bulletin* 9 (1983): 383–438. **altered pain threshold:** E. F. Torrey, "Headaches After Lumbar Puncture and Insensitivity to Pain in Psychiatric Patients," *New England Journal of Medicine* 301 (1979): 110. **"Chronic or process":** Seidman. **"Schizophrenic patients":** T. E. Goldberg and D. R. Weinberger, "Methodological Issues in the Neuropsychological Approach to Schizophrenia," in Nasrallah and Weinberger. **"The more severe":** D. Rogers, "The Motor Disorders of Severe Psychiatric Illness: A Conflict of

Paradigms," *British Journal of Psychiatry* 147 (1985): 221–32. **"selective, integrative":** D. R. Roberts, "Schizophrenia and the Brain," *Journal of Neuropsychiatry* 5 (1963): 71–79. **"able to correlate":** P. D. MacLean, "Psychosomatic Disease and the 'Visceral Brain,'" *Psychosomatic Medicine* 11 (1949): 338–53. **limbic system dysfunction:** E. F. Torrey and M. R. Peterson, "Schizophrenia and the Limbic System," *Lancet* 2 (1974): 942–46. **brain tumors:** N. Malamud, "Psychiatric Disorders with Intracranial Tumors of the Limbic System," *Archives of Neurology* 17 (1967): 113–23. **Cases of encephalitis:** J. R. Brierley et al., "Subacute Encephalitis of Later Life Mainly Affecting the Limbic Areas," *Brain* 83 (1960): 357–68. **epilepsy, when it originates:** N. Malamud, "The Epileptogenic Focus in Temporal Lobe Epilepsy from the Pathological Standpoint," *Archives of Neurology* 14 (1966): 190–95; M. A. Falconer, E. A. Serafetinides, and J. A. N. Corsellis, "Etiology and Pathogenesis of Temporal Lobe Epilepsy," *Archives of Neurology* 10 (1964): 233–48. **limbic electrical activity:** R. G. Heath, *Studies in Schizophrenia: A Multidisciplinary Approach to Mind-Brain Relationships* (Cambridge: Harvard University Press, 1954); R. G. Heath, "Correlation of Electrical Recordings from Cortical and Subcortical Regions of the Brain with Abnormal Behavior in Human Subjects," *Confina Neurologia* 18 (1958): 305–15; R. R. Monroe et al., "Correlation of Rhinencephalic Electrograms with Behavior," *EEG and Clinical Neurophysiology* 9 (1957): 623–42; C. W. Sem-Jacobsen, M. C. Peterson, and J. A. Lazarte, "Intracerebral Electrographic Recordings from Psychotic Patients During Hallucinations and Agitation: Preliminary Report," *American Journal of Psychiatry* 112 (1955): 278–88; C. W. Sem-Jacobsen et al., "Electroencephalographic Rhythms from the Depths of the Parietal, Occipital, and Temporal Lobes in Man," *EEG and Clinical Neurophysiology* 8 (1956): 263–78; J. F. Kendrick and F. A. Gibbs, "Origin, Spread and Neurosurgical Treatment of the Psychomotor Type of Seizure Discharge," *Journal of Neurosurgery* 14 (1957): 270–84; J. Hanley et al., "Spectral Characteristics of EEG Activity Accompanying Deep Spiking in a Patient with Schizophrenia," *EEG and Clinical Neurophysiology* 28 (1970): 90; J. Hanley et al., "Automatic Recognition of EEG Correlates of Behavior in a Chronic Schizophrenic Patient," *American Journal of Psychiatry* 128 (1972): 1524–28. **Patients with temporal lobe epilepsy:** P. Flor-Henry, "Psychosis and Temporal Lobe Epilepsy: A Controlled Investigation," *Epilepsia* 10 (1969): 363–95; P. Flor-Henry, "Schizophrenic-like Reactions and Affective Psychoses Associated with Temporal Lobe Epilepsy: Etiological Factors," *American Journal of Psychiatry* 126 (1969): 400–4. **"The evidence for":** H. A. Nasrallah, "Cerebral Hemisphere Asymmetries and Interhemispheric Integration in Schizophrenia," in Nasrallah and Weinberger.

physical anomalies: J. D. Guy, L. V. Majorski, C. J. Wallace, et al., "The Incidence of Minor Physical Anomalies in Adult Male Schizophrenics," *Schizophrenia Bulletin* 9 (1983) 571–82. **unusual fingerprint:** For a review of these studies see E. F. Torrey and M. R. Peterson, "The Viral Hypothesis of Schizophrenia," *Schizophrenia Bulletin* 2 (1976): 136–46. **"substantial evidence":** T. F. McNeil, "Perinatal Factors in the Development of Schizophrenia" in H. Helmchen and F. Henn, eds., *Biological Perspectives of Schizophrenia* (Chichester: John Wiley and Sons, 1987). **seasonal excess:** Two recent reviews of this rapidly expanding literature are T. N. Bradbury and G. A. Miller, "Season of Birth in Schizophrenia: A Review of Evidence, Methodology and Etiology," *Psychological Bulletin* 98 (1985): 569–94, and J. H. Boyd, A. E. Pulver, and W. Stewart, "Season of Birth: Schizophrenia and Bipolar Disorder," *Schizophrenia Bulletin* 12 (1986): 173–86. **single major cause:** L. Thomas, *The Medusa and the Snail: More Notes of a Biological Watcher* (New York: Viking, 1981). **more inbreeding:** A. H. Ahmed, "Consanguinity and Schizophrenia in Sudan," *British Journal of Psychiatry* 134 (1979): 635–36. **genetics plays some role:** See S. Kessler, "The Genetics of Schizophrenia: A Review," *Schizophrenia Bulletin* 6 (1980): 404–16; D. K. Kinney and S. Matthysse, "Genetic Transmission of Schizophrenia," *Annual Review of Medicine* 29 (1978): 459–73. **abnormal eye movements:** P. S. Holzman et al., "Eye Tracking Dysfunctions in Schizophrenic Patients and Their Relatives," *Archives of General Psychiatry* 31 (1974): 143–51. **Genetic markers:** For a review see L. Erlenmeyer-Kimling, "Biological Markers for the Liability to Schizophrenia," in Helmchen and Henn, op. cit.; see also D. K. Kinney, B. T. Woods, and D. Yurgelun-Todd, "Neurologic Abnormalities in Schizophrenic Patients and Their Families," *Archives of General Psychiatry* 43 (1986): 665–68. **"something necessary":** R. Cancro, "Genetic Evidence for the Existence of Subgroups of the Schizophrenic Syndrome," *Schizophrenia Bulletin* 5 (1979): 453–59; see also S. S. Kety et al., "The Biologic and Adoptive Families of Adopted Individuals Who Became Schizophrenic: Prevalence of Mental Illness and Other Characteristics," in L. C. Wynne, R. L. Cromwell, and S. Matthysse, *The Nature of Schizophrenia* (New York: Wiley, 1978). The findings of the Denmark study have been disputed by T. Lidz, S. Blatt, and B. Cooke, "Critique of the Danish-American Studies of the Adopted-away Offspring of Schizophrenic Parents," *American Journal of Psychiatry* 138 (1981): 1063–68. **"If schizophrenia is a myth":** S. S. Kety, "From Rationalization to Reason," *American Journal of Psychiatry* 131 (1974): 957–63. **genetic predisposition:** See A. L. Notkins, "The Causes of Diabetes," *Scientific American* 241 (1979): 62–73. **excess of dopamine:** D. H. Langer, G. L. Brown, and J. P. Docherty, "Dopamine Receptor Supersensitivity and

Schizophrenia: A Review," *Schizophrenia Bulletin* 7 (1981): 208–24; see also R. J. Wyatt, "The Dopamine Hypothesis: Variations on a Theme," *Psychopharmacological Bulletin* 22 (1986): 923–27; and S. H. Snyder, "Schizophrenia," *Lancet* 2 (1982): 970–73. **MAO research:** R. J. Wyatt, S. G. Potkin, and D. L. Murphy, "Platelet Monoamine Oxidase Activity in Schizophrenia: A Review," *American Journal of Psychiatry* 136 (1979): 377–85; L. E. DeLisi et al., "A Probable Neuroleptic Effect on Platelet Monoamine Oxidase in Chronic Schizophrenia," *Psychiatry Research* 4 (1981): 95–107. **serotonin:** L. E. DeLisi et al., "Increased Whole Blood Serotonin Concentrations in Chronic Schizophrenic Patients," *Archives of General Psychiatry* 38 (1981): 647–50. **"have crossed the threshold":** T. H. Maugh, "Biochemical Markers Identify Mental States," *Science* 214 (1981): 39–41. **high doses of niacin:** A. Hoffer, *Niacin Therapy in Psychiatry* (Springfield, IL: Charles C. Thomas, 1962). **Linus Pauling:** L. Pauling, "Orthomolecular Psychiatry," *Science* 160 (1968): 265–71. **fill a textbook:** D. Hawkins and L. Pauling, *Orthomolecular Psychiatry: Treatment of Schizophrenia* (San Francisco: Freeman, 1973). **attempts to replicate:** J. H. Autrey, "Workshop on Orthomolecular Treatment of Schizophrenia: A Report," *Schizophrenia Bulletin* No. 12 (original series) (1975): 94–103. **Gluten:** F. C. Dohan, "Cereals and Schizophrenia: Data and Hypothesis," *Acta Psychiatrica Scandinavica* 42 (1966): 125–52; F.

C. Dohan, "Wartime Changes in Hospital Admissions for Schizophrenia," *Acta Psychiatrica Scandinavica* 42 (1966): 1–23. **gluten-free and milk-free diet:** F. C. Dohan and J. C. Grasberger, "Relapsed Schizophrenics: Earlier Discharge from the Hospital after Cereal-Free, Milk-Free Diet," *American Journal of Psychiatry* 130 (1973): 685–88; M. M. Singh and S. R. Kay, "Wheat Gluten as a Pathogenic Factor in Schizophrenia," *Science* 191 (1976): 401–2; S. R. Potkin et al., "Wheat Gluten Challenge in Schizophrenic Patients," *American Journal of Psychiatry* 138 (1981): 1208–11; L. H. Storms, J. M. Clopton, and C. Wright, "Effects of Gluten on Schizophrenics," *Archives of General Psychiatry* 39 (1982): 323–27. **search for food allergies:** H. G. Kinnell, E. Kirkwood, and C. Lewis, "Food Antibodies in Schizophrenia," *Psychological Medicine* 12 (1982): 85–89. **zinc or copper:** D. Shore et al., "CSF Copper in Chronic Schizophrenia," *American Journal of Psychiatry* 140 (1983): 754–57; S. G. Potkin et al., "CSF Zinc in Ex-Heroin Addicts and Chronic Schizophrenia," *Biological Psychiatry* 17 (1982): 1315–22. **Viral particles:** V. M. K. Morozov, "On the Problem of the Virus Etiology of Schizophrenia," *Korsakov Journal of Neuropathology and Psychiatry* 54 (1954): 732–34 (in Russian). **"encephalitis and schizophrenia":** I. Hendrick, "Encephalitis Lethargica and the Interpretation of Mental Disease," *American Journal of Psychiatry* 84 (1928): 989–1014. For a summary of evidence for viral theories, see E. F. Torrey and M. R. Peterson, "The Viral Hypothesis of Schizophrenia," *Schizophrenia Bulletin* 2 (1976): 136–46; Torrey and Kaufmann; and E. F. Torrey, R. Rawlings, and I. N. Waldman, "Schizophrenic Births and Viral Diseases in Two States," submitted for publication. **Finland:** S. A. Mednick, R. A. Machon, M. Huttunen, et al., "The 1957 Helsinki Type A-2 Influenza Epidemic and Adult Seasonality," submitted for publication. **Immunological theories:** For a good summary of this literature, see L. E. DeLisi, "Neuroimmunology: Clinical Studies of Schizophrenia and Other Psychiatric Disorders," in Nasrallah and Weinberger. **"Schizophrenia is":** D. R. Weinberger, "Implications of Normal Brain Development for the Pathogenesis of Schizophrenia," *Archives of General Psychiatry* 44 (1987): 660–69. **"These findings":** N. Andreasen, H. A. Nasrallah, V. Dunn, et al., "Structural Abnormalities in the Frontal System in Schizophrenia," *Archives of General Psychiatry* 43 (1986): 136–44. **"We believe":** J. Chamberlain, *On Our Own: Patient-Controlled Alternatives to the Mental Health System* (New York: Hawthorn, 1978), p. xvi. **1968 study:** G. W. Brown and J. L. T. Birley, "Crises and Life Changes and the Onset of Schizophrenia," *Journal of Health and Social Behavior* 9 (1968): 203–14. **"stressful life events":** B. D. Dohrenwend and G. Egri, "Recent Stressful Life Events and Episodes of Schizophrenia," *Schizophrenia Bulletin* 7 (1981): 12–23. **"No study found":** J. G. Rabkin,

"Stressful Life Events and Schizophrenia: A Review of the Literature," *Psychological Bulletin* 87 (1980): 408–25. **"There is no good":** C. C. Tennant, "Stress and Schizophrenia: A Review," *Integrative Psychiatry* 3 (1985): 248–61. **"only 15.4 percent":** R. Gruen and M. Biron, "Stressful Life Events and Schizophrenia," *Neuropsychobiology* 12 (1984): 206–8. **during World War II:** F. C. Dohan, "Wartime Changes in Hospital Admissions for Schizophrenia: A Comparison of Admissions for Schizophrenia and Other Psychoses in Six Countries During World War II," *Acta Psychiatrica Scandinavica* 42 (1966): 1–23. **"Today of course":** J. G. Hall, "Emotions and Immunity," *Lancet* 2 (1985): 326–27. **the memoirs:** D. P. Schreber, *Memoirs of My Nervous Illness* (1903), translation and introduction by I. Macalpine and R. A. Hunter (London: William Dawson & Sons, 1955). **"conflict over unconscious homosexuality":** I. Macalpine and R. A. Hunter in Schreber. **"I seldom see":** Letter from Sigmund Freud to Karl Abraham in E. Jones, *The Life and Work of Sigmund Freud*, vol. 2 (New York: Basic Books, 1955), p. 437. **Freud sided with Abraham:** Jones, vol. 2, pp. 46–48. **"the unceasing terror":** N. Fodor, "Prenatal Foundations of Psychotic Development," *Samiksa* 11 (1957): 1–43. **"relationship of":** H. S. Sullivan, *The Interpersonal Theory of Psychiatry* (New York: W. W. Norton, 1953). **"dominated by":** P. Robinson, "Mr. Interpersonal Relations," *Psychology Today*, March,

1982. **"a homosexual" and episodes of schizophrenia:** Ibid. **"This book is":** R. Abrams, review of L. B. Boyer and P. L. Giovacchini, *Psychoanalytic Treatment of Schizophrenic, Borderline, and Characterological Disorders,* in *American Journal of Psychiatry* 138 (1981): 267. **"All mothers":** T. Tietze, "A Study of Mothers of Schizophrenic Patients," *Psychiatry* 12 (1949): 55–65. **"the majority":** S. Arieti, "Schizophrenia," in S. Arieti, ed., *The American Handbook of Psychiatry*, vol. 1 (New York: Basic Books, 1959), p. 469. **"strange, near-psychotic":** T. Lidz, S. Fleck, and A. R. Cornelison, *Schizophrenia and the Family* (New York: International University Press, 1965), p. 327. **"an extremely noxious":** T. Lidz, B. Parker, and A. R. Cornelison, "The Role of the Father in the Family Environment of the Schizophrenic Patient," *American Journal of Psychiatry* 113 (1956): 126–32. **"double-bind":** G. Bateson, D. D. Jackson, J. Haley, et al., "Toward a Theory of Schizophrenia," *Behavioral Science* 1 (1956): 251–64. **later essay:** G. Bateson, "The Birth of a Matrix or Double Bind and Epistemology," in M. M. Berger, ed., *Beyond the Double Bind* (New York: Brunner Mazel, 1978). **As early as 1951:** C. T. Prout and M. A. White, "A Controlled Study of Personality Relationships in Mothers of Schizophrenic Male Patients," *American Journal of Psychiatry* 107 (1951): 251–56. **subsequent studies:** See, for example, J. Block, V. Patterson, J. Block, et al., "A Study of Parents of

428

NOTES TO PAGES 164–185

Schizophrenic and Neurotic Children," *Psychiatry* 21 (1958): 387–97. **"a single-minded":** W. R. McFarlane, ed., *Family Therapy in Schizophrenia* (New York: Guilford Press, 1983), p. 8. **"The idea that":** W. R. McFarlane and C. C. Beels, ibid., p. 311. **"there is as yet":** S. R. Hirsch, "Do Parents Cause Schizophrenia?" *Trends in Neurosciences* 2 (1979): 49–52. **"Neither has anyone":** Ibid. **"fake disease":** T. Szasz, *Schizophrenia: The Sacred Symbol of Psychiatry* (New York: Basic Books, 1976). **"Long before":** M. Barnes and J. Berke, *Mary Barnes: Two Accounts of a Journey Through Madness* (New York: Ballantine Books, 1971), pp. 75–76. **"I don't think":** "Britain's Offbeat Psychoanalyst," *Newsweek,* November 1, 1982, p. 16. **"Insanity is terrific":** D. Previn, *Bog-Trotter* (New York: Doubleday, 1980), p. 64. **"No trial":** E. F. Torrey, "A Fantasy Trial About a Real Issue," *Psychology Today,* March 1977, p. 22.

CHAPTER 7: THE TREATMENT OF SCHIZOPHRENIA

"To lighten": Charles Dickens, "A Curious Dance Around a Curious Tree," in *Household Words,* 1852. This epigraph was borrowed from N. Andreasen, *The Broken Brain* (New York: Harper & Row, 1984). **"as a suffering":** W. J. Annitto, "Schizophrenia and Ego Psychology," *Schizophrenia Bulletin* 7 (1981): 199–200. **minimal level of knowledge:** R. L. Taylor and E. F. Torrey, "The Pseudo-regulation of American Psy-

chiatry," *American Journal of Psychiatry* 129 (1972): 658–62. **demonstrated many times:** See E. F. Torrey, *The Mind Game: Witchdoctors and Psychiatrists* (New York: Emerson Hall, 1972) for a review of studies in this area. **"the combination of drug":** B. Pasamanick, F. R. Scarpitti, and S. Dinitz, *Schizophrenics in the Community: An Experimental Study in the Prevention of Hospitalization* (New York: Appleton-Century-Crofts, 1967), p. ix. **half of all state:** D. J. Knesper, "Psychiatric Manpower for State Mental Hospitals," *Archives of General Psychiatry* 35 (1978): 19–24. **"Three-fourths of all":** T. B. Moritz, "A State Perspective on Psychiatric Manpower Development," *Hospital and Community Psychiatry* 30 (1979): 775–77. **have been well documented:** See E. F. Torrey and R. L. Taylor, "Cheap Labor from Poor Nations," *American Journal of Psychiatry* 130 (1973): 428–34. **"What does mean":** B. J. Ennis, *Prisoners of Psychiatry* (New York: Harcourt Brace Jovanovich, 1972); for a more complete discussion of this problem see the chapter on the Principle of Rumpelstilskin in E. F. Torrey, *The Mind Game* (New York: Emerson Hall, 1972). **The Tennessee statute** is TCA 33-604. **The Nevada statute** is 433A, Care of the Mentally Ill. **The Texas statute** is from the laws on the mentally ill. **basic legal safeguards:** The President's Commission on Mental Health recommended that such safeguards be extended to all states; see *Report of the President's Commission on Mental Health,* Vol. 1 (Washington, D.C.: U.S. Government Printing Office, 1978), pp. 42–44. **penicillin exerts:** J. Davis, "Maintenance Therapy and the Natural Course of Schizophrenia," *Journal of Clinical Psychiatry* 46 (1985): 18–21. **John Davis:** J. M. Davis, "Overview: Maintenance Therapy in Psychiatry: I. Schizophrenia," *American Journal of Psychiatry* 132 (1975): 1237–45. **80 percent relapsed:** N. Capstick, "Long-Term Fluphenazine Decanoate Maintenance Dosage Requirements of Chronic Schizophrenic Patients," *Acta Psychiatrica Scandinavica* 61 (1980): 256–62. **the difference between:** "Fluphenazine Levels—Short and Long," *Biological Therapies in Psychiatry* 4 (1981): 33–34. **In another experiment:** J. Turbott, J. Villiger, and L. Hunter, "Neuroleptic Serum Levels by Radioreceptor Assay in Patients Receiving Intramuscular Depot Neuroleptics," *British Journal of Psychiatry* 146 (1985): 439–42. **Megadose fluphenazine:** S. J. Dencker, P. Enoksson, R. Johansson, et al., "Late (4–8 Years) Outcome of Treatment with Megadoses of Fluphenazine Enanthate in Drug-Refractory Schizophrenics," *Acta Psychiatrica Scandinavica* 63 (1981): 1–12; and also S. Steiner and C. Nagy, "Follow-up Study of 281 Schizophrenic Patients Treated with High Dosage Fluphenazine Decanoate," *International Pharmacopsychiatry* 16 (1981): 184–92. **two groups of investigators:** T. Van Putten, P. R. A. May, and S. R. Marder, "Response to Antipsychotic Medication: The Doctor's and the Consumer's View," *American Jour-*

nal of Psychiatry 141 (1984): 16–19; T. P. Hogan, A. G. Awad, and M. R. Eastwood, "Early Subjective Response and Prediction of Outcome to Neuroloptic Drug Therapy in Schizophrenia," *Canadian Journal of Psychiatry* 30 (1985): 246–48. **intermittent medication:** M. I. Herz, H. V. Szymanski, and J. C. Simon, "Intermittent Medication for Stable Schizophrenic Outpatients: An Alternative to Maintenance Medication," *American Journal of Psychiatry* 139 (1982): 918–22. **for loxapine:** L. Sperry, B. Hudson, and C. H. Chan, "Loxapine Abuse," *New England Journal of Medicine* 310 (1984): 598. **"The antipsychotic agents":** R. J. Baldessarini, "The Neuroleptic Antipsychotic Drugs," *Postgraduate Medicine* 65 (1979): 108–28. **may be indistinguishable:** For an excellent discussion of this problem see A. Rifkin, "The Risks of Long-Term Neuroleptic Treatment of Schizophrenia: Especially Depression and Akinesia," *Acta Psychiatrica Scandinavica* Supplementum 291, 63 (1981): 129–36. **"I am unfortunate":** H. R. Rollin, *Coping with Schizophrenia* (London: Burnett Books, 1980), pp. 164–65. **"Whereas I lived":** *National Schizophrenia Fellowship Newsletter,* April 1980. **beta blockers:** J. J. Ratey, P. Sorgi, and S. Polakoff, "Naldolol as a Treatment of Akathisia," *American Journal of Psychiatry* 142 (1985): 640–42. **one study:** T. Van Putten, P. R. A May, and S. R. Marder, "Akathisia With Haloperidol and Thiothixene," *Archives of General Psychiatry* 41 (1984): 1036–39. **clonidine:** "Clonidine (Catapres) for Akathisia," *Biological Therapies in Psychiatry* 8 (1985): 22–23. **Kraepelin described:** R. S. Garber, "Tardive Dyskinesia," *Psychiatric News* May 4, 1979, p. 2. **researchers found involuntary movements:** M. Jones and R. Hunter, "Abnormal Movements in Patients with Chronic Psychiatric Illness," in G. E. Crane and R. Gardner, eds., *Psychotropic Drugs and Dysfunctions of the Basal Ganglia: A Multidisciplinary Workshop,* Publication No. 1938 (Washington, D.C.: U.S. Public Health Service, 1969); D. G. C. Owens and E. C. Johnstone, "The Disabilities of Chronic Schizophrenia—Their Nature and the Factors Contributing to Their Development," *British Journal of Psychiatry* 136 (1980): 384–95; E. C. Johnstone and D. G. C. Owens, "Neurological Changes in a Population of Patients with Chronic Schizophrenia and Their Relationship to Physical Treatment," *Acta Psychiatrica Scandinavica* Supplementum 291, 63 (1981): 103–10; D. G. C. Owens and E. C. Johnstone, "Spontaneous Involuntary Disorders of Movement," *Archives of General Psychiatry* 39 (1982): 452–61. **13 percent:** D. V. Jeste and R. J. Wyatt, "Changing Epidemiology of Tardive Dyskinesia: An Overview," *American Journal of Psychiatry* 138 (1981): 297–309. **10 to 20 percent range:** APA Task Force on the Late Neurological Effects of Antipsychotic Drugs, "Tardive Dyskinesia: Summary of a Task Force Report of the American Psychiatric Association," *American Journal of Psychiatry* 137 (1980):

1163–72. **Some preliminary evidence:** "Tardive Dyskinesia: More Longitudinal Data," *Biological Therapies in Psychiatry* 10 (1987): 5–8. **"While the problem":** Task Force Report of the American Psychiatric Association, op. cit. **neuroleptic malignant syndrome:** J. L. Levinson, "Neuroleptic Malignant Syndrome," *American Journal of Psychiatry* 142 (1985): 1137–45. **Interactions:** These are taken from M. A. Rizak and C. D. M. Hillman, eds., *The Medical Letter Handbook of Drug Interactions* (New Rochelle, NY: The Medical Letter, 1983) and C. Salzman and S. A. Hoffman, "Clinical Interaction Between Psychotropic and Other Drugs," *Hospital and Community Psychiatry* 34 (1983): 897–902. Another good source of information on drug interactions is A. F. Shinn and R. P. Shrewsbury, *Evaluations of Drug Interactions* (St. Louis: C. V. Mosby Co., 1985). **Use in pregnancy:** "Psychotropic Drugs and the Fetus," *Biological Therapies in Psychiatry* 7 (1984): 13–14. **best study:** M. I. Herz and C. Melville, "Relapse in Schizophrenia," *American Journal of Psychiatry* 137 (1980): 801–5. **"it is extremely":** M. Herz, "Prodromal Symptoms and Prevention of Relapse in Schizophrenia," *Journal of Clinical Psychiatry* 46 (1985): 22–25. **"In the first stage":** M. Lovejoy, "Recovery from Schizophrenia: A Personal Odyssey," *Hospital and Community Psychiatry* 35 (1984): 809–12. **"It is still":** R. Diamond, "Drugs and the Quality of Life: The Patient's Point of View," *Journal of Clinical Psychiatry* 46 (1985): 29–35.

"so that a good stew": M. Shafii, "A Precedent for Modern Psychotherapeutic Techniques: One Thousand Years Ago," *American Journal of Psychiatry* 128 (1972): 1581–84. **"Then Avicenna":** Ibid. **"The newly approved":** "Generic Drugs," *The Medical Letter* 28 (1986): 1–2. **One recent study:** R. S. Winslow, V. Stillner, and D. J. Coons, "Prevention of Acute Dystonic Reactions in Patients Beginning High-Potency Neuroleptics," *American Journal of Psychiatry* 143 (1986): 706–10. **enhance the effectiveness:** N. Manos, J. Gkiouzepas, and J. Logothetis, "The Need for Continuous Use of Antiparkinsonian Medication with Chronic Schizophrenic Patients Receiving Long-term Neuroleptic Therapy," *American Journal of Psychiatry* 138 (1981): 184–88; see also "When Antiparkinson Drugs are Withdrawn," *Biological Therapies in Psychiatry* 5 (1982): 2–3. **lithium is effective:** F. P. Zemlan, J. Hirschowitz, F. J. Sautter, et al., "Impact of Lithium Therapy on Core Psychotic Symptoms of Schizophrenia," *British Journal of Psychiatry* 144 (1984): 64–69. **can be given once daily:** "Lithium Dosing Schedule," *Biological Therapies in Psychiatry* 9 (1986): 41. **general consensus:** R. D. Goldberg and N. D. Spence, "Safety of the Combination of Lithium and Neuroleptic Drugs," *American Journal of Psychiatry* 143 (1986): 882–84. **Lithium interactions:** Rizak and Hillman; Salzman and Hoffman. **excited or violent:** E. Klein, E. Bental, and B. Lerer, "Carbamazepine and Haloperidol vs. Placebo and Haloperidol in Excited Psychoses," *Archives of General Psychiatry* 41 (1984): 165–70; V. M. Neppe, "Carbamazepine in the Psychiatric Patient," *Lancet* 2 (1982): 334; H. P. A. Hakola and V. A. Laulumaa, "Carbamazepine Treatment of Violent Schizophrenics, *Lancet* 1 (1982): 1358. **carbamazepine interactions:** Rizak and Hillman. **clozapine:** "Clozapine, A Non-Neuroleptic Antipsychotic Drug," *Biological Therapies in Psychiatry* 8 (1985): 33–34. **one study:** J. Gerlach, K. Behnke, J. Heltberg, et al. "Sulpiride and Haloperidol in Schizophrenia," *British Journal of Psychiatry* 147 (1985): 283–88. **"impulsively aggressive":** P. J. Sorgi, J. J. Ratey, and S. Polakoff, "Beta-Adrenergic Blockers for the Control of Aggressive Behaviors in Patients With Chronic Schizophrenia," *American Journal of Psychiatry* 143 (1986): 775–76; see also "Propranolol (Inderal) for Schizophrenia: A Review and New Data," *Biological Therapies in Psychiatry* 9 (1986): 13–14. **Valproic acid:** S. Puzynski and L. Klosiewicz, "Valproic Acid Amide as a Prophylactic Agent in Affective and Schizoaffective Disorders," *Psychopharmacology Bulletin* 20 (1984): 151–59. **Clonazepam:** B. S. Victor, N. A. Link, R. L. Binder, et al., "Use of Clonazepam in Mania and Schizoaffective Disorders," *American Journal of Psychiatry* 141 (1984): 1111–12. **alprazolam:** O. M. Wolkowitz, D. Pickar, A. R. Doran, et al., "Combination Alprazolam-Neuroleptic Treatment of Positive and Negative Symptoms of Schizophrenia," *American Journal of Psychiatry*

143 (1986): 85–90. **Treatment of "negative" symptoms:** J. G. Csernansky, K. Brown, and L. E. Hollister, "Is There Drug Treatment for Negative Schizophrenic Symptoms?" *Hospital Formulary* 21 (1986): 790–92. **"are inaccessible to":** S. Freud, "On Narcissism," 1914. In *Collected Papers,* vol. 4 (London: Hogarth Press), p. 31. **best-known of these studies:** P. R. A. May, *Treatment of Schizophrenia: A Comparative Study of Five Treatment Methods* (New York: Science House, 1968). **"Analysis of variance":** P. R. A. May, et al., "Schizophrenia: A Follow-up Study of the Results of Five Forms of Treatment," *Archives of General Psychiatry* 38 (1981): 776–84. **"psychotherapy alone":** L. Grinspoon, J. R. Ewalt, and R. I. Shader, *Schizophrenia: Pharmacotherapy and Psychotherapy* (Baltimore: Williams & Wilkins, 1977), p. 154. **"There is no scientific":** D. F. Klein, "Psychosocial Treatment of Schizophrenia, or Psychosocial Help for People with Schizophrenia?" *Schizophrenia Bulletin* 6 (1980): 122–30. **"outcome for patients":** J. M. Davis et al., "Important Issues in the Drug Treatment of Schizophrenia," *Schizophrenia Bulletin* 6 (1980): 70–87. **"checked the therapeutic":** I. Macalpine and R. A. Hunter, in D. P. Schreber, *Memoirs of My Nervous Illness* (1903), translation and introduction by I. Macalpine and R. A. Hunter (London: William Dawson & Sons, 1955), p. 23. **"analogous to pouring":** R. E. Drake and L. I. Sederer, "The Adverse Effects of Intensive Treatment

of Chronic Schizophrenia," *Comprehensive Psychiatry* 27 (1986): 313–26. **"psychotic breaks":** S. W. Hadley and H. H. Strupp, "Contemporary Views of Negative Effects in Psychotherapy," *Archives of General Psychiatry* 33 (1976): 1291–1302. **"there is some":** *Report of the President's Commission on Mental Health* (Washington, D.C.: U.S. Government Printing Office, 1978), vol. 4, p. 1766. **"recent evidence suggests":** G. L. Klerman, "Pharmacotherapy and Psychotherapy in the Treatment of Schizophrenia" (Paper presented at the Annual Meeting of the American Psychiatric Association, San Francisco, 1980). **"To offer traditional":** T. C. Manschreck, "Current Concepts in Psychiatry: Schizophrenic Disorders," *New England Journal of Medicine* 305 (1981): 1628–32. **"sixteen either failed":** D. F. Klein, "Psychosocial Treatment . . ." **"most controlled evaluations":** L. Mosher and S. J. Keith, "Psychosocial Treatment: Individual, Group, Family, and Community Support Approaches," *Schizophrenia Bulletin* 6 (1980): 10–41. **One study of aftercare:** M. W. Linn et al., "Day Treatment and Psychotropic Drugs in the Aftercare of Schizophrenic Patients," *Archives of General Psychiatry* 36 (1979): 1055–66. **group psychotherapy may precipitate:** I. Sale et al., "Acute Psychosis Precipitated by Encounter Group Experience," *Medical Journal of Australia* 1 (1980): 157–58. **"Because group therapy":** S. J. Keith and S. M. Matthews, "Schizophrenia: A Review of Psychosocial Treatment Strategies" in Williams and Spitzer, p. 76. **proponents of orthomolecular:** M. A. Lipton and G. B. Burnett, "Pharmacological Treatment of Schizophrenia," in L. Bellak, ed., *Disorders of the Schizophrenic Syndrome* (New York: Basic Books, 1979). **Gluten-free diets:** See references in chapter 6. **hemodialysis:** See S. Sidorowicz et al., "Clinical Trial of Hemodialysis in Chronic Schizophrenia," *Acta Psychiatrica Scandinavica* 61 (1980): 223–27; S. C. Schulz et al., "Dialysis in Schizophrenia: A Double-blind Evaluation," *Science* 211 (1981): 1066–68.

CHAPTER 8: THE ORGANIZATION OF PSYCHIATRIC SERVICES FOR SCHIZOPHRENIA

"With the knowledge": J. A. Talbott, "Deinstitutionalization: Avoiding the Disasters of the Past," *Hospital and Community Psychiatry* 30 (1979): 621–24. **"In some of":** A. Deutsch, *The Shame of the States* (New York: Harcourt, Brace and Company, 1948), p. 28. **"Conditions in":** Ibid., p. 98. **"main line":** *Action for Mental Health* (New York: John Wiley and Sons, 1961), p. xiv. **"move the care":** F. D. Chu and S. Trotter, *The Madness Establishment* (New York: Grossman Publisher, 1974), p. 19. **"It is clear":** Ibid. **"no plans":** Ibid., p. 26. **a NIMH study:** *Medical World News,* April 12, 1974, p. 51. **"that some centers":** Chu, p. 32. **"The only people":** E. F. Torrey and R. L. Taylor, "A Minuet of Mutual

Deception: NIMH and the Community Mental Health Centers" (NIMH Memorandum, May 8, 1972). J. Reich, "Care of the Chronically Mentally Ill: A National Disgrace," *American Journal of Psychiatry* 130 (1973): 911–15. **"there is no":** D. Scully and C. Windle, "An Empirical Study of the Impact of Federally Funded Community Mental Health Centers on State Mental Hospital Utilization" (NIMH Memorandum, November, 1973). **"The deficiencies":** Chu. **between 1970 and 1975:** H. H. Goldman, D. A. Regier, C. A. Taube, et al., "Community Mental Health Centers and the Treatment of Severe Mental Disorder," *American Journal of Psychiatry* 137 (1980): 83–86. **In 1978:** "Provisional Data on Federally Funded Community Mental Health Centers 1977–78" (NIMH Report, 1980). **"would enable":** "Directions," a newsletter of The Park Center, December, 1983. **Governor Robert D. Orr:** Letter from the Governor to E. Fuller Torrey and Sidney M. Wolfe, March 21, 1986. **"Now is":** W. C. Young, "Down the Tube with Outpatient Psychotherapy," *POCA Press* 17 (1986): 11–13. **from 37,000 to 3,000 patients:** P. J. Hilts, "Mental Care Revolution: Clearing 'Warehouses,'" *Washington Post,* Oct. 27, 1980, pp. A1–3. **In New York State:** B. Pepper and H. Ryglewicz, "Testimony for the Neglected: The Mentally Ill in the Post-Deinstitutionalized Age," *American Journal of Orthopsychiatry* 52 (1982): 388–92. **$2.3 billion:** *Selected State and Federal Government Agency Mental*

Health Expenditures Incurred on Behalf of Mentally Ill Persons. Final report, National Association of State Mental Health Program Directors, Washington, D.C., June, 1985. **"Instead of":** F. Padavan, "Focus on Mental Health," *The New York Times,* December 17, 1985, p. A27. **"The single":** E. F. Torrey and S. M. Wolfe, *Care of the Seriously Mentally Ill: A Rating of State Programs* (Washington, D.C.: Health Research Group, 1986). J. R. Elpers, "Dividing the Mental Health Dollar: The Ethics of Managing Scarce Resources," *Hospital and Community Psychiatry* 37 (1986): 671–72. **45 changes:** A. E. Moran, R. I. Freedman, and S. S. Sharfstein, "The Journey of Sylvia Frumkin: A Case Study for Policymakers," *Hospital and Community Psychiatry* 35 (1984): 887–93. M. A. Test, "Continuity of Care in Community Treatment," in L. I. Stein, ed., *Community Support Systems for the Long-term Patient* (San Francisco: Jossey-Bass, 1979). E. F. Torrey, "Continuous Treatment Teams," *Hospital and Community Psychiatry* 37 (1986): 1243–47. **A recent study:** R. D. Miller, "Commitment to Outpatient Status: A National Survey," *Hospital and Community Psychiatry* 36 (1985): 265–67. **Saskatchewan:** C. M. Smith, "From Hospital to Community," *Canadian Journal of Psychiatry* 24 (1979): 113–20. **Maryland:** W. Weintraub, H. T. Harbin, J. Book, et al., "The Maryland Plan for Recruiting Psychiatrists into Public Service," *American Journal of Psychiatry* 141 (1984): 91–94. **Dane County:** A recent description of this program is L. I. Stein and M. A. Test, eds., *The Training in Community Living Model: A Decade of Experience* (San Francisco: Jossey-Bass, 1985).

CHAPTER 9: WHAT THE PATIENT NEEDS

"Expecting the . . .": J. Halpern, P. R. Binner, C. B. Mohr, et al., *The Illusion of Deinstitutionalization* (Denver: Denver Research Institute, 1978). **"To expect":** J. A. Talbott, "Deinstitutionalization: Avoiding the Disasters of the Past," *Hospital and Community Psychiatry* 30 (1979): 621–24. **"graduated independent":** "Diabetic Lay Dead at Group Home 3 Days," *Washington Post,* April 19, 1986, p. C3. **"the police found":** "21 Ex-Mental Patients Taken From 4 Private Homes," *The New York Times,* August 5, 1979, p. B3. **In one study:** H. R. Lamb, "Board-and-Care Home Wanderers," *Hospital and Community Psychiatry* 32 (1981): 498–500. **Fairweather Lodges:** G. W. Fairweather, ed., *The Fairweather Lodge: A Twenty-Five-Year Retrospective.* (San Francisco: Jossey-Bass, 1980). **"the presence of":** *There Goes the Neighborhood* (White Plains, NY: Community Residences Information Services Program, 1986). **"an inability to engage":** Social Security Administration, Department of Health and Human Services, *Supplemental Security Income Regulations.* These regulations are available in all Social Security offices. **between 400,000:** See J. R. Anderson, "Social Security and SSI Benefits for the Mentally Disabled," *Hospital and Community Psychiatry* 33 (1982): 295–98; Anderson's figures are for all the mentally disabled, of whom schizophrenics are the largest proportion. **$2.3 billion:** *Selected State and Federal Government Agency Mental Health Expenditures Incurred on Behalf of Mentally Ill Persons.* Final report, National Association of State Mental Health Program Directors, Washington, D.C., June, 1985, pp. 132, 135. **one-half million:** H. H. Goldman and B. Runck, "Social Security Administration Revises Mental Disability Rules," *Hospital and Community Psychiatry* 36 (1985): 343–45. **SSI appeals process:** See Anderson for an excellent description of this. **6 percent:** R. J. Turner, "Jobs and Schizophrenia," *Social Policy* 8 (1977): 32–40. **"in the morning":** H. R. Lamb and Associates, *Community Survival for Long-term Patients* (San Francisco: Jossey-Bass, 1976), p. 8. **Some other countries:** B. J. Black, "Substitute Permanent Employment for the Deinstitutionalized Mentally Ill," *Journal of Rehabilitation* 43 (1977): 32–35. **"I get lost":** S. E. Estroff, *Making It Crazy: An Ethnography of Psychiatric Clients in an American Community* (Berkeley: University of California Press, 1981), p. 233. **"I just can't":** C. Smith, "Schizophrenia in the 1980's," presented at the Alberta Schizophrenia Conference, May, 1986. **Tennessee state hospital:** J. P. McEvoy, A. Hatcher, P. S. Appelbaum, et al., "Chronic Schizophrenic Women's Attitudes Toward Sex, Pregnancy,

Birth Control, and Childrearing," *Hospital and Community Psychiatry* 34 (1983): 536–39. **"vividly described":** M. B. Rosenbaum, "Neuroleptics and Sexual Functioning," *Integrative Psychiatry* 4 (1986): 105–6. **Dr. Werner M. Mendel:** "Managing Dependency in a Psychiatric Patient," *Audio-Digest* 6 (1977): 16. **In one study:** G. Hogarty and S. Goldberg, "Drug and Sociotherapy in the Post-Hospital Maintenance of Schizophrenia," *Archives of General Psychiatry* 24 (1973): 54–64. **"It is tempting":** L. Mosher and S. J. Keith, "Psychosocial Treatment: Individual, Group, Family, and Community Support Approaches," *Schizophrenia Bulletin* 6 (1980): 10–41. **formal class:** C. Pilsecker, "Hospital Classes Educate Schizophrenics About Their Illness," *Hospital and Community Psychiatry* 32 (1981): 60–61. **the following problems:** A. K. McCarrick, R. W. Manderscheid, D. E. Bertolucci, et al., "Chronic Medical Problems in the Chronic Mentally Ill," *Hospital and Community Psychiatry* 37 (1986): 289–92. **"provide the glue":** A. E. Moran, R. I. Freedman, and S. S. Sharfstein, "The Journey of Sylvia Frumkin: A Case Study for Policymakers," *Hospital and Community Psychiatry* 35 (1984): 887–93. **studies done at Thresholds:** J. Dincin and T. F. Witheridge, "Psychiatric Rehabilitation as a Deterrent to Recidivism," *Hospital and Community Psychiatry* 33 (1982): 645–50. **"These findings":** T. F. Witheridge and J. Dincin, "The Bridge: An Assertive Outreach Program in an Urban Setting," in L. I.

Stein and M. A. Test, eds., *The Training in Community Living Model: A Decade of Experience* (San Francisco: Jossey-Bass, 1985).

CHAPTER 10: WHAT THE FAMILY NEEDS

"Lunacy, like the rain": *The Philosophy of Insanity* by an inmate of the Glasgow Royal Asylum for Lunatics at Gartnavel, 1860. Used as an epigraph by Albert Deutsch, *The Shame of the States* (New York: Harcourt, Brace and Company, 1948). **"Of all types":** C. Creer and J. K. Wing, *Schizophrenia at Home* (London: Institute of Psychiatry, 1974), p. 66. **"seemingly endless questions":** Anonymous, "You Do Believe Me—Don't You?" *National Schizophrenia Fellowship News,* April, 1980. **"One lives closeted":** M. Cecil, "Through the Looking Glass," *Encounter,* December, 1956, pp. 18–29. **"Because it's happened":** T. P. Laffey, "Effects of Schizophrenia on the Family with the Relatives Viewed as Cosufferers" (thesis, University of Canterbury, Christchurch, New Zealand, 1978), p. 35. **Several studies:** A. E. Davis, S. Dinitz, and B. Pasamanick, *Schizophrenics in the New Custodial Community: Five Years After the Experiment* (Columbus: Ohio State University Press, 1974); J. K. Wing, *Schizophrenia and Its Management in the Community* (pamphlet published by National Schizophrenic Fellowship, 1977); A. B. Hatfield, "Help-Seeking Behavior in Families of Schizophrenics," *American Journal of Community*

Psychology 7 (1979): 563–69. **An excellent description:** L. Wilson, *This Stranger, My Son* (New York: Putnam, 1968). **"We had moved":** Ibid., p. 178. **"You know, Dad":** Wechsler, *In a Darkness,* p. 27. **" 'I read a book' ":** Wilson, *This Stranger, My Son,* pp. 123–24. **"My mother died":** M. C., personal communication, New York. **"Badly treated families":** W. S. Appleton, "Mistreatment of Patients' Families by Psychiatrists," *American Journal of Psychiatry* 131 (1974): 655–57. **"Once you have":** A. C., personal communication, Maryland. **"One of our":** H. B. M. Murphy, "Community Management of Rural Mental Patients," Final Report of USPHS Grant (Rockville, MD: National Institute of Mental Health, 1964). **"Well, I guess":** G. L., personal communication, Maryland. **Several observers have noted:** W. W. Michaux et al., *The First Year Out: Mental Patients After Hospitalization* (Baltimore: Johns Hopkins Press, 1969). **"Several relatives mentioned":** Creer and Wing, p. 33. **"You've got to reach":** Laffey, p. 40. **"Recognizing that a person":** H. R. Lamb and Associates, *Community Survival for Long-term Patients* (San Francisco: Jossey-Bass, 1976), p. 7. **"A neutral":** Wing, *Schizophrenia,* p. 29. **"Superficially she *was*":** O. Sacks, *The Man Who Mistook His Wife for a Hat* (New York: Summit Books, 1985), pp. 70–74. **function at a higher:** See D. E. Kreisman and V. D. Joy, "Family Response to the Mental Illness of a Relative: A Review of the Literature," *Schizophrenia Bulletin* 10 (1974): 34–57; J. Dincin, V. Selleck, and S. Streicker, "Restructuring Parental Attitudes—Working with Parents of the Mentally Ill," *Schizophrenia Bulletin* 4 (1978): 597–608. **"I found structure":** A. H., personal communication, Washington, D.C. **"What saved me":** M. Sechehaye, *Autobiography of a Schizophrenic Girl* (New York: Grune & Stratton, 1951), p. 22. **"My wife will cook":** Creer and Wing, p. 30. **"The second practical":** Anonymous, personal communication, California. **"Look at the person":** Anonymous, personal communication, Davis, California. **"My son seemed":** A. H., personal communication, Washington, D.C. **"Patients tended to":** Wing, *Schizophrenia,* p. 27. **"I would have been":** H. R. Rollin, ed., *Coping with Schizophrenia* (London: Burnett, 1980), p. 158. **"A more realistic":** Creer and Wing, p. 71. **"One patient returned home":** Ibid., p. 22. **"One young man":** Ibid., p. 11. **"One lady said":** Ibid., p. 8. **"Leave me alone":** B. B., personal communication, New York. **"When our son was":** L. Y., personal communication, San Jose, California. **"The most remarkable lesson":** L. M., personal communication, Florida. **"Part of the peculiar":** Wing, *Schizophrenia,* pp. 28–29. **"It's so annoying":** Creer and Wing, p. 10. **arrest rate:** L. Sosowsky, "Explaining the Increased Arrest Rate Among Mental Patients: A Cautionary Note," *American Journal of Psychiatry* 137 (1980): 1602–5. **One man smashed:** G. E. Whitmer, "From Hospitals to Jails: The Fate of California's Deinstitutionalized Mentally Ill," *American Journal of Orthopsychiatry* 50 (1980): 65–75. **One study:** J. A. Yesavage, "Inpatient Violence and the Schizophrenic Patient: An Inverse Correlation Between Danger-Related Events and Neuroleptic Levels," *Biological Psychiatry* 17 (1982): 1331–37. See also K. E. Weaver, "Increasing the Dose of Antipsychotic Medication to Control Violence," *American Journal of Psychiatry* 140 (1983): 1274. **In another study:** Whitmer; see also Creer and Wing. **form of currency:** J. I. Benson and J. J. David, "Coffee Eating in Chronic Schizophrenic Patients," *American Journal of Psychiatry* 143 (1986): 940–41. **excessive amounts of coffee:** B. DeFreitas and G. Schwartz, "Effects of Caffeine in Chronic Psychiatric Patients," *American Journal of Psychiatry* 136 (1979): 1337–38. **absorption of antipsychotic drugs:** "Coffee, Tea and Antipsychotic Drugs Revisited," *Biological Therapies in Psychiatry* 4 (1981): 42–43. **One study:** J. R. Hughes, D. K. Hatsukami, J. E. Mitchell, et al., "Prevalence of Smoking Among Psychiatric Outpatients," *American Journal of Psychiatry* 143 (1986): 993–97. **A study:** See M. Galanter, "Psychological Induction into the Large Group: Findings from a Modern Religious Sect," *American Journal of Psychiatry* 137 (1980): 1574–79; See also M. Galanter et al., "The 'Moonies': A Psychological Study of Conversion and Membership in a Contemporary Religious Sect," *American Journal of Psychiatry* 136 (1979): 165–70. For a particularly cogent analysis, see also S. V. Levine, "Role of Psychiatry in the Phenomenon of Cults," *Canadian Journal of Psychiatry* 24 (1979): 593–603; **there may be some advantages:** See S. V. Levine, "Role of Psychiatry." **"jumped on one":** Laffey, p. 26. **"I often wonder" and "We all do stupid":** Laffey, p. 24. **"Surely you will do":** L. Wilson, p. 176. **"One thing that":** N. Dearth, B. J. Labenski, M. E. Mott, et al., *Families Helping Families: Living with Schizophrenia* (New York: W. W. Norton, 1986), p. 45. **One study of:** J. F. Thornton et al., "Schizophrenia: Group Support for Relatives," *Canadian Journal of Psychiatry* 26 (1981): 341–44. **only 6 percent:** S. Sharfstein and A. Beigel, "Less Is More? Today's Economics and Its Challenge to Psychiatry," *American Journal of Psychiatry* 141 (1984): 1403–8. **"by teaching the patients":** I. R. H. Falloon, J. L. Boyd, C. M. McGill, et al., "Family Management in the Prevention of Exacerbations of Schizophrenia," *New England Journal of Medicine* 24 (1982): 1437–40. **"provides evidence that":** M. J. Goldstein and J. A. Doane, "Family Factors in the Onset, Course and Treatment of Schizophrenic Spectrum Disorders," *Journal of Nervous and Mental Disease* 170 (1982): 692–700. **"the parents":** D. Goleman, "Schizophrenia: Early Signs Found," *The New York Times,* December 11, 1984.

CHAPTER 11: LEGAL AND ETHICAL DILEMMAS IN SCHIZOPHRENIA

"When I tell": H. R. Rollin, ed., *Coping with Schizophrenia* (London: Burnett Books, 1980), p. 153. **His many books:** T. S. Szasz, *Law, Liberty and Psychiatry* (New York: Macmillan, 1963) and *Psychiatric Slavery* (New York: Free Press, 1977). **"The goal should":** B. J. Ennis, *Prisoners of Psychiatry* (New York: Harcourt Brace Jovanovich, 1972). **Psychiatric Terror: How Soviet Psychiatry Is Used to Suppress Dissent:** (New York: Basic Books, 1977). **In one study:** J. P. McEvoy et al., "Measuring Chronic Schizophrenic Patients' Attitudes Toward Their Illness and Treatment," *Hospital and Community Psychiatry* 32 (1981): 856–58. **Even Szasz:** M. C. McDonald, "The Chodoff-Szasz Clash," *Psychiatric News,* November 5, 1975. **"Patients wander":** L. M. Siegel, "Feeling the Chill," *The New York Times,* March 3, 1981, p. A19. **"The liberty":** A. A. Stone, "A Response to Comments on APA's Model Commitment Law," *Hospital and Community Psychiatry* 36 (1985): 984–89. **"a man barricaded":** C. Holden, "Broader Commitment Laws Sought," *Science* 230 (1985): 1253–55. **"Public defender":** D. A. Treffert, "The Obviously Ill Patient in Need of Treatment: A Fourth Standard for Civil Commitment," *Hospital and Community Psychiatry* 36 (1985): 259–64. **"significant deterioration":** Holden. **"A large number":** H. R. Lamb and M. M. Mills, "Needed Changes in Law and Procedure for the Chronically Mentally Ill," *Hospital and Community Psychiatry* 37 (1986): 475–80. **"The two warring":** Holden. **"Almost all crimes":** S. Brill, "A Dishonest Defense," *Psychology Today,* November, 1981, pp. 16–19. **"the line between":** C. Holden, "Insanity Defense Reexamined," *Science* 222 (1983): 994–95. **"To deprive any citizen":** *Wyatt* v. *Stickney,* 325 F. Supp. 781 (MD Alabama, 1971). **"when there is":** P. S. Appelbaum and T. G. Gutheil, "The Boston State Hospital Case: 'Involuntary Mind Control,' the Constitution, and the 'Right to Rot,' " *American Journal of Psychiatry* 137 (1980): 720–23. **Rogers suit:** "Mental Patients Win Drugs Ruling," *The New York Times,* December 4, 1983, p. A45. See also T. G. Gutheil, "*Rogers* v. *Commissioner:* Dénouement of an Important Right-to-Refuse Treatment Case," *American Journal of Psychiatry* 142 (1985): 213–16. **"mental illness often":** J. Gross, "New York Court Says Mentally Ill Have Right to Refuse Medication," *The New York Times,* June 11, 1986, p. A1. **"right to rot":** Appelbaum and Gutheil. **"will suffer if a liberty":** R. Michels, "The Right to Refuse Psychoactive Drugs," *Hastings Center Report* 3 (1973): 8–11. **improves their thinking:** See D. L. Braff and D. P. Saccuzzo, "Effect of Antipsychotic Medication on Speed of Information Processing in Schizophrenic Patients," *Archives of General Psychiatry* 139 (1982): 1127–30. **could not be medicated:** S. Schultz, "The Boston State Hospital Case: A Conflict of Civil Liberties and True Liberalism," *American Journal of Psychiatry* 139 (1982): 183–88. **an additional $35,-350:** G. Byrne, "Refusing Treatment in Mental Health Institutions: Val-

ues in Conflict," *Hospital and Community Psychiatry* 32 (1981): 255–58. **only 27 percent:** J. P. McEvoy. **"The state must":** F. Padavan, "Focus on Mental Health," *The New York Times,* December 17, 1985, p. A27. **"most patients":** M. Irwin, A. Lovitz, S. R. Marder, et al., "Psychotic Patients' Understanding of Informed Consent," *American Journal of Psychiatry* 142 (1985): 1351–54. **useful discussion:** D. V. Jeste and R. J. Wyatt, *Understanding and Treating Tardive Dyskinesia* (New York: Guilford Press, 1982), pp. 294–96. **Vermont recently:** A. A. Stone, "Vermont Adopts Tarasoff: A Real Barn Burner," *American Journal of Psychiatry* 143 (1986): 352–55. **"I was never":** N. Dearth, B. J. Labenski, M. E. Mott, et al., *Families Helping Families* (New York: W. W. Norton, 1986), p. 61. **"Experimentation which is":** *Report of the President's Commission on Mental Health* (Washington, D.C.: U.S. Government Printing Office, 1978), p. 1439. **lumbar punctures:** E. F. Torrey, "Headaches After Lumbar Puncture and Insensitivity to Pain in Psychiatric Patients," *New England Journal of Medicine* 301 (1979): 110. **Gottesman's calculations:** I. I. Gottesman, *Schizophrenia and Genetic Risks* (Arlington, VA: National Alliance for the Mentally Ill, 1984).

CHAPTER 12: THE HISTORY AND DISTRIBUTION OF SCHIZOPHRENIA

"I doubt if ever": J. Hawkes, "On the Increase of Insanity," *Journal of Psy-*

chological Medicine and Mental Pathology 10 (1857): 508–21. **Kraepelin wrote:** E. Kraepelin, *Dementia Praecox and Paraphrenia* (Edinburgh: Livingstone, 1919), p. 232. **"schizophrenia has existed":** D. V. Jeste et al., "Did Schizophrenia Exist Before the Eighteenth Century?" *Comprehensive Psychiatry* 26 (1985): 493–503. **"the longest of all":** Jeste et al., quoting Celsus. C. V. Haldipur, "Madness in Ancient India: Concept of Insanity in Charaka Samhita (1st Century A.D.)," *Comprehensive Psychiatry* 25 (1984): 335–44. **"fright, loss of a sense":** Jeste et al. **Poor Mad Tom:** N. Bark, "Did Shakespeare Know Schizophrenia? The Case of Poor Mad Tom in King Lear," *British Journal of Psychiatry* 146 (1985): 436–38. **Karl Jaspers:** Cited in A. Jablensky, "Epidemiology of Schizophrenia: A European Perspective" *Schizophrenia Bulletin* 12 (1986): 52–73. **Psychiatrist Edward Hare:** E. Hare, "Epidemiological Evidence for a Viral Factor in the Aetiology of Functional Psychosis," in P. V. Morozov, ed., *Research on the Viral Hypothesis of Mental Disorders* (Basel: S. Karger, 1983), p. 57. **"Medieval people":** J. Kroll and B. Bachrach, "Medieval Visions and Contemporary Hallucinations," *Psychological Medicine* 12 (1982): 709–21. **"For several days":** Quoted in R. A. Hunter and I. Macalpine, *Three Hundred Years of Psychiatry 1535–1860* (London: Oxford University Press, 1963), p. 155. **Felix Platter:** Jeste et al. **Thomas Willis:** P. F. Cranefield, "A Seventeenth Century View of Mental Deficiency and

Schizophrenia: Thomas Willis on 'Stupidity or Foolishness,' " *Bulletin of the History of Medicine* 35 (1961): 291–316. **Smoking was thought:** Anonymous, "Dr. Samuel Johnson on Insanity," *American Journal of Insanity* 3 (1847): 285–87. J. Haslam, *Observations on Insanity*, 2nd ed. (London: F. & C. Rivington, 1809), pp. 64–67. **"The alarming increase":** Haslam, Preface. **Halliday noted:** A. Halliday, *A Letter to Lord Robert Seymour with a Report of the Number of Lunatics and Idiots in England and Wales* (London: Thomas & George Underwood, 1829). **J. C. Prichard:** *A Treatise on Insanity* (London: Sherwood, Gilbert & Piper, 1835). **"I doubt if ever":** Hawkes. **"Formerly insanity":** Renaudin, "Observation Deduced from the Statistics of the Insane," *Journal of Mental Science* 7 (1862): 534–46. **The number of those hospitalized:** K. Gorwitz, "A Critique of Past and Present Mental Health Statistics in the United States and a Blueprint for Future Program Development" (Dissertation, School of Hygiene and Public Health, Johns Hopkins University, 1966). **this number had skyrocketed:** H. M. Pollock and B. Malzberg, "Trends in Mental Disease," *Mental Hygiene* 21 (1937): 456–70. **"The successive reports":** W. J. Corbet, "On the Increase in Insanity," *American Journal of Insanity* 50 (1893): 224–35. **Rothman:** D. J. Rothman, *The Discovery of the Asylum* (Boston: Little, Brown, 1971). **"It is suggested":** J. Cooper and N. Sartorius, "Cultural and Temporal Variations in Schizophrenia: A Speculation on the Importance of Industrialization," *British Journal of Psychiatry* 130 (1977): 50–55. **"Four Shillings Act":** Hare, "Was Insanity on the Increase?" **"If the evidence":** Jablensky. **"if from this center":** W. A. White, "The Geographical Distribution of Insanity in the United States," *Journal of Nervous and Mental Disease* 30 (1903): 257–79. **The states with the greatest:** Torrey, *Schizophrenia and Civilization* (New York: Jason Aronson, 1980). **"The evidence that":** M. L. Kohn, "Social Class and Schizophrenia: A Critical Review and a Reformulation," *Schizophrenia Bulletin* 7 (1973): 60–79. **Five separate studies:** See M. Kramer, B. M. Rosen, and E. M. Willis, "Definitions and Distribution of Mental Disorders in a Racist Society," in C. V. Willie, B. M. Kramer, and B. S. Brown, eds., *Racism and Mental Health* (Pittsburgh: University of Pittsburgh Press, 1973); and M. Kramer, "Population Changes and Schizophrenia, 1970–1985," in L. Wynne et al., eds., *The Nature of Schizophrenia* (New York: Wiley, 1978). **careful study in Rochester:** *Report of the President's Commission on Mental Health* (Washington, D.C.: U.S. Government Printing Office, 1978). **in Texas and in Louisiana:** Kramer, Rosen, Willis; E. G. Jaco, *The Social Epidemiology of Mental Disorders: A Psychiatric Survey of Texas* (New York: Russell Sage Foundation, 1960). **label a black patient:** J. Fischer, "Negroes and Whites and Rates of Mental Illness: Reconsideration of a Myth," *Psychiatry* 32 (1969): 428–

46. multisite NIMH study: J. K. Myers, M. M. Weisman, G. L. Tischler, et al., "Six-Month Prevalence of Psychiatric Disorders in Three Communities," *Archives of General Psychiatry* 41 (1984): 959–67. This study reports all prevalence rates for populations age 18 and over; these cannot be directly compared with rates per total population, but can be converted into an approximation by taking two-thirds of the rate for 18 and over. For example, the NIMH study found a schizophrenia prevalence rate in New Haven of 11.0 per 1,000 for the population 18 and over; two-thirds of this would be 7.4 per 1,000 for the total population. **Tennessee:** W. F. Roth and F. H. Luton, "The Mental Health Program in Tennessee," *American Journal of Psychiatry* 99 (1943): 662–75. **rural North Carolina:** D. Blazer, L. K. George, R. Landerman, et al., "Psychiatric Disorders: A Rural/Urban Comparison" *Archives of General Psychiatry* 42 (1985): 651–56. **Studies have recently:** E. F. Torrey, "The Geographical Distribution of Schizophrenia" *British Journal of Psychiatry* 150 (1987): 598–608. **Yugoslavia is:** See P. V. Lemkau et al., "Selected Aspects of the Epidemiology of Psychoses in Croatia, Yugoslavia: I. Background and Use of Psychiatric Hospital Statistics," *American Journal of Epidemiology* 94 (1974): 112–17; and the two articles which follow in the same journal. **India is another:** The Indian studies are reviewed in Torrey, "The Geographical Distribution of Schizophrenia." **"insanity is a disease":** A.

Halliday, *Remarks on the Present State of the Lunatic Asylums in Ireland* (London: John Murray, 1808). **"it is remarkable":** Anonymous, "Lunatic Asylums in Ireland," *American Journal of Insanity* 21 (1864): 298–300. **"the insane have all but doubled":** W. J. Corbet, "On the Increase in Insanity," *American Journal of Insanity* 50 (1893): 224–35. **three times higher:** D. Walsh, *The 1963 Irish Psychiatric Hospital Census* (Dublin: Medico-Social Research Board, 1970). **The area studied:** E. F. Torrey, M. McGuire, A. O'Hare, et al., "Endemic Psychosis in Western Ireland," *American Journal of Psychiatry* 141 (1984): 966–69. **4 percent of the people:** D. Walsh, "Epidemiological Methods Applied to an Irish Problem," in D. Leigh and J. Noorbakhsh, eds., *Epidemiological Studies in Psychiatry* (London: World Psychiatric Association, 1974). **As early as 1850:** G. N. Grob, *Mental Institutions in America* (New York: Free Press, 1973). **"in the Irish":** H. M. Swift, "Insanity and Race," *American Journal of Insanity* 70 (1913): 143–54. **"the Irish-born":** H. M. Pollock, quoted by H. B. M. Murphy, "Alcoholism and Schizophrenia in the Irish: A Review," *Transcultural Psychiatric Research Review* 12 (1975): 116–39. **children of the Irish immigrants:** B. Malzberg, "A Statistical Study of Mental Diseases Among Natives of Foreign White Parentage in New York State," *Psychiatric Quarterly* 10 (1936): 127–42. **"far larger increase":** D. H. Tuke, "Increase of Insanity in Ireland," *Journal of Mental*

Science 40 (1894): 549–58; see also A. O'Hare and D. Walsh, *Activities of Irish Psychiatric Hospitals and Units 1973 and 1974* (Dublin: Medico-Social Research Board, 1978). **later onset in Ireland:** H. B. M. Murphy. **Northern Ireland:** W. R. Dawson, "The Relation Between the Geographical Distribution of Insanity and That of Certain Social and Other Conditions in Ireland," *Journal of Mental Science* 57 (1911): 571–97; see also H. B. M. Murphy and G. Vega, "Schizophrenia and Religious Affiliation in Northern Ireland," *Psychological Medicine* 12 (1982): 595–605.

CHAPTER 13: MOTHERS MARCH FOR MADNESS: HOW THE SYSTEM CAN BE CHANGED

"We have traveled": A. Deutsch, *The Mentally Ill in America* (New York: Columbia University Press, 1937), p. 518. **"are not falling":** M. Starin, "What Mental Illness Doesn't Destroy, the System Does," *Poughkeepsie Journal,* January 18, 1984, p. 5. **college freshmen:** O. Wahl, "Public vs. Professional Conceptions of Schizophrenia," *Journal of Community Psychology* 15 (1987): 285–91. **One poll:** C. Holden, "Giving Mental Illness Its Research Due," *Science* 232 (1986): 1084–86. **in one study:** G. Gerbner et al., "Health and Medicine on Television," *New England Journal of Medicine* 305 (1981): 901–4. **"although audiences tended":** Quoted in J. A.

Talbott, ed., *The Chronic Mental Patient* (Washington: American Psychiatric Association, 1978), p. xiii. **research achievement awards:** In 1977 the National Mental Health Association (NMHA) McAlpin Research Achievement Award was given to Drs. Lyman Wynne and Margaret Singer for their work on communication among family members which may contribute to the development of schizophrenia; see *Research on Mental Health: Progress and Promise* (NMHA, Washington, D.C., 1978). **Japan:** "Violation of Human Rights in Japanese Mental Hospitals," *Lancet* 2 (1986): 701. **Soviet abuse of psychiatry:** S. Bloch and P. Reddaway, *Soviet Terror: How Soviet Psychiatry Is Used to Suppress Dissent* (New York: Basic Books, 1977). See also V. Nekipelov, *Institute of Fools* (New York: Farrar, Straus and Giroux, 1980). **In Italy:** For summaries of the Italian experiment, see K. Jones and A. Poletti, "The Italian Experience in Mental Health Care," *Hospital and Community Psychiatry* 37 (1986): 795–802; and C. Zimmermann-Tansella, L. Burti, C. Faccincani, et al., "Bringing into Action the Psychiatric Reform in South-Verona: A Five-Year Experience," *Acta Psychiatrica Scandinavica* Supplementum 316 (1985): 71–86. **"a minority within minorities":** *Report of the President's Commission on Mental Health,* vol. 2 (Washington, D.C.: U.S. Government Printing Office, 1978), p. 362.

INDEX